God and Government

God and Government

Biblical Principles for Today: An Introduction and Resource

CORNELIS VAN DAM

WIPF & STOCK · Eugene, Oregon

GOD AND GOVERNMENT
Biblical Principles for Today: An Introduction and Resource

Copyright © 2011. Cornelis Van Dam. All rights reserved. Except for brief quotations in critical publications or reviews, no part of this book may be reproduced in any manner without prior written permission from the publisher. Write: Permissions, Wipf and Stock Publishers, 199 W. 8th Ave., Suite 3, Eugene, OR 97401.

Wipf & Stock
An Imprint of Wipf and Stock Publishers
199 W. 8th Ave., Suite 3
Eugene, OR 97401
www.wipfandstock.com

ISBN 13: 978-1-61097-326-7

Manufactured in the U.S.A.

Unless otherwise indicated, all Scripture quotations are from the Holy Bible, New International Version®. NIV®. Copyright © 1973, 1978, 1984 by Biblia, Inc.™ Used by permission of Zondervan Publishing House. All rights reserved.

Scripture quotations marked ESV are from The Holy Bible, English Standard Version,® (ESV®) copyright © 2001 by Crossway Bibles, a publishing ministry of Good News Publishers. Used by permission. All rights reserved.

The Scripture quotation marked NASB is from The New American Standard Bible,® copyright © 1960, 1962, 1963, 1968, 1971, 1972, 1973, 1975, 1977, 1995 by The Lockman Foundation. Used by permission.

Scripture quotations marked RSV are from The Holy Bible, Revised Standard Version, copyright © 1946, 1952, 1971 by the Division of Christian Education of the National Council of the Churches of Christ in the United States of America. Used by permission. All rights reserved.

Other versions mentioned but not quoted include NET (The Net Bible) and the NKJV (New King James Version).

All royalties generated from the sales of this book go to the ARPA Canada (Association for Reformed Political Action—http://arpacanada.ca).

For Ed and Audrey Vanwoudenberg
loving, inspiring, and ardent activists for God's rights in the nation

Contents

Preface / xiii
Abbreviations / xv

PART A BACKGROUND / 1

1 THE HERITAGE OF THE WESTERN WORLD

Christianity / 3
    Democracy / 4
    Law / 7
    Freedom / 12
Humanism / 17
    Democracy, Law, and Liberty / 18
The Nature of the Conflict / 22
Suggested Reading / 24

PART B BASIC PRINCIPLES / 25

2 THE ORIGIN AND TASK OF CIVIL GOVERNMENT

The Origin of Civil Government / 27
God's Servant for Good / 30
    Limitations / 32
    The First Task of Civil Government / 34
    Other Duties of Government / 40
    Summary of Duties / 42
Concluding Comments / 45
Suggested Reading / 46

3 CHURCH AND STATE

Some Historical Background / 47
    Early History / 47
    Subsequent Developments / 52

The Role of the State / 54
   The Duty of the State Redefined / 54
   Three Approaches / 57
     Voluntaryism and Pluralism / 57
     Theonomy / 59
     Principled Pluralism / 64
The Bible and Pluralism / 66
   Church and Kingdom / 66
     Old Testament / 66
     New Testament and Today / 68
   Church and State / 70
     Biblical Distinctions / 71
     The Rule of Law / 73
     The Church's Duty / 74
Suggested Reading / 76

4 Human Rights, Moral Norms, and Toleration

Human Rights / 78
   The Reformation's Understanding of Human Rights / 78
   The Enlightenment's Understanding of Human Rights / 80
   The Current Dilemma / 82
Moral Norms / 83
   Where God's Norms are Found / 85
     The Bible / 85
     Natural Law / 87
Toleration / 89
   Keeping the Civil Peace / 90
   Finding a Justifiable Civic Consensus / 92
     Preconditions / 92
     Obstacles to Remove / 94
     Contributions Christians Can Make / 95
   Government as God's Servant / 97
Suggested Reading / 101

Part C Some Current Issues / 103

5 Life and Death

Abortion / 105
   The Bible and the Unborn Child / 106
   The Duty of Government / 108

Euthanasia / 112
    The Bible and Euthanasia / 113
    The Duty of Government and Secular Arguments / 115
Capital Punishment / 118
    The Bible and Capital Punishment / 119
    The Duty of Government and Secular Arguments / 122
Suggested Reading / 125

6   Marriage and Family

The Original Design and Blessing of Marriage / 128
    A Helper Suitable for Him / 129
    Marriage and Procreation / 130
    Marriage Defined / 131
Biblical Norms for Marriage and Family and the Role
        of the State / 132
    Divorce and a Weakened Commitment to Marriage / 132
    Same-sex Marriage / 135
        Consequences of Same-sex Marriage / 135
        The Role of Government / 138
    Children 141
        A Blessing / 141
        Nurturing and Educating Children / 143
Suggested Reading / 145

7   Work and Rest

Work / 147
    The Divine Mandate / 147
    Some Implications of this Mandate / 148
    Work as a Blessing in a Sinful World / 150
    The Task of Government / 152
Rest / 156
    A Creation Ordinance / 156
    A Covenant Sign for the People of God / 157
    The State and Sunday—A Brief Historical Overview / 159
        The Roman Empire / 159
        Medieval Europe / 160
        The Reformation / 161
        Subsequent Developments in the United States
            and Canada / 162
        Summary / 164

The State and Sunday Today / 165
    A Creation Ordinance with Benefits / 165
    Objections and Concerns / 166
    The Task of Government / 167
Suggested Reading / 169

8 THE ENVIRONMENT

The Bible and the Environment / 172
    Whose World is It? / 172
    Rule Creation / 173
    Fill the Earth and Subdue It / 174
        "Be Fruitful and Increase in Number" / 174
        Fill and Subdue the Earth / 176
        Tend the Garden / 177
    Other Biblical Principles / 179
Radical Environmentalism / 180
The State and the Environment / 183
    Climate Change / 183
    Energy Resources / 186
    The Obligations of the State / 188
The Way Forward / 191
    Limitations / 191
    A Holistic Christian Approach / 192
Suggested Reading / 196

9 MULTICULTURALISM

What is a Nation? / 197
    Nationhood is a Divine Ordinance / 198
        The Beginning of Nations / 198
        The Nation of Israel / 199
    The Principles Involved / 199
Multicultural Israel / 200
    The Situation in Ancient Israel / 201
        A Multi-ethnic Society / 201
        Resident Aliens / 202
        Foreigners / 204
    The Principles Involved / 205

The Current Multicultural Challenge / 207
    Who are We? The Importance of a National Identity / 207
    Pitfalls of Multiculturalism / 210
        Are Cultures Morally Equivalent? / 211
        Can Diverse Cultures Always Co-exist Peacefully? / 213
        Must One Respect the Culture to Respect the Person? / 214
    Welcoming Immigrants: The Need to Assimilate / 215
        Admitting Immigrants / 216
        Helping Immigrants / 218
Suggested Reading / 221

PART D   WORKING FOR CHANGE / 223

10 Getting Involved

The Biblical Demand / 225
    Jeremiah's Letter to the Exiles / 225
    Salt and Light / 227
    Jesus is Lord / 228
The Practical Necessity / 230
    The Democratic Reality / 230
    The Christian Heritage / 231
Give to Caesar what is Caesar's . . . / 233
    Give to Caesar / 234
    Give to God / 236
Securing and Preserving Freedom / 238
    Living the Faith / 239
    Defending Freedom / 242
Special Issues / 246
    Compromise / 247
        Is Compromise Biblical? / 247
        Incrementalism / 250
        In Conclusion / 251
    Civil Disobedience / 251
The Return of the King / 253
Suggested Reading / 255

11 RESOURCES: A SELECTION OF HELPFUL ORGANIZATIONS

America / 256
- Acton Institute / 256
- Alliance Defense Fund / 257
- American Family Association / 258
- Americans United for Life / 258
- Brookings Institution / 259
- Cato Institute / 260
- Center for Bioethical Reform / 260
- The Center for Public Justice / 261
- Citizen Link / 262
- Heritage Foundation / 262
- National Association of Evangelicals / 263
- Witherspoon Institute / 263

Canada / 264
- Association for Reformed Political Action Canada / 264
- Campaign Life Coalition / 265
- Canadian Centre for Bioethical Reform / 265
- Canadian Centre for Policy Studies / 265
- Cardus / 266
- Centre for Faith and Public Life / 266
- Christian Heritage Party of Canada / 267
- Christian Legal Fellowship of Canada / 267
- Fraser Institute / 268
- Institute for Marriage and Family Canada / 269
- Justice Centre for Constitutional Freedoms / 269
- Manning Centre / 269

Britain / 270
- Jubilee Centre / 270

Questions for Further Discussion / 273
Bibliography / 279
Scripture Index / 301

Preface

WE LIVE IN A time of rapid cultural change with new economic challenges. People look to their governments for leadership and solutions. But what can and should government do to meet the difficulties that beset a nation? What can citizens expect from their elected representatives? What is reasonable? And what should citizens do? What are their responsibilities?

This book addresses such fundamental issues through the eyes of Scripture and against the backdrop of North America's dual heritage of Christianity and humanism. Government, politics, and the Bible do not seem like a good mix. But as this book aims to show, the Bible has much wisdom to teach us about the place and role of government and its citizens. It may seem radical at times, but it is eminently sensible and has stood the test of time on numerous occasions. Biblical principles work because God knows how his world and his servant governments are supposed to function. After all, he ordained the governing authorities and the principles enunciated in his Word are timeless. They are still practical today.

The emphasis in this book is on introducing the fundamental biblical principles. Working out these principles in greater detail in all kinds of different scenarios is best left to experts in the relevant fields. I have written this book as an Old Testament professor who firmly believes that this part of Scripture has much to teach us today, also in the areas of government and politics. My intent is to outline the biblical fundamentals on government and to motivate the reader to get involved where possible in the political processes of the day. Our legislators need the input and help from their informed Christian constituents.

Much of this book has its origin in speeches and presentations I have made in different forums over the years in which the political principles and challenges of the day were discussed. Most recently these activities have taken place with ARPA Canada (Association for Reformed Political Action; http://arpacanada.ca).

Since the intent of this book is not only to inform but also to initiate reflection, deliberation, and action, questions for discussion have been included at the back. Hopefully they will help reinforce key concepts and provide a starting point for delving further into the topics that have been dealt with.

The research and writing of this book would not have been possible without the help of others. I am grateful to the Board of Governors of the Canadian Reformed Theological Seminary for granting me sabbatical time to work on this project and to ARPA Canada for their support of this endeavor. I would also like to express my appreciation for the feedback received on an earlier draft of this work from those associated with ARPA Canada: Mark Penninga, executive director, André Schutten, Ontario director, John Voorhorst, board chairman, and fellow board members: Bruce DeBoer, Neil Dykstra, Bryan Grim, James Teitsma, and Ralph Vis. Furthermore, I also benefited from the comments and questions of Dr. Frederika Oosterhoff and Rob Wildeboer who both read the entire manuscript as well, and Dr. Peter Buist and Dr. Margaret Helder who gave comments on chapter 8. Needless to say I alone am responsible for the views presented.

I am grateful to Christian Amondson, Assistant Managing Editor at Wipf and Stock who accepted the manuscript for publication and exhibited incredible patience while the manuscript was being prepared. My sincere thanks also go to Margaret Van der Velde, librarian at the Canadian Reformed Theological Seminary. She is always willing to help.

Last, but certainly not least, I would like to thank my dear wife, Joanne, for her feedback, proofreading, understanding, and loving forbearance as this project worked its way to completion.

May this contribution to the discussion of God and government serve the praise of the supreme Ruler of all those in authority on earth.

Abbreviations

ECNT	Baker Exegetical Commentary on the New Testament
ESV	English Standard Version (2001)
ERE	*Encyclopaedia of Religion and Ethics*. 13 vols. Edited by J. Hastings. New York: Charles Scribner's Sons, 1908–1926
NASB	*The New American Standard Bible* (1995)
NCE	*New Catholic Encyclopedia*. Edited by W. J. McDonald et al. 15 vols. New York, 1967
NET	*The Net Bible* (1996–2007)
NICOT	The New International Commentary on the New Testament
NIDOTTE	*New International Dictionary of Old Testament Theology and Exegesis*. Edited by W. A. VanGemeren. 5 vols. Grand Rapids: Zondervan, 1997
NIGTC	The New International Greek Testament Commentary
NKJV	*New King James Version* (1982)
COS	*The Context of Scripture*. Edited by W. W. Hallo. 3 Vols. Leiden: Brill, 2007–2011
NIV	*The New International Version* (1984)
RPP	*Religion Past and Present: Encyclopedia of Theology and Religion*. 10 vols. to date. Edited by Hans Dieter Betz, Don S. Browning, Bernd Janowski, Eberhard Jüngel. Leiden: Brill, 2007–2011
RSV	*The Revised Standard Version* (1971)

TLOT	*Theological Lexicon of the Old Testament*, edited by Ernst enni, with assistance from Claus Westermann. Translated by Mark E. Biddle. 3 vols. Peabody, MA: Hendrickson, 1997

Transliterations from Hebrew or Greek follow the general purpose style guidelines in P. A. Alexander et al, ed. *The SBL Handbook of Style*. Peabody, MA: Hendrickson, 1999, 28–29.

Part A

Background

1

The Heritage of the Western World

To understand the Western world and in particular our own country, we need to know its past. Unless we are aware of the forces that have shaped the present, we are unable think intelligently about the future of our nation. So, what basic influences have molded our nation, our political system, and our present culture? On what heritage has this country been built? And what are the present dynamics and dominant forces at work determining its future?

Two conflicting elements of our heritage as a nation warrant our attention: Christianity and secular humanism. Both have had a profound influence on how we view government and govern ourselves as a democracy. To try to understand our heritage and current situation, we will focus on three important areas: democracy, law, and freedom. This chapter will consider these areas first from the perspective of Christianity and then from that of secular humanism. Some concluding observations will follow.

CHRISTIANITY

There is no denying the enormous influence of Christianity on all aspects of our Western culture. Such an impact is not surprising given the fact that political and church histories have been intertwined for much of the pre-Enlightenment period. When we speak of the influence of Christianity we really mean the influence of the Bible. Throughout the past centuries Christians have generally accepted the Bible according to its own testimony as the inspired Word of God. As such the divine Word had absolute authority and it revealed God's will for mankind. It was like a lamp before one's feet showing society the way to go (Ps 119:105). The principles taught in the Bible therefore also affected political issues. What are these principles? Are they still relevant for us today? These are some of the questions we will consider in the first part of this book.

Democracy

With respect to democracy, or rule by the people, it is commonplace to say that democracy originated in the city state of Athens during the fourth century B.C. This is true. It is not always recognized, however, that Christianity also contributed to the rise of democracy. The Bible, in its teaching about the nature of man, shows the necessity for democratic principles, and in its guidelines for governing in both state and church, mandates important democratic features. In other words, one can argue that important elements of democracy are compatible with Scripture and that Christianity has played a significant role in the realization of Western democracies.

With respect to the nature of man, Scripture makes clear that "all have sinned and fall short of the glory of God" (Rom 3:23) and that the human "heart is deceitful above all things and beyond cure" (Jer 17:9). If such is the human condition, then it follows that "the best form of government is one that prevents any one sinner from gaining absolute control over the rest; and if all are potential recipients of God's saving grace, then the best government is the one that permits each person to contribute the most to the well-being of his fellows."[1] Democracy comes closer to fulfilling these requirements than any other political system.

Not surprisingly then, God stipulated a political system for ancient Israel that had significant democratic features. An important national body was the assembly of the elders of Israel which was accountable to the people because the people had a say as to who would belong to this assembly (cf. Deut 1:13;16:18). This body had both political and judicial powers. Politically it represented, among other things, the interests of the nation and tended to counter the centralization of power. It was this body of the elders, speaking for the people, that asked for a king (1 Sam 8:4–5) and saw to the anointing of the monarch (2 Sam 5:3). Although the influence of the elders waned during the monarchy, the national assembly could still have considerable

---

1. Montgomery, "Demos and Christos," 25.

influence as to who would be king (1 Kgs 12:20; 2 Chron 23:3) and the elders were on occasion still able to serve the king with their counsel (1 Kgs 20:7–8). There were also important democratic elements in the justice system. The people as a whole had the responsibility to purge the evil from their midst (cf. Deut 13:5; 17:7; also 6:6–9; 16:19–20) and justice was normally administered through judges appointed by the people (Deut 16:18; cf. 1:1, 13).[2]

These democratic elements in Israel were carried over into the Judaism of intertestamental and New Testament times. The Christian church also had important democratic elements in its governance. The congregation participated in determining who its ruling and teaching elders would be (Acts 14:23 NIV text note).[3] These elders had the oversight of the flock (Acts 20:28) and would deal with matters that needed their judgment. However, the first line of responsibility for maintaining justice and righteousness rested with the congregation (Matt 18:15–18). When the congregation was unable to resolve the matter, it would go to the elders, the official address of the church (Matt 18:17). Also among the churches, there was a desire to reach consensus on difficult issues by having representatives of the churches meet together in a council to discuss the issues and come to an agreement (Acts 15).

It should be stressed that these democratic elements need to be understood within the context of both ancient Israel and the early church. In both cases the people who were entrusted with what we would call democratic privileges were in a covenant relationship with God. This had at least two obvious implications. First, the will of the people and decisions made were always to be subject to God's wishes. Some of the implications of this truth will become clear under the next heading when we consider the West's indebtedness to principles of law and order derived from the Bible. The second implication of

---

2. Van Dam, *The Elder*, 6–7, 58–59, 68–73. For more on democracy in ancient Israel, see, e.g., Wolf, "Traces of Primitive Democracy in Ancient Israel," 98–108; Gordis, "Democratic Origins in Ancient Israel - the Biblical '$ĒDĀH$,'" 369–88. Also see J.G. McConville, *God and Earthly Power*, 94–98; Ska, "Biblical Law and the Origins of Democracy," 146–58.

3. See also Titus 1:5; 2 Cor 8:19. The basic meaning of the Greek verb used, *cheirontoneō*, is "stretch out the hand, for the purpose of giving one's vote in the assembly." Liddell, Scott, and Jones, *A Greek-English Lexicon*, 1986a; see further Merkle, *The Elder and Overseer*, 128–29. See further on this issue, Knight III, *The Pastoral Epistles*, 288 and Marshall, *The Pastoral Epistles*, 152.

having democratic privileges while being in covenant with God is that God himself wanted his people to be involved and ready to assume responsibility for the direction of their society and the maintenance of righteousness and justice in the land. His people were not to sit on the sidelines. Indeed, God intended that they be a kingdom of priests (Exod 19:6; cf. 1 Pet 2:5). It is, for example, telling that the detailed Levitical legislation was addressed, not just to the priests, but to the entire nation (e.g., Lev 1:2; 4:2). Every individual had to understand and be involved in the running of society and that included being knowledgeable even of what was expected of the priests. This was in stark contrast to the ignorance in which other nations kept their people.[4]

While the democratic principles derived from the New Testament are applicable in the first place to the life of the church, those deriving from ancient Israel can have implications for society at large. After all, ancient Israel was not just the chosen people of God, but it also functioned politically and judicially as a nation among other nations. For this reason, principles such as the democratic involvement of the people in the political and judicial processes for the well-being of their nation have continuing relevance today.

It would take us far beyond the scope of this introduction to relate in detail how democratic principles have come to us today mediated and facilitated in part by the Old and New Testament Scriptures.[5] History has shown that Western Christendom undoubtedly provided the womb within which the democratic system and vision gestated. The gestation period through the first Christian centuries was complex, but by the time of the Reformation new ways of thinking about the state were triggered by the desire to reform the church. Luther's emphasis on the priesthood of all believers countered the accepted hierarchical mind-set in the church. However, this emphasis also had vast implications for the role of Christians in matters of state.[6] Calvin's contribution to democracy can perhaps be shown with reference to two key teachings: the absolute sovereignty of God and the right of rebellion against unjust rulers. God's sovereignty meant among other things that man's chief end was to live for God and his glory. If a ruler

---

4. Milgrom, *Leviticus 1–16*, 143–44.

5. See for an overview Strohm, "Democracy and Christianity," 792–94.

6. De Gruchy, *Christianity and Democracy*, 8, 57–73.

claimed absolute sovereignty and prevented the true worship of God then resistance to such rulers and their overthrow was justified. This struggle against tyranny was a powerful catalyst for the development of democracies in countries influenced by the ideas of Luther and Calvin.[7] We will be returning to the right of rebellion later in this chapter. Calvin himself seems to have favored a mix of aristocracy and democracy. Important for him was the preservation of liberty.[8]

Factors other than those just mentioned undoubtedly played a role as well in the development of democracies, but it is nevertheless striking that in all the varied history and circumstances of the nations involved, it was the Protestant rather than the Roman Catholic nations that first saw the creation of democracies. From Europe the new political ideas carried over to the New World, and both Canada and the United States have benefited. Although the processes and histories are different, yet both nations owe much to their Christian heritage for their democratic systems of government.[9]

Law

Central to any Christian understanding of law is the sovereignty of God. He determines what is right and wrong. He sets the standards for justice and righteousness for all of life. With his own hand he wrote on tablets of stone his law and commands for his people Israel (Exod 24:12; 31:18). He also wrote his will on the consciences of all mankind (Rom 2:15; cf. 1:21–32). He is the judge of heaven and earth (Gen 18:25) and all will ultimately appear before his judgment seat (Acts 10:42; Rom 14:10; 2 Cor 5:9).

It is not surprising then that a judge in Israel fulfilled his office on behalf of God whom he ultimately served. Moses charged the judges to adjudicate fairly and not to be afraid of men because "judgment

---

7. De Gruchy, *Christianity and Democracy*, 75–80. Especially influential in the early period were Theodore Beza, who developed Calvin's thoughts and made use of Lutheran thinking, and Johannes Althusius. See Witte, *The Reformation of Rights*, 81–207.

8. Calvin, *Institutes*, IV.xx.8. The edition used is McNeill, ed., Battles, trans., *Calvin: Institutes of the Christian Religion*. Calvin's mix of aristocracy and democracy is essentially representative democracy. See Hudson, "Democratic Freedom," 190–91; also see McNeill's introduction to John Calvin, *On God and Political Duty*, xxii–xxiii. This article was reprinted in McNeill, "Calvin and Civil Government," 260–74.

9. See further, e.g., De Gruchy, *Christianity and Democracy*, 81–94.

belongs to God" (Deut 1:17). In a similar vein, many years later, King Jehoshaphat told the judges: "Consider carefully what you do, because you are not judging for man but for the Lord, who is with you whenever you give a verdict" (2 Chron 19:6). Indeed, the concept of the judges representing God and administering his justice was so important that appearing before the judges could be described as appearing before God (Exod 22:8–9).[10]

No rule of law is possible without a law-abiding citizenry and God certainly wanted his people involved. There were at least four ways in which the Lord accomplished this.

First, as we saw earlier, they were to be part of the process of appointing judges. The people would choose the men whom Moses then would appoint (Deut 1:1, 13–16; cf. 16:18).

Second, the people were also expected to fight corruption and not tolerate any injustice. This is evident from the way judicial guidelines were given to the people as a whole, even though their first relevance was for the judges. Such rules included not denying justice to the poor, not taking bribes, and not perverting justice (Exod 23:6–8; Deut 16:19–20).

A third way the people were to be involved with the maintenance of the rule of law was by participating in the trials that took place in the city gates and by being honest witnesses (cf. Exod 23:1–3). The gross injustices that later took place in Israel's history would never have been possible if the people as a whole had not perverted justice and taken bribes. One thinks, for example, of how Queen Jezebel apparently had little difficulty in rounding up the necessary false witnesses in order to proceed with the judicial murder of Naboth (1 Kgs 21:9–13). So important did God consider the integrity of the justice system that he warned his people that if they did not purge evil from the land and punish offenders, then the Lord would punish the community as a whole and fulfill his covenant curses (cf. Lev 18:26–28; 26:3–45; Deut 28).

A fourth way for the people to maintain justice in the land was to be law-abiding citizens and to teach their children the way God wanted them to live (Deut 6:4–9). The better the law was known, the less opportunity there would be for corruption to go unchallenged. It

---

10. The NIV translates the phrase in question "before the judges." Literally it reads: "before God" (RSV).

is significant that King Jehoshaphat included in his work of reformation the instruction of the entire nation in the law (2 Chron 17:7–9).

In the New Testament era, the situation of God's people was vastly different but there were nevertheless many similarities. Among these was the command to obey the law and honor those in authority, even if the authorities themselves were hostile to the gospel. The Lord Jesus set the tone by saying: "Give to Caesar what is Caesar's, and to God what is God's" (Matt 22:21). The apostle Paul maintained that "Everyone must submit himself to the governing authorities, for there is no authority except that which God has established. The authorities that exist have been established by God. . . . For he is God's servant to do you good. But if you do wrong, be afraid, for he [the one in authority] does not bear the sword for nothing. He is God's servant, an agent of wrath to bring punishment on the wrongdoer" (Rom 13:1, 4; cf. 1 Tim 2:2; 1 Pet 2:13–17).

There were however limits to the obedience to be given. If a choice had to be made between obeying God or man, then God was to be obeyed and the human command disobeyed (Acts 4:19; 5:29). We will be returning to the role of government and the obedience owed to it later in this chapter. Suffice it for now to note that God's people were directed to respect the rule of law in both the Old and New Testament.

In the centuries following New Testament times important developments took place with respect to the church and the civil authorities which directly impacted on the administration of law. It will be helpful for understanding our present context to have a bird's eye view of this development. When the Christian religion became the official religion of the Roman Empire in 380 A.D., there was in effect a subordination of the Christian church to the Roman emperor. Instead of being head of the official pagan religion, the emperor was now head, not only of the political order, but also of the Christian church. As a result, he convened many of the church's councils. One of logical results of this development was the gradual fusion of Roman law and Christian legal concepts.[11] The subordination of the church to the civil authorities was not a desirable situation for the church is to be accountable to Christ and independent of the civil authorities.

---

11. Witte Jr., "Introduction," 8–9; Helmholz, "Western Canon Law," 80; for the survey that follows, also see Witte Jr., "Law and Legal Theory," 218–26.

Beginning in the eleventh century, the church gradually wrested itself free from its civil rulers and established its legal autonomy. The church then claimed jurisdiction over many aspects of life and developed an elaborate system of canon law which impacted on many of the civil issues of the day.[12] The Reformation of the sixteenth century, however, rightly challenged the underlying premises of this system of canon law. The church is the body of Christ whose task it is to preach the gospel and take care of everything that pertains to this. Civil law and the governing of society are not in the province of the church but of the state. It is the civil authorities who are to be God's servant for matters of state.

The Reformation resulted in the state taking over many of the earlier civil jurisdictions of the church in such areas as marriage, family, and property law. The old Roman Catholic canon law however remained integral to the legal codes of the West in both Roman Catholic and Protestant jurisdictions. In this way much of the biblical influence that had made itself felt in canon law came into general Western law. To be sure, in the Protestant states, specifically Protestant views found legal expression, such as in laws governing marriage and divorce.[13]

With respect to the legal heritage of the English speaking world, canon law retained its place in the ecclesiastical courts for quite some time, but the influence of English common law prevailed over that of canon law in the secular courts.[14] This common law ultimately goes back to the law book of King Alfred, who ruled England from 871–901 A.D. In his Book of Laws (or Dooms) he drew on earlier laws which were indebted to biblical principles of law.[15] The legal systems of Canada (except for Quebec) and the United States have their origins in English common law. The Puritan desire to make New England a new Israel governed by the Old Testament laws of God is well-known. The effort failed. Nevertheless, biblical influences in law both in the United States and Canada are undisputed. Needless to say, the positive influences of a Judeo-Christian heritage do not necessarily make society Christian

---

12. Witte Jr., "Introduction," 10–13.

13. Witte Jr., "Introduction," 15–18. For biblical influence in Europe's laws via the canon law, see also, e.g., Isaacs, "The Influence of Judaism on Western Law," 385–87, 391–97.

14. Helmholz, "Western Canon Law," 81, 84.

15. See Perks, *Christianity and Law*, 17–23, 60–73.

today.[16] Nevertheless, as this historical account shows, Christianity and the Bible have had a significant influence on Western law.

Because Calvin's influence was considerable in the Protestant Reformation, it is appropriate to mention here that he considered biblical law to consist of the moral, ceremonial, and judicial laws. The ceremonial law was fulfilled in Christ. The judicial law could not be binding on all nations since they are free to make laws fitting for themselves as long as they satisfy the rule of love. It is the moral law, summarized in the Ten Commandments and in the law of love, that remains in force and is of particular relevance for this discussion.[17]

Calvin, and others following him, distinguished three uses of the moral law. The first, the pedagogical or theological use, is that the law shows God's righteousness and our sins. The second, the civil or political use, is that the law restrains evil doers. The third, the didactic, is that it admonishes believers and urges them to do good.[18] Keeping these three uses in mind is helpful in making the necessary distinctions when dealing with issues of law, also in the case of the government. For the government, the civil use of the law is paramount, although the other uses are not irrelevant if the government is to be God's servant.

One final note on law. Without taking away from the influence of Christianity on our legal heritage, it should be noted that God has written on the hearts of men an understanding of his will so that their consciences testify for or against them (Rom 2:14–15; cf. 1:21–32). This means that much of what is written, for example, in the Ten Commandments is not really new or surprising to the natural man. Even someone who does not believe in God senses the correctness of, for example, not murdering, not committing adultery, and not stealing. This observation has led Calvin, for instance, to consider the Ten Commandments as both expressing and clarifying natural law engraved on human hearts. In other words, there was an innate recognition even by fallen sinful man that God's law is true. Calvin,

---

16. For the failed Puritan effort, and the biblical influences admittedly present in the United States, see Noll, Hatch, and Marsden, *The Search for Christian America*, 28–47, 137–40; Gaer and Siegel, *The Puritan Heritage*, 65–104; on Canada, see, e.g., Noll, *What Happened to Christian Canada?* and "Canada's Christian Heritage Web Site."

17. Calvin, *Institutes*, IV.xx.15.

18. Calvin, *Institutes*, II.vii.6–13.

however, also noted that because of our dullness and arrogance, "the Lord has provided us with a written law to give us a clearer witness of what was too obscure in the natural law."[19]

Freedom

Another area wherein the Bible and Christianity have had considerable influence is in the notion of freedom and the development of civil and ecclesiastical liberties which we can enjoy today. We can thank the Reformation and especially Calvin for bringing these biblical concepts to the foreground.

Before discussing freedom as a political idea, it may be good to begin by orientating ourselves briefly on what Scripture says about liberty. In this way we will understand something of the general biblical framework within which the reformers worked. Freedom is a very important biblical theme. God does not want his creation to be in bondage. Since the essence of bondage in Scripture is enslavement to sin and death, the essence of true freedom is deliverance from them.

An important biblical image of bondage and liberty is ancient Israel's enslavement in Egypt under a cruel Pharaoh and the Lord's subsequently delivering his people. There are several important concepts that these events highlight.

First, this Egyptian bondage, although political, is also illustrative of the bondage of sin. When God set Israel free from Egypt, he also set it free from the sin that it had enmeshed itself in while in that country (cf. Josh 24:14–15; Ezek 20:7). This reminds us that there is a correlation between sin and bondage, be it spiritual or political. When Israel many years later refused to heed God's commands then they eventually ended up in political bondage again as exiles in Babylon.

Second, when God set his people free he brought them into a renewed covenant relationship with himself. We see this in an especially clear way after the Exodus deliverance from Egypt. Israel's freedom did not mean that she was now "on her own" and had achieved some sort of autonomy. No. Rather, instead of being claimed by Pharaoh, the gods of Egypt, and sin, the Lord Almighty claimed Israel for himself at Mount Sinai (cf. Exod 19:4–6).

---

19. *Institutes* II.viii.1. See also the extensive footnote in McNeill and Battles, *Calvin: Institutes*, 367–68 note 5.

Third, true freedom is found in doing the will of God. When God renewed his covenant at Sinai, then in order to keep his people free he gave them his law. The Ten Commandments are prefaced with God's self-identification as Israel's Savior. "I am the Lord your God, who brought you out of Egypt, out of the land of slavery" (Exod 20:1). The implication is: therefore do my will as found in the commandments that follow and remain free. As the Psalmist put it: "I will walk about in freedom, for I have sought out your precepts" (Ps 119:45). If mankind does what God designed it to do, namely to obey God, then it will find true freedom and joy (cf. Ps 119:14). Life will be protected and marriages will be secure, to mention only two examples. Furthermore, God's law is designed to give his people as much material freedom as possible. Think, for example, of the legislation by which the Lord set people free from their debts, especially during the year of Jubilee (Deut 15:1–18; Lev 25). He did not want his people in bondage forever.

All the above general points are important for understanding what the Bible considers true freedom to entail. They need to be kept in mind when specific current issues are discussed and the notion of freedom is raised.

With respect to political liberty, an additional point, not related to the Exodus, is that each office or institution in Israelite society had its specific authority and clearly demarcated role. If an office or institution took on more power to itself than was called for, then tyranny and oppression resulted. In this connection one can think of the important role of the elders in Israel. In many ways, they as lower magistrates were to be guardians of Israel's freedom. When their place in Israelite society weakened, the monarchy easily abused its power and justice was perverted. It is not by chance that the prophetic warnings against the oppression of the poor and needy coincide with the times when the monarchy controlled most of life and the place of the elders was limited and weak.

By the time of the Reformation, the need for each institution in society to recognize the restrictions of its authority had been adequately illustrated in the history of the relationship of church and state. Initially the Christian church had essentially been under the authority of the Roman emperor and the civil state. But the church managed to establish its legal autonomy and even claimed jurisdiction over many aspects of civil life. Indeed, Pope Innocent III (1198–1216) claimed to rule not only over the church but also over the world for he exercised considerable political power.[20] The Reformation, by returning to Scripture and its teachings, ended much of the abuse of power that both state and church had been guilty of and helped to open the way to true liberty.

It was in particular Calvin who gave biblical notions of freedom a new relevance. He did so by making central in his theology the doctrine of the sovereignty of God. God's Word rules over both the church and the state. Both are subject to God and his ordinances. This meant that ultimate authority could never rest in a human being or in a human word, action, or institution. Also, both the state and the church have their mandate from God. Neither is to meddle in the affairs of the other. They stand equally before God.

Important for understanding all of this is the concept of covenant. All of creation and its relations exist in covenant with God. To use the example of government, both the ruler and those ruled exist under God, in covenant with him and with each other. Each party of the covenant has its own specific responsibilities. All creation and all humans are called to serve God as his creatures. But they are also called to serve each other, both as rulers and as subjects. The horizontal human relationships should reflect something of the vertical relationship with God, especially in honoring the rule of love.[21]

We will be considering the task of government in chapter 2. But for our purposes here it is important to note that the ruler or government has a task from God. The laws of the land are the common point of agreement between the ruler and those ruled. There is a legal framework, implying the consent of those ruled. Calvin wanted the people to be able to choose their rulers to prevent tyranny.[22] Calvin detested despotism. It violated human dignity. "No kind of government is more happy than one where freedom is regulated with becoming moderation and is properly established on a durable basis."[23]

---

20. De Gruchy, *Christianity and Democracy*, 63; also see a summary of his career in Rusch, "Innocent III," 710–11.

21. See Wells, "Reformational Thought," 36–40; De Gruchy, *Christianity and Democracy*, 93; for more detail, Witte, *The Reformation of Rights*, 123–34, 181–84.

22. Calvin on Micah 5:5 as quoted by Wells, "Reformational Thought," 38.

23. Calvin, *Institutes*, IV.xx.8.

Should there be an abuse of power then passive disobedience is legitimate. A biblical example is the refusal of the Hebrew midwives to obey Pharaoh's command to kill new born boys. But sometimes God "raises up open avengers from among his servants, and arms them with his command to punish the wicked government and deliver his people, oppressed in unjust ways, from miserable calamity."[24] Calvin is very careful not to encourage the despising of the authority of those set in positions of power. Ultimately it is for the Lord to avenge and for the subjects to obey and suffer. Calvin did not advocate popular uprising or rebellion. He did not think that private citizens had the right to rebel. But obedience to men must not become disobedience to God.[25] Calvin therefore also wrote that

> if there are now any magistrates of the people, appointed to restrain the willfulness of kings ... I am so far from forbidding them to withstand, in accordance with their duty, the fierce licentiousness of kings, that, if they wink at kings who violently fall upon and assault the lowly common folk, I declare that their dissimulation involves nefarious perfidy, because they dishonestly betray the freedom of the people, of which they know that they have been appointed protectors by God's ordinance.[26]

These words of Calvin, present already in the first edition of the *Institutes* (1536), show his abiding conviction that no one is above the law and that the lower magistrates who represent the people can oppose tyrannical rulers and bring them to justice.

This view of Calvin was very influential in the subsequent struggles for securing liberty, especially for the people in the Netherlands and Scotland. By restricting the right of opposing the rulers to lawfully established lower magistrates, Calvin placed the right of resistance within the accepted political framework. In this way, his thinking served as a foundation for constitutional democracy where each person would have the freedom of conscience to serve God.[27]

---

24. Calvin, *Institutes* IV.xx.30.
25. Calvin, *Institutes* IV.xx.31, 32.
26. Calvin, *Institutes*, IV.xx.31.
27. See McNeill and Battles, *Calvin: Institutes*, 1518–19, note 54; Wells, "Reformational Thought," 38–39; Bremmer, *Reformatie en Rebellie*, 13–16.

In the Netherlands the largely Calvinist rebellion against Spain, headed initially by Prince William I of Orange (1533-1584), led to Dutch independence and much religious freedom and toleration. In Scotland, John Knox (1514?-1572) went further than Calvin. In his view, if the nobles did not act against an unfaithful ruler, then the common people could do so.[28] The thinking was that if the covenant between the king and the people is broken, it is no longer binding on the people. Eventually the rebellions in Scotland led to the firm establishment of the Reformation in that country. The situation in sixteenth and seventeenth century England was complex and need not detain us here. But, in the end, one can say that Calvinist influence had been critical for the eventual further limitation of monarchial power.[29]

The Reformation in France did not establish freedom of conscience. The infamous 1572 Saint Bartholomew's Day Massacre of French Calvinists, called Huguenots, ended any hopes for religious liberty in that country. One result of the massacre was the appearance of several writings justifying rebellion against the monarch. One of these was the publication in 1579 of *A Defence of Liberty Against the Tyrants* under the pseudonym of Junius Brutus. In it the probable author, Philippe du Plessis-Mornay, argued for the right of resistance. He noted that the king has a covenant with God and with the people. God gives the king his task according to his law and the king and the people have the holy obligation to keep it. Should the king not do so, the magistrates had the duty to resist such a king. The possibility of resistance by private individuals is, however, not excluded. If it is clear that such individuals are called by the Lord and fight the Lord's cause and not their own, then even armed resistance from private citizens can be warranted.[30] This position was of great influence, also in the American Revolution and some of its features are reflected in the Declaration of Independence.[31]

---

28. Reid, *Trumpeter of God*, 150–51; Kelly, *The Emergence of Liberty*, 54–56.

29. Kelly, *The Emergence of Liberty*, 113–14 and cf. 77–113. For seventeenth century England, especially through the work of John Milton, see Witte, *The Reformation of Rights*, 209–75.

30. Brutus, *A Defence of Liberty*, 1–51. See also Bremmer, *Reformatie en Rebellie*, 19–24.

31. Kelly, *The Emergence of Liberty*, 47, 132–35; Also see the introduction by Goodrum in Brutus, *A Defence of Liberty*, v.

It is difficult to overestimate the influence that Calvinism had on the promotion of liberty in the Western world. It has been correctly stated that "the model of the covenant of people under God, where each has a proper place and where God alone is Lord, is the foundation of liberty in social association."[32] Samuel Rutherford stated that the covenant between God and the ruler and the people meant that when the law was violated by the ruler, one's resistance to the ruler was an assertion of the law. The law is king.[33] The idea of a limited sovereignty, of a government under law, as well as the right of resistance when the government does not conform to the law, have not unjustly been called the twin pillars on which democracy, and the accompanying democratic freedom, rest.[34]

It is not by chance that the countries most influenced by the Protestant Reformation, and especially Calvinism, have experienced the greatest liberty in the sixteenth and seventeenth and subsequent centuries. This is also part of the Christian heritage of North America.[35]

We now turn to the second major element in the heritage of the Western world, namely secular humanism.

HUMANISM

We understand humanism as a way of thinking and acting that places human interests and values in the center. Key concerns are autonomous human dignity and freedom. Man is the measure of all things. Followed through consistently, this way of thinking is antithetical to biblical teaching in that it denies the sovereignty of God. Humanism shows much faith in the ability of human reason as the source of truth and considers mankind capable of meeting all life's challenges. An important manifestation of humanistic thinking was that of the Enlightenment, a diverse philosophical movement originating at the end of the seventeenth century. Although the movement was not a

---

32. Wells, "Reformational Thought," 39–40. See also De Gruchy, *Christianity and Democracy*, 80.

33. Rutherford, *Lex Rex*, 54. The title *Lex Rex* translates as "the law is king."

34. See Hudson, "Democratic Freedom," 181.

35. See De Gruchy, *Christianity and Democracy*, 76; for the Christian and Calvinist influence in the founding of the United States, see, e.g., Kelly, *The Emergence of Liberty*, 119–37 and DeMar, *America's Christian History*.

single unified entity, all Enlightenment humanists stressed reason over faith, criticized revelation and religion, and went against the traditional religious and political order of the day. Their ideas have had an enormous impact.

Since no one doubts the pervasive influence of humanistic presuppositions on political thinking and acting in North America, our treatment of the influence of humanism and the Enlightenment on our political culture will be less extensive than our coverage of Christianity's influence. Because ideas about democracy, law, and liberty are intricately related to each other in humanistic thought, we will treat these themes together under one heading. Humanistic thinking with respect to human rights will be dealt with in chapter 4.

Democracy, Law, and Liberty

We have seen how notions of democracy, law, and liberty are in many ways compatible with biblical principles and form part of the Christian heritage of the West. However, the ideals of modern democracy have also humanistic roots which have secularized these traditions. This humanism has a continuing and direct impact today.

It is very interesting to see how the influence of Christianity in Britain and in America curbed some of the excesses of Enlightenment thinking as it affected the French Revolution of 1789–1799. It is, however, beyond the limits of this introduction to trace these developments and their impact.[36] For our purposes we can restrict ourselves to the major humanistic and Enlightenment principles and show how they continue to affect thinking about issues relating to government in the Western world today.

The cornerstone of democracy from an Enlightenment perspective was the desire and right of an individual to life, liberty and the pursuit of happiness. In order to be able to pursue these goals free from the constraints of state control, one needed to insist that the power of the state was not based on divine right, but on the sovereign will of the people themselves. However, not only the state was a potential hindrance to one's claiming one's natural rights; also the constraints of traditional Christianity had to be cast aside.[37]

---

36. See, for example, the survey in De Gruchy, *Christianity and Democracy*, 95–128.
37. De Gruchy, *Christianity and Democracy*, 96–97.

These Enlightenment principles came out in their most extreme form in the events constituting the French Revolution with its cry of "liberty, equality, and fraternity!" The *Declaration of the Rights of Man and of the Citizen* approved by the National Assembly of France in 1789 clearly shows what happens when man is made the measure of all things. With respect to our present concerns the following from this *Declaration* can be noted.[38]

> Article 3: The principle of all sovereignty resides essentially in the nation. No body nor individual may exercise any authority which does not proceed directly from the nation.

Although the preface speaks of "the Supreme Being," it is clear that God's sovereignty is denied with the exclusive claim made in this article that all sovereignty resides essentially in the nation.

> Article 4: Liberty consists in the freedom to do everything which injures no one else; hence the exercise of the natural rights of each man has no limits except those which assure to the other members of the society the enjoyment of the same rights. These limits can only be determined by law.

Liberty is completely open-ended. There is no higher moral compass here but what man decides. This becomes even more obvious in the following article.

Article 6: Law is the expression of the general will. . . .

Only people can decide what is legitimate or not. Sovereignty lies with mankind. No appeal can be made to an authority like the Bible. God has been excluded from the legal issues of the day. One consequence is that law no longer has an unchanging foundation. What is legal becomes arbitrary and dependent on the current human whim. Dependence on a corrupted and sinful human nature for discerning what is right and wrong does not bode well for the upholding of true justice and righteousness. What can be illegal one day can become legal the next or vice versa. Relying on human criteria alone also means there is no universal standard for justice and ultimately nothing is sacred or inviolable.

---

38. The translations used in quoting from the *Declaration of the Rights of Man and of the Citizen* are from *Human and Constitutional Rights Documents*. For the original French version see Van Asbeck, *The Universal Declaration of Human Rights*, 48–51.

These humanistic principles of democracy, law and liberty are, for the most part, muted in the constitutional documents of the United States and Canada but are nevertheless clearly present. We read in the American Declaration of Independence (1776):

> We hold these truths to be self-evident: that all men are created equal; that they are endowed by their Creator with certain inalienable rights; that among these are life, liberty, and the pursuit of happiness. That, to secure these rights, governments are instituted among men, deriving their just powers from the consent of the governed.

Note that although the Creator is mentioned, the powers of the government do not derive from God but "from the consent of the governed." That means that also the power to make laws for the nation depend on the consent of the governed. There is no constitutional basis for laws needing to comply with the demands of the living God. The rights to liberty and to the pursuit of happiness are to be interpreted similarly, without any overriding moral compass to define the extent of the liberty or the pursuit of happiness. With the denial of God's sovereignty, human sovereignty takes its place.

In Canada's past, the nation's constitutional affairs were dealt with in the British Parliament until 1982. In that year, Canada finally received her own constitution in The Constitution Act, 1982. The Preamble of Part I of this Act, entitled Canadian Charter of Rights and Freedoms, states that "Canada is founded upon principles that recognize the supremacy of God and the rule of law." One would think that this basis should be the point of departure for coming to judicial decisions based on the Charter. This however has not happened. The judiciary has virtually ignored "the supremacy of God." It is the concept of human dignity that has been recognized by the Supreme Court of Canada as the underlying principle upon which Canadian society is built.[39] In other words, also in Canada, man is sovereign and not God, and this ultimately defines Canada as "a free and democratic society" (Article 1 of this Charter).

It is important to note that all the inter-related ideas concerning democracy, law, and liberty are centered in the sovereignty of man. It is man's desire for and right to life, liberty, and happiness that is the foundation of current thinking on government related issues in

---

39. See Sossin, "The 'supremacy of God,'" 227–41.

the Western world today. This is a complete turnabout and revolution from acknowledging God's sovereignty in all issues of life as had been the case when Christian thinking dominated the West. The difference between the Christian world view with God as sovereign and consistent humanistic and Enlightenment thinking where man is sovereign could not be greater. If the world-view of mankind alone as sovereign is carried through to its logical conclusion, the implications are enormous. This point will become clear when we deal with current issues in chapters 5 to 9.

For now, it is good to remember that this man-centered thinking emerged within a Christian matrix, and also that in God's providence some of the practical results of humanistic thinking have had beneficial effects and are consistent with biblical principles. For example, although there is a world of difference between the biblical covenant concept under a sovereign God and a humanistic social contract, yet the idea of a social contract of the people with the government finds its roots in a biblical covenant ideal. Due in part to Christian influence, the social contract notion has the benefit of clearly outlining the duties and responsibilities of government and citizens over against each other.[40] Another example is the concern for human rights. This is a good thing. Although humanistic thought bases human rights in mankind itself rather than in God's just demands in the Ten Commandments, yet the concern for human rights and the resulting safeguarding of human liberties are to be applauded and are consistent with Christianity.[41]

In other cases, the Christian matrix within which the Enlightenment arose provides a corrective force. According to humanistic thinking, man is sovereign and only needs to obey laws to which he has given his voluntary assent. However, if such thinking were taken to its logical conclusion there would be chaos and anarchy. And so, although the rule of law as a higher authority above man is antithetical to humanistic presuppositions, yet it is needed to keep order. Such a notion of the rule of law, that is, of law being above and standing in

---

40. See De Gruchy, *Christianity and Democracy*, 91–92; Tödt, "Freedom: Theological," 351–52. Also see, e.g., *Social Contract: Essays by Locke, Hume, and Rousseau*.

41. For human rights see further chapter 4.

judgment of all, is a result of the biblical influence of Christianity.[42] And so, although Christianity's influence is waning in the Western world, the residual presence of Christian principles still has an effect in mitigating some of the possible disastrous consequences of a completely man-centered world view followed to its logical conclusion.[43]

THE NATURE OF THE CONFLICT

The two main influences on our Western political heritage, Christianity and humanism, are based on two profoundly different premises. Christianity recognizes the authority and sovereignty of God as revealed in his Word whereas humanism insists on the priority and sovereignty of the people. Contrary to widely held notions, not only Christianity but also humanism is religious in nature. After all, in humanism there is a virtual deification of man. Instead of the Creator being worshipped and obeyed, it is man, the creature, who sets the norms and expects unconditional obedience. This demands faith, because evidence for the validity of this worship of a fallen creature is wanting, as is evident from two other features of humanism as a religion.[44]

Like the biblical religion, humanism also looks forward to a utopian future, although humanism bases its hope for a perfect society of peace and justice solely on man and not on the redeeming work of God in Jesus Christ. A related indicator of the religious nature of humanism is its optimistic faith in human progress. Contrary to the historical evidence, there is always the hope that things will get better through the efforts of man and that utopia can be reached.[45] Much faith is needed for this since history has shown the futility of human striving for perfection. God's work of salvation as detailed in his Word is needed.

There is much truth in the statement of Harold Berman that "liberal democracy was the first great secular religion in Western history—the first ideology which became divorced from traditional

---

42. De Gruchy, *Christianity and Democracy*, 91–94; also see Koyzis, *Political Visions and Illusions*, 129.

43. See also the discussion in Witte Jr., "Law and Legal Theory," 225.

44. See on these and related issues Koyzis, *Political Visions and Illusions*, 186–202.

45. See for these two characteristic features of modern ideology Watkins, *The Age of Ideology*, 7–8.

Christianity."⁴⁶ It has further been pointed out that secular faiths or ideologies can be characterized as having a militantly revolutionary character.⁴⁷ This is certainly true of humanism. With its stress on the sovereignty of man and the exultation of reason over faith it stands in diametric opposition to Christianity. Indeed, Guillaume Groen van Prinsterer, the nineteenth century Dutch Protestant political thinker, eloquently showed that the humanism that led to the French Revolution and that is still a formative political notion today is based on the rejection of the God of the Bible. This humanistic way of thinking is, therefore, in the process of overturning the Christian foundations of Western civilization.⁴⁸ It is truly revolutionary in the full meaning of the term.

To be sure, humanism promotes some wonderful ideals like justice, liberty, toleration, and morality. But, these are not original to humanism. They have been taken from Christianity. However, when humanism has been consistently true to its secularist presuppositions, (and thankfully it is not always consistent), it has cut these ideals from faith in God and rooted them in faith in the basic goodness of man. The result then is that instead of justice came injustice; instead of liberty, compulsion; instead of toleration, persecution; and instead of altruism, egoism.⁴⁹

What we see today is, therefore, basically the struggle between faith in man and faith in the God of Scripture. It is at bottom a religious conflict. As we go through the various topics in this book, this will become more and more clear. There is no such thing as religious neutrality.⁵⁰

---

46. Berman, "Religious Foundations," 38 as quoted by De Gruchy, *Christianity and Democracy*, 57.

47. Watkins, *The Age of Ideology*, 3–4.

48. G. Groen van Prinsterer, *Unbelief and Revolution: A Series of Historical Lectures* (1847), 191–215, 263, as translated and found in the second half of Harry Van Dyke, *Groen Van Prinsterer's Lectures on Unbelief and Revolution* (Jordan Station ON: Wedge, 1989). According to Groen van Prinsterer the revolutions in The Netherlands (sixteenth century), England and the American colonies were different in essence and principle from the French Revolution. Groen van Prinsterer, *Unbelief and Revolution*, 262–63.

49. The French Revolution illustrates this truth. Groen van Prinsterer, *Unbelief and Revolution*, 187–88, 231–56 as translated and found in the second part of Van Dyke, *Groen Van Prinsterer's Lectures on Unbelief and Revolution*.

50. This truth was clearly brought to the fore by Abraham Kuyper, who was much

SUGGESTED READING

De Gruchy, John W. *Christianity and Democracy*. Cambridge: Cambridge University Press, 1995. A scholarly work exploring the relationship of Christianity and democracy.

DeMar, Gary. *America's Christian History: The Untold Story*. Powder Springs, GA: American Vision, 2008 (1995). A popular study underlining the influence of Christianity in American history.

Kelly, Douglas F. *The Emergence of Liberty in the Modern World: The Influence of Calvin on Five Governments from the 16th through 18th Centuries*. Phillipsburg, NJ: P&R, 1992. A clear testimony to the impact of Calvin's thinking on civil government.

Van Dyke, Harry. *Groen van Prinsterer's Lectures on Unbelief and Revolution*. Jordan Station, ON: Wedge Publishing Foundation, 1989. A translation and analysis of Groen Van Prinsterer's classic work, illustrating the roots of the French revolution (and thereby much current political thinking) in unbelief.

Witte Jr., John and Frank S. Alexander, eds. *Christianity and Law: An Introduction*. An authoritative collection of essays by experts on the influence of Christianity on the development of Western law.

---

influenced by Groen van Prinsterer. By insisting on the sovereignty of God over all creation, Kuyper showed that also in political and governmental matters there is the antithesis between faith in God and man. He founded the Anti-Revolutionary Party, and was Prime Minister of the Netherlands from 1901 to 1905. See, e.g., Abraham Kuyper, "Maranatha," in *Abraham Kuyper: A Centennial Reader*, ed. James D. Bratt (Grand Rapids, MI: Eerdmans, 1997), 206–28.

Part B
Basic Principles

2

The Origin and Task of the Civil Government

THERE SEEMS TO BE a love-hate relationship with government in society today. People love the government for the benefits it gives and they readily turn to the government in time of need. However, many are loath to respect it for the authority it has over them, especially at income tax time. How should we consider government? Is it just an evil necessity or is there more to it?

This chapter mainly considers the biblical norms for government and what ideally should be the situation. Subsequent chapters will deal more fully with the actual circumstances of governing in a post-modern democracy and the challenges these realities present for Christians.

THE ORIGIN OF CIVIL GOVERNMENT

The origin of all governing authorities is God. Romans 13:1 states that "there is no authority except that which God has established. The authorities that exist have been established by God." This truth was graphically illustrated in Old Testament times when God told the prophet Jeremiah to pass on his message to no fewer than five kings. These were the kings of Edom, Moab, Ammon, Tyre, and Sidon whose envoys were then in Jerusalem. The message was that God had made the earth and its people and he could give it to anyone he pleased. He would, therefore, now hand over all their countries to his servant Nebuchadnezzar, king of Babylon. They would have to serve him (Jer 27:5–6). In a similar vein, Daniel confessed that God "sets up kings and deposes them" (Dan 2:21, also see v. 37). He also prophesied to King Nebuchadnezzar that he would be driven from his palace and live with the wild animals "until you acknowledge that the Most High is sovereign over the kingdoms of men and gives them to anyone he wishes" (Dan 4:25, 32; 5:21). God, and he alone, is the source of all governing authority. It is not in the first place the sword of men or the power of those who rule, but it is God who is sovereign and almighty. He puts governments in their place, although he uses human agents to fulfill his purposes.

An early hint of government is found in Scripture after the Noachian flood. The antediluvian world with its sin, corruption, and violence had been destroyed. Then, among other things, God decreed that "whoever sheds the blood of man, by man shall his blood be shed; for in the image of God has God made man" (Gen 9:6). These words imply that those who would execute the murderer would themselves not be guilty of crime when punishing the offender. This divine decree is a new development since God had previously protected the life of the murderer Cain so that his next of kin could not take it (Gen 4:15). God's post-flood decree would therefore suggest that a higher authority, removed from the family circle, would now have to be responsible for administering justice. As noted, it is God himself who established such a higher authority in government.[1]

It is noteworthy that Scripture does not distinguish between different types of government, some to be obeyed and others not. All governing authorities are ultimately established by God and thus need to be honored. Ancient Israel was ruled by judges, kings, and foreign monarchs, but God expected his people to obey these diverse authorities (cf. Judg 2:16–22; Prov 24:21; Jer 29:7). It is the same in New Testament times. The Lord Jesus recognized the Romans as legitimate governors of the land and taught that the appropriate tribute be paid to Caesar (Matt 22:16–22). When Christ appeared before Pontius Pilate he told the Roman governor: "You would have no power over me if it were not given to you from above" (John 19:11), meaning from God. Christ thus recognized that he was standing before the judge who was placed there by God himself.

The apostles understood their Master's teaching. Paul's command is clear: "Everyone must submit himself to the governing authorities . . . . he who rebels against the authority is rebelling against

---

1. For discussions on Gen 9:6 and civil government see, e.g., James, "Divine Justice," 201–5 and Aalders, *Genesis*, 1:202–5 Also with God's recognition of the avenger of blood, next of kin to the one killed, the role of government was indispensable (Num 35:12, 24–25). Also see chapter 5 note 36 and pp. 120–21.

what God has instituted, and those who do so will bring judgment on themselves (Rom 13:1–2). Obedience was urged, without any apparent qualification or exception.² To Timothy, Paul wrote: " I urge, then, first of all, that requests, prayers, intercession and thanksgiving be made for everyone—for kings and all those in authority, that we may live peaceful and quiet lives in all godliness and holiness. This is good, and pleases God our Savior" (1 Tim 2:1–3). Paul exhorted Titus: "Remind the people to be subject to rulers and authorities, to be obedient" (Titus 3:1). Peter also exhorted his readers: "Submit yourselves for the Lord's sake to every authority instituted among men: whether to the king, as the supreme authority, or to governors.... Show proper respect to everyone... fear God, honor the king" (1 Pet 2:13–14, 17). However, the authority of civil government over its people is never absolute. Should a choice have to be made, then "we must obey God rather than men" (Acts 5:29). The issue of civil disobedience will be considered in Chapter 10.

In summary, government derives its authority from God. Regardless of the type of administration it is, all authority finds its origin in the Almighty. This was true of Pilate and the Roman emperor in New Testament times. It is also true of dictatorships and democracies of our day. All this is not to say that God approves of every form of government or of everyone who holds governmental office.³ It does mean that God is the one who has ordained the institution of government and that all authority to rule comes from him. In our democratic context, we need to mindful that ultimately it is not the voters who put governments in power, but, at the end of the day, it is the sovereign God of heaven and earth who does so. It is, therefore, ultimately to him that government is responsible. Furthermore, since God is the origin of government, we are to obey and honor those set over us by God, unless obedience to the authorities means disobedience to God. Also we must thank God for his provision of government and the gifts that accompany it. After all, government is to be God's servant for good.

---

2. Murray notes possible reasons for reminding the Christians to be subject to the authorities such as perverted notions of freedom with respect to the lordship of Christ. Murray, *Romans*, 2.146–47.

3. See Koyzis, *Political Visions and Illusions*, 249.

GOD'S SERVANT FOR GOOD

If government owes its position to God, then one can expect that God wants his interests served and that he gives the essence of its mandate. Romans 13 is instructive on these points.

> Everyone must submit himself to the governing authorities, for there is no authority except that which God has established. The authorities that exist have been established by God. Consequently, he who rebels against the authority is rebelling against what God has instituted, and those who do so will bring judgment on themselves. For rulers hold no terror for those who do right, but for those who do wrong. Do you want to be free from fear of the one in authority? Then do what is right and he will commend you. For he is God's servant to do you good. But if you do wrong, be afraid, for he does not bear the sword for nothing. He is God's servant, an agent of wrath to bring punishment on the wrongdoer. Therefore, it is necessary to submit to the authorities, not only because of possible punishment but also because of conscience. This is also why you pay taxes, for the authorities are God's servants, who give their full time to governing. Give everyone what you owe him: If you owe taxes, pay taxes; if revenue, then revenue; if respect, then respect; if honor, then honor (Rom 13:1–7).

Notice how the governing authorities are characterized "as God's servant" (v. 4). There are at least two basic implications that follow from this characterization. First, as servant of God, the civil authorities are subservient to God and must, therefore, recognize his higher authority. Civil government can never consider itself as an autonomous power. As servants of the Almighty, they are duty bound to recognize and enforce God's ordinances and seek to do his will. Second, being servants of God implies that governments will have to give account to God for the manner in which they have sought to honor their Master, God in heaven, and for the way they have dealt with the people entrusted to them (cf. Ps 58, 82).

In general, the task of the ruling authorities is to be "God's servant to do you good." Government must seek the well-being of the people, but this is not the same as government simply being in the service of the people and doing their will. As those placed in authority by God, ideally the norm for government to follow should ultimately be not what the people want, but what God desires. As servant of God, government receives its mandate from above and not, in the first place, from the people. As such government should seek the well-being not only of the majority, but of all the people in the land.

Being God's servant to do good to the population means that government must ensure justice. Government is "God's servant, an agent of wrath to bring punishment on the wrongdoer" (Rom 13:4). A similar description is found in 1 Peter 2:14 where governors are characterized as those "who are sent by him to punish those who do wrong and to commend those who do right." Clearly, a central and critical duty of government is to restrain evil and punish the evil doer. This responsibility can include taking the life of those who committed crimes worthy of death "for he does not bear the sword for nothing" (Rom 13:4). Such capital punishment would be in line with God's directive in Genesis 9:6. "Whoever sheds the blood of man, by man shall his blood be shed; for in the image of God has God made man." However, before such an ultimate penalty can be exacted, it must meet the standards of God's justice which includes the principle of needing two witnesses for a conviction (Deut 19:15). In any case, government as God's servant has the general task to maintain justice and order. This duty indicates that government is necessary to restrain the natural tendency of man to do evil and that maintaining justice is central to the task of government.

The fact that government "does not bear the sword for nothing" (Rom 13:4) shows that it can use coercion to do its duty. Indeed, government is the only part of society that can legitimately use armed force to enforce justice. Individuals have no such right or duty. They are to avoid violence. As a matter of fact, in the larger context of Romans 13 we read the admonition: "Do not take revenge, my friends, but leave room for God's wrath, for it is written: 'It is mine to avenge; I will repay,' says the Lord. On the contrary: 'If your enemy is hungry, feed him; if he is thirsty, give him something to drink. In doing this, you will heap burning coals on his head. Do not be overcome by evil, but overcome evil with good'" (Rom 12:19–21; cf. Matt 5:39). It is also telling that when Peter cut off the ear of the high priest's servant (John 18:10), Christ said: "Put your sword back in its place, for all who draw the sword will die by the sword" (Matt 26:52). Government, however, is to bear the sword and this must not be done in vain. God has different expectations from government than from private individuals and citizens.⁴

Finally, it should be noted that government as God's servant is under the authority of the risen Christ. Since the Lord Jesus has ascended into heaven he sits at the right hand of God the Father. He rules creation for the Father until the day of his return in glory (cf. 1 Cor 15:24). Christ has been given all authority on heaven and on earth (Eph 1:20–21; Matt 28:18). He is "the ruler of the kings of the earth" (Rev 1:5). And so the ruling authorities today are under the kingship of Jesus Christ, whether they recognize it or not for "God placed all things under his feet and appointed him to be head over everything" (Eph 1:22). Indeed, "in him all things hold together" (Col 1:17).⁵

Limitations

The general description of the duty of government in Romans 13 and elsewhere suggests that the task of the governing authorities is a relatively limited one. To a modern mind this may seem strange. Today government intrusion into the lives of its citizens grows continually. Virtually every aspect of our existence is touched by state controls and laws. To be sure, the desirability of this is being debated. On the one side of the political spectrum are those who would want the government to be even more involved in assuring adequate guarantees for the well-being of its citizens, particularly in matters of health care, minimum incomes, and redistribution of wealth. Such notions are typically classified as belonging to liberalism or in its more extreme forms, to socialism. On the other side are those who want government activity to be limited to the basic essentials such as law and order, defense, and providing for the most needy in society. Such views tend to be associated with conservatism.

How should Christians consider the scope of the task of government? Since it is critical to know what the Bible teaches, we must try to distance ourselves from modern problems and streams of political thought so that we can first listen to what God's Word has to tell us. It

---

4. See on this point Julian Rivers, "Government," 144.

5. Oliver O'Donovan rightly insists on the political significance of Christ's resurrection, ascension, and kingship over the nations. O'Donovan, *The Desire of the Nations*, 120–57. Christ is officially recognized as the ultimate ruler in both the Irish and British constitutions. See Rivers, "Disestablishment and the Church of England," 70–71. This official recognition is a vestige of the European time of Christendom.

will then become clear that no single political philosophy, be it liberalism or socialism or conservatism really captures the biblical message of the scope of the duty of government. We must go beyond these human ideologies.⁶

Scripture makes clear that a government's task has limitations. Only God is sovereign and he is the source of all authority. The civil authorities are his servants (Rom 13:4). A servant can only do what his master or lord gives him authorization for. Governments must therefore be mindful of their limitations and be careful not simply to assume more and more power to themselves. The question whether it is legitimate for a government to take on more power needs to be asked constantly. After all, there are other divinely ordained authority structures that need to be respected. This was already clear in Old Testament times. A king could not simply do what he wished. When King Uzziah entered the temple of the Lord to burn incense in the Holy Place he overstepped his authority. Burning incense was the prerogative of the priest and not the king. He was chased out of the temple and God struck him with leprosy (2 Chron 26:16–21). Other areas of authority that needed to be safeguarded included the family and the home. For example, a creditor could not simply enter someone's home in order to get a pledge for a loan (Deut 24:10–11). He had no authority inside the home and thus had to remain outside and respect his limitations, even as a creditor. In the New Testament it is striking how the apostolic admonitions in letters like Ephesians, Colossians, and Titus show the different societal relationships which exist and need to be honored. The apostle addresses office bearers and those subject to them, parents and children, masters and servants, rulers and citizens, and elders and members of the congregation. Nothing suggests that those in authority in one relationship are subordinate to those in other relationships. Each relationship, whether of the home, or place of work, or church, is independent and accountable in the first place to God from whom their authority comes.⁷

Such diversity in societal relationships has been called sphere-sovereignty by Abraham Kuyper. The point he made was that under

---

6. For a Christian treatment and evaluation of the different political ideologies, see Koyzis, *Political Visions and Illusions*.

7. See Eph 6:1–9; Col 3:18–4:1; Titus 2:1–3:2. For this example, see Van Riessen, *The Society of the Future*, 74.

the overarching lordship of Christ each sphere or sector of life has its own authority and responsibilities. Thus the state should not seek totalitarian control of another sphere, like the family or church or economic life.[8] The term sphere sovereignty has been criticized because sovereignty belongs to God alone and the reality of life does not always allow us to fully separate the different sectors of life—to mention but two objections. It is therefore better to describe the point made as differentiated authority or differentiated responsibility.[9] The concept that lies behind the terms sphere sovereignty, or differentiated authority, is an important one and it actually has a long history in Western thought.[10] We do well to maintain it. This notion will help us to understand more fully the positive duty of government and the inherent limitations in its role. After all, not only government, but also the citizens have responsibilities and the government should not interfere with these. We will be returning later in this chapter to the concept of differentiated responsibility or authority.

The First Task of Civil Government

As noted earlier, the ruling authority "is God's servant to do you good. But if you do wrong, be afraid, for he does not bear the sword for nothing. He is God's servant, an agent of wrath to bring punishment on the wrongdoer" (Rom 13:4). In view of this biblical description, one can argue that the first task of government is to establish justice and righteousness and to maintain the same. Government can use the power of the sword as necessary to achieve this end.

In this connection, questions come up. What is the "good" that Romans 13:4 refers to? ("He is God's servant to do you good.") What is justice? Practically every government and ideology speak of pursuing justice and righteousness. But justice and what's good for the people will be interpreted quite differently by a Chinese Communist government and a Western democracy. Closer to home, a liberal lawgiver will have an idea of justice which is different from that of his conservative

---

8. See especially Kuyper, "Sphere Sovereignty," 461–90.

9. For a critique on sphere sovereignty, see, e.g., Douma, *Another Look at Dooyeweerd*, 58–65. For a critique and a defense for speaking of "differentiated authority" and "differentiated responsibility" see Koyzis, *Political Visions and Illusions*, 229–43.

10. See, e.g., Wells, "Reformational Thought," 42–46; cf. also Spykman, "Sphere-Sovereignty," 163–208.

colleague on a variety of issues that may need to be decided. So what are the norms of justice which a government must follow? In a way, the answer is straightforward and simple. If government is God's servant, then it is God's sense of justice and righteousness that must be honored and pursued. This chapter will therefore deal in general with some of the important elements of God's norms for society. The following chapters will consider special issues and difficulties that come up for a democratic government to consistently implement God's standards for justice in a secular culture.

If government is to maintain justice as God's servant, then it needs to heed God's norms as set out in his Word. Such obedience should be done in the realization that God is the Creator and he knows exactly what his creation and humanity needs. It is therefore important that his standards for society be honored. What does God's demand for justice entail? The biblical concept of justice and righteousness means to act in accordance with the law and revealed will of God. And basic to God's law is the command to love him and our neighbor. Justice and love are, therefore, not opposing concepts. They can be mentioned in one breath, so to speak: "maintain love and justice" (Hos 12:6) or in parallelism: "the Lord loves righteousness and justice; the earth is full of his unfailing love" (Ps 33:5; cf. Isa 61:8; Jer 9:24). Since government must maintain justice which is closely related to love, the command to love the neighbor has relevance for the governing authorities as well.

The Lord, therefore, never tired in urging his Old Testament people to uphold his demands for society. "Let justice roll on like a river, righteousness like a never-failing stream!" (Amos 5:24). Typical is also the proclamation through the prophet Isaiah. "Take your evil deeds out of my sight! Stop doing wrong, learn to do right! Seek justice, encourage the oppressed. Defend the cause of the fatherless, plead the case of the widow" (Isa 1:16–17). The government, the king in this case, should have set the example and led the people in God's ways. But in the days of the prophets the situation was dismal.

It will be instructive to look at some biblical examples of what actually happened when governments no longer honored justice and righteousness as determined by God's law.[11] A consideration of the devastating effects of disobedience to God's directives will help us to

---

11. For what follows, see, e.g., McIlroy, *A Biblical View of Law and Justice*, 89–113 and Birch, *Let Justice Roll Down*, 259–69.

appreciate the importance of maintaining God's principles and norms for society today. One will notice that in a sense there is nothing new under the sun (Eccl 1:9).

A lack of government leadership in exercising true justice and righteousness impacted the life of the people in different ways. Not surprisingly the effect was also evident in the courts and judicial system. The prophets confronted those responsible "who acquit the guilty for a bribe, but deny justice to the innocent" (Isa 5:23). "You who turn justice into bitterness and cast righteousness to the ground. ... you hate the one who reproves in court and despise him who tells the truth. You trample on the poor ... For I know how many are your offenses and how great your sins. You oppress the righteous and take bribes and you deprive the poor of justice in the courts" (Amos 5:7, 10-11, 12). God held the rulers responsible. "Listen, you leaders of Jacob, you rulers of the house of Israel. Should you not know justice, you who hate good and love evil; who tear the skin from my people and the flesh from their bones ... Hear this, you leaders of the house of Jacob, you rulers of the house of Israel, who despise justice and distort all that is right; who build Zion with bloodshed, and Jerusalem with wickedness. Her leaders judge for a bribe" (Micah 3:1-2, 9-11).

As could be expected, lack of justice in high places and the courts also had detrimental effects in economic life. For example, it was God's will for Israel that the ancestral land given to each tribe and family should remain with them in perpetuity (Lev 25). This prevented the accumulation of property to the detriment of the poor in society. However, God's just wishes had not been heeded. The consequences were the loss of family land and abject poverty. The economic fallout was addressed by the prophets. Their message was clear for those in power who exploited the poor. "The Lord enters into judgment against the elders and leaders of his people: 'It is you who have ruined my vineyard; the plunder from the poor is in your houses. What do you mean by crushing my people and grinding the faces of the poor?' declares the Lord, the Lord Almighty" (Isa 3:14-15). God "looked for justice, but saw bloodshed; for righteousness, but heard cries of distress. Woe to you who add house to house and join field to field till no space is left and you live alone in the land" (Isa 5:7-8).

Needless to say such unjust economic measures left many marginalized in the life of the nation. But it is instructive how each disadvantaged individual is precious to the Lord. "He upholds the cause of the oppressed and gives food to the hungry. The Lord sets prisoners free, the Lord gives sight to the blind, the Lord lifts up those who are bowed down, the Lord loves the righteous. The Lord watches over the alien and sustains the fatherless and the widow, but he frustrates the ways of the wicked" (Ps 146:7–9).

Another result of government not honoring its duty to maintain and promote God's righteousness and justice was that the worship of God became superficial and formalistic throughout the land. This could be expected. With no moral leadership, the God of justice was no longer taken seriously by those who set the course for the nation. If God was no longer honored by the leaders, why should the people who follow them honor him? God can only be truly worshipped if true justice is promoted. But the opposite was happening and so lip service to God, religious formalism, and hypocrisy set in. Therefore God said through Amos: "I hate, I despise your religious feasts; I cannot stand your assemblies. . . . Away with the noise of your songs! I will not listen to the music of your harps. But let justice roll on like a river, righteousness like a never-failing stream!" (Amos 5:21, 23–24). Not only was the true God worshipped in a formalistic way, but gods like Baal were also worshipped in direct violation of the first commandment. Yet, the people were so calloused by sin that they nevertheless still went to the Lord's temple. God then said through Jeremiah: "Will you steal and murder, commit adultery and perjury, burn incense to Baal and follow other gods you have not known, and then come and stand before me in this house, which bears my Name, and say, 'We are safe'—safe to do all these detestable things?" (Jer 7:9–10). The temple would be destroyed (Jer 7:14). When a nation is not led by a government committed to true justice and righteousness, even the religious life of a nation becomes poisoned and corrupt.

These devastating effects on ancient Israelite society of government judicial negligence underscore the importance of the civil authorities promoting justice and righteousness today.

Maintaining justice in the land starts with acknowledging the sovereignty of God since he sets the norms. This acknowledgment is implied in the official national motto of the United States of America: "In God we trust." These words are found on the nation's currency and are also engraved above the Speaker's podium in the national House of Representatives in Washington. The Canadian Charter of Rights and Freedoms (1982) has a Preamble which acknowledges God's sovereignty by stating that "Canada is founded upon principles that recognize the supremacy of God and the rule of law." If God is to be recognized as supreme in North America, then the country's elected representatives have the first responsibility to set the moral compass of the country. It will not do to let the courts decide on the direction of a nation. We must remember that "righteousness exalts a nation, but sin is a disgrace to any people" (Prov 14:34; cf. Ps 33:12).

A government's responsibility begins with how it conducts itself. It must be obvious that the manner in which government does its business is above reproach, transparent, and accountable. The importance of the government's setting the example for the nation in how it manages its own responsibilities with integrity cannot be overestimated. A government that acts according to the highest moral principles gives a credible model for the nation to follow and so exerts a strong moral leadership. It goes a long way to raising the ethical level of a nation.

A government that sets a high moral bar will also make sure that the credibility of the judicial system is protected and maintained. Such credibility is enhanced when judges are appointed who realize that their task, when judging a particular case, is to interpret law and not to create new law according to the current moral whims of the majority. This practice of creating new law has, human nature being what it is, invariably led to lower moral standards for the nation.[12] Judicial activism also undermines confidence in the judicial process for one never knows for sure whether the law will be upheld or not. The elected representatives making up the legislative branch of government have the responsibility to pass new laws as necessary to enable the courts to judge consistent with the standards God has set.

With respect to maintaining justice by means of the courts, many other things could be mentioned. For example, it is important that processes of reconciliation and forgiveness be implemented where possible; that punishment be in proportion to the crime, and so on. But all these issues essentially fall under the government's responsibility to make it possible for judges to do their work consistent with God's law.[13]

---

12. See, e.g., Bork, *Coercing Virtue* and Leishman, *Against Judicial Activism*.

13. For biblical principles of law, see, e.g., Burnside and Baker, eds, *Relational*

With respect to the economic life of a nation, government has the obligation to set fair rules for commerce so that the rights of the economically weak in society are protected. Also, the civil authorities should allow the necessary freedom and possibilities to those who are able to create employment opportunities and take advantage of market conditions that promote the economic well being of the nation. All should share in times of prosperity. The government has an obligation to make sure that there are no uncared-for poor and needy in the land.[14]

Regarding North America's Christian heritage, governments have the obligation to protect this important treasure. Government by its very size and power leads a nation. When matters of national significance happen, the state should not be ashamed to acknowledge its dependence on the God of heaven and earth and offer prayer of thanksgiving in times of national rejoicing and petition for help and comfort in times of national tragedy. An example of how not to do it concerns a commemorative service for the 229 people killed in the crash of Swissair Flight 111 off Peggy's Cove, Nova Scotia. The Canadian federal government specifically denied a Christian minister the right to read from the New Testament or mention Jesus Christ during the official government-sponsored service held on September 9, 1998.[15] Government needs to create an environment where the Christian gospel can be freely preached. The next chapter will explore further the relation of church and state.

When a government is servant for good (Rom 13:4) and a country is ruled with justice and righteousness, then God promises that "the fruit of righteousness will be peace; the effect of righteousness will be quietness and confidence forever" (Isa 32:17). This also counts for governments and countries today.[16]

Justice, Montgomery, *The Law Above the Law* and McIlroy, *A Biblical View of Law and Justice*.

14. For biblical economic principles, see, e.g., Chewning, ed., *Biblical Principles and Economics* and Boersema, *Political-Economic Activity*; specifically on poverty, A. Kuyper, *The Problem of Poverty*, and Beisner, *Prosperity and Poverty*.

15. See, e.g., Corbella, "Christ's Name Banned from Memorial."

16. See also Rouvoet, *Reformatorische Staatsvisie*, 88.

Other Duties of Government

Moving beyond the immediate concerns of the core task of upholding justice and righteousness, we now consider other tasks that flow from these basic responsibilities. But first we need to place government in the larger framework of society and nation. How do individuals and other organizations in society relate to the government? Is the government the all-controlling head of everything or is its place more modest? Do organizations in society exist due to the good graces of the government or do they have their own right to exist? Should all of society look to government to sustain them or should government involvement be minimal? How we answer these questions will profoundly influence how we perceive the task of government.

The Bible teaches that each person has his or her own responsibilities. God created humans after his image and gave them a task in his world (Gen 1:26–30). He blessed the first couple and said to them: "Be fruitful and increase in number; fill the earth and subdue it. Rule over the fish of the sea and the birds of the air and over every living creature that moves on the ground" (Gen 1:28). So he entrusted to them and their descendants the right to exercise dominion over creation as well as to build and preserve it. This charge is often called the cultural mandate, with culture being understood in a very broad sense as encompassing all human activity that serves God's plan for his creation. This includes building families and other social units such as cities and governments. It also involves extracting from creation something of the potential that God put into it in terms of working the soil, building civilizations, inventing, making music, and doing science. The fall into sin brought much misery and struggle, but God kept the world from destruction, promised redemption from sin and Satan (Gen 3:15), and so made it possible for the cultural mandate to be maintained (cf. also Gen 9:1–7). Since the cultural mandate is a charge given to all humanity, everyone has his or her own responsibilities which, for example, no government can take away. This basic point would seem to argue for a society in which each person and organizational unit has the maximum possible freedom in the different aspects and relationships of life in order to be able to fulfill God's expectations for his or her life.[17]

---

17. Veling, *De Dienst Van de Overheid*, 34. On differentiated responsibilities, see also Rivers, "Government," 149–51.

The different relationships of life, such as a family, a business enterprise, a church, or an educational institution, all have their own specific needs and responsibilities which no one else can see to and assume for them. Differentiated responsibility suggests limitations to what government should be busy with. This point needs to be reaffirmed. One cannot expect government to do everything and assume all kinds of responsibilities that are not inherent to the core tasks of governing. Indeed, it is dangerous for a government to act as if it is omnipotent and has the solution for all types of problems and troubles in human society. It is relatively easy to create the myth that government will solve all difficulties. But there is a high price to be paid for this myth. It requires that people surrender their freedom and responsibilities to the state. The more government is asked to do, the more freedom needs to be given up by the population. However, to relinquish one's responsibilities so that the government can take care of the country's citizens is a denial of one's own obligations and duties to God. One must be ever vigilant of an all-powerful government as the examples of totalitarian states elsewhere remind us.

Even though democratic processes provide some guarantees against such excesses, yet the danger is not imaginary that even in a democratic society certain ways of thinking of how society should be organized can become so commonplace that government is tempted to impose them on the entire country and thereby rob many of their freedom. For example, in some circles it is becoming quite acceptable to assume that government has the duty to take care of pre-school children by providing subsidized day care facilities for all. Everyone would pay for this through taxation. However, taking care of pre-school children is a responsibility God has given to parents in the first place and not to the government. The state has no business in taking on this role for all the country's children but should rather seek to strengthen the family unit by making it economically attractive for a parent to stay at home to nurture the children. Children are also the beneficiaries when God's plan for the family unit is honored. The role of government should be limited.

On the other hand, while we must be vigilant against government assuming too many responsibilities, we must also not expect too little from this servant of God for our good (Rom 13:4). In many areas of life, a government is the only realistic body to assume certain responsibilities. Two examples come to mind. Only government with its authority and coercive power can see to it that the differentiated responsibilities and authorities in society are protected and able to function. Put differently, only government can make sure that the family unit, commercial enterprises, churches, and educational institutions (to mention the major players) all function as they should and contribute to the wholeness, proper functioning, and peace in society. Sin is very disruptive and in human relationships is never absent. Government has the duty to restrain sin and its effects and to let the different spheres of responsibility and authority function as God intended.[18]

A second example is that government can often best undertake mega economic projects that will be advantageous for the nation. The ongoing James Bay Project, a gigantic hydro-electric development in northern Quebec that has been under construction for over thirty years, would be inconceivable without long term sustained government funding. Perhaps in general it could be said that as long as government does not interfere in the God-given responsibilities of individuals and families and other societal organizations, government should be free to work for the common good where it can.

Summary of Duties

Government has ultimately been given its responsibilities by God and, therefore, those in government hold their office as a trust and stewardship from God. He expects government to rule and give leadership on his behalf. The duties of government are many and complex, but its accountability to God must never be forgotten. What follows is an attempt at listing responsibilities which rightly belong to government. There are arguably five major areas under which various relevant duties can be noted. Since the first responsibility of maintaining justice and righteousness can be conceived of as quite comprehensive, more could have been placed under it. The following breakdown is only one possible way of organizing the material. It is merely intended to help focus on the different areas of responsibility and not to provide a comprehensive inventory of duties. Some of the points raised will be

---

18. See, e.g., on this Koyzis, *Political Visions and Illusions*, 252–60.

The Origin and Task of the Civil Government 43

looked at more closely in the following chapters. The duties, following biblical principles, can be listed as follows:[19]

1. *Maintain justice and righteousness.*
    a. guard against the open and public transgression of God's law and promote good public morals (Deut 17:18–20; 2 Sam 23:3–4; Ps 2:10–12);
    b. maintain the rule of law (Rom 13:1–4);
    c. combat violence and injustice in society (Rom 13:1–4);
    d. promote peace in society (1 Tim 2:2);
    e. conduct the affairs of government with integrity and transparency (2 Sam 23:3–4);
    f. levy and collect taxes so government has the resources to do its duty (Rom 13:6–7);
    g. work for the general good and not for special lobby or interest groups which only seek benefits for themselves (Prov 29:4; Isa 1:23);
    h. ensure an impartial judiciary (Exod 23:6–9; Prov 24:23–25) that understands its task to interpret and apply law and not to work on creating new statues;
    i. ensure that punishment as determined by law should be in proportion to the crime (Exod 22:1, 4).
2. *Safeguard persons and their societal relationships and organizations so that they have the freedom to do their part of the cultural mandate.*
    a. protect persons and organizations against threats from a third party (cf. Isa 10:1–2);
    b. maintain full protection and freedom to the Christian church to preach the gospel and provide freedom for all faiths provided they honor the rules of a free society (1 Tim 2:2; Matt 13:30);

---

19. The major categories are from Veling, *De Dienst Van de Overheid*, 52–53, 56; see also Kuiper, *Dienstbare Overheid*, 36–40; Redekop, *Politics Under God*, 69–81.

    c. maintain rules and laws which promote the harmonious living and working together of society, both on a personal level as well as organizationally, both socially and economically (1 Tim 2:2);

    d. create new structures as necessary to allow relationships within society to flourish;

    e. ensure an adequate military force to defend the nation and meet its security needs (cf. Ps 72);

    f. help other nations by providing peace keeping forces.

3. *Create the conditions to make possible the doing of one's cultural mandate should current conditions make it impossible or should the work to be done be so important that government cannot risk leaving it undone or done inadequately.*

    a. combat poverty with appropriate programs that encourage employment and prevent destitution (Ps 82:3–4; Prov 14:31);

    b. combat exploitation and discrimination against those who are at the bottom of the social and economic ladders (Ps 82:3–4);

    c. provide training and essential services where needed or have them provided;

    d. provide care for the sick, aged, and handicapped as required (Deut 10:18);

    e. stimulate cultural activities that are consistent with the country's Christian heritage (cf. Phil 4:8).

4. *Co-ordinate activities of citizens and their organizations, for example, by laying down ground rules for such activities.*

    a. ensure that the various government departments, and regulatory and administrative agencies are consistent and fair in the decision-making process. The same policies and rulings need to be applied to all irrespective of race, culture, or religion (Ps 99:4).

5. *Do what no one else is doing through negligence or lack of opportunities.*

a. make higher education possible and accessible;
  b. protect the environment with a view to sustainable development (cf. Exod 23:10–11; Deut 20:19–20; Ps 8).

CONCLUDING COMMENTS

Government as established by God has an awesome responsibility. Those who govern are accountable to Almighty God. It is, therefore, important for Christians to give respect, honor and obedience to those in authority. Their task is difficult and they need our prayers (1 Tim 2:1–2).

The duties of government are many and varied. But so many responsibilities do not necessarily translate into an intrusive government. It is striking, to give one example, that the Bible indicates that rulers should be concerned about the plight of the poor (Ps 72). The problem of poverty is thus justifiably on the agenda of government. However, this does not necessarily mean that government has to look after each impoverished person. There are social networks which God has put in place to take care of that. The family is important in this regard (1 Tim 5:8).[20] But government has to see to it that what God has put in place actually functions. Those who govern have, therefore, been charged to "maintain the rights of the poor and oppressed" (Ps 82:3). They need to make sure that the rights of the poor are actually being honored.

The tendency today is to look to government for the solution to all society's problems. The attitude is often: "let the government take care of it." We need to realize that government has limitations. In some countries, such as the Netherlands, the realization is growing that the enormous bureaucratic welfare system that has grown over the last five decades or so is not sustainable in the foreseeable future. In such situations, governments need to make painful decisions on prioritizing cutbacks to its social programs and encouraging other sectors of society such as the family, the church, and the business world to assume their responsibilities. There is something very good about the realization that government cannot do everything. Other spheres of

---

20. See for the Old Testament background Cornelis Van Dam, *Perspectives on Worship, Law and Faith: The Old Testament Speaks Today* (Kelmscott, Western Australia: Pro Ecclesia, 2000), 67–69.

responsibility and authority need to be mobilized to step to the plate and make a contribution for the good of society.

Finally, one must realize that government regardless of its wealth and power is ultimately not able to save society and humanity, and solve its problems. The only lasting solution is Jesus Christ. He is the ultimate ruler and he will one day return to establish a renewed creation. Human beings can strive and hope for utopia, but they cannot establish a perfect world. Fallen humanity's legacy of sin creates problems such as wars, environmental disasters, and skewed population growth. It is only because of the patience and benevolence of Almighty God that such disasters are ameliorated by human efforts, but the lasting solution is elsewhere. This sense of realism is important in a Christian view of government.

SUGGESTED READING

Grudem, Wayne. *Politics According to the Bible: A Comprehensive Resource for Understanding Modern Political Issues in the Light of Scripture.* Grand Rapids, MI: Zondervan, 2010. An up-to-date comprehensive resource giving both general principles as well as specific direction on the place and task of government.

Meeter, H. Henry. *The Basic Ideas of Calvinism.* 6th ed. Rev. by Paul Marshall. Grand Rapids: Baker, 1990. A classic exposition with a major emphasis on the political ideas of Calvin.

Koyzis, David T. *Political Visions and Illusions: A Survey and Christian Critique of Contemporary Ideologies.* Downers Grove: InterVarsity, 2003. A comprehensive survey and Christian critique of key political ideologies.

Spencer, Nick and Jonathan Chaplin, ed. *God and Government.* London: SPCK, 2009. An interesting collection of essays exploring the proper function of government.

Van Dam, Cornelis. *God and Government: A Biblical Perspective on the Role of the State.* Lethbridge, AB: ARPA Canada, 2009. Available at http://arpacanada.ca. A presentation made to Members of Parliament and Senators in the Canadian Parliament in Ottawa.

3

Church and State

THE ISSUE OF THE relationship between the church and state has been and continues to be a contentious one. This chapter will consider some of the background to the present situation, the different approaches to the issue of church and state, and how the responsibilities of each institution can best be seen and implemented.

SOME HISTORICAL BACKGROUND

Early History

In the first centuries of its existence, the state often persecuted the Christian church. When Emperor Constantine made Christianity a legal religion in 313 AD, the church was beholden to him and, given the political realities of the time, Constantine had considerable influence on the church.[1] Imperial dominance eventually resulted in a long struggle, with the church seeking supremacy over the emperor. The church's power over secular authorities peaked under two medieval popes: Pope Gregory VII (1073–1085) who excommunicated the emperor, Henry IV, and forced him into a humiliating submission, and Pope Innocent III (1198–1216) who was the most successful in asserting papal power over secular authorities.[2] However, during the late Middle Ages civil rulers slowly gained a stronger position over against

---

1. For a nuanced and interesting description of the era and Constantine's role, see Leithart, *Defending Constantine*.

2. See, e.g., Walker, et al., *A History of the Christian Church*, 275–77, 368–69. More specifically, see, e.g., Pope Gregory VII's *Dictatus Papae* (1075) which asserted papal sovereignty over church and state. For the text see O'Donovan and O'Donovan, eds, *From Irenaeus to Grotius*, 242–43.

the Roman church due to a variety of circumstances and this trend has continued to the present time.

Today the Roman Catholic Church has no civil authority except in Vatican City. It needs to be noted though that the Roman Church has never disowned the belief that civil authority is to be subservient to that of the church. The papal coronation ceremony reflects this conviction. A new pope is crowned with the words: "Receive the tiara adorned with three crowns and know that you are Father of Princes and Kings, Ruler of the World, Vicar of Our Savior Jesus Christ in earth, to whom is honor and glory in the ages of ages"[3] This Roman Catholic view is to be rejected for it does not properly acknowledge the authority and task which God has given to civil government.

In the time of the Reformation, Protestants took different approaches to the problem of the relation of church and state. In the chaotic situation of his day, Luther, and those who followed him, entrusted the care of the church to the different civil authorities that make up present day Germany. The territorial princes basically organized church life and even appointed men to govern the church. The long term result of this was that the Lutheran church became a church under the authority of the state. One eventual consequence of this status of the church was that during the Nazi regime, Hitler's goal to control the church was simplified and many church leaders acknowledged his authority over the church.[4]

In England, Parliament honored the selfish wishes of King Henry VIII in his political struggle against the papacy by passing the Act of Supremacy (1534) which made the king and his successors head of the church at the expense of the pope. It was however understood that the administration of the Word and sacraments was not hereby given to the king. The new status of the monarch was also reflected in the Thirty-nine Articles of the Church of England (1571). Today the ruling British monarch remains the supreme governor of the Church

---

3. See Nabuco, "Papal Ceremony and Vesture," 972 and also, e.g., the Syllabus of Errors (issued by Rome in 1864) which asserted the Pope's temporal authority over all civil rulers. For an overview of the Roman Catholic position, see Van Ruler, *Calvinist Trinitarianism and Theocentric Politics*, 160–61.

4. Those who resisted formed the Confessing Church and eventually, in cooperation with other churches, the Barmen Declaration was drafted in 1934. It insisted that only Christ is the source of authority and truth for the church. See Peet, "The Protestant Churches in Nazi Germany," 440–41, 463–65, 487–89, 526–27.

of England, the established church, and bishops are appointed by the crown. A political system that makes the church subordinate to the state has been called Erastian, after the sixteenth century theologian Thomas Erastus who promoted this view. This is still the official situation in England with respect to the Anglican Church. The idea of an established church is however to be rejected because it wrongly presupposes that in a Christian nation church and state are co-extensive. As we shall see later in this chapter, the Bible teaches that the civil magistrate and the church are separate entities and each has been given its own specific task.

It has taken quite some centuries for the church and state to find their proper roles in society. Each has its own God-given office and duty. The state should not dominate the church and neither should the church do so to the state. When the church takes upon itself responsibilities that belong to the state, strange situations can arise. This truth is evident, for example, from events in the Netherlands of the sixteenth century. In October, 1566, an influential Reformed theologian, Petrus Dathenus, proposed in an ecclesiastical assembly in Ghent in the southern Netherlands that Philip of Spain be offered three million gold guilders in return for freedom of worship. But in December of that year, the Synod meeting in Antwerp acknowledged the legitimacy of armed rebellion and decided to use the money that had already been collected for recruiting troops! A subsequent ecclesiastical assembly on December 17 entrusted two ministers of the gospel with organizing an armed resistance against the authorities. In January, 1567, the Reformed Churches in the Southern Netherlands met again in Antwerp to discuss, among other points on their agenda, the collection of money and the raising of troops to fight for the church against the occupying power of Spain. The troops were mustered and by March of that year, the Spanish forces massacred this army of 3,000.

That such military matters were on the agenda of ecclesiastical assemblies shows that there was little clarity on the separation of the duties of the state and the church. This clarity was, however, forthcoming. In 1571, Prince William of Orange lost his bid to have the Reformed Synod of Emden give full and open support to his cause to liberate the Netherlands from the Spanish yoke. This struggle for liberation was a matter dear to the synodical delegates and they fully supported the prince. However, as an ecclesiastical assembly they refused the request of the Prince. In 1574 the Synod of Dordrecht decided that ecclesiastical assemblies could only deal with ecclesiastical matters.[5]

The struggle of the Dutch Calvinists to rightly discern the task of the church and the state raises the question how Calvin dealt with this problem. Calvin recognized that church and state are two different jurisdictions. In his *Institutes* he wrote that "Christ's spiritual Kingdom and the civil jurisdiction are things completely distinct." Calvin had no desire to establish a theocracy. "It is a Jewish vanity to seek and enclose Christ's Kingdom within the elements of this world."[6] The civil government has authority in the temporal things of this life, and the church in matters spiritual. Each has its own specific task. The government, therefore, has no right to meddle in the affairs of the church. However, civil government as a servant of God does have a duty towards God. It owes its position to God who is sovereign. For that reason the government must do God's will. Indeed, Calvin placed the governing authorities under the obligation to both tables of the Ten Commandments; that is, government should see as its duty to enforce also the first four commandments. The implication is state involvement in preventing idolatry, false worship, swearing, and the desecration of the day of rest.[7]

In order to appreciate Calvin's thinking and the influences that helped mold it, we need to place ourselves in the world in which he lived. In Calvin's day, all of society was considered Christian. As we have seen there was as yet no clear demarcation between the duties of the state and the church. However, since all of society was deemed Christian, it was considered obvious that the Christendom that had existed for over a thousand years should be maintained. As a result there was widespread agreement that one of the most important tasks of the state was to maintain the true religion and the Christian church. Calvin too saw it as the duty of government to rightly establish religion, meaning the true Christian faith.[8] It was therefore not strange that also "Calvin was convinced, and all the Reformers shared this

---

5. For the above, see the dissertation of Ruys Jr., *Petrus Dathenus*, 64–75; Janse, *Burgerlijke of Kerkelijke Politiek*, 34–40; Jansen, *Korte Verklaring Van de Kerkenordening*, 134–35; Parker, *The Dutch Revolt*, 120–21.

6. Both quotations are from *Institutes* IV.xx.1. The edition quoted is McNeill, ed., Battles, trans., *Calvin: Institutes of the Christian Religion*.

7. *Institutes* IV.xx.3,9.

8. *Institutes* IV.xx.3.

conviction, that it was the duty of a Christian magistrate to put to death blasphemers who kill the soul, just as they punished murderers who kill the body."[9] Calvin's active involvement for the execution of heretic Servetus is a well-known example of how Calvin was a child of his times in this respect. In a treatise written after the execution, he vigorously defended that it was just to put heretics and blasphemers to death since God required it.[10]

Although Calvin himself did not include the magistrate's duty of eradicating false religion in his Geneva Confession of 1536 (Article 21),[11] other Reformed creeds did. Calvin's thinking found its way into the Belgic Confession, Article 36, which in its original 1561 wording read in part that the government's "task of restraining and sustaining is not limited to the public order but includes the protection of the church and its ministry in order that all idolatry and false worship may be removed and prevented, the kingdom of Antichrist may be destroyed, the kingdom of Christ may come, the Word of the gospel may be preached everywhere, and God may be honored and served by everyone, as he requires in His Word." The Westminster Confession includes in its original 1647 text of Article 23 the following description of the task of civil government. "It is his duty to take order, that unity and peace be preserved in the Church, that the truth of God be kept pure and entire, that all blasphemies and heresies be suppressed, all corruptions and abuses in worship and discipline prevented or reformed, and all the ordinances of God duly settled, administered, and observed." Creedal statements such as the Scottish Reformed Confession of Faith (1560) and the Second Helvetic Confession (1566) expressed similar sentiments.

It is clear that there is an inconsistency and a tension here. The government and the church are to be separate and each is to have its own jurisdiction and yet the government is expected to remove and destroy idolatry and false worship (Belgic Confession) and sup-

---

9. Wendel, *Calvin*, 97. For the context of the times, also see McGrath, *A Life of John Calvin*, 120.

10. "Whoever shall now contend that it is unjust to put heretics and blasphemers to death will knowingly and willingly incur their very guilt." Calvin in his *Defensio orthodoxae fedei de sacra Trinitate* (1554) as quoted in Schaff, *Modern Christianity*, 8:791; see further De Greef, *The Writings of John Calvin*, 163–64. For the letter Calvin wrote to Farel (August 20, 1553) see John Calvin, *Letters of John Calvin*, 2:417.

11. On the authorship of the Geneva Confession, see Cochrane, ed., *Reformed Confessions*, 119.

press heresies and prevent corruption in the church (Westminster Confession). As we shall see, further reflection on the issue led to the conclusion that the Scriptural justification for an active state role in maintaining the purity of the church was inadequate and needed to be reconsidered. Furthermore, experience taught that entrusting the civil government with the duty to establish the true religion was not always good for the church. For example, although the cause of the Reformation in the Netherlands benefited greatly from a government that helped maintain Calvinist orthodoxy over against Arminian threats, all was not well. There even came a point when the government ruled over the church. From 1619 to 1789, the civil authorities did not allow a Reformed synod to be convened.[12] Similarly, the Scots found out that entrusting the civil authorities with prerogatives in ecclesiastical matters meant, for example, that Oliver Cromwell could disrupt and suppress General Assembles from 1650–1658.[13]

As time went on further clarity into what God expected of government in this area came about so that some of the tensions and inconsistencies could be addressed and to a certain extent removed.

Subsequent Developments

As society more and more lost its Christian character, the weakness of the biblical foundations for an active role of the civil authorities in suppressing heresy became increasingly evident. Over time, especially in the nineteenth and twentieth centuries, it became clear for many that the confessional basis which gave legitimacy to the civil authorities to protect and enforce the doctrine of the church could not be maintained. We need not go into all the details of this development here. The chief arguments that played a role in the discussion will be considered shortly. Suffice it for now to note the following.

With respect to the Westminster Confession, the original 1647 reading of Chapter XXIII.3 on the civil magistrate states:

> The civil magistrate may not assume to himself the administration of the Word and sacraments, or the power of the keys of the kingdom of heaven: yet he hath authority, and it is his

---

12. For other examples of government control, see Bolt in van Ruler, *Calvinist Trinitarianism and Theocentric Politics*, xxv.

13. Rankin, *The Church of Scotland*, 2:528, 532. See also Morris, *Theology of the Westminster Symbols*, 571–72.

duty, to take order, that unity and peace be preserved in the Church, that the truth of God be kept pure and entire, that all blasphemies and heresies be suppressed, all corruptions and abuses in worship and discipline prevented or reformed, and all the ordinances of God duly settled, administered, and observed. For the better effecting whereof, he hath power to call synods, to be present at them, and to provide that whatsoever is transacted in them be according to the mind of God.[14]

Both in Scotland, and even earlier in the American colonies, the duty of the magistrates with respect to suppressing heresy and abuse in worship was redefined.[15] In a nineteenth century American revision, a new and completely rewritten Chapter XXIII.3 was approved. It has been adopted and is now commonly held by American orthodox churches in the Presbyterian family. The revision reads as follows:

> Civil magistrates may not assume to themselves the administration of the Word and sacraments; or the power of the keys of the kingdom of heaven; or, in the least, interfere in matters of faith. Yet, as nursing fathers, it is the duty of civil magistrates to protect the church of our common Lord, without giving the preference to any denomination of Christians above the rest, in such a manner that all ecclesiastical persons whatever shall enjoy the full, free, and unquestioned liberty of discharging every part of their sacred functions, without violence or danger. And, as Jesus Christ hath appointed a regular government and discipline in his church, no law of any commonwealth should interfere with, let, or hinder, the due exercise thereof, among the voluntary members of any denomination of Christians, according to their own profession and belief. It is the duty of civil magistrates to protect the person and good name of all their people, in such an effectual manner as that no person be suffered, either upon pretense of religion or of infidelity, to offer any indignity, violence, abuse, or injury to any other person whatsoever: and to take order, that all religious and ecclesiastical assemblies be held without molestation or disturbance.[16]

14. Schaff, *The Creeds of Christendom*, 3:653.

15. For a convenient summary of the main actions taken in America and England and Scotland, see Schaff and Schaff, "Westminster Standards," 325–26.

16. For the text, see, e.g., "American Revisions to the Westminster Confession of Faith" at the Orthodox Presbyterian Church website. Similarly see, e.g., "The Westminster Confession of Faith," at the Presbyterian Church in America website. The Reformed Presbyterian Church in North America specifically rejects the controverted part of Chapter 23 of the 1647 Westminster Confession in its Testimony to

It is clear that the task of government with respect to the church is much more modest in this revision.

A similar development took place in Holland. In 1905 the General Synod of the Reformed Churches in the Netherlands deleted from Article 36 of the Belgic Confession any reference to the civil government having as its duty to suppress false religion. It did this by simply removing the words struck through in the following rendition of the relevant part of Article 36.[17]

> Their task [i.e. the civil government's] of restraining and sustaining is not limited to the public order but includes the protection of the church and its ministry in order that ~~all idolatry and false worship may be removed and prevented, the kingdom of antichrist may be destroyed~~ the kingdom of Christ may come, the Word of the gospel may be preached everywhere, and God may be honored and served by everyone, as he requires in his Word.

English-speaking Reformed churches which have their historic roots in the Netherlands have adopted or accepted this change as well.

However, not all agreed that these revisions were justified. The Free Church of Scotland retains the original 1647 reading of the relevant part of Chapter XXIII on the civil magistrate.[18] Another example can be found in the Netherlands. Those aligned with the Staatkundig Gereformeerde Partij, a political party, maintain the original text of Article 36 of the Belgic Confession.[19]

THE ROLE OF THE STATE

The Duty of the State Redefined

What were the biblical reasons for the revision of the Reformed and Presbyterian confessional formulations so that the duty of civil government no longer included the suppression of heresy and the punishment of heretics? In answering this question we first need to

---

that Article. See "The Constitution of the Reformed Presbyterian Church."

17. See in English, Godfrey, "Church and State in Dutch Calvinism," 240.

18. "The Westminster Confession of Faith," in the Free Church of Scotland website.

19. See K. van der Zwaag, *Onverkort of gekortwiekt?* 387–404.

consider how the original confessional statements were justified from Scripture.

The Scottish Confession of Faith (1560) speaks of the civil magistrate in Chapter 24. "Moreover we state that the preservation and purification of religion is particularly the duty of kings, princes, rulers and magistrates. They are not only appointed for civil government but also to maintain true religion and to suppress all idolatry and superstition. This may be seen in David, Jehoshaphat, Hezekiah, Josiah, and others highly recommended for their zeal in that cause."[20] Also the Belgic Confession (1561), Article 36, uses the Old Testament to define the task of the civil authorities. The Scripture passages referred to include 1 Kings 15:12 which speaks of King Asa's removal of male cult prostitutes and idols from the land, and 2 Kings 23 which details Josiah's reforms, including the slaying of the priests of the high places in Samaria.[21] Similarly the Westminster Confession refers to King Josiah, as well as to the death penalty exacted by the authorities in ancient Israel for blasphemers and false prophets (Lev 24:16; Deut 13:5–6).[22]

There are however great difficulties with this approach for one cannot equate the special position of Israel's theocratic kings with the rulers of our present age. This equation obliterates the vast differences between Israel's identity as a special nation called by God to be his holy people in whose midst he lived and a modern nation that has no such relationship with God. Today no nation can be identified as the special people of God.

No ruler today, therefore, stands in the same position as the Davidic kings who could be actively involved in Israel's worship of God and the reformation of their religion. King David, for example, organized liturgical matters (1 Chron 23–25) and made preparations for the construction of the temple (1 Chron 29) which was built and dedicated by Solomon (2 Chron 3–6). The office of the Davidic kings spoke of and pointed to the great King Jesus Christ. Psalm 2, for example, speaks of God establishing his king, his son, on Zion, his holy

---

20. Cochrane, *Reformed Confessions*, 183.

21. These passages are found in text of Dordrecht (1619) of the Belgic Confession as found in Bakhuizen van den Brink, *De Nederlandse Belijdenisgeschriften*, 142.

22. For the passages associated with the original Chapter 23 of the Westminster Confession, see Schaff, *The Creeds of Christendom*, 3:653.

hill. For that reason, King Solomon is described as sitting on the Lord's throne (1 Chron 29:23; 2 Chron. 9:8). Israel's king had to maintain the right worship of God and the pious kings who opposed idolatry are praised for it. The force of law was employed to maintain the holiness of the people of God and the death penalty was applied as necessary.

This use of civil law to maintain the discipline and sanctity of the chosen nation, in essence the church, is no longer the right of any civil authority today. The discipline of the people of God, the church, is a spiritual one, exercised by the sword of the Spirit, the Word of God (Eph 6:17; Heb 4:12–13; 2 Cor 10:4) and the extreme punishment is excommunication (Matt 18:17–18; 1 Cor 5:5). Such ecclesiastical discipline and punishment must always be distinguished from that exercised by civil authorities to whom God has even given the power of the sword (Rom 13:4).

Besides appealing to the Old Testament and equating the situation then with the present age, Calvin and others also sought justification from the New Testament. In the parable of the great banquet, the master tells his servant to "go out to the roads and country lanes and make them come in, so that my house will be full" (Luke 14:23). In his commentary on this passage, Calvin stated: "I do not disapprove of the use which Augustine frequently made of this passage against the Donatists, to prove that godly princes may lawfully issue edicts, for compelling obstinate and rebellious persons to worship the true God and to maintain the unity of the faith." This parable, however, does not speak of forcing those invited to come against their will. Rather, it tells us that when those who had first been invited did not want to come, others were invited from the streets and lanes of the city. And when there was still room, then the servant had to go out to the highways and hedges so that those people, who lived there unsheltered, be urged, yes compelled, to come because they would not otherwise dare to enter such a home since they considered themselves unworthy of this honor. There is no reference to the use of outward force against those privileged enough to be initially invited.

Indeed, there are indications in the New Testament which argue against such coercion. For example, the Lord Jesus said to Pontius Pilate, "My kingdom is not of this world. If it were, my servants would fight to prevent my arrest by the Jews. But now my kingdom is from another place" (John 18:36). The power of the kingdom of God is the gospel (cf. Rom 1:16). Faith overcomes the world, not the sword (1 John 5:4; cf. Zec 4:6).

The biblical support for the state having to see to the purity and doctrinal soundness of the church is weak at best. It is understandable that Presbyterian and Reformed confessions were revised in light of the biblical evidence. Indeed, as will become more clear, the state does not have the duty to coerce or seek to change the religious convictions of its citizens. It is the task of the church to change human hearts by preaching the gospel and making disciples of all nations (Matt 28:19–20).[23]

The issue of the respective duties of church and state is however not a simple one. For the question of the relationship of these two entities involves the larger concern of how the duty and responsibility of the civil authorities relate to the Bible and the Christian faith. Can the civil government be neutral over against the claims of Scripture, and more importantly the claims of God himself? Many different positions have been taken on this issue. For our purpose, to try to get some clarity on the matter, we will consider three important positions: voluntaryism and pluralism, theonomy, and principled pluralism.

Three Approaches

Voluntaryism and Pluralism

Already in the sixteenth century, the idea that the state had nothing to do with the church took root. This notion has historically been called voluntaryism. It was a reaction against the then commonly accepted idea of a Christian nation and the assumption that everyone was a member of a church—the ideal of Christendom with its unified society of state and church. The idea of voluntaryism was to remove and disentangle completely the church and state from each other. There was to be no state control of the church and the church was not to influence politics. This meant that the church should not be supported by the state, but by the willing contributions of those who were members of the church. Church membership should be completely voluntary and one could decide not to be a member. Using taxation money to support the church should cease since it gave the state control over

---

23. For more on this issue, see, e.g., Poythress, *The Shadow of Christ in the Law of Moses*, 289–310.

the church and it forced non-church members to support the church through the taxes they paid. Thus voluntaryism advocated the total and complete separation of church and state. The one has nothing to do with the other. Civil government exists only to maintain social order and to preserve societal peace. The state must never interfere in matters of conscience and religion.

There was initially much opposition to voluntaryism, one argument being that the moral health of society would be threatened if complete freedom of association were to be allowed. Furthermore, a uniformity of belief was considered necessary for a viable social order. Thomas Hobbes in 1651 defended the unrestricted sovereignty of the state which he called Leviathan, after the biblical monster, symbolizing total power and authority. In his view the church should be an arm of the state. There should be no association of any kind without the state.[24] However, freedom of association did carry the day and society became more diverse.

Today important ideas of voluntaryism are promoted under the name of pluralism. And it must be acknowledged that our times are ripe for the entrenchment of this political philosophy. The process of secularism has deeply impacted society. Church attendance is a far cry from what it was a century ago, or even several decades ago. This decline has also meant a decline of Christian influence in political life and in the market place of ideas. Coupled with secularization is the tremendous growth of a variety of religions in North America which has historically been dominated by Christian thinking. The ongoing immigration from different parts of the world with different religious traditions keeps fueling this diversity of faiths and world views. As a result of these realities, pluralism and multiculturalism are embraced as a way of keeping society happy. Each segment of society is free to do its own thing and is expected to be tolerant of others who think and live differently. It is clear that when pluralism is subscribed to consistently, there is no room for the absolutes of God's law. Relativism is the order of the day and a wide diversity of values and morals is tolerated.

---

24. For a brief overview of the history of voluntaryism, see Adams, *On Being Human Religiously*, 61–64; Thomas Hobbes famously spoke of voluntary associations outside state control as "worms in the entrails of the natural man," the natural man being the society of men. Hobbes, *Leviathan*, 221.

There are good things to be said about voluntaryism and pluralism. Voluntaryism forced a a more clear perception of the place and duties of the state and church. It is very good that the days when the state was heavily involved in the matters of the church are over. The tasks of the state and church are quite distinct and should be clearly differentiated.

All this is not to say that what has now resulted in a secular pluralism is the ideal. This is certainly not the case. The current pluralism has considerably weakened any commitment to Christian ethics and biblical norms for society. It is one thing for church and state each to have their legitimate authority in the areas assigned to them by God. It is entirely another to endorse a pluralism that seems to lack any normative biblical guidelines for society. A Christian cannot accept this as the ideal environment in which government is to function. The Bible teaches that God is sovereign and that his norms for society should be honored. This brings us to theonomy. It is in some ways the opposite of secular pluralism.

Theonomy

The word "theonomy" comes from two Greek words meaning "God" and "law". The term has come to designate an approach to politics which is also known as Christian Reconstruction. This is not a monolithic movement, but the general idea is that God's Word and law is authoritative for all of life and therefore also for the life of a nation. Unless there is biblical evidence to the contrary, one needs to presume that Old Testament law which gives policy directives applicable to different classes of individuals is still morally binding today. After all, Christ said: "Do not think that I have come to abolish the Law or the Prophets; I have not come to abolish them but to fulfill them. I tell you the truth, until heaven and earth disappear, not the smallest letter, not the least stroke of a pen, will by any means disappear from the Law until everything is accomplished" (Matt 5:17–18). This passage is interpreted to mean that Christ upheld the moral validity of the law so that unless God revealed otherwise, civil governments today are under obligation to uphold this law. "The civil precepts of the Old Testament . . . are a model of perfect social justice for all cultures, even in the punishment of criminals."[25] This means

---

25. Bahnsen, "The Theonomic Position," 24, also see 40–41; Bahnsen, "The

that the death penalty needs to be exacted today for crimes such as blasphemy (Lev 24:10–16), adultery and unchastity (Lev 20:10), rape (Deut 22:25), homosexuality (Lev 18:22), and Sabbath breaking (Exod 31:14).[26]

Theonomy does distinguish between social and political ethics. In other words, not all sins against God's law are properly treated as crimes to be punished by the state. The coercive power of the state must only be used to enforce God's criminal law.[27] For example, the state can not use its power to force people to worship God or to redistribute wealth to assist the poor. The task of the state does not include the enforcement of religious belief and the forced redistribution of wealth by taxation or economic barriers. The needs of the poor should be met by voluntary personal charity (1 Cor 13:3), obeying the principles of God's laws on lending and gleaning (Exod 22:25; Lev 19:9–10), and the church's diaconal ministry (1 Cor 16:1–2; Rom 15:25–27).[28] The state's authority is limited and should only be used to enforce God's criminal law. Since Scripture is not a textbook on statecraft, research is needed to distill the necessary abiding principles from the Bible. The fact that God's law was to be an example for the nations (Deut 4:5–8) underlines its continuing authority and relevance for government today.

This position of theonomy is further premised on the fact that Christ is king (Matt 28:18–20; Rev 1:5), and therefore those in civil authority need to acknowledge his supremacy and perform their public tasks in obedience to him. However, given the secularization of current society, what can believers do to correct the situation and make the government see its obligation to God? Adherents of theonomy answer that God's Word forbids the use of violence or revolution to effect change and that the law of God is not to be imposed by force

---

Theonomic Reformed Approach," 113–15, 132–39, 142. These detailed articles by Bahnsen are an excellent summary of the theonomic position and are, to my knowledge, his last detailed surveys of theonomy. Bahnsen died in December 1995.

26. Bahnsen, "The Theonomic Position," 51; Bahnsen, "The Theonomic Reformed Approach," 132–39. A list of crimes worthy of capital punishment today can be found in Bahnsen, *Theonomy in Christian Ethics*, 445–46.

27. Bahnsen, "The Theonomic Position," 41–52; Bahnsen, "The Theonomic Reformed Approach," 125–28.

28. Bahnsen, "The Theonomic Position," 45 n.19; similarly Bahnsen, "The Theonomic Reformed Approach," 129.

on an unwilling population. God's people are to rely on evangelism, prayer, re-education, and gradual legal and legislative reform to bring about a reformation of the political order.[29]

The late Rousas John Rushdonny and the late Greg Bahnsen are especially noted representatives of this theonomic approach.[30]

Theonomy is opposed to secular pluralism. At first glance theonomy holds great attraction for serious Christians because it rightly emphasizes that the authorities are in God's service. This needs to be constantly remembered. Furthermore, the theonomic stress on the authority of God's law is welcome in an age of relativism and libertarianism. The difficulty, however, arises when one gets to the details. Is it really the task of civil government today to uphold the penal penalties given to ancient Israel? Theonomy asserts this to be the case, but such a view overlooks the special place of Israel as a theocratic nation. Israel was the people of God, the congregation of the Creator of heaven and earth. From all the nations on earth, God had claimed this people (Lev 20:24) and also claimed them as the place where he would live. In their midst was his holy tabernacle and later the temple. He therefore demanded that his people be perfect and blameless (Gen 17:1; Deut 18:13). They were to be holy as the Lord their God was holy (Lev 19:2; 20:7). The land of promise which God gave his chosen people also was to be kept holy lest God's judgment come upon them and the land (Zec 2:12; Deut 24:4; Ezek 36:17–19).

In order to maintain the holiness of God's people and the land, unrepentant sinners were to be completely removed and this was to be done by means of the death penalty. It was like being excommunicated from the church. In the Old Testament, church and nation were in many respects the same. God, therefore, tailored the penalties for transgression according to this reality. Since God lived in their midst, there was absolutely no room within his people for such as blasphemers, idolators, adulterers, and murders. They had to be completely removed. In this connection, one must remember that the death penalty was the ultimate penalty for an unrepentant sinner. Where there was sorrow for sin, the death penalty could be stayed, except for murder.[31]

---

29. Bahnsen, "The Theonomic Position," 52–53; Bahnsen, "The Theonomic Reformed Approach," 139–41, 143.

30. Representative writings include: Rushdoony, *The Institutes of Biblical Law*; Bahnsen, *Theonomy in Christian Ethics*.

31. On adultery, e.g., compare Lev 20:10 (Deut 22:22) and Prov 6:32-35 which

These principles for maintaining holiness are relevant for ecclesiastical discipline for which the New Testament church is responsible and not the civil government. The church is where the living God dwells today (2 Cor 6:16–18; Eph 2:21). She is the new Israel (Gal 6:16; 1 Pet 2:9–10). Also in her midst unrepentant sinners cannot be tolerated and such people must be removed completely out of the midst of the holy congregation. This removal is now done by excommunication (Matt 18:15–18; 1 Cor 5, cf. Lev 18:8, 29). This same degree of holiness was not and cannot be expected of those who do not believe (cf. Matt 5:47–48). This does not mean that the civil authorities should not seek to maintain God's will respecting human life, human authority, marriage, property, and the punishing of transgressors. But the Old Testament penalty of death cannot simply be transposed to today because the situation and context are vastly different. Also other penalties found in the Old Testament law cannot simply be transferred to the present time for the same basic reason. It also needs to be kept in mind that the Old Testament does not always provide concrete penalties for specific crimes and some flexibility came into play.[32]

All of this, therefore, shows that theonomy has an incorrect understanding of the words of the Lord Jesus in Matthew 5. When he said that he had not come to abolish but to fulfill the law and that nothing will disappear from the law until everything is accomplished (Matt 5:17–18), he did not mean to underline the duty of the civil authorities to enforce the Old Testament penal code. Rather, he meant that the law retains its full authority and he as the Savior shows that by deepening the seriousness of maintaining the law. When Christ fulfilled the law he ensured that the law received the full obedience that it warranted and he brought to light the true and deepest meaning of the law. As Christ's further words show, the tremendous depth of obedience and holiness that God now demands of his covenant nation in the New Testament goes beyond what he asked of his Old Testament

---

suggests that compensation could be considered instead of the death penalty; cf. on David's adultery with Bathsheba 2 Sam 12:13. Also cf. Num 15:27–31. Murder was clearly punishable by death (Gen 9:6; Num 35:31–34). See also McKeating, "Sanctions Against Adultery," 57–72.

32. See on these and related issues Longman III, "God's Law and Mosaic Punishments Today," 41–54; also see Johnson, "The Mosaic Penal Sanctions," 171–92. On excommunication taking the place of the death penalty, see, e.g., Johnson, "The Mosaic Penal Sanctions," 181, 189–90.

people. It is not enough not to commit physical adultery. Even looking lustfully at a woman means you have transgressed the law. Outward obedience of the law may have been sufficient for ancient Israel but not for the new Israel on whose hearts the law has been written. Perfection is required (Matt 5:19–48; cf. Jer 31:33). In view of the finished work of Christ and the coming of the Holy Spirit, much more is now asked of God's people today than the outward obedience championed by legalists such as the Pharisees in Christ's day.[33]

Another valid criticism of theonomy is that it restricts the role of government too much. Contrary to theonomy, the task of government goes beyond simply enforcing certain laws. For example, it is true that in an ideal world, the family, the church, and neighbors would voluntarily take care of the needy—a situation theonomy envisages for society today. But we do not live in an ideal world and a song like Psalm 72 specifically notes that the ideal king will "deliver the needy who cry out, the afflicted who have no one to help. He will take pity on the weak and the needy and save the needy from death. He will rescue them from oppression and violence, for precious is their blood in his sight" (Ps 72:12–14). Indeed, can and should the government not take over the care of the poor if families and churches no longer do this?[34] The broad mandate given to government as "God's servant to do you good" (Rom 13:4) suggests a positive answer. Romans 13 speaks of more than just the administration of justice. Government is a benevolent institution given by God for the benefit of society.[35]

The classic Reformed confessions express the place of the Old Testament law well. Not the exact letter of the law (such as the precise penalty) is necessarily relevant, but its principles need to be applied today. The Westminster Confession of Faith (Article 19.4) correctly states that God gave to Israel "also, as a body politic, . . . sundry judicial laws, which expired together with the State of that people; not obliging any other now, further than the general equity thereof may require." The phrase "general equity" refers to the general moral principles un-

---

33. See. e.g., Ridderbos, *Matthew*, 98–99; Knudsen, "May We Use the Term 'Theonomy'?" 17–37.

34. See Paul G. Schrotenboer, "The Principled Pluralist Response to Theonomy," 60.

35. Delving further into the topic of the state assisting the poor is beyond the scope of this chapter. See further on these issues Keller, "Theonomy and the Poor," 280–87.

derlying the judicial laws.[36] Article 25 of the Belgic Confession carries a similar message.[37]

This brings us to principled pluralism.

Principled Pluralism

Principled pluralism recognizes the pluralism of contemporary society but contends that biblical norms need to be recognized and applied in order for government and society to function according to God's will. When this is done, society benefits for God established the norms for humans to live together peacefully and for the benefit of each other. Principled pluralism has the following distinctive basic principles.

There is no morally neutral ground. All of life is religious in nature and both Christians and non-Christians have religious presuppositions which they bring into the public square. Also secularism and the denial of God's relevance for public life is a religious system. It is, therefore, impossible to restrict religion to the private personal sphere of home and church and to insist that the public square is without religious convictions. Principled pluralism opposes a secularized public square which bans religious voices and practices except its own. Christians have the obligation to influence the public discourse in a biblical direction. Principles derived from Scripture need to be part of the debate in the public square so that arguments can be made for a public policy according to the overriding norms of God's Word.

Although God's special revelation in the Bible is normative for all of life, God has revealed enough of his eternal power and divine nature in creation and in the nature of things to render all people without excuse. He has written his law in their conscience (Rom 1:18–21; 2:14–15). In this way God has a claim on all creation, including the civil authorities. Before his throne they are without excuse if they suppress the truth and refuse to see the light of God's gracious demands and promote sin (Rom 1:18–19).

---

36. See further Fergusson, "An Assembly of Theonomists?" 315–49; also, Zorn, *Christ Triumphant*, 180–201.

37. Article 25 of the Belgic Confession reads as follows: "We believe that the ceremonies and symbols of the law have ceased with the coming of Christ, and that all shadows have been fulfilled, so that the use of them ought to be abolished among Christians. Yet their truth and substance remain for us in Jesus Christ, in whom they have been fulfilled. In the meantime we still use the testimonies taken from the law and the prophets, both to confirm us in the doctrine of the gospel and to order our life in all honesty, according to God's will and to His glory." *Book of Praise*, 510.

The civil government is God's servant to maintain justice and righteousness (Rom 13:1–5). To understand this mandate properly, one must realize that God gave each person an office or offices in life, be it as a parent, a church member, a plumber, a husband, or whatever. If a government is to maintain justice, it must see to it that these offices can be exercised. "The state should safeguard the freedom, rights, and responsibilities of citizens in the exercise of their offices within their various life-spheres according to their respective religious convictions. The government is obliged to respect, safeguard, preserve or, where lost, to restore, and to promote the free and responsible exercise of these other societal offices. That is what God commands the state to do to fulfill the biblical idea of public justice."[38]

Principled pluralism affirms that a government's authority is limited because God has ordered society in such a way that different structures make up the whole. These structures, such as civil government, the family, church, and the market place, each have their own sphere of authority which should not be transgressed by another societal structure or sphere. Government has the duty to recognize this diverse reality and to promote the well being of the different spheres of authority found within society by safeguarding their existence and ensuring their continued health. We have seen the basic biblical evidence for the different spheres of authority and the limitations of the state's jurisdiction in chapter 2.

Principled pluralism also recognizes that civil government does not have the authority to decide what constitutes true religion. For that reason, government cannot favor one religion over another or enforce, for example, the religion of secularism in society. Within certain limits, such as the need to restrain evil, all religions must be treated alike and be given the same freedom and opportunities.

These basic ideas were championed by Abraham Kuyper and are defended in North America by his spiritual disciples such as those associated with The Center for Public Justice in Washington.[39]

---

38. Spykman, "The Principled Pluralist Position," 92.

39. For Kuyper, see Bolt, "Abraham Kuyper and the Search for an Evangelical Public Theology," 141–61; for The Center of Public Justice, see their website: http://www.cpjustice.org. Also see Spykman, "The Principled Pluralist Position". An important journal, *First Things* once edited by the late Richard John Neuhaus, has as its purpose "to advance a religiously informed public philosophy for the ordering of society." See http://www.firstthings.com.

A major advantage of principled pluralism is that it recognizes the different spheres of authority in society and thus offers some safeguard against an authoritarian and totalitarian state. These different spheres of authority, such as family, church, and voluntary organizations can also mediate between the megastructures of our time such as the modern state and the international corporation and the individual lives of the citizens. These mediating structures can give a sense of stability and connectedness to society.[40]

Principled pluralism has been criticized for being inconsistent. If God's Word is normative for all of life, then how is it possible, for example, to tolerate evil? Let us now turn to an assessment of principled pluralism in the light of Scripture. In the next chapter we will consider the practical implications.

THE BIBLE AND PLURALISM

The purpose of this section is not to repeat what has been discussed elsewhere with respect to the government being a servant of God with the basic mandate to uphold justice in the land. Our concern here is to see whether principled pluralism can be called a Christian or biblical approach to the task of government and the world of politics, especially with a view to tolerating false religion and evil. It will be helpful to approach this issue by first considering the biblical distinction of church and kingdom, and then moving on to apply our findings to the relationship between church and state.

Church and Kingdom

OLD TESTAMENT

In its broadest sense the kingdom of God refers to God's sovereign control and dominion over all his creation. For this reason the Psalmist jubilates: "How awesome is the LORD Most High, the great King over all the earth! . . . Sing praises to God, sing praises; sing praises to our King, sing praises. For God is the King of all the earth" (Ps 47:2, 6–7). More specifically God's reign comes to a concrete expression where he is acknowledged as Lord and King. However, not all on earth recognize his kingship. That refusal to honor his rule began with the fall

---

40. Spykman, "The Principled Pluralist Position," 94–97. Spykman also refers to the work of Richard Neuhaus and Peter Berger on "mediating structures."

into sin in paradise. But God is sovereign and he will have all peoples and nations bow down before him (Isa 45:23)![41]

To begin that process of all creation recognizing his lordship, God called Abraham and his descendants as his special people who would recognize his sovereign rule. In this way, this people would be a blessing and a light for all the nations on earth (Gen 12:3; Deut 4:5–8; Isa 51:4). They were to be an example of God's gracious kingdom, a first installment, so to speak, of God's reclaiming all of humanity to recognize his rule. And so God claimed the promised seed of Abraham, Israel, at the Sinai to be his kingdom of priests and a holy nation (Exod 19:6). God was their king, enthroned between the ark's cherubim (Ps 99:1). When he gave them the Promised Land, his kingdom took on a tangible form. After some time, God's anointed representatives ruled as kings on the Lord's throne in the capital city of Zion (Ps 2; 1 Chron 28:5; 29:23). These were kings in the line of David, to whom God had promised an everlasting throne (1 Sam 7). As a theocratic king, David placed a high priority on ensuring proper worship of God within his kingdom, as seen in his care for the ark and his desire to build a temple for the Lord (2 Sam 6–7). Subsequent kings were judged in part by how they dealt with issues of worship (e.g., 1 Kings 15:11–15; 2 Kings 16:2–4). In the Old Testament, the people of the kingdom were those who lived under the rule of the theocratic king. However, this people could not simply be equated with the church.

The church was the assembly of God's people but the territorial kingdom ruled by Israel's monarch included more than those who belonged to this assembly. Although the king who ruled in Zion was the theocratic head of the people of God, he was also the king of a kingdom which included more than the chosen people of God. In his latter capacity he tolerated what he could not tolerate as head of the elect nation. It is noteworthy that the Lord never commanded his king in Zion to force all his subjects to recognize the reign of the true God and to worship him. There was, for example, no compulsion for the aliens and strangers to convert to faith in the true God so that all could participate of the Passover. No, only those who were circumcised, either as being part of a covenantal household or through conversion, could participate (Exod 12:48–49). But God was merciful and he protected those who lived as strangers and aliens under his theocratic king (cf.

---

41. See Zorn, *Christ Triumphant*, 1–2.

Lev. 19:33). God tolerated these unbelievers, presumably because God wanted people to recognize his royal rule and worship him, not of compulsion, but of love, as the love of a child for his heavenly father (cf. Exod 4:22–23; Deut 6:5; Prov 23:26).

Although God desired his people, as a visible expression of his rule on earth, to be a blessing to the nations, the Davidic kingship and Israel failed in this respect.[42] The corruption and sin of the pagan countries around Israel deeply affected God's people. It was clear that someone who was greater than fallible human kings was required to establish God's kingdom on earth in perfection. The promised great Son and Lord of David was needed (2 Sam 7:12–16; Isa 9:6–7). Eventually the Lord punished his people by sending them into exile. But God never lost sight of the great goal that all nations and peoples should recognize his rule. Even in exile he reaffirmed the promises of the coming Messianic king (Ezek 34:22–24). The Christ would come to pay for all the sins of his people and establish God's kingdom in perfection in this world (Isa 53; Jer 33:15, 20–22).

New Testament and Today

A remnant returned from exile (Isa 10:20–22). Not all who were of Israel had actually been part of the true Israel. To the descendants of this remnant, the Christ came. John the Baptist announced his coming with the words: "Repent, for the kingdom of heaven is near" (Matt 3:2).[43] The Christ came at God's appointed time. He was born in Bethlehem of David's line in fulfillment of the prophecies (Matt 2:4–5). He too heralded the coming of God's kingdom with the words: "Repent, for the kingdom of heaven is near" (Matt 4:17). The present reality of the kingdom was obvious when Christ countered Satan's power by casting out demons (Matt 12:22–28). As the promised Messiah he also raised the dead, healed the sick, and forgave sins (Matt 11:1–6). In short, the promised kingdom, the visible expression of God's rule for the deliverance of his people, came in Christ, the Son of God. To overcome the incalculable debt of sin owed to God, he gave his life as a ransom for many (Mark 10:45). His sacrifice is sufficient

---

42. The Lord did send his prophet Jonah to Nineveh. He went unwilling and under divine compulsion, but the preaching bore fruit (Jonah 3).

43. The expression "the kingdom of heaven" means the same as "the kingdom of God."

to atone for the sins of the whole world (1 John 2:1). When he had fulfilled his messianic task by suffering, dying on the cross, and rising from the dead (Luke 24:44–48), the progress of the kingdom took on new dimensions.

The manifestation of God's kingdom was to be removed from the confines of the land of Israel and become worldwide. As victorious Lord he declared to his disciples before his ascension into glory: "All authority in heaven and on earth has been given to me. Therefore go and make disciples of all nations, baptizing them in the name of the Father and of the Son and of the Holy Spirit, and teaching them to obey everything I have commanded you. And surely I am with you always, to the very end of the age" (Matt 28:18–20). The world-wide church means that Christ's world-wide kingdom has been established. But this is only a small beginning of what the future will bring. One day Christ will return and establish his kingdom in full perfection and all knees will bow and recognize his rule (Isa 45:23; Phil 2:9–10; Rev 1:7). "Then the end will come, when he hands over the kingdom to God the Father after he has destroyed all dominion, authority and power" (1 Cor 15:24).

In the New Testament and today, the relationship between the church and the kingdom is close, but they are not identical.[44] The church is the people or citizens of the kingdom. As was the Israel of old, so the church today is called a kingdom of priests and a holy nation (Exod 19:6; 1 Pet 2:9). The church is the gathering of those who accept Jesus as Lord and do his will (John 14:15; 1 Cor 12:3). The kingdom of God therefore becomes visible in the church. As citizens of the kingdom, those in the church show something of the love of God and his righteousness and so function as a light in the world of darkness and as the salt of the earth (Matt 5:13–20).

But, the kingdom is not confined to the church. The kingdom is wherever Christ, the king, is obeyed and is active in his redeeming work. Christ is head of both the church and his kingdom (Eph 1:22; Col 2:10). Since all authority has been given to him (Matt 28:18), the extent of Christ's kingdom is the entire world. And so, wherever his authority is acknowledged, his kingdom blessings follow. This truth applies also to governments which are his servants (Rom 13:4).

---

44. For the relationship of church and kingdom see Ridderbos, *The Coming of the Kingdom*, 342–56.

Christ is patient and long-suffering over against unbelief and rebellion against his rule. He has never instructed any state or government to force people to acknowledge him as Lord or to compel citizens to be members of the church by the power of the sword. Such a means of conversion is the teaching of Islam,[45] but it is foreign to Scripture. The power of the kingdom of God is the Word of God. This is the sword of the Spirit (Eph 5:17). Where there is unbelief, Christ withholds his wrath so that the gospel, his Word, can have an opportunity to impact the lives of those not yet redeemed (2 Pet 3:9). He tolerates the weeds, the unbelievers, growing alongside the pure wheat of his people. On the Day of Judgment the great separation will take place (Matt 13:24–30, 36–43).

Today the people of God, the citizens of the kingdom, live in the expectation of the coming of the day of Christ, his final appearing, when he will establish his kingdom in all perfection. Until that day comes, the church is to be at work by using the sword of the Spirit, the proclamation of the gospel, and having its redeeming power work in the world. Where the gospel is accepted, the blessings of the kingdom follow such as the deliverance from the bondage of sin and the fear of death. Christ, however, does not promise a fully realized perfect kingdom here on earth through the efforts of his kingdom subjects. Rather he urges perseverance, watchfulness, faithfulness, and continuing in prayer in the face of affliction (Matt 24–25; Luke 18:1–8). But the people of God can labor in the sure knowledge that the victory over sin and death has been won and that the kingdom will come in full glory on the day of Jesus Christ. A new heaven and a new earth will appear where righteousness dwells (2 Pet 3:13).

Having seen the grand narrative of God's church and kingdom and how they relate to each other, we will now consider some aspects more closely in order to determine what principles we can deduce from the Bible respecting the place and duties of the institutions of the church and the state and how they interface with each other.

Church and State

Our brief survey of church and kingdom showed that the kingdom is broader than the church and that God tolerated more in the kingdom

---

45. *The Qur'an*, Surah 2:216, 9:5, 29; Riddell and Cotterell, *Islam in Context*, 61 and Hartwig, "Spread by the Sword?"

than he could in the church. Indeed, in the widest sense of the term, God's kingdom refers to all creation for he rules over all of it. There is a background to God's current patience and tolerance. At a certain point in the early history of the world, God could no longer bear the sin being committed and so he destroyed and cleansed the world with a great flood in the days of Noah (Gen 6:5–8). However recognizing the evil nature of the human heart, God said he would never again so destroy the world (Gen 8:21). He would be patient and gather together his people who would exhibit his rule and kingdom by their obedience to his will. Through the line of Shem and Abraham, God worked towards the realization of his plan of the redemption of creation through the work of Christ.

BIBLICAL DISTINCTIONS

When God gathered his chosen people, his demands were clear. They had to be completely dedicated to his service. However, God recognized that within his kingdom of Israel, there was not only his holy nation, the church, but, as noted earlier, there were also others who did not really belong to the assembly of God's people.[46] They nevertheless lived within the kingdom of God on earth as established in Israel. To these people the LORD showed great forbearance. They were not forced to become worshippers of the God of Israel nor did God give any command to that effect to Israel's rulers. However, they were expected to obey the prohibitive commands of God's moral law. They could not, for example, indulge in sexual sin (Lev. 18:24–30), blaspheme God's name (Lev 24:15) or sacrifice their children to the false god Molech. (Lev 20:2). The people in whose midst they lived, as well as the land, was holy and they had to respect that. Indeed, God had expressly commanded that all the idolatrous nations living in Canaan had to be wiped out for the land was to be holy (Deut 7; cf. Ps. 78:54; Zec. 2:12). There was, however, no such command for territories outside Canaan that were later conquered to be under Israel's rule.

It is noteworthy that after David defeated Moab, the Aramaean kingdoms of Hadadezer (Damascus and Maacah), Edom, and the Ammonites,[47] there is no hint anywhere in Scripture that he worked to remove all idolatry and false worship. Also no special attempt was

---

46. For a discussion on Israel's mixed population, see Chapter 9.
47. See 2 Sam 8:2–14; 10:6–19; 12:26–31.

made to compel these people to become worshippers of the true God. Since David's office as a godly king over these gentile peoples roughly parallels the office of government today, this tolerance points to a principle that can apply to government today.

Indeed, state tolerance of false religion is not in disagreement with Scripture. God is long-suffering and patient. "He causes his sun to rise on the evil and the good, and sends rain on the righteous and the unrighteous" (Matt 5:45). He allows the good grain as well as the weeds to grow together, until the time of harvest. Then God himself will separate the two in the final Day of Judgment (Matt 13:36–43). Government can tolerate what the church cannot endure. Each has its own office and calling. In a modern pluralistic society, the following words of Christ are relevant: "do to others what you would have them do to you" (Matt 7:12). If one asks freedom of worship for oneself, then it should also be granted to others.[48]

As head of the church, Christ tolerates no ungodliness and sin. The church on earth must act accordingly. As head and ruler of his kingdom Christ is patient and bears with the weakness of the sinful human heart. His servants, the civil governments, must do likewise even as they are obligated to seek true righteousness and justice for the country entrusted to their rule.

Besides the principle of toleration, there is the related principle of the civil authority being distinct from the religious authority in Israel. Even though church and state were very closely related, they were not identical. Each had its own jurisdiction. This has important implications. Even in Israel, which was a theocracy, there were clear limitations to what the king as civil ruler could do. Although the theocratic king had priestly and prophetic aspects to his office, he nevertheless remained in the first place the civil ruler in charge of the judicial and political affairs of the nation. Although the priests were vital in the theocracy, Israel as a theocracy was not a priest state as found in other ancient near Eastern countries such as Egypt. Priestly authority was limited to all things related to the administration of the sacrificial service of reconciliation, including instruction in the ways of the Lord. And so there were clear distinctions. Religious matters were in the province of the priests and the civil ones were the responsibility of

---

48. See Douma, *Politieke Verantwoordelijkheid*, 127; Van Middelkoop, *Reformatie en Tolerantie*, 20; Spykman, "The Principled Pluralist Position," 85–86.

the king. Accordingly, in the time of King Jehoshaphat the civil courts were organized specifically along the lines of religious and civil matters (2 Chron 19:11; cf. 1 Chron 26:30, 32).

We need to value the biblical principle that is involved here. Scripture gives no justification for a modern theocratic state such as we find in some Islamic jurisdictions. The Bible indicates that there is to be a clear separation of what we today call church and state, or spiritual authority and civil authority. Christ's teaching affirmed this when he said "My kingdom is not of this world. If it were, my servants would fight to prevent my arrest by the Jews. But now my kingdom is from another place" (John 18:36). Such thinking is completely contrary to, for example, the Muslim idea of a jihad or holy war that is necessary to establish their kingdom in the here and now.[49]

All of this underlines the fact that the state is not given the duty to force people to love God and to worship him. The state is permitted to tolerate things that the church cannot tolerate. There is, however, more to this larger issue.

The Rule of Law

Another important principle in considering the relation of church and state is the rule of law. The Davidic king was not to be autocratic and self-seeking, thinking himself to be more worthy than those around him. He was God's representative in the theocracy, sitting on God's throne (1 Chron 29:23) and therefore a servant of God who needed to submit to God's law. The Lord even stipulated that when the king assumed the throne of the kingdom then he "is to write for himself on a scroll a copy of this law, taken from that of the priests, who are Levites. It is to be with him, and he is to read it all the days of his life so that he may learn to revere the LORD his God and follow carefully all the words of this law and these decrees and not consider himself better than his brothers and turn from the law to the right or to the left" (Deut 17:18–20). In this way God's will would be done for his chosen nation in his kingdom. With all the plurality that may have existed in Israelite society, above it all was the law of God. It needed to be heeded for the well-being of the people.

---

49. See further on these issues, e.g., Verbrugh, *Universeel en Antirevolutionair*, 1.126–28.

Israel's rulers were not the only ones who were accountable to God. Pagan ones were as well. For example, Daniel told King Nebuchadnezzar that God had put him in power (Dan 2:37–38) and so God warned the monarch through Daniel that unless he acknowledged God's supreme place and repented of his sins in ruling, he would be driven from the throne to live with the wild animals (Dan 4:24–27). There was accountability that had to be acknowledged.

Today, rulers are to be servants of God in the first place and as such also have an obligation to heed the abiding principles of God's Word for the good of society. Thus, when government makes decisions pertaining to morals and issues on which the Word of God gives clear direction, it should not set itself above the norms which God has revealed. It is the duty of government to restrain sin and evil (Prov 14:33; Rom 13:4). How does the calling of the church factor into this obligation of the government?

The Church's Duty

Clearly the task of the church is to preach the gospel and administer the reconciliation that God offers to mankind. The church's "job description" was given by the risen Christ prior to his ascension when he said: "All authority in heaven and on earth has been given to me. Therefore go and make disciples of all nations, baptizing them in the name of the Father and of the Son and of the Holy Spirit, and teaching them to obey everything I have commanded you. And surely I am with you always, to the very end of the age" (Matt. 28:18–20). The church is to proclaim the glad tidings of salvation and gather God's people together. The state must give the church the freedom and opportunity to do its calling of spreading the gospel. That gospel includes the proclamation of Christ's kingship, a message the state must hear from the church or its members so that it understands its servant role.[50]

The church's task with respect to the state is not to make official pronouncements about the political issues of the day and to get

---

50. "The service rendered by the state to the church is to facilitate its mission." O'Donovan also notes that in view of Christ's victory and the coming of his kingdom, the church must seek to change the state's "self-understanding and its manner of government to suit the dawning age of Christ's own rule. The church has to instruct it in the ways of the humble state." O'Donovan, *The Desire of the Nations*, 217, 219. On the question of how government should realize its evangelical obedience and humble state in a pluralist society, see Chaplin, "Political Eschatology and Responsible Government," 289–90.

involved in crafting government policy. The church as an institution has neither the charge nor expertise to do so.[51] It is also not the task of the church to try to rule over the government (the Roman Catholic ideal).[52] The state has its own God-given responsibilities. However, the church does have the duty to train and equip its members so that they can function meaningfully in today's secular society as citizens of Christ's kingdom and so influence also politics. Scripture is certainly relevant for the affairs of the state, but it is not the calling of the church as a corporate body to interfere in the political process and attempt to apply the biblical principles to the government agenda. That is the responsibility of Christians in all walks of life, also those involved in politics.

All of this does not mean that the church should always remain silent. There can be unusual circumstances when the church needs to speak up by means of the pulpit or otherwise in order to protect its God-given mission to preach the gospel and condemn sin where sin needs to be condemned. There can also be occasions when the government invites input from interested parties on new legislation which is of great interest to the church. Churches should then participate and make a case for the application of biblical principles on the issues of the day.[53]

In summary, the church's duty is to preach and safeguard the gospel and seek the spiritual well-being of its members. The resources and gifts of the church should focus on these central concerns. With respect to its task over against the government, the church must also

---

51. For a strong plea to recognize the spirituality of the church whose teachings, though meaningful for government, offer no blueprint for politics, see Hart, *A Secular Faith*. In taking this stance, Hart followed the heritage of Gresham Machen. See Hart, *Defending the Faith*, 133–59. See also VanDrunen, "The Two Kingdoms and the *Ordo Salutis*," 207–24, esp. 222–23 and Gamble, "Presbyterianism, Politics, and Westminster Theology," 91, 94. Both the Presbyterian and Reformed traditions recognize the need for the church as an institution to deal only with ecclesiastical matters. See, *The Westminster Confession of Faith* XXXI.4 and the *Church Order of Dort*, Art. 30.

52. See footnotes 1 and 2 of this chapter.

53. The *Westminster Confession of Faith*, XXXI.4, makes allowance for special circumstances. See Williamson, *The Westminster Confession of Faith*, 327. Although careful not to have the church engage in politics, John Murray did appear to go further in insisting on the duty of the church to proclaim the whole counsel of God also when it involves exposing and opposing legislation not according to the Word of God. See Murray, *The Claims of Truth*, 253–59.

lead the way in instructing its members to be good citizens and to be obedient to those in authority over them. Furthermore, the church is called to pray for those who rule over them (1 Tim 2:1-4). Such prayer includes the petition that the state may continue to protect the freedom and ministry of the church so that the gospel can continue to be proclaimed. When that proclamation is blessed, it will eventually have a salutary effect on society and government.

In our current age of secularization, it is easy for the people of God to grow weary in seeking the best for those who rule over them. But, one must realize that there are usually no quick fixes to the dilemmas of evil and sin in society and often incremental change is all that is possible. But the church need never become despondent. It has every reason to be encouraged for an important truth is that God is supreme ruler over everything already. In a broad sense his kingdom encompasses the entire universe. The battle against evil has been won (Col 1:13-20; 2:15). One day God's kingdom will arrive in full perfection when all will recognize him as Lord and Master.

Now that we have seen the main principles that inform the relationship between church and state, we need to discuss in more detail the very real and pressing issues that face the church and state in our day, issues such as human rights, the general moral decline, and how far toleration should be permitted to go.

SUGGESTED READING

Hall, David W. *Calvin in the Public Square: Liberal Democracies, Rights, and Civil Liberties.* Phillipsburg, NJ: P&R, 2009. An accessible overview of Calvin's thought and influence.

Marshall, Paul. *God and the Constitution. Christianity and American Politics.* Lanham, MD: Rowman & Littlefield, 2002. Covers the topic well and also encourages Christians to get involved politically.

Monsma, Stephen V. and J. Christopher Soper. *The Challenge of Pluralism. Church and State in Five Democracies.* 2nd ed. Lanham, MD: Rowman & Littlefield, 2009. A survey of how the United States, the Netherlands, Australia, England, and Germany deal with the religious convictions of their citizens and the demands of public policy.

Pennings, Ray. *Church and Ceasar. A Legal Primer for Church Office-bearers*. Grand Rapids, MI / Mitchell, ON: Reformation Heritage Books / Free Reformed Publications, 2008. A useful, popularly written primer for office-bearers.

Smith, Gary Scott, ed. *God and Politics: Four Views on the Reformation of Civil Government: Theonomy, Principled Pluralism, Christian America, National Confessionalism*. Phillipsburg, NJ: Presbyterian and Reformed, 1989. A very helpful collection in bringing clarity to the different viewpoints.

4

Human Rights, Moral Norms, and Toleration

EVERYONE SEEMS TO BE talking about human rights. It is a central part of the current political discourse. But what do these rights entail? Do those speaking about human rights all mean the same? How does a concern for human rights impact one's view on morals and toleration? In trying to answer these and related questions, we will first get our bearings with a brief historical overview and subsequently address issues of political ethics and toleration.

HUMAN RIGHTS

The history of human rights is complex and fascinating.[1] Our concern is with the early modern period during which two basic approaches to human rights came to the foreground. The one understanding was influenced by the Protestant Reformation, the other by the Enlightenment.

The Reformation's Understanding of Human Rights

The Reformation was a movement which directed people back to the Bible. The reformers, particularly Calvin and those influenced by him, critically examined the duties and authority of the church and state, as well as other institutions, in the light of Scripture. Their study led them to oppose the abuse of power and tyranny by the state and the church. Freedom from this abuse from government and the clergy was the cry of the day. However, such freedom was not unlimited. It was freedom as defined by the Word of God. Indeed, to do justice to the

---

1. See, e.g., the overview in Witte, *The Reformation of Rights*, 20–37.

Reformation's understanding of freedom and human rights, we need to begin with God and his revelation.

God and his rights came first in the thinking of the Reformers. God has the right to be obeyed by mankind whom he had created to honor him and to give him glory (Ps 86:9, 10; 1 Cor 10:31). Humanity's obligation to obey God includes heeding the divine demand to love one's neighbor. Only when one's duty to God and the neighbor is understood can one speak of human rights. They are grounded in the duties and responsibilities we owe to God and our neighbor, as defined in God's law. It is normative.

More specifically, therefore, loving God means obeying the first four of the Ten Commandments—to worship God alone and to do so according to his will, to honor his name, and to maintain his day of rest. The love for the neighbor means obeying the last six commandments—to honor father and mother and all authority, not to murder, not to commit adultery, not to steal, not to bear false witness, and not to covet. All these duties demanded by God translate into rights. After all, if God commands, who is able to deny one the duty of obedience? It is such a person's right. So, if one wants to love God according his will, then no one has the jurisdiction to take away one's right to honor God. That right, therefore, includes the right to worship God alone, the right to be free from the bondage of false gods and false oaths, and the right to enjoy rest and worship on the day of rest. Because God commands it, he has a right to this obedience. Similarly, if one wishes to love one's neighbor in accordance with the divine demand, no one can take that right away. Indeed, one's God-given duty to the neighbor means that the neighbor has the right to see the results of that duty. "One person's duties not to kill, to commit adultery, to steal, or to bear false witness thus gives rise to another person's rights to life, property, fidelity, and reputation."[2]

The Reformation also pointed out that every person is made in God's image (Gen 1:27; 9:6). This fact has several implications and consequences. It sets human beings and human life apart from all creation. Humanity has a special place in the world and cannot, for example, be placed on the same level as animal or plant life. God's law therefore protects human life and its relationships, and sets the norms for human behavior. Furthermore, being made in God's image means

2. Witte, *The Reformation of Rights*, 29.

that one must have the freedom to obey God and do his will. Another consequence of being made in God's image is that all people are equal before God and before their neighbor. All must therefore have an equal standing before the state and the state must treat all equally. The practical result must be that the rights of everyone are equally protected and promoted. One important reason for this is so that all can perform the responsibilities that their rights assume, namely to love God and their neighbor according to the divine norms. This duty calls for laws that curb and restrain sin for according to Scripture all are inclined to evil (e.g., Rom 3:10–12).

The biblical truths that the Reformation rediscovered created a keen awareness of the right of all citizens to serve God according to their wishes. Indeed, it was their duty to do so. These basic teachings helped to fuel the struggle for freedom against Roman Catholic tyranny in France, the Netherlands, and Scotland. Their God-given rights and privileges were worth fighting for.

The background for the modern enlightenment ideas of rights and freedoms is radically different.

The Enlightenment's Understanding of Human Rights

Whereas the Reformation appealed to God's Word, the Bible, for direction, the thinkers of the Enlightenment based their ideas of human rights in human nature itself. Philosophers like Jean-Jacques Rousseau argued that each individual was "by nature equal in virtue and dignity and was vested with inherent and unalienable rights of life, liberty, and property."[3] By nature all were capable of choosing their own means of happiness without being compelled by an external agent such as law. "In their natural state, the state of nature, all persons were free to exercise their natural rights fully."[4] The underlying assumption in this view is the autonomy and sovereignty of man. He is his own master and beholden to no one. Even God is essentially out of the picture.

Although the Enlightenment had a very high view of man's inherent goodness and ability both to choose and work out his own happiness, it did nevertheless recognize the necessity for rational persons to move from the state of nature to a well-ordered society. They did so by entering into a social contract; that is, by agreeing to a political con-

3. Witte Jr., "Rights," 706.
4. Witte Jr., "Rights," 706.

stitution by which they could be governed. But, a key demand was that certain inalienable rights would be preserved. This notion is reflected in the American Bill of Rights (1791) and the Canadian Charter of Rights and Freedoms (1982). Both of these documents guarantee such basic rights as freedom of religion, speech, and assembly.[5]

The Enlightenment view of human rights as based in human nature itself remains a very powerful force today. In 1948 the General Assembly of the United Nations proclaimed its Universal Declaration of Human Rights. The preamble begins with the words that "recognition of the inherent dignity and of the equal and inalienable rights of all members of the human family is the foundation of freedom, justice and peace in the world."[6] On this basis, more declarations and documents were agreed to. In 1966 the United Nations promulgated two international covenants which took as their starting point the inherent dignity and the equal and inalienable rights of all members of the human family. These covenants were The International Covenant on Economic, Social, and Cultural Rights and The International Covenant on Civil and Political Rights. In 1981, the United Nations issued the Declaration on the Elimination of all Forms of Intolerance and Discrimination Based on Religion or Belief and in 1989 the Vienna Concluding Document followed. It provided support for the protection of religious rights for individuals and groups.[7]

Western nations such as the United States and Canada show a growing concern for human rights within their borders. Quasi-legal human right commissions are starting to appear in the United States, while in Canada both federal and provincial Human Rights Commissions have been playing a prominent role in rights issues since that country's adoption of its Charter of Rights and Freedoms. In both nations much litigation and court action is premised on the protection of one's rights.[8] Society seems to function on the assump-

---

5. For the American Bill of Rights, see Witte, *The Reformation of Rights*, 31; for the Canadian Charter of Rights and Freedoms, see "The Canadian Charter of Rights and Freedoms," in *Part I of the Constitution Act, 1982*. It is noteworthy that the rights listed in the Bill of Rights (1791) had already been formulated by Calvinists in the prior two centuries but their presuppositions were rather different. Witte, *The Reformation of Rights*, 31–32, 34.

6. Van Asbeck, *The Universal Declaration of Human Rights*, 90.

7. Witte Jr., "Rights," 707.

8. See Levant, "Human Rights Commissions in the United States."

tion that all will be well if only human rights are maintained. Human rights seem to be considered the salvation of society. The difficulty is that without the restraints of divine norms and accompanying responsibilities, there is no limit to what could be declared to be one's rights and privileges. Indeed, imagined rights can even be detrimental to society.

The Current Dilemma

When two say the same, it is not necessarily the same. Christians support much of the concern to protect human rights. Indeed, as we have just seen, there is a Christian background to this issue for at the heart lies the need to have freedom to serve God according to his Word. However, Enlightenment and humanistic thinking places the human being and his right to freedom and happiness in the center. When one consistently applies these man-centered principles in the pursuit of human rights, then God is excluded and one can end up defending as a right what is actually sinful in God's eyes. Two hot button issues of our day, the right to an abortion and gay rights illustrate the problem. Such issues pit conservative Christians against those aligned with liberal Christianity and humanism. From a biblical and Christian perspective, God's command not to murder means that humans have the right to life. That right includes the unborn (cf. Ps 139:13–16). As a right given by God, no one can take that right away. God's prohibition of homosexual behavior (Lev 18:22; cf. Rom 1:21–27) entails the right to be free from being exposed to homosexual sin and from being subjected to education from a homosexual perspective.

Because the struggle for human rights has both Christian and humanistic roots, both sides can appeal to relevant official political declarations or documents. Those Americans who wish to have God in the picture can appeal to the Declaration of Independence (1776) which states in the second paragraph: "We hold these truths to be self-evident: that all men are created equal; that they are endowed by their Creator with certain inalienable rights; among these are life, liberty, and the pursuit of happiness." Does reference to the Creator not indicate that he has made man after his own image and given him his dignity and task which is to serve God? Canadian Christians can appeal to the preamble of their Charter of Rights and Freedoms (1982) which says that "Canada is founded upon principles that recognize the supremacy of God and the rule of law." After that statement is made, the rights and freedoms are dealt with.[9] Does the reference to the supremacy of God not underline the need to interpret the rights and freedoms in the light of his Word? On the other hand, secularists can focus on the human rights as such and understand them without reference to God. This is indeed what has by and large happened in North America. Legally God the Creator does not function in the American courts and the Canadian reference to the supremacy of God in its Charter of Rights and Freedoms has also proven to be an empty gesture with no legal consequences.

This leaves a dilemma. Whose norms will now determine a human right? What is to be the moral basis of a democratic society that does not want to acknowledge God as it enacts legislation? This question needs to be considered.

MORAL NORMS

In this time of relativism, it should be stressed that there are absolutes. There is a right and a wrong. The very fact that we have a judicial system which punishes those who transgress the norms society has set illustrates the need for a basic recognition of a right and a wrong. It is currently politically correct to keep religion out of the public square. The credo of our times professes religion to be a personal matter and holds that society functions according to norms that are neutral. However, such reasoning is fallacious. There are no neutral norms for everyone functions under basic religious presuppositions. This cannot be avoided for humans are religious beings.[10]

Western society fears any constraints to its perceived right to moral freedom. Such a right to choose rests on the essentially religious belief that man can make his own moral decisions and that he has the right to pursue his own happiness as he sees fit. This is an article of faith for it cannot be proven that such thinking is either correct or beneficial. Indeed, much evidence to the contrary exists. The conviction that God's Word gives us the norms needed for a moral life is also a religious presupposition that needs to be taken in faith. So, we

---

9. See for The Declaration of Independence, Van Asbeck, *The Universal Declaration of Human Rights*, 37, and for the Canadian Charter, "The Canadian Charter of Rights and Freedoms."

10. See the helpful discussion in Koyzis, *Political Visions and Illusions*, 65–68.

are back to the basic choice of humanism and Christianity as guiding principles for society. Both humanism and Christianity rest on essentially religious presuppositions and their standards are determined accordingly.

The norm for secular humanism is ultimately the will of the people. Whatever the nation desires is the way to go. The norm of God's Word has been excluded and so everything is relative. If the opinion makers or the majority of people want a particular right, then it is theirs to take. Man is the measure of all things as he seeks ways and means to pursue his happiness. Of course this frame of mind is antithetical and hostile to Christianity's claim that only God's intentions for his creation are proper and right. For that reason, Christians will never give up the struggle against the abandonment of God's norms for society today as the fight against abortion and gay activism show. After all, Christians argue, should God's rights as Creator and Ruler of all not take precedence over all human rights? Also, God bestowed the rights by giving his law to men. Rights are grounded in man's duties to God.

It is remarkable that one of the panels of the Jefferson Memorial in Washington, D.C., gives a quotation of Thomas Jefferson in which he links God to the gift and right of liberty in a manner inconceivable today. The quotation is taken from a larger context. The portion actually appearing on the memorial is in italics. "*Can the liberties of a nation be thought secure when we have removed* their only firm basis, *a conviction* in the minds of the people *that these liberties are the gift of God? That they are not to be violated but with his wrath? Indeed I tremble for my country when I reflect that God is just: that his justice cannot sleep forever.*"[11]

What must a democratically elected government do in its capacity as a servant of God? Government has the responsibility to recognize and safeguard the human rights which God has given—rights given on the basis of the duties humans owe to God. Wherever possible, government should give positive leadership in enacting laws that reflect the will of God. It is simply not true that right and wrong, and good and bad, can only be determined by the will of the majority. The government must give ethical leadership. The theory is, however, simpler than the reality of dealing with a culture that is not Christian. In

---

11. See Thomas Jefferson, "Quotations on the Jefferson Memorial."

our times many assume that there is no absolute truth or morality. The question, therefore, comes up how a democratically elected government is to guide a nation morally. It should be noted that the issue is not whether the government guides the people morally. Government always does so by the laws it passes. The concern is how government as a servant of God can be instrumental in encouraging a positive godly moral conduct.

Government cannot, of course, compel people to become Christians. The great commission to spread the gospel and call people to repentance has been given to the church (Matt 28:19–20), and not to the government. In chapter 3 we have seen how this difference between the responsibilities of church and state has meant the toleration of unbelievers within Israel and the toleration of unbelief today. However, the principle that government cannot compel people to adhere to the Christian religion also means that government has no jurisdiction to force people to accept the beliefs and practices of the religion of secular humanism. Yet, there is no escaping the fact that government constantly makes moral decisions. It legislates morality.[12] If a nation rejects God's Word as authoritative, what norms should government use? Is humanism then the default norm?

Let us consider these issues by first considering the two sources for knowing the moral mind of God and then how government is to make use of them.

Where God's Norms are Found

THE BIBLE

The Bible is of course the primary source for knowing the will of God, both for public and private life. In it God shows the way and details what he expects from his creation. His Word is to be a lamp before our feet and a light on our life path (Ps 119:105). There the norms and principles for his justice and righteousness are to be found as detailed in the law of Moses. "Righteousness exalts a nation, but sin is a disgrace to any people" (Prov 14:34). The Ten Commandments give a summary of what God expects from his creation.

---

12. Montgomery, "Should We Legislate Morality?" 69–79. Also Stott, *Issues Facing Christians Today*, 45–61.

These commandments are therefore very relevant for society today. For that reason, North America with its Christian heritage has laws against stealing and murder, to mention but two examples. One must, however, be very careful how one applies biblical law to today's context. A moment's reflection will make one realize that a government cannot enforce all the Ten Commandments. A government's ability and jurisdiction is limited. The state cannot enforce, for example, the commandment not to covet (Exod 20:17). After all, a government is unable to look into the hearts and minds of its citizens and compel its citizens not to desire their neighbor's property. Furthermore, as we have seen in chapter 3 it is not in the province of the civil government to enforce the commandment not to worship other gods (Exod 20:3) and compel its citizens to believe in the God of the Bible and become Christian. It is up to the church to spread the gospel and urge people to believe and be saved (Matt 28:19). In addition, as we also saw in the preceding chapter, we cannot simply apply Old Testament law as given at the Sinai to society today, as those of theonomic persuasion would like to do. Distinctions need to be made.[13] Not everything that Scripture commands is the duty of and enforceable by the government today. To put it differently, not all sins against the law of God are necessarily crimes to be punished by the state.[14]

It is, nevertheless, important to recognize that the principles of God's justice and righteousness as expounded in both the Old and New Testament remain applicable. A thorough study of God's law shows principles that apply to areas of life such as family, economics, business, education, and justice.[15] Ideally government should integrate these principles into the laws of the land. Such an inclusion of godly principles will be a blessing for the country. Indeed, God's laws given to Israel were to be the envy of the nations around it. When God

---

13. In the classic confessions of the Reformation, three basic distinctions have been made in biblical law: the moral law, the ceremonial law, and the civil law. See Westminster Confession of Faith, Chapter 19, *The Thirty-Nine Articles of the Church of England*, Article 7.

14. See Frame, "Toward a Theology of the State," 224; Bahnsen, "The Theonomic Position," 42–46; also cf. McIlroy, *A Biblical View of Law and Justice*, 162–65. See also very pointedly Colijn, *Van de Overheid en's Heeren Wet*, 9–16. Colijn, a consistent Calvinist, was Prime Minister of the Netherlands during the depression years of the 1930's.

15. See, e.g., Burnside, *God, Justice, and Society*, Schluter and the Cambridge Papers Group, *Christianity in a Changing World* and notes 13 and 14 in chapter 2.

exhorted Israel to keep his law, he added that: "this will show your wisdom and understanding to the nations, who will hear about all these decrees and say, 'Surely this great nation is a wise and understanding people . . . And what other nation is so great as to have such righteous decrees and laws as this body of laws?'" (Deut 4:6, 8). God's just law made Israel a light to the nations (cf. Isa 51:4). So, far from being irrelevant, God's law as given in Old Testament times is of great value for it shows divine principles which can be a blessing to all areas of life.

Unfortunately, current Western society has little patience with being told what God's will as revealed in Scripture is all about. Our culture is in the process of turning its back to God and his clear demands. However, even in the current context, God has not left himself without a witness for there is a second way in which he reveals his will.

NATURAL LAW

The expression "natural law" as used here is that knowledge of the law which God has written in human hearts so that they know what he requires. We read in Romans 2:14–15 that "when Gentiles, who do not have the law, do by nature things required by the law, they are a law for themselves, even though they do not have the law, since they show that the requirements of the law are written on their hearts, their consciences also bearing witness, and their thoughts now accusing, now even defending them."

For our purpose it is important to note the following. First, those who do not have the (Mosaic) law of God in written form, nevertheless have the basic requirements of the law written on their hearts. In other words, they possess the basic divine moral directives in some form even though it will not be in the detail that the written Word provides. The fact that "they are a law for themselves" underlines that having the basic requirements of the law written on their hearts is part of their nature as humans. Second, those without the written law are, therefore, without excuse. Indeed, their consciences bear witness and even accuse them when they go against the natural law. It is important to realize that Romans 2:14–15 indicates that the human conscience is not the source of moral norms. Rather, the conscience passes judgment on whether one has adhered to the norms given by what is written in one's heart.[16]

The reality of this natural law in those who are not Christian is evident from the fact that even societies unfamiliar with the Bible have laws against theft, murder, and false witnessing. God has inscribed his basic requirements in human hearts. One can consider this natural law as part of God's self-revelation through creation. These are certain self-evident truths based on the nature of creation and our being humans. There is the obvious value of life (as opposed to death), liberty (as opposed to bondage), reward for work done (as opposed to fruitless toil), rest (as opposed to working ceaselessly), human relationships (as opposed to living in isolation), and human dignity (as opposed to being without any self-worth).[17] To recognize such truths from observing creation and the nature of reality is to recognize what God the Creator is telling us through his handiwork. God reveals something of his power and divine nature, and hence his will, by the way he has made this world (Rom 1:20). This is therefore an objective standard by which to measure human desire and behavior. Right would be what is in agreement and conformity with creation and its design and wrong would be that which goes contrary to it.

Because natural law and the revelation of God and his glory and majesty through creation are known to all people, government has the obligation to legislate accordingly. Scripture even states that because of this revelation people are without excuse if they insist on going against God's norms and choose wickedness rather than God's wisdom. Indeed, God will punish those who suppress his truth. Romans 1:18–20 says that "The wrath of God is being revealed from heaven against all the godlessness and wickedness of men who suppress the truth by their wickedness, since what may be known about God is plain to them, because God has made it plain to them. For since the creation of the world God's invisible qualities—his eternal power and divine nature—have been clearly seen, being understood from what has been made, so that men are without excuse." Because of God's revelation through his creation and natural law, government has the

---

16. See for this understanding of the passage, e.g., Schreiner, *Romans*, 121–24. Also see Calvin, *Institutes*, IV.xx.16 and Hesselink, *Calvin's Concept of the Law*, 238–51.

17. See, e.g., McIlroy, *A Biblical View of Law and Justice*, 35. For what follows I am dependent on McIlroy, *A Biblical View of Law and Justice*, 163–65.

obligation to legislate as closely as is politically possible to God's norms in those areas of life over which God gave government jurisdiction.

To do this is not an easy feat in a society that wants liberty from all normative restraints. Both in the United States and Canada, society is by and large not in the mood to submit itself to God's ways. We live in post-Christian times. If society wants to go its own way, what should government do then? This issue brings us to the topic of toleration.

TOLERATION

When a democratically elected government is unable, due to political realities, to pass laws that are consistent with God's expectation for his creation, then the unavoidable result is that such a government is forced to tolerate what should not be tolerated. This is an undesirable state of affairs, but such a situation is not unusual in a fallen world where sin against God is common place. Even in ancient Israel, a theocratic state chiefly composed of those who were expected to confess the LORD as their God and obey him, God as their King tolerated much due to the hardness of men's hearts. For example, God had instituted marriage and designed it to be for life. However, due to the hardness of human hearts and the reality of sin God permitted divorce (Deut 24:1–4; Matt 5:31–32), in spite of the fact that he hated it (Mal 2:16). So most Western countries have decriminalized adultery and passed liberal divorce legislation in view of the increasing inability of their citizens to honor the institution of marriage. Notice, however, that from a Christian perspective this is a toleration of an evil which ideally should not be tolerated. It is toleration and acquiescence, not approval. It is a giving in to human weakness, not legislation that a Christian is proud of. Yet Christians are in principle for such toleration because it follows the example of God himself. It also recognizes that the duty of government is to rule over all its citizens, also those who reject the norms given by God. Allowances need to be made for those who refuse to live according to God's norms. Not every sin against God can or needs to be criminalized and punished by the state.

However, what if society strays far from biblical norms and those so obviously reinforced by natural revelation with respect to matters of fundamental importance? The protection of human life, a key government obligation, and marriage, the basic institution of society, come to mind as current examples. In Canada it is legal to end human life before birth and to engage in same-sex marriage. The situation in the United States is not much different. What is the duty of the state and what are the duties of Christians in such a context? To answer these questions, two issues need to be addressed. When government goes against the principles held by many of its citizens, civil strife can result. This raises the matter of needing to keep the civic peace. However, more needs to be done. A second issue is that a nation should also work at reaching a justifiable civic consensus on the moral issues of the day and not simply follow a path that seems most expedient politically.

Keeping the Civil Peace

When the state tolerates practices that go against God's norms—practices it has the duty to ban for the sake of justice, Christians will use all legal means to oppose such evil. As a result real tensions and strife can develop in society. The state, however, has the obligation to keep the civil peace (cf. 1 Tim 2:1–2).[18] Whenever there are competing groups in society with conflicting norms and morals, things can easily get out of hand. Government has the duty to recognize the situation for what it is and try to maintain societal harmony. In an increasingly multicultural society, this becomes more difficult. Government needs to reckon with real and profound differences generated by different faiths, competing morals, and disparate living styles. This reality will not disappear overnight. There must, therefore, be toleration and room for this diversity for society to function in peace.[19] If the state would be intolerant of diversity, it would be forced to exercise coercion to bring everyone into line with its particular vision for society.[20] Such action would result in abuse of state power and an intolerable loss of freedom.

The need to maintain a status quo which is abhorrent and sinful in the eyes of committed Christians brings up the issue of responsibility and conscience. It needs to be stressed that government toleration

---

18. For what follows, see *passim* Paas, *Vrede Stichten*, 409–11; also see Kuiper, *Dienstbare Overheid*, 70.

19. The toleration in Calvinist Netherlands in the seventeenth century was due in no small part to the need to keep concord and peace within a diverse population. See, e.g., Frijhoff, "Religious Toleration in the United Provinces," 31–37.

20. Van Ruler, *Calvinist Trinitarianism and Theocentric Politics*, 187. Also, e.g., Sampson, *Sustaining Democracy*, 10–12.

does not necessarily imply or assert personal ethical approval by all those in government. Given the democratic realities of the day, it can happen that legislation is passed which the president or prime minister would prefer not to have as law. Such a situation is especially possible whenever there is a minority government in Canada. One needs to remember that a tolerant living together as citizens of the same country is a matter of civic justice which recognizes the reality of a fallen world and which enables society to function more or less peacefully. Government toleration of what some will consider reprehensible behavior neither implies nor requires the moral approval of all citizens. If that were the case, those with the most political power would impose their beliefs and practices on minorities against their will. Then all citizens would need to be taught to be morally tolerant of whatever the current majority finds acceptable. Such an approach would result in the loss of the basic freedoms of conviction and religion. In the diverse reality of today, the legal framework of society needs to be based on principles that protect the consciences of the individual and limit the power of the state.[21]

Such an ordering of a democratic nation in today's context does, therefore, entail the official toleration of sin because the jurisdiction and the ability of the state are limited. Government has neither the authority nor the capability to work repentance. It does not have the task to seek the conversion of the population. Of course, this inability on the state level does not absolve a nation from guilt. Scripture teaches that such a society can expect God's wrath (cf. Rom 1:18). But this toleration is the best the government can do under the circumstances. Ideally it is toleration and acquiescence, but not approval. This is how it should be. The influence of secular humanism can, however, result in legislation that goes against God's norms but is passed under the cover of human rights. When legislators pass laws on that basis, God is not pleased.

This brings us to another issue. Toleration cannot be unlimited and unconditional. A nation that allows this will end up destroying itself because it lacks any semblance of moral order or restraint. And so, although toleration is necessary, government has the obligation to lead and provide positive moral direction. It must do everything possible to restrain sin and evil as revealed by God both in Scripture and

---

21. See also Koyzis, *Political Visions and Illusions*, 204–5.

natural law. North American culture has deep roots in Christianity which has served the United States and Canada well. To jettison this heritage in the name of limitless moral toleration is to invite disaster. There is no such thing as a purely neutral state, for every law passed with moral implications steers society in a certain direction. The moral course of the nation needs to be openly discussed in the public square so that society can move to a justifiable civic consensus on the ethical issues of the day.

Finding a Justifiable Civic Consensus

For a truly civic consensus to emerge in a democratic society, it is of critical importance that government ensures a fair and open debate on the issues of the day. To have such discussions we need to consider the preconditions as well as the conditions that are necessary to foster and make possible such a civic discourse.

PRECONDITIONS

A prerequisite is that no segment of society has an unfair advantage in molding the minds of the people in framing the issues and crafting the solution. What are the most important means by which the minds of the people are shaped? The two most influential ones over which government exercises considerable control are the educational institutions and the media. Both are critically important in shaping worldviews and influencing religious and moral preferences. As the guarantor of justice, government has the duty to ensure that these areas are accessible to the entire population without prejudice. In this way one can expect public debate to be inclusive and reflective of the population as a whole.

With respect to education, it is in the first place a parental responsibility. The children belong to those who brought them into this world. They do not belong to the state. Parents therefore have the right to educate their children and to have them educated in accordance with their beliefs and preferences. The state or public education system may not be a good fit. Because public education is dominated by secular humanism, many parents cannot in good conscience send their children there. If they choose to send them to a private Christian school, they end up being penalized financially since they already pay for the public education through their taxes and in addition need to finance the education that they are comfortable with. To ensure a level playing field for influencing the minds of the young, government should make certain that in one way or another the education tax dollar follows the child so that all parents, also the poor, can have their children educated in accordance with their beliefs and principles.

Education is no small matter and the concerns are real. It is well known that public schools are not neutral but promote secular humanism. There are different ways to present facts. For example, a public school will tend to present the scientific theory of evolution as if it were a fact which discredits the biblical account of creation. A Christian school can be expected to teach science from a biblical worldview. Teaching morals is implicit in many subjects. For example, sex education in a public school will tend to be free of moral overtones so that students can decide for themselves when to engage in sexual activity. The push in many quarters for the inclusion of educational material approving gay marriage is another example indicating that secular schools are not morally neutral.[22] Christian schools will handle these topics quite differently and encourage chastity and teach biblical principles relating to the gift of sex.

All parents who are not in favor of having their children indoctrinated in secular humanism but in Judaic-Christian values should have the right to transmit these values to their children. They will one day express them in the public square as they join in the conversation to reach a civic consensus for the direction of their nation. To deprive these children of such an education is unjust. It can also be argued that having the tax dollar follow the wishes of the parents is in accord with the United Nations Convention on the Rights of the Child (1989).[23]

Another prerequisite for laying the groundwork for enabling a fair and open public discourse is that the media are equally accessible to all segments of society. The mass media are very powerful molders

---

22. For the American situation, see, e.g., Baklinski, "California Passes Bill Mandating Pro-gay Teaching." For a Canadian example, Craine, "Toronto School Board: Parents Can't Opt Kids Out of Pro-homosexual Curriculum."

23. On the American scene, see, e.g., Spykman, "The Principled Pluralist Position," 98–99. For the United States and Canada, Koyzis, *Political Visions and Illusions*, 255–58. The United Nations Convention on the Rights of the Child (1989) states that the education of the child shall be directed to "the development of respect for the child's parents, his or her own cultural identity, language and values . . . ." (Art. 29.1.c).

of the public mind. It is, therefore, the duty of government to ensure that all views in society can be heard through them. It seems that most North American media are in the control of left-leaning liberal elite.[24] This situation is especially true for Canada. For example, Christian broadcasters have difficulty getting airtime which is controlled by the Canadian Radio-television and Telecommunications Commission (CRTC). This commission reports to Parliament and part of its mandate is to ensure that the broadcasting systems serve the Canadian public. Questions are often raised whether this is being accomplished. For example, in August of 2008, the CRTC approved a Canadian pay-television pornography channel, but some months later denied two applications for Christian radio stations. When pressed for comment a spokesman said it was "unlikely that a single-faith station could be balanced" without some programming on other faiths.[25] Christians clearly have a lower priority for the CRTC than those addicted to porn. Government should not let this happen. North American mainline media tend to have an anti-Christian bias and it is important that government provide equal opportunity for Christian reporting and media.

Having considered two important preconditions necessary for a fair civic discourse, let us now consider the conditions essential for such a conversation to take place.

Obstacles to Remove

Two important and inter-related obstacles hinder an open discussion in the public square. They are the false notion that religion must be excluded from any debate and that the debate needs to be politically correct.

The duties of church and state are different and should not be confused. Chapter 3 has dealt with that. Each institution has its own calling. However, the separation of church and state does not mean that one cannot bring one's cherished and deeply held Christian con-

---

24. See, e.g., the detailed study of American media by Groseclose and Milyo, "A Measure of Media Bias," 1191–1237. Canada's national broadcaster, the Canadian Broadcasting Corporation, is noted for its liberal bias. See, e.g., Cooper, *Sins of Omission*. On the anti-evangelical bias of Canadian media in general see Haskell, *Through a Lens Darkly*.

25. Green, "Christians Livid as CRTC Denies Religious Radio, but OKs Porn TV."

victions into the public square. Christians have an obligation to do so for they believe that God's Word holds answers for our society. Secular humanists also engage in the public square because they are convinced that they have the answers. Humans are religious in nature and both Christians and secular humanists have deeply held convictions and visions on life which they bring into the discussion. There is no such thing as a person who is truly neutral. This reality needs to be acknowledged. Everyone is shaped by underlying convictions whether they are recognized as such or not.[26] There must, therefore, also be room for Christians to participate in a meaningful way in the public square.

Political correctness is another obstacle that needs to be removed. The input of Christians is vitally important and must be meaningful and not be filtered out of the media by some notion of political correctness. Political correctness affirms that anything that could offend political sensibilities, such as matters of race, sex, culture, or religion, should be eliminated from public discourse. The result has been the stifling of meaningful debate in the mainline media on some of the hot-button issues of the day such as abortion and same-sex marriage. Society needs to move beyond the prejudices and intolerance of political correctness and have open discussion so all parties involved, also those whose voice is not appreciated by the majority, have a chance to say their part. By shutting out those disagreeing with current cultural norms, the public square is impoverished and society is the worse for it. Indeed, the exclusion of religious values has resulted in what has been called "the naked public square,"[27] although, as we have seen, everyone has religious values whether they acknowledge them as such or not.

Contributions Christians Can Make

An open debate on the issues of the day that involves all parties is necessary to come to a civic consensus which is justifiable. The contribution of Christians who understand the principles of God's law for society is absolutely critical to this discussion. The Bible makes clear the superiority and benefits of the principles of biblical law.

---

26. See also Van Ruler, *Calvinist Trinitarianism and Theocentric Politics*, 159.
27. See Neuhaus, *The Naked Public Square*.

Prior to their entry into the Promised Land, God told Israel that when they do his will as a nation, they will be the envy of the peoples around them and they will say of Israel: "Surely this great nation is a wise and understanding people" (Deut 4:6). Doing the will of God is wise and shows understanding for the issues of life. Israel was to be "a light for the Gentiles, to open eyes that are blind, to free captives from prison and to release from the dungeon those who sit in darkness" (Isa 42:6–7). All this underlines the uniqueness of God's law for society. It alone can bring true freedom and righteousness—contrary to the claims of those rulers who deny the true God.[28]

Given society's hostility to involving the biblical religion in public debate, it makes little sense for Christians simply to appeal to divine authority as found in Scripture, just as it would make little sense for a Muslim merely to appeal to the Qur'an in our current culture. Christians should show and demonstrate that the principles of God's law are simply the best way for any society and in this way attempt to bring society's norms as close as possible to the norms of God as revealed in the Bible. The empirical evidence for the superiority of God's ways is evident in the created world and the human conscience also testifies to it.[29]

Chapters 5 to 9 will illustrate this point. It will also become clear that it is not just reason but religious motivations that undergird discussions in the public square. There is, therefore, a spiritual and directional diversity.[30] Christians with strongly held religious convictions should, therefore, not feel inhibited but fully participate in the debates of the day. It only needs to be recognized that in a secular democracy opposing factions will live in constant tension between what is accepted as public policy and what is perceived to be right and wrong from a biblical point of view.[31] There is no easy way out of this dilemma, especially because the worldviews and directions represented are often mutually exclusive, although there are significant

---

28. Such as Hammurabi's claims, as noted by McConville, *Deuteronomy*, 104–5.

29. For a discussion of how the Christian religion can be the cement that holds a tolerant and pluralistic society together, see Paul Roy Fries, "Religion and the Hope for a Truly Human Existence," 196–98. Also see Bolt, "The Background and Context of Van Ruler's Theocentric (Theocratic Vision)," xl.

30. The expression comes from Mouw and Griffioen, *Pluralisms and Horizons*, 87–89.

31. Turnau III, "Speaking in a Broken Tongue," 364–67, 370–72.

exceptions. Christians, secular humanists, and Muslims, for example, all have very different ideas about how society should be ordered, but Christians and humanists will agree on basic rights issues over against Muslims; and Christians and Muslims will agree on same-sex marriage over against those pleading for these "rights."

It is important that Christians recognize the dilemma of competing, deeply held religious views and ethics for what it is and work tirelessly to show, where possible, with the empirical evidence on hand, that the biblical way is the best for society. Chapter 10 will consider how Christians can be most effective in making their contribution to the discussions.

Government as God's Servant

It needs to be noted at the outset that any government is God's servant for God is sovereign and he has ultimately placed all civil authorities in power. In biblical times even heathen rulers were characterized as being in God's service, in spite of their religious orientation. God called the founder of the Persian Empire, Cyrus the Great, his shepherd and his anointed (Isa 44:28; 45:1). Cyrus decreed that the Jewish exiles could return to Jerusalem and rebuild their temple (Ezra 1). God also used Roman Emperor Augustus as his servant. This emperor ordered a census to be taken thereby ensuring that Joseph and Mary would be in Bethlehem for the birth of the Messiah as foretold by Micah (Luke 2:1–5; Micah 5:2). Even pagan rulers are ultimately in the service of God.

We need to remember this truth in our day when Christians can become frustrated with democratic governments that are either unable or reluctant to exercise their biblical mandate of upholding justice as God's servant (Rom. 13:3–4). In today's political climate the ideal of a government espousing and defending biblical values is not always possible. Even if a president or prime minister is a dedicated Christian who would wish to lead the country according to his most cherished convictions, this may not be doable in a secular democracy. Yet, the state remains the servant of God and Christians need to recognize that and not dismiss the civil authorities as an intolerable evil because human rights are center stage rather than God's rights. God who is sovereign also uses rulers of secular democracies today for his purposes.

The task of government in ensuring justice implies limitations to toleration and what are perceived to be human rights. In any diverse democratic society one cannot expect everyone to agree on a common ethic and worldview. There are secularists, racists, Christians, Muslims, and many other definable groups, each with their differing views on a host of issues relating to the public square. Government cannot be all things to all people but must provide moral leadership. In countries with a strong Christian heritage, the traditional Judeo-Christian values should be determinative. These values have historically been an indispensable part of the unity binding a nation together and the matrix that provided toleration and freedoms that we enjoy today. Using Judeo-Christian values as normative will not please everyone and some will feel discriminated against. But such limitations to toleration and freedom are unavoidable. The goal of these constraints is to provide a coherent public order of justice, to restrain evil, and to encourage virtue.

Do such limitations spell the end of toleration and liberty? Does it mean the domination of one group of society over another? No. Government has an inherently limited role and government should not interfere in matters of personal responsibility or the responsibility of other players in society. The state needs to recognize the concept of differentiated responsibilities. However, where freedoms impinge on the rights of others, limitations must necessarily be enforced. For example, it is one thing to decriminalize homosexual activity. People have their own personal responsibilities and government should not legislate what cannot be enforced. It is, however, another to force gay values on children through school curricula. More examples will be given in subsequent chapters.

Furthermore, government must provide moral leadership in ensuring justice and not leave it to the courts to determine what rights trump other rights. There is a trend both in the United States as well as in Canada for the courts to effect moral change through judicial activism.[32] Courts tend to be elitist and out of touch with the aspirations of the people. However, there is no doubt about the corrosive effect on the morals of a nation when legal decisions on human rights void long standing biblical principles. But the courts should not set new

---

32. See, e.g., Bork, *Coercing Virtue*, 21–105 and Leishman, *Against Judicial Activism*.

national moral directions. It is the duty of the elected representatives of the people to legislate the ethical direction of the country in matters such as abortion and same-sex marriage. The nation as a whole which elects their representatives tends to be more conservative than the courts in the moral issues of the day. As servant of God, government must live up to its responsibility and lead the nation in a godly direction and restrain evil.

At this point, secular humanists will raise an objection. What right does the government have to impose its morality on the country? In response, it can be noted that no government can change anyone's morals, values, or heart's desires. No government, however, is neutral. Everything that humans do is motivated by values and morals of one kind or another. Two major forces that currently have tremendous implications for the direction of North America nation are Christianity and secular humanism. On many issues they stand over against each other. Government has the obligation to do what is best for the nation. The next five chapters will show that following the principles of God's law will make human life better. These principles can be summarized as loving God and one's neighbor. This is the chief demand of the law (Matt 22:36–40). "Do to others what you would have them do to you" (Matt 7:12).

Government is unable to make human hearts love God and the neighbor and it must, therefore, tolerate much evil. By nature, the human heart is sinful and is inclined to self-love, rather than a love for God and the neighbor (Rom 8:7; Titus 3:3). Not surprisingly, the current emphasis on human rights has encouraged individualism and the demand for virtual unfettered freedom to pursue one's happiness. But a caring and united society cannot be built on such an egoistic basis. When the individual comes first, the relationship to others suffers and society becomes more and more fragmented. Government must, therefore, show the way as best as it can. What better way is there than to utilize the time-tested Christian heritage of biblical morals and principles that have historically shaped so much of the life and institutions of North America? The American and Canadian democracies owe much to their Christian heritage. It has been a powerful force for good.[33] Even the leftist German philosopher Jürgen Habermas

---

33. Redekop, *Politics Under God*, 92–94; Stavleu, "De Bijbel as Inspiratiebron Voor Politiek," 9–10.

famously proclaimed: "Christianity, and nothing else, is the ultimate foundation of liberty, conscience, human rights, and democracy, the benchmarks of Western civilization. To this day, we have no other options [than Christianity]. We continue to nourish ourselves from this source. Everything else is postmodern chatter."[34] As servant of God, government has the calling to protect the national treasure of the Christian heritage and apply its honored principles to the problems of the day.[35] One cannot exclude government from obeying God. Society needs a positive moral compass. "To deny political authority obedience to Christ is implicitly to deny that obedience to society, too."[36]

There is no such thing as a neutral morality. All of life is shaped by religious presuppositions. North America is currently reaping the bitter fruits of idolizing human rights and all the freedoms needed to pursue one's imagined happiness. These fruits include a growing lawlessness, lack of respect for authority, the breakdown of the family unit, the killing of the unborn, and the promotion of gay lifestyles that are harmful both to good morals and good health.

Government has a moral obligation to show God-honoring leadership wherever possible so that biblical principles of justice and righteousness be promoted in all areas of life. This will honor God and be a blessing to the nation. As wise King Solomon put it: "Righteousness exalts a nation, but sin is a disgrace to any people" (Prov 14:34). It is God's standard of righteousness that is in view since it is "the duty of all men" to "fear God and keep his commandments" (Eccl 12:13).

The next four chapters will consider the task of government with respect to the following foundational gifts which God gave at creation and which make life on earth possible: the gift of human life, marriage and family, work and the day of rest, and the environment. Subsequently, chapter 9 will consider another essential and basic gift of God, namely, nationhood. This topic will give occasion to discuss some biblical principles to meet the challenges posed by multiculturalism. With each issue there will be strong empirical evidence suggesting that the biblical way is the best route for society to follow. Government

---

34. Quoted by Hayward, "Our Forgotten Christian Heritage." Also see Nazir-Ali, "Breaking Faith with Britain," and D'Souza, *What's So Great About Christianity*, 43–81.

35. See also O'Donovan, *The Desire of the Nations*, 233, 249.

36. O'Donovan, *The Desire of the Nations*, 246.

needs to take such evidence into account and build on it as it tries to fulfill its God-given task. But, as the last chapter will show, for such a government to be successful, it will need the help of Christian citizens who are active in influencing the nation's culture in a godly direction.

SUGGESTED READING

Audi, Robert and Nicholas Wolterstorff. *Religion in the Public Square: The Place of Religious Convictions in Political Debate.* Lanham, MD: Rowman & Littlefield, 1997. A scholarly debate by two authorities.

Farrow, Douglas, ed., *Recognizing Religion in a Secular Society: Essays in Pluralism, Religion, and Public Policy.* Montreal & Kingston: McGill-Queen's University Press, 2004. A stimulating collection of essays by a wide variety of experts.

McIlroy, David. *A Biblical View of Law and Justice.* Milton Keynes, UK: Paternoster, 2004. A very accessible and useful work.

Penninga, Mark. *Building on Sand: Human Dignity in Canadian Law and Society.* Winnipeg: Premier / ARPA, 2009. An exposé of the inadequacy of making secular ideas of human dignity the basis for understanding human rights.

Witte Jr., John. *The Reformation of Rights: Law, Religion, and Human Rights in Early Modern Calvinism.* Cambridge: Cambridge University Press, 2007. An important scholarly study.

Part C

Some Current Issues

5

Life and Death

THE PROTECTION OF HUMAN life lies at the core of a government's responsibility. Without this basic safeguard, the normal functioning of society falters and life becomes tenuous and cheap. While most will agree in a general sort of way that this is the task of government, disagreement erupts when one gets to the specifics. This chapter briefly considers the hot button issues of abortion, euthanasia, and capital punishment. Our concern is not to outline and document the ongoing battles surrounding these issues, but first of all to provide a biblical perspective on the matter itself. Knowing what the Bible says is crucial considering the mixed and often contradictory messages coming from different churches. Next, we will also consider what the government's role should be. Chapter 10 will deal with the part that Christians should play to address these and other issues discussed in the next four chapters.

ABORTION

The present topic is obviously not spontaneous abortion as in a miscarriage, but abortion as the active taking away of human life at the very beginning of its existence. It is a medical intervention that terminates a pregnancy. The number of abortions performed in North America is astounding. From 1973, when the American Supreme Court legalized abortion, to March 2011, there have been over 53 million reported abortions in the United States and counting. In Canada with its much smaller population, the situation is just as dismal with over 3 million abortions reported from 1969, the year abortion was decriminalized, to 2005.[1] While it seems to be politically correct to support abortion, the question that needs to be answered is: what does the Bible say?

The Bible and the Unborn Child

Those in favor of giving women access to abortion will protest that the heading speaks of the unborn child. What is not born is only a fetus, not a child. Pro-abortion advocates even appeal to Scripture, in particular to Exodus 21:22–25 as translated, for example, in the Revised Standard Version. This passage then states that

> When men strive together, and hurt a woman with child, so that there is a miscarriage [lit. "and her children come out" C.V.D.], and yet no harm follows, the one who hurt her shall be fined, according as the woman's husband shall lay upon him; and he shall pay as the judges determine. If any harm follows, then you shall give life for life, eye for eye, tooth for tooth, hand for hand, foot for foot, burn for burn, wound for wound, stripe for stripe.

This translation is interpreted to mean that since the mishap involving the woman "only" resulted in a miscarriage and no further harm was done to her, a fine would suffice. If however the woman herself would have been harmed, then the rule life for life would apply. Pro-abortion advocates therefore conclude that the life of the unborn is less than human because the penalty for the death of a fetus is just a fine. There is no demand of life for life. So, aborting the unborn is permissible because God does not regard the life within the womb as a human being no matter how far the pregnancy has gone.

There is however no linguistic justification for understanding what took place as a miscarriage. What happened was that "her children come out." This is literally what the original Hebrew text says. In all likelihood, the interpretation of miscarriage has been influenced by the fact that laws which legislate a fine for miscarriages due to an injury inflicted by someone else were well-known in the ancient Near East, both preceding and following the time of Moses.[2] The actual

---

1. For the American statistics see National Right to Life, "Abortion Statistics." For the Canadian statistics see Statistics Canada, "Canada Abortion Rates 1974 to 2005."

2. Hoffner, "Hittite Laws," §§ 17–18; Roth, "The Laws of Hammurabi," §§ 209–14; Roth, "The Middle Assyrian Laws," A §§ 21, 50–52; Roth, "The Laws of Lipit-Isthar," §§ d-f.

words of Scripture however take precedence over whatever perceived ancient analogies may be found. Often God's law shows striking differences with those of the ancient world in which Israel lived. This is one such instance.

In the biblical law of Exodus 21, the normal words for child and going out are used. The plural "children" probably indicates an indefinite singular.[3] The verb is used elsewhere of a child coming out of the womb in birth (Gen 25:25–26; 38:28–30; Job 1:21; Jer 1:5). Never does the word "come out" refer to a miscarriage unless this is specifically stated (as in Num 12:12). Furthermore, there is a special word in Hebrew for miscarriage, but it is not used in Exodus 21. It is found in Exodus 23:26 "none will miscarry or be barren in your land" (also, e.g., Hos 9:14). The sense of the passage in question is that a pregnant woman, who has been hit, gives birth prematurely. Many translations go in this direction (e.g., NASB, NKJV, NIV, ESV, NET).

Two further comments are in order. First, the fine is imposed because there is no serious physical harm to either the mother or child. Over against the objection that it makes no sense to impose a fine when all is well, the mother and unborn child were exposed to danger and an unnatural premature birth is very stressful. As a result, the husband is allowed to sue the one who injured his wife and the judges will see to it that the fine is reasonable. Second, the text states that "if there is a serious injury, you are to take life for life" (Exod 21:23). Since the context speaks of a premature birth, this rule applies equally to mother and child. If the mother dies, so shall the guilty one; but, also if the child dies. The life of the unborn child is valued just as highly as that of the mother in this legislation. In today's context, the conclusion is obvious. Abortion is murder.

The fact that the unborn is human life is fully supported by the testimony of Scripture elsewhere. David saw himself as being in the womb of his mother before he was born. As he confessed to God: "You created my inmost being; you knit me together in my mother's womb. I praise you because I am fearfully and wonderfully made; your works are wonderful, I know that full well. My frame was not hidden from you when I was made in the secret place. When I was woven together in the depths of the earth" (Ps 139:13–15). This personal identity started from the moment of conception, as is clear from David's penitential

---

3. See, e.g., Joüon, *A Grammar of Biblical Hebrew*, 2:503.

prayer to God when he confessed that he was "sinful from the time my mother conceived me" (Ps 51:5; also see Job 10:8–11). That the fetus is a human being is clear furthermore from the fact that life in the womb before birth is described as a child or baby (Gen 25:22; Luke 1:41). Also, God said to Jeremiah that he knew him before he was formed and before he was born God had set him apart as a prophet for the nations (Jer 1:4–5). Obviously God saw in the womb a human being. A final example will suffice. The eternal Son of God took upon himself our human nature (Phil 2:6–7). When did that occur? That happened at Christ's conception through the working of the Holy Spirit (Luke 1:35). At that moment he became a true human. Since he was like us in all things, can we not assume that our humanity also starts at the moment of our conception? Indeed, is human life not a continuum?[4]

In conclusion, taking the life of an unborn is ending a human life. Human life should be protected not killed. What if a continued pregnancy endangers the life of the mother? This is a very rare situation but it can occur when the fertilized egg implants itself in the fallopian tubes instead of the womb. Since the life of the unborn child cannot be saved and the mother's life is threatened, it is ethically justified to remove the new life.[5]

As a secondary consideration, science has confirmed the biblical message that the unborn are persons in their own right. The pro-abortion argument that a woman can make her own decisions as to what she does with her body overlooks the reality that the unborn is a new human entity which is not part of her. It is scientifically indisputable that the unborn child has its own genetic makeup and is therefore not part of the mother's body in the same sense that her liver or legs are.[6]

The Duty of Government

Given the biblical testimony, it is small wonder that the early Christian church countered the generally permissive pagan culture of their day and prohibited abortion. Two early Christian documents dating from

---

4. Much more could be said with respect to the biblical data; e.g., O'Donovan, *The Christian and the Unborn Child*, 14–16; Frame, *The Doctrine of the Christian Life*, 717–24 and Frame, "Abortion from a Biblical Perspective," 43–75.

5. See further, Frame, *The Doctrine of the Christian Life*, 726–27.

6. See the clear explanation as relayed in Grudem, *Politics According to the Bible*, 161–62. For more detail, George and Tollefsen, *Embryo*.

the early second century, but drawing on Christian sources going back to the first century, explicitly condemn abortion and set the tone for subsequent history. Both the *Didache* or *Teaching of the Twelve Apostles* (2.2) and the *Epistle of Barnabas* (19.5) mention in a list of prohibitions: "You shall not murder a child, whether by abortion or by killing it once it is born."[7] Subsequent Christian writings consistently maintained this position. By the third century Christianity's influence had grown to the extent that it apparently contributed to anti-abortion legislation in the Roman Empire.[8] Once Christianity became a legalized religion, there was a great influx of new members, probably not all sincerely committed, and abortion became a practical issue within the church. But, the church fathers continued to characterize abortion as murder. It is noteworthy that concern for the unborn set the Christian position on abortion apart from pagan reasons for opposing abortion. Pagan antiabortion thinking mentioned the well-being and rights of the state, the father, the family, and occasionally the woman, but never those of the unborn child. Christian thinking however considered the fetus as an independent creation of God and not, as pagans assumed, simply a part of the mother's body.[9]

All of this is relevant for the present context. Throughout the centuries Christian influence in Western society has meant the outlawing of abortion on demand. That has changed by the rise of secularism and what can be described as neo-pagan way of thinking. In ways similar to their ancient counterparts in the Roman empire, also today it is not the unborn child that is the focus of attention, but the perceived rights of others, especially now the woman's right to choose. It is considered her right to freedom of choice. But it has been aptly noted that the call for freedom by pro-abortion groups "reflects not a responsible Christian attitude toward freedom but a secularly informed libertinism."[10] All ethical choices are ultimately based on foundational presuppositions. As heirs of centuries of Christian thinking which has been a great blessing to society, government today has no excuse to evade their obligation to oppose abortion on demand and lead the way into true freedom. This is the freedom that liberates unborn children

---

7. See Niederwimmer and Attridge, *The Didache*, 88–90.
8. Gorman, *Abortion and the Early Church*, 49–62.
9. Gorman, *Abortion and the Early Church*, 77.
10. Gorman, *Abortion and the Early Church*, 99.

from death in what should be the safest place on earth, the mother's womb. It is also the freedom that liberates pregnant women from violence against themselves and against their identity as a woman and potential mother. Many studies show that abortions have severe negative consequences for those who have had them, both physical and psychological.[11]

Christian citizens will continue to make this issue a big priority as efforts are ongoing to stop the large scale killing that goes on. It is clearly against God's will and should therefore be abhorrent to any human being with a God-given conscience. It should be a source of great embarrassment to our Western civilization that millennia ago a pagan Assyrian culture known for its violence and cruelty nevertheless had a strict law against willful abortion. It was considered such a heinous offense for a mother to abort her own offspring that the worst possible punishment was reserved for such a person. She was to be impaled alive if she survived the abortion and denied burial. Even if she died in aborting her child, her dead body was to be impaled and also denied burial.[12] Although these ancients did not have God's written revelation, they forbade in this instance by nature what God's law required (cf. Rom 2:14). How culpable our society and government, privileged with a Christian heritage, are on this score in not forbidding this evil but rather funding and encouraging it!

Government cannot ignore this willful killing. The situation in Canada is especially reprehensible. There is no legislation on abortion and no government dares to tackle the issue because the perception is that the subject has become taboo in the public square. Even if the majority of the population are in favor of unlimited abortion—a debatable point—government has the obligation to oppose the practice and lead the nation in a pro-life direction on an ethical issue as basic as this one. It has been correctly stated that "one cannot do ethics by majority vote."[13] In the United States pro-life legislation has been

---

11. Martinuk, "Women Who Have Abortions Face Numerous Health Issues," 6. Also see the extensive resources in "Effects of Abortion."

12. Roth, "The Middle Assyrian Laws," A § 53. These laws date about the eleventh century B.C.

13. Somerville, "Birth, Death, and Technoscience," 101. In an American Pew Research Center poll dated March 3, 2011, support for legal abortion rose to 54%. However, a Rasmussen Reports poll released March 13, 2011, showed that 65% would support a law requiring women who seek an abortion to wait three days and

passed in numerous states, but there are few signs of any legislative movement in Canada.[14]

The argument is often made that Christians should not impose their moral views on others. But this argument ignores the fact that all laws set standards of behavior based on certain moral convictions such as laws against stealing and murder. If the unborn is human, then the unborn child should be protected. Government therefore has an obligation to act on the abortion issue. It is central to its mandate to protect life, especially that of the defenseless and weak. Steps that can be taken include stopping the promotion of abortion by education and other means, defunding abortions, and prohibiting abortion except to save the life of the mother.[15]

The reason the battle is so difficult is that this is part of a spiritual battle being waged for the soul of a nation. It is, for example, telling that in public debate about abortion, the mainline media consider it politically incorrect to mention the real health dangers that abortion presents. One is considered prejudiced and biased to raise such concerns. Why cannot all the facts and figures be put on the table in the public square? The reason seems to be that passionately held beliefs motivate those who defend abortion. These beliefs really amount to the religion of secular humanism where human rights and absolute freedom to do whatever one wishes are the greatest good regardless of the consequences to others. This amounts to human rights being a modern idol which dictates policy even to our demonstrable hurt. The hurt does not stop at the murder of countless defenseless unborn children and the violence done to the person undergoing abortion. It also manifests itself in very different ways, for example, in an eroding of the value of human life as seen in debates about euthanasia. Another negative consequence is the skewed demographics with a population

---

receive counseling on other options, with only 24% opposing. Gilbert, "Americans Favor Laws Reducing Abortion." In Canada, polls taken over thirty years show a majority opposed to unrestricted abortion. "Thirty Years of Surveys Show Canadians Oppose Unrestricted Abortion."

14. Gilbert, "Roundup: Sudden Surge of Pro-Life Legislation." Canada's Prime Minister, Stephen Harper, has stated on January 19, 2011, that he would refuse to address the issue of abortion, even if his party won a majority in the next election. See Peter Mansbridge and Stephen Harper, "Interview with Stephen Harper." At the time of writing and with a majority, the Harper government shows no sign of changing this position.

15. See further Grudem, *Politics According to the Bible*, 169–77.

that is top heavy with a growing proportion of elderly. This situation in turn necessitates a high level of immigration with all the accompanying challenges to keep a country's economy viable.[16] Following God's will for his creation is best for society, also in the twenty-first century.

EUTHANASIA

The discussions concerning euthanasia are complex and confusing. It is therefore important to clearly define what we mean. For our purposes, euthanasia can be defined as "a deliberate act that causes death undertaken by one person with primary intention of ending the life of another person, in order to relieve that person's suffering."[17] This definition therefore excludes the justified withdrawing or withholding of medical treatment that results in death. It also excludes treatment to relieve pain, even if that could shorten the life span, as long as the treatment is not given with the primary intention of killing the patient. It is best not to speak of passive euthanasia to describe justified withdrawal of life support. Doing so opens the door to an easier acceptance of active euthanasia. After all, if a medical practitioner has already been doing passive euthanasia, then why not go one step further and allow active euthanasia? The two are, however, fundamentally different. Only in active euthanasia, and what is here simply called euthanasia, is the purpose to kill the person in order to relieve suffering.

Euthanasia is rapidly becoming a contentious issue for at least three reasons. First, in this day of claiming one's rights, more and more people want the right to be able to end their lives when they wish. Is my life not my own? Can I not decide when to terminate it? Second, medical advances resulting in longer life spans also play a part in the debate. Because people live longer on average there is an increased risk of suffering from dementia or other debilitating sicknesses. Should one then not be able to end the misery of poor health and dependency on others when one wishes? A third factor in the mix is economics, namely the spiraling health costs to care for an aging population. As the baby boomers get older and infirm and the cost of taking care of them continues to rise, the pressure for euthanasia

---

16. See, e.g., Colson, "Illegal Immigration." For more on the perils of declining fertility, see chapter 6, p. 16.

17. This definition and the immediately following discussion are from Margaret Somerville, "The Secular Case."

will grow. As Governor Richard D. Lamm of Colorado put it in 1984: "We've got a duty to die and get out of the way . . . and let the other society, our kids, build a reasonable life."[18]

Since 1947, public opinion has moved towards a greater acceptance of euthanasia. In 2002, the Netherlands and Belgium legalized it.[19] Euthanasia is illegal in the United States and Canada, but patients can self-administer lethal doses of drugs under physician supervision under the provisions of Death With Dignity Acts in the American states of Oregon (1994) and Washington (2008), and in Montana, a judge ruled this to be legal (2008). There is no comparable legislation in Canada. However, the debate in North America is ongoing. But since human wisdom does not have the final say, we need to consider Scripture on this subject.

The Bible and Euthanasia

Several key biblical truths are helpful for navigating the thorny issues raised by euthanasia.

First, life is a gift of God and is to be protected. The Creator blew the breath of life into the nostrils of the first human being, Adam, whom he made in his own image (Gen 1:26–27; 2:7). For that reason, human life is to be protected and not destroyed. As God told Noah, and through him all humanity: "Whoever sheds the blood of man, by man shall his blood be shed; for in the image of God has God made man" (Gen 9:6). The protection of human life was also articulated in the sixth commandment: "You shall not murder" (Exod 20:13); that is, take away human life illegally, in transgressing God's law.

It needs to be noted that the value of human life is not absolute in the sense that human life is always inviolable and may never be surrendered. Scripture teaches otherwise. "Greater love has no one than this, that he lay down his life for his friends" (John 15:13). One can give one's life for the cause of God's work (Judg 16:28–30 and Heb 11:32; Rom 16:3–4; Rev 12:11). Furthermore, a believer in God's promises of life eternal does not need to hang on to this present life at

---

18. National Desk, "Gov. Lamm Asserts Elderly, If Very Ill, Have 'duty to Die.'"

19. See David W. Moore, "Three in Four Americans Support Euthanasia" and Blizzard, "Canadians and the Ethics of Euthanasia." The Dutch Bill, Termination of Life on Request and Assisted Suicide (Review Procedures) Act, became law on April 1, 2002 and the Belgian Euthanasia Act 2002 on September 23 of that year.

all costs. The apostle Paul longed to depart from this present life and be with Christ but he realized that he still had a task in this life (Phil 1:22–26). Ultimately, the value of human life is relative, but as a gift of God it needs to be appreciated, nurtured, and protected.

Second, God is sovereign over life and death. "In his hand is the life of every creature and the breath of all mankind" (Job 12:10). And so our times are indeed in his hand (Ps 31:15). As sovereign Lord, he gives life in the miracle of conception and he takes life away according to his purpose. No human being has the right to take the life of someone else to end suffering for that person has also been made in God's image and is as such under the protection of his law (Gen 9:6). Indeed, to take someone's life is to usurp God's sovereignty over life and death.

Third, suffering and trouble is part of life in a groaning creation (cf. Rom 8:18–22). This reality brings enormous difficulties for those whose lives are impacted. We cannot always fathom why the Lord allows grief and hurt, but when he does we as creatures are to submit to his ways. As Job put it: "Shall we accept good from God, and not trouble?" (Job 2:10). We are also to help and care for each other. The fear of suffering should never be used to justify euthanasia. "Although it may sometimes appear to be an act of compassion, killing is never a means of caring. . . . To deal with suffering by eliminating those who suffer is an evasion of moral duty and a great wrong."[20]

Fourth, over against the argument that a disabled person no longer has a sufficient quality of life to make living worthwhile, stands the testimony of Scripture that the Messiah will not break a bruised reed or snuff out a smoldering wick (Isa 42:3; Matt 12:20). A bruised reed is, pragmatically speaking, good for nothing. It cannot serve as a support and is useless. But for the Messiah, nothing is useless and he spares the bruised reed. A wick that smolders gives very little light and is about to go out. It is a picture of life nearly at its end. But the Messiah does not end the life, but spares it. If the Lord has pity on the weak, "useless," and suffering, we should do likewise. And with respect to the quality of life, the Lord has a purpose for every person. He can give the disabled and mentally challenged much joy in life and also make them into very special blessings for others as those who nurture children with significant disabilities know. They can, for example, show much

---

20. Arkes, "Always to Care, Never to Kill."

love and cheer and so enrich the quality of the lives of those around them. Those who have given palliative care to dying loved ones often testify to the same enrichment. Also those being cared for can experience this part of life's journey in a positive way. One's idea of what constitutes quality of life is very subjective and can undergo quite a dramatic positive transformation when faced with unexpected sickness or the sudden need to care for loved ones who are challenged in many ways. The same goes for the person who experiences crippling disabilities but discovers God's purpose for life. The life story and work of the well-known quadriplegic Joni Eareckson Tada amply illustrates this point.

Furthermore, death is a horror and an enemy. It has entered the world because of sin and does not really belong to life (Rom 5:12). No one should be exposed to this enemy before their time. Christians know that this enemy has been defeated (1 Cor 15: 26, 54–57), but it remains an enemy. Dying is going through a valley of death although God's presence and eternity with Christ is assured (Ps 23:4; Phil 1:23). While the Christian has this hope, the Bible teaches that all men pass from this life through death to another existence about which Scripture does not tell us much. But, choosing death is not an escape from trouble into nothingness. All will appear before God's throne and one's existence continues after death (Rev 20:11–15; Matt 25:41–46).[21] Society should reflect on the profundity of death. Killing a fellow human, supposedly for his good, is no small matter.

The Duty of Government and Secular Arguments

From a biblical perspective it is obvious that government has the duty to protect life and to oppose any legalization of euthanasia. It is a sad commentary on the secularized state of the Western world that killing a fellow human being to relieve suffering is gaining acceptance. This is particularly deplorable in a time when palliative care and pain relief has never been better.

To put the issue in perspective, it should be noted that never in the history of Western civilization since the days of Constantine has human life seemed so expendable. Prior to the twentieth century, it was difficult to find discussions on euthanasia. Euthanasia, when

---

21. See further Gootjes, *Both in Life and Death*, 19–23.

found at all, was associated with pagan societies.[22] But even ancient pagan Greek society provided for and protected the sick. With the Hippocratic Oath physicians pledged not to give lethal drugs to their patients, even if asked. This heritage from the past has had a positive influence on Western medicine.[23]

Since the Bible no longer holds the authoritative place in society that it once held, it is good to note additional reasons that should give pause to the legalization of euthanasia and prevent its becoming law. These reasons are interrelated and could be summed up as follows.

First, "legalizing euthanasia would damage important foundational societal values and symbols that uphold respect for human life."[24] Medicine and law are important institutions for maintaining respect for human life and shaping positive ethical attitudes in a secular pluralistic society. To allow people to kill each other would dramatically affect the underlying rationale for these institutions, seriously undermine their ability to promote the value of human life, and erode the public trust in the medical and legal profession. Indeed, one could argue that the prohibition against intentional killing is fundamental to our whole legal system. The 1993–94 British House of Lords Select Committee on Medical Ethics declared that this prohibition is "the cornerstone of law and of social relationships."[25] Not surprisingly then, both the American Medical Association and the Canadian Medical Association are against euthanasia, although the Canadian organization seems more open to the possibility of change. Furthermore, "surveys consistently show that physicians in various countries are more opposed to euthanasia than the general public. For instance, a 2009 survey by the British Royal College of Physicians showed 73 per cent of its members opposed euthanasia, whereas up to 82 per cent of the British general public approved of it."[26]

22. Rose, "Euthanasia," 599–600.
23. Wiesing, "Hippocratic Oath," 154–55.
24. Somerville, "The Secular Case," 20.
25. Dobbin and et al., "Memorandum by the All-Party Parliamentary Pro-Life Group (August 2004)," § 2.
26. Somerville, "Euthanasia Would Hurt Doctors." For the American Medical Association and the Canadian Medical Association, see respectively American Medical Association, "Opinion 2.21 - Euthanasia," American Medical Association, "Opinion 2.211 - Physician-Assisted Suicide," and Canadian Medical Association, "Euthanasia and Assisted Suicide (Update 1998)."

Second, if euthanasia were to be legalized, life would simply be a commodity that could be done away with at will. Human life and its value would be reduced in a purely materialistic sense. "Life, however, is not simply a 'good' that we possess. We are living beings. Our life is our person. To treat our life as a 'thing' that we can authorize another to terminate is profoundly dehumanizing. Euthanasia, even when requested by the competent, can never be a humanitarian act, for it attacks the distinctiveness and limitations of being human. Persons—ourselves and others—are not things to be discarded when they are no longer deemed useful."[27]

Third, over against arguments about patient autonomy and the right to choose, one should realize that "the concept of autonomy, in particular the right to refuse medical treatment, is designed not to give persons a right to decide whether to live or die but to protect them from the unwanted interferences of others. The concept is rooted in the notion of the intrinsic value and dignity of the human person and thus can be overridden when autonomy is exercised in ways which contravene this notion or place other members of society at risk of harm."[28]

Fourth, it would be impossible to prevent abuse once euthanasia is allowed, even in very specialized circumstances. Abortion was at first allowed for very specific circumstances, but soon became widely available. British organizations dealing with hospices and palliative care argued that once euthanasia is accepted it "is uncontrollable for philosophical, logical and practical reasons rather than slippery slopes of moral laxity or idleness. Patients will almost certainly die without and against their wishes if such legislation is introduced."[29] Indeed, the developments in the Netherlands show that once euthanasia is legalized, its application expands. The evidence demonstrates that killing patients without their explicit request or consent is rampant in that country. Indications are that the situation is no better in Belgium.[30]

---

27. Arkes, "Always to Care, Never to Kill," 46.

28. Dobbin and et al., "Memorandum by the All-Party Parliamentary Pro-Life Group (August 2004)," § 16.

29. Dobbin and et al., "Memorandum by the All-Party Parliamentary Pro-Life Group (August 2004)," § 25.

30. See, e.g., Grudem, *Politics According to the Bible*, 182–83; for Belgium, Hilary White, "Over 30% of Euthanasia Cases in Belgian Region Did Not Give Consent: Study." Also see for both countries Broeckaert and Janssens, "Palliative Care and

When an aging population, scarce and costly health-care resources, and euthanasia come together, the mix is deadly. "It's cheaper to kill people than to care for them when they're dying."[31]

Fifth, if British statistics from a 2003 survey are any indication, patients are not exactly clamoring for the right to kill themselves, and the relatives of patients are even less inclined to see their loved ones die. There is no reason to think that the British are unique in this respect. In this survey, doctors commented that in their experience, requests for euthanasia were "cries for help that have been resolved with good symptom control."[32] The reserve to euthanasia of those directly affected stands in contrast to the high British general public approval of euthanasia mentioned earlier.

It has been well said that "euthanasia and physician-assisted suicide are simplistic, wrong and dangerous responses to the complex reality of human death. They involve taking people who are at their weakest and most vulnerable, who fear loss of control or isolation and abandonment—who are in a state of intense 'pre-mortem loneliness'— and placing them in a situation where they believe their only alternative is to be killed or kill themselves."[33] Government, as servant of God to do good (Rom 13:4), has the duty to care for its weakest and most vulnerable citizens and to lead the way in setting a positive moral tone for the future. Euthanasia is never an option.

CAPITAL PUNISHMENT

Capital punishment or the death penalty for murder is largely out of favor in today's Western world. Canada abolished the death penalty in 1976 because of three concerns: the concern for wrongful convictions, the concern of the state taking the lives of individuals, and the concern about its value as a deterrent for crime. Initially the law abolishing capital punishment had exceptions, but these were removed in 1998 so that the repeal of this form of punishment for all crimes was complete.[34] Canada is not alone in taking this position. As of 2006, 86 na-

---

Euthanasia: Belgian and Dutch Perspectives," 35–69.

31. Kathleen Foley as quoted by Hunter, "If Life is Cheap, Death is Cheaper."

32. Dobbin and et al., "Memorandum by the All-Party Parliamentary Pro-Life Group (August 2004)," §§ 37–38.

33. Somerville, "The Secular Case," 23.

34. Department of Justice, "Capital Punishment in Canada."

tions have abolished the death penalty for all offences, including every nation on the European continent, except Belarus. Other nations have retained the death penalty but have not used it in over ten years. This means that 122 of 193 sovereign states, the approximate world total, can be considered either legally or in reality abolitionist. The death penalty is in force in the United States and, among others, in China, Japan, India, and all Islamic nations.[35]

In the United States the situation is complex because of shared responsibilities on the federal and state level. In 1972 the American Supreme Court overturned state death penalty laws because none provided adequate protection against capricious or discriminatory administration. State laws were rewritten to meet the new standards and 38 states, as well as the federal government, now allow capital punishment. The majority of the population is in support of the death penalty. However, the fear of wrongful conviction has resulted in states imposing moratoria on executions and the number of death sentences imposed has gone down considerably.

What are Christians to think about the death penalty? Two basic issues need to be resolved. First, does the state have the God-given authority to punish and take lives? If so, is the death penalty appropriate for murders? What does the Bible say about these and related issues?

The Bible and Capital Punishment

The oldest recorded biblical law dealing with the death penalty for murder was relayed to Noah by God himself. The context is significant. The LORD had brought a flood upon the earth that wiped out virtually the entire human race because of their sin (Gen 6:7). Noah and his family who survived in the ark were the only humans left on earth. At this new beginning, God made a covenant with them and so with all humanity. The original creation mandate given to Adam and Eve was repeated (Gen 1:28; 9:1–2) and among other things God also said:

> Whoever sheds the blood of man, by man shall his blood be shed; for in the image of God has God made man.(Gen 9:6)

---

35. For the data in what precedes and the following paragraph, see Owens, "Death Penalty: Law," 704–5.

Several important principles are here articulated. First, the severity of the punishment matches the heinousness of the crime. The crime is murder since the expression "shedding the blood of man" is used for premeditated killing (Gen 37:22). The punishment suits the offense according to the principle of "life for life, eye for an eye" (Exod 21:23–24). Second, the seriousness of taking human life is grounded in man's being made in the image of God. In a sense, God is implicated in each murder for he made man after his image and in his likeness (Gen 1:26–27). This crime, therefore, is not just against man, but also against God. He himself will therefore demand an accounting. "From each man . . . I will demand an accounting for the life of his fellow man" (Gen 9:5). Third, nevertheless, not God, but man is to execute the punishment and avenge the murder. "By man shall his blood be shed" (Gen 9:6). Clearly, if man is to ensure justice, then God gives man the power to do so in his behalf. Luther correctly said that hereby "temporal government was established, and the sword placed in its hand by God."[36] This command that the murderer's blood be shed laid the foundation for civil government and a well-ordered society in which life could be protected and evil restrained. Fourth, since God spoke these words to Noah and so to all mankind at a new beginning of human history on a cleansed earth, the divine ordinance "whoever sheds the blood of man, by man shall his blood be shed," is normative for all men in all times and places.

The death penalty for murder was reinforced in God's subsequent revelation to his people Israel.[37] Intentional killing was to be punished by death (Exod 21:12, 14, 23). There was to be no difference between the native-born Israelite and the foreigner. Both had to be put to death if convicted (Lev 24:17, 21–22). However, if the killing was done unintentionally, and "God lets it happen, he is to flee to a place I will designate" (Exod 21:12–14). The Lord designated six strategically located cities as places of refuge so that if someone accidentally killed his neighbor without premeditated malice, then he could flee to such

---

36. As quoted in Keil and Delitzsch, *Commentary on the Old Testament*, 1.97. Also see chapter 2, note 1.

37. The death penalty also functioned as the maximum punishment possible for rebellion against many of God's ordinances. This served in essence as excommunication by death from the holy assembly, the people of God in the Old Testament. For this reason, the penalty of death for these offences can no longer be applied by the state today. See further Van Dam, *The Elder*, 12, 83–85.

a city to save his life. "Otherwise, the avenger of blood might pursue him in a rage, overtake him if the distance is too great, and kill him even though he is not deserving of death, since he did it to his neighbor without malice aforethought" (Deut 19:6; also see Num 35:6–34).

God did not establish the position of "avenger of blood" in Mosaic law, but recognized the figure as a reality in ancient tribal society. Such a person, usually the nearest of kin, would be responsible for taking vengeance on behalf of the one killed in order to exact from the wrongdoer his life as satisfaction for the murder committed. This ancient practice is likely reflected in Cain's fear for his life after his murder of Abel (Gen 4:14). The Lord however did not simply recognize the custom of blood vengeance. He regulated it and basically placed this practice under his law which allowed the one who accidentally killed to flee to a city of refugee. There the one pursued could count on the normal judicial process and not be left to the mercy of the avenger of blood. If he was not guilty, his life would be spared, but he had to stay inside the city of refuge until the death of the high priest. Should he be found guilty of intentional killing, the avenger of blood became the executioner. But, the avenger of blood could not take the law into his own hands. The court decided on the fate of the one charged with murder. The activity of the avenger of blood was regulated under the auspices of the civil authorities (Num 35:9–28; Deut 19:11–13). The practice of avenging blood by the closest relative eventually died out in Israel.

Another important aspect of the death penalty is the need for at least two witnesses in order to convict someone of murder. "On the testimony of two or three witnesses a man shall be put to death, but no one shall be put to death on the testimony of only one witness" (Deut 17:6; similarly 19:15; Num 35:30). If the verdict was guilty, the witnesses were to cast the first stones to execute the death penalty. However, the rest of the people also participated (Deut 17:5–7). If there were no witnesses, or only one, then in order to conclude the matter, an oath could be administered before God who sees all things (1 Kgs 8:31–32; Prov 15:3). In any case, Israel knew that if a court was powerless due to human limitations, the Lord could still punish the wicked (cf. Lev 17:10).

Negligence leading to death could also be a reason for capital punishment. If a bull killed someone, it had to be killed and the owner was not liable. However, if the bull had had a history of goring, the owner had to be put to death as well as the animal. But, if payment was demanded, the owner could redeem his life by paying whatever was demanded (Exod 21:28–32). This example shows that the law took into account the circumstances and death was not an automatic penalty.

The New Testament does not really address the death penalty as an issue. It is clear from Romans 13 that the government, as servant of God, has the power of the sword to punish evil doers. The ruling authority is "God's servant, an agent of wrath to bring punishment on the wrongdoer" (Rom 13:4). The apostle Paul underlined this truth by saying: "If, however, I am guilty of doing anything deserving death, I do not refuse to die" (Acts 25:11). Also Peter exhorted: " Submit yourselves for the Lord's sake to every authority instituted among men ... who are sent by him to punish those who do wrong and to commend those who do right" (1 Pet 2:13–14).

The Duty of Government and Secular Arguments

If Scripture is to be the norm for society, then the state has the duty to maintain the death penalty for murder. After all, God mandated this for all humanity after the great flood (Gen 9:6). The state has the duty to protect the lives of its people and so punish the evil doer, but it must do so in accordance with the Word of God. That truth has several consequences for today's society.

First, the state needs to maintain justice in the land. In other words, vigilante justice, where people take the law into their own hands, can never be justified. The activities of the avenger of blood in ancient Israelite society were carefully circumscribed by God's law to the effect that the avenger had to be under the law of the land. Those who today appoint themselves to kill abortionists, for example, act against God's revealed will. Such action can never be justified from the Bible. The courts of the land determine guilt or innocence. If one is convinced that the courts do not judge rightly, one can consider legal options. Failing that, one can comfort oneself with the fact that the Lord sees everything that happens and he is the ultimate judge who will one day make his judgment known (Ps 96:13).

Second, biblical principles teach us to be both nuanced about the way we speak of the death penalty for murder and forthright in recognizing the enormity of the loss of human life. The distinction between meditated and premeditated killing is important and has consequences for the punishment. However, one is culpable, even if the killing was not planned. For example, the one who reached the city of refuge and was cleared of any guilt for premeditated murder still had to suffer virtual imprisonment in the city of refuge. He could not leave it without risking his very life (Num 35:26–27). That resulted in quite an upheaval in his life. There was therefore a considerable consequential cost to his killing. Similarly, in the case of the owner of the animal which killed someone, there were considerable consequences. If the owner was unaware of the bellicose nature of the animal, he was innocent, but he nevertheless suffered the loss of a valuable animal. If he was negligent, he could be put to death; but, his life could also be redeemed with money (Exod 21:28–30). The death penalty was not always required but the taking of a human life was considered to be a very serious matter for such a life was made in God's image (Gen 9:6). The one responsible for the death of a fellow human needed to suffer the consequences for it. If this principle were to be applied today, it would help put an end, for example, to relatively low sentences for careless driving causing death.[38]

Third, no death penalty can be exacted based solely on circumstantial evidence. The biblical requirement is two or three witnesses. The gravity of witnessing was underlined by the fact that the witnesses were the first to carry out the sentence (Deut 17:6–7; 19:15). A human life can only be taken if there is absolute certainty of premeditated killing. If this principle had been followed in North America, the incidence of wrongful punishment would have been far less than has been shown to be the case. Also the presence of DNA at a murder scene does not act as a witness to conclusively prove guilt. It is circumstantial evidence that needs to be interpreted. It is not a direct testimony as DNA could be, for example, to prove paternity. The biblical solution to current concerns for the potential of unjust punishment in murder trials is the requirement of two or three witnesses who can testify to what they saw.

Fourth, God's law dictated that if the death penalty was determined to be the judicial solution, then it had to be carried out immediately (Deut 17:6–7). The current norm of convicted killers

---

38. See also Burnside, *God, Justice, and Society*, 264–65.

languishing for a long time on death row after the judicial process has run its course is not in accord with biblical principles. For example, in California the leading causes of death among inmates on death row are apparently "old age, suicide, and execution, in that order. Actual execution is a very distant third place."[39]

Since the Enlightenment, several objections against the death penalty for murder have been raised from a humanist perspective. Is this not cruel and unusual punishment? Indeed, is the rule: "life for life, eye for eye, tooth for tooth" and so on (Exod 21:23–24) not unduly harsh? However, one should realize that this rule limited the punishment according to the injury in view. It restrained the anger of the one offended and restricted the options for retribution. Also, it did not allow the wealthy to simply pay a fine for an offense (as happened with Israel's neighbors), but compelled them to satisfy the requirements of justice with punishment appropriate for the crime or violation. The rule was therefore quite enlightened and, if followed today, would match the punishment with the crime and prevent both too little and too much punishment. Biblical wisdom states that "a man reaps what he sows" (Gal 6:7).

Other common objections include that a person should be rehabilitated and not killed. But this notion ignores God's preeminent right to justice and is premised on the unbiblical idea of the basic goodness of man (cf. Rom 3:10–12). Many protest that there is no proof that capital punishment acts as a deterrent. Such a statement is counter-intuitive and where meaningful statistics are available has been shown to be misleading.[40] However, this argument is ultimately irrelevant for the fact of the matter is that God has entrusted the state with the sword to execute the convicted murderer. The state therefore has the full right to proceed to capital punishment if the biblical safeguards have been met. In this way the governing authorities reflect something of God's abhorrence of murdering someone made in his image. Another common objection is that the sixth commandment forbids killing. However, this is not quite accurate. The sixth commandment

---

39. Gleason, *The Death Penalty* on Trial, 85.

40. Sweden abolished the death penalty in 1921 but it had been rare since 1865. Norway abolished it in 1905 but had been little used for 30 years prior. Compared to England and Wales, which still had the death penalty, the murder rate of these Scandinavian countries was much higher in those years. See for more detail Taylor, "The Death Penalty," 14–16.

forbids murder (the Hebrew word for illegal killing, ratsakh, is used in the original text). This commandment does not outlaw all killing. When God gives the state the authority to execute convicted murderers, it is not transgressing the sixth commandment.

More objections have been raised,[41] but Scripture is clear on the need and justice of the death penalty for murder. Society benefits when God's ordinances are honored.

In conclusion, government has the duty to protect human life. Realizing this responsibility means opposing abortion and euthanasia, but honoring the biblical demand for capital punishment where the biblical safeguards have been met.

SUGGESTED READING

Abortion

Frame, John M. *The Doctrine of the Christian Life*. Phillipsburg, NJ: P&R, 2008, pages 717–732. A short but very lucid treatment.

Ganz, Richard L, ed. *Thou Shalt Not Kill: The Christian Case Against Abortion*.New Rochelle, NY: Arlington House, 1978. A solid collection of articles covering biblical, medical, and legal aspects of abortion.

Gorman, Michael J. *Abortion and the Early Church: Christian, Jewish, and Pagan Attitudes in the Greco-Roman World*. Downers Grove, Ill: InterVarsity Press, 1982. An interesting and informative study of how the early Christians approached abortion.

Schlossberg, Terry and Elizabeth Rice Achtemeier. *Not My Own: Abortion and the Marks of the Church*. Grand Rapids, MI: Eerdmans, 1995. It addresses the important issue of churches being indifferent to or actually supporting abortion and shows how this position cannot be maintained.

Stewart, Gary P. et al. *Basic Questions on Suicide and Euthanasia. Are They ever Right?* Bio Basics Series. Grand Rapids, MI: Kregel, 1998.

---

41. See, with rebuttals, for example, Grudem, *Politics According to the Bible*, 190–200 and Gleason, *The Death Penalty on Trial*, 57–98.

Stott, John. *Issues Facing Christians Today: A Major Appraisal of Contemporary Social and Moral Questions*. Basingstoke, UK: Marshalls, 1984, pages 280–300. A helpful overview.

Euthanasia

Evangelical Fellowship of Canada. *In the Shadow of Death: A Christian Perspective on Euthanasia and Assisted Suicide*. Markham, ON: Faith Today Publications, 2006. Available at http://www.evangelicalfellowship.ca/page.aspx?pid=190. This background discussion paper by The Centre for Faith and Public Life of the Evangelical Fellowship of Canada outlines the main issues and gives Christian direction.

Frame, John M. *Medical Ethics: Principles, Persons, and Problems*. Phillipsburg, NJ: Presbyterian and Reformed Publishing Company, 1988. A wide-ranging treatment from a biblical perspective of ethical problems encountered in medical treatment. It includes a valuable "Report of the Committee to Study the Matter of Abortion" presented to the Thirty-eight General Assembly of the Orthodox Presbyterian Church (May 24–29, 1971).

Gootjes, N. H. *Both in Life and Death. Biblical Notions in Connection with Today's Tendency Towards Euthanasia*. London, ON: Inter-League Publication Board, 1994. A very accessible biblical introduction to the issues surrounding euthanasia.

Wyatt, John. "Euthanasia and Assisted Suicide." *Cambridge Papers* 19:2 (June 2010). Available at http://www.jubilee-centre.org. A clear and concise treatment of the background and ongoing developments in the euthanasia debate to demonstrate the preciousness and inter-dependence of human life.

Capital Punishment

Bedau, Hugo Adam. *The Death Penalty in America: Current Controversies*. New York, NY: Oxford University Press, 1997. A comprehensive overview reflecting contemporary issues.

Gleason, Ron. *The Death Penalty on Trial: Taking a Life for a Life Taken*. Ventura, CA: Nordskog, 2008. A clear and incisive biblical explanation of some of the major issues in the debate.

Grudem, Wayne, *Politics According to the Bible: A Comprehensive Resource for Understanding Modern Political Issues in Light of Scripture*. Grand Rapids, MI: Zondervan, 2010, pages 186–201.

Ingram, T. Robert, ed. *Essays on the Death Penalty*. Houston, TX: St. Thomas Press, 1971. Eight studies on various aspects of the death penalty.

Megivern, James J. *The Death Penalty: An Historical and Theological Survey*. New York, NY: Paulist Press, 1997. A detailed scholarly study from early Christianity to the end of the twentieth century.

6

Marriage and Family

When it comes to marriage, many in today's society are confused about the identity, place, and role of this institution. Quite a few in our postmodern culture are bewildered and asking basic questions such as: what actually is marriage anyway? If two people love each other, what's wrong with pre-marital sex and living together? If you happen to be married and don't want to be married anymore, why not opt out and divorce? And if just about anything goes, as seems to be the case today, what is wrong with same-sex marriage? Furthermore, if marriage is up to society to define, why not include polygamy? The scope of this current confusion is unprecedented in the history of Western society and it coincides with society's leaving its Christian moorings and embracing the logical consequences of human autonomy with man as the measure of all things.

To know what marriage is really all about, we need to listen to the One who designed it and gave it to us. Marriage is not a human fabrication but it is God's creational gift.

This chapter takes a brief look at the original design and blessing of marriage, the current challenges, and the role of government in meeting those challenges.

THE ORIGINAL DESIGN AND BLESSING OF MARRIAGE

When God created all things in the beginning, he crowned his work with the creation of man and with the institution of marriage. On the sixth day of creation, "God created man in his own image, in the image of God he created him; male and female he created them. God blessed them and said to them, 'Be fruitful and increase in number; fill the earth and subdue it.'" (Gen 1:27–28). For the first time male and female are mentioned. This is quite remarkable because on the preceding day when God had created the sea creatures and birds there is no mention of male and female although God had then also blessed them and commanded them to be fruitful and increase in number (Gen 1:22). Obviously sexual differences are presupposed among the animals in order to enable procreation, but this fact is not stated in so many words. Sexual differentiation is specifically mentioned only with respect to humanity. This reference to male and female pointed ahead to a relationship that is completely unique in all creation, the relationship of holy marriage, established by God himself.

This uniqueness is evident from the way God instituted marriage. The order of events is instructive. Prior to the gift of wedlock, God first had man name the animals which he brought to him. Why did God do this? It was to help man realize his special place in creation. By naming the animals, Adam became aware of his special identity. He was not an animal. He was of a different order. He stood above the animals and had dominion over them as evidenced by his giving them each its name. Furthermore, by observing that all the animals he named were paired as male and female he became aware of his own exceptional status and loneliness, being a male all by himself. Being the only human, he was unable to find a complement to himself. He was a male, but there was no female. All of this stresses the uniqueness of what was coming: human marriage.

The way God prepared Adam for marriage underscored Adam's humanity. Adam was not an animal. There was no counterpart for him in the animal world. Sexual relations among animals are of a completely different order than those among humans. God established holy wedlock for men and women. A consequence of this reality—to give but one example—is that one cannot use evidence of animal sexual behavior to rationalize it in human intercourse. This approach is often taken in same-sex marriage debates to justify homosexual activity for humans on the ground that it occurs in the animal world. The underlying premise that man is simply another animal is fallacious as the opening chapters of Genesis make clear.

A Helper Suitable for Him

When Adam realized in a very profound way that he was indeed alone, God made clear to him the first purpose of marriage, namely, having someone to share life with. So God made a helper suitable for him. This helper was by God's design of the opposite gender, a woman, Eve. She was his true counterpart. How man jubilated when he received woman from the hand of God: "This is now bone of my bones and flesh of my flesh; she shall be called 'woman,' for she was taken out of man" (Gen 2:23). Together they formed one whole, a complete unit. "For this reason a man will leave his father and mother and be united to his wife, and they will become one flesh" (Gen 2:24). So marriage brings together male and female in a beautiful unity and wholeness because this is how God designed and made it. They fit together.[1]

She is "a helper suitable for him" (Gen 2:18). What does that mean and what does that indicate about the marriage relationship? The original Hebrew used for "helper suitable for him" indicates someone who will correspond to Adam and be neither inferior nor superior to him. She will be his equal, his counterpart.[2]

In marriage, sex differences bind together into one beautiful unity that excludes loneliness and gives a safe and secure haven for social and sexual intimacy. According to God's design a profound joy is found in that intimacy for a wholeness is experienced that those who are alone miss. Part of the happiness of marriage is that within the safe confines of marriage where love and faithfulness have been pledged to each other, God's gift of sex can be enjoyed.

Marriage and Procreation

This divine gift means that there is far more to God's design for marriage than just making two individuals feel good as they form an emotional, spiritual, and physical unity. God's design of sex includes receiving children.[3]

---

1. Cf. "Only a being made from 'ādām can and ought to become someone with whom 'ādām longs to *re*unite in sexual intercourse and marriage, a *re*union that not only provides companionship but restores 'ādām to his original wholeness. The woman is not just 'like himself' but 'from himself' and thereby a complementary fit to himself. She is a complementary sexual 'other.'" Gagnon, *The Bible and Homosexual Practice*, 60–61.

2. Any suggestion that the term "helper" suggests subordinate status is refuted by the fact that this same word frequently describes the Lord's relationship to Israel. He is Israel's helper (e.g. Exod 18:4; Deut 33:7, 26, 29).

3. Those who are unable to beget offspring can therefore feel deprived and experience this inability as a real burden. However a childless marriage is still a purposeful union and a gift of God in which husband and wife can help each other to live

When a couple marries, the relationship of husband and wife overrides the relationship with one's parents. "A man will leave his father and mother and be united to his wife, and they will become one flesh" (Gen 2:24). With marriage, one goes away from the parental home and a new and permanent relationship of husband and wife takes its place. Within that family setting, new life is received by means of the gift of sex. The children who are born experience the blessings of having a father and a mother who are biologically their parents. In that intimate family setting, children learn the basics that will enable them to function productively in society, such as understanding authority structure, relating socially to others, and being an effective member of the community. It all starts in the home and the home as God has designed it is based on a marriage bond. Such a home that works according to God's design is a strong protective bulwark for the child or children, because marriage by definition is a trust relationship, a love commitment to one another as husband and wife for life. It is, to use the words of Scripture, a covenant (Mal 2:14).

As with anything that is beautiful and well-designed, once you start tampering with it, it breaks. And when something as beautifully designed as marriage breaks, it, like a magnificent vase that is broken, becomes quite a mess. And unfortunately we live in a fallen world. However, God in his Word gives guidelines so that his creational gifts of marriage and family can be protected.

Marriage Defined

In light of what has already been said, marriage can be defined as follows. It is "an exclusive heterosexual covenant between one man and one woman, ordained and sealed by God, preceded by a public leaving of parents, consummated in sexual union, issuing in a permanent mutually supportive partnership, and normally crowned by the gift of children."[4] Current issues surrounding marriage need to be considered in the light of this definition because it is consistent with the biblical testimony.

---

faithfully before God.

4. The definition is from Stott as noted in Köstenberger, "Marriage and Family in the New Testament," 244.

BIBLICAL NORMS FOR MARRIAGE AND FAMILY
AND THE ROLE OF THE STATE

After the fall into sin, the Lord gave clear direction for marriage and family, first to Israel and then to the New Testament church and so to the entire human race. As God's gift at creation to all humanity, the place of marriage and family is integral to the proper functioning of society. There is no getting around this reality. If society does not honor God's designs for marriage and family, much can go wrong, since marriage and family occupy a central place.

The family is society's basic building block and is truly a divine gift. Studies have confirmed what is already clear from Scripture. The benefits of marriage include the following. Men and women who marry are ordinarily better off as a result. Marriage protects and promotes the well-being of children and thereby promotes the common good of civil society. Marriage is also a wealth-creating institution, increasing human and social capital. A nation with strong marriages and families will more easily and readily protect their responsibilities and liberties from government encroachment and thereby foster limited government.[5]

Within the confines of this book, we will briefly consider God's will for marriage and family in the context of current issues, society's apparent struggle or inability to meet biblical standards, and the role of the state in safeguarding and promoting the well-being of these institutions. The issues considered are divorce, cohabitation, same-sex marriage, and the gift of children.

Divorce and a Weakened Commitment to Marriage

God intended marriage to be a lifelong bond. He therefore forbade adultery (Exod 20:14) which broke the marriage covenant by either the husband or wife being sexually unfaithful. In Old Testament times, such a marriage was ended with the death of the guilty (Deut 22:22–24). Sexual relations that were punished by death also included incest, homosexuality, and bestiality (Exod 22:19; Lev 18:6–29; 20:12–17). These activities are still abhorrent to God (Rom 1:26–27; 1 Cor 6:13–20; Gal 5:19).

---

5. See, e.g., how these benefits are articulated in the well researched and documented work of Aguirre and et al., *Marriage and the Public Good*.

The death penalty for adultery is no more, but adultery can still end a marriage (Matt 5:32). In the Old Testament, divorce was also tolerated for "some indecency" (Deut 24:1), literally "nakedness," a very vague description of something objectionable. Exegetes remain divided about its precise meaning. One thing is very clear. God hates divorce, but he allowed it under some circumstances and still allows it due to the hardness of men's hearts (Matt 19:8; 1 Cor 7:13–15).[6]

Today divorce is widespread in North American society. Divorce laws are liberal and the divorce rates reflect it. For both Canada and the United States the latest figures available (2003) indicate that the divorce rate for all marriages was about 38 to 40%.[7] The big losers are the children who are usually caught in the middle and they suffer much grief. These children often become a problem for society and they are more likely to have to cope with poverty and abuse. They also have no good model on which to build their own future with a marriage partner and the problems tend to get repeated in the next generation. Study after study has shown the enormous cost of divorce, emotionally, financially, and socially.[8]

Another phenomenon in the weakening of marriage is the soaring rate of cohabitation.[9] As one can expect, when God's creation ordinance of marriage is not honored, negative consequences follow. The relationship of couples living together without the commitment needed for marriage are less solid with the resulting negative fallout for any children that are involved. Cohabitation also fares less well in terms of accumulating wealth and does not lead to stable marriages.[10]

Obviously government has an enormous stake in healthy marriages. Solid marriages and families help make a strong society. What can government do? Government should ensure that public policy

---

6. Van Dam, *Divorce and Remarriage* and Ciampa and Rosner, *The First Letter to the Corinthians*, 302–3.

7. Statistics Canada, "Divorces (March 9, 2005)" and Hurley, "Divorce Rate: It's not as High as You Think (April 19, 2005)."

8. See, e.g., Aguirre and et al., *Marriage and the Public Good*, 15–17.

9. See, e.g., the statistics and supporting studies in Popenoe, "Cohabitation," 431.

10. For studies on cohabitation see, e.g., Gardoski, "The Implications of Living Together Before Marriage," 106–13, Popenoe, "Cohabitation," Hayward and Brandon, *Cohabitation in the 21st Century*, and Institute of Marriage and Family Canada, "Cohabitation Statistics."

and law support or reinforce the important place of marriage and family. Tax laws, for instance, should favor marriage over cohabitation and promote the interests of a traditional family. Divorce laws should be made more stringent. For example, the whole issue of no-fault divorce should be re-examined since it is dubious that it has contributed to more stable marriages. Also, the need of a mandatory period of counseling prior to divorce proceedings should be entertained. Divorce should be discouraged wherever possible. At the end of the day, divorce can be necessary in a sinful world, but the law should not needlessly facilitate it. Also, the well-being of children still at home should be a high priority.[11]

Government's obligation however goes further than dealing with divorce and cohabitation laws. God's Word enjoins us to pray for those in authority over us so that "we may live peaceful and quiet lives in all godliness and holiness" (1 Tim 2:2). In the corrosive, oversexed, and individualistic culture of today, where pornography is pervasive and readily available, godly, principled government leadership is needed more than ever in encouraging upright morals and in countering the current permissive mind-set where everything seems to go.[12] Such leadership would seek to enact laws encouraging and favoring marriage and discouraging cohabitation (as, for example, in coed university dorms). It would also legislate to make the creation, distribution, and marketing of pornography illegal because of its addictive and destructive nature. Such state leadership would support and promote "godliness and holiness" and a more biblical view of marriage as God intended it. Given the monumental shift in morals and the democratic context, such state leadership will be very difficult to achieve.[13] But as a servant of God, government has the duty to pursue it. Furthermore,

---

11. For the task of government, see, e.g., Aguirre and et al., *Marriage and the Public Good*, 23–25 and Brandon, *Just Sex*.

12. For the enormous costs of pornography for the individual, marriage, family, and society, see Eberstadt and Layden, *The Social Costs of Pornography*. For the pervasive and corrosive nature of the current immoral culture, see Kupelian, *The Marketing of Evil*, 61–81, 127–48.

13. For an overview of the challenges and the probable direction of government policy in an age of individualism which craves for maximum sexual freedom, see Kuehne, *Sex and the iWorld*, 73–93. For suggestions of legislation, see the previous footnote and Eberstadt and Layden, *The Social Costs of Pornography*, 49–51 and Grudem, *Politics According to the Bible*, 242–44.

as can be expected, when society's norms are close to God's standards, there is great benefit for all.

As many studies have shown,[14] it is in the best interest of society to heed God's will for his institution of marriage, and not seek to redefine it as is now happening in both Canada and the United States.

Same-sex Marriage

For any government or court to redefine marriage is the height of folly and arrogance. This gift of God, designed by him to fit perfectly the needs of the human race and until recently the marital norm for every society, is recklessly being cast aside for the sake of perceived human rights. The driving force behind this development has been the gay rights movement. Although only representing a small fraction of the population, gay activists have been very successful in using the courts and legislatures to legitimize in society what was once universally considered sinful. Although the Parliament of Canada voted overwhelmingly in favor of maintaining traditional marriage in 1999, a few years later, in 2005, it legalized same-sex marriage. All this was accomplished "without an electoral mandate, without the benefit of serious social-scientific research, without adequate democratic deliberation, without the normal process of judicial appeal."[15] Same-sex marriage is also making headway in the United States. Early in 2011 President Obama "has determined that the Defense of Marriage Act — the 1996 law that bars federal recognition of same-sex marriages— is unconstitutional and has directed the Justice Department to stop defending the law in court."[16]

CONSEQUENCES OF SAME-SEX MARRIAGE

What is at stake in these developments is nothing less than revolutionary. First, homosexual activity is condemned in the Bible (Gen 19; Lev 18:22; Rom 1:26–27) and has therefore been forbidden in Western legal codes until recently.[17] This activity is contrary to God's goal in his creation of male and female. Recognizing the activity as legitimate

---

14. See the references in notes 5, 9, 10, and 12 above.
15. Cere, "War of the Ring," 11.
16. Savage and Stolberg, "In Shift, U.S. Says Marriage Act Blocks Gay Rights."
17. For a full discussion, answering modern objections, see Gagnon, *The Bible and Homosexual Practice* and De Young, *Homosexuality*.

is consciously going against God's creation gift of marriage. When government sanctions sin, misery follows. In this particular case, it has been well documented that homosexual activity has some very real negative effects. First, medical consequences include a far higher risk of shortened life expectancy, hepatitis, esophageal cancer, and AIDS. Second, societal endorsement of homosexuality will increase pedophilic activity. Third, affirming homosexuality encourages sexual promiscuity and undermines sexual fidelity since homosexual relationships are often short lived. Fourth, approving homosexual behavior can mean the total annihilation of gender distinctions and norms leading to increased sexual confusion among the young and a further erosion of Christian ethical standards. Fifth, the legal endorsement of homosexual behavior results in the public marginalization of all those who regard such behavior as sinful. Last but not least, the homosexual suffers when society no longer calls his behavior sinful and when mainline liberal churches endorse it. A sin needs to be called a sin so that people know where they stand with respect to their relationship with God.[18]

The second element that makes same-sex marriage so revolutionary is not only tolerating what is sinful but the reshaping of marriage itself. An institution granted at creation and meant for male and female and for procreation is being usurped to satisfy fallacious human notions of justice and rights. "The recasting of marriage in non-procreative terms . . . eliminates the only institution society has that upholds a child's right to the care of his or her own parents. Indeed, it opens to question the legal foundation of the child-parent bond, and of the parental claim to the child over against that of some other party, such as the state."[19]

Not surprisingly then, the first to feel the effects of same-sex marriage are the children. Gay marriage is all about adult interests and goals. Children, if they are involved, come in second place. But sometimes a child is desired and gotten through adoption or reproductive technology. However, as can be expected when God's ordinance is treated with contempt, studies have shown that children are better off with a father and a mother than with two fathers or two mothers.

---

18. For details substantiating the negative effects of homosexual behavior which have been listed, see Gagnon, *The Bible and Homosexual Practice*, 471–85.

19. Farrow, *Nation of Bastards*, 13.

Also, the bond that binds biological parents to their children translates into more effective care for their offspring than is the case with non-biological same-sex parents and their adopted children.[20] But more is involved. A child has an inherent right to know who its parents are.[21] When marriage is restricted to the union of a man and woman, that right of children is a societal norm. "It is a fundamental purpose of marriage to give children both a mother and a father, preferably their own biological parents. Changing the definition of marriage to include same-sex couples would overtly and directly contravene both the right and the norm and would mean marriage could no longer function to affirm the biological bond between parents and their children."[22]

Another consequence of same-sex marriage is that the fatherhood role of men will be frustrated and so will the motherhood role of the women. Same-sex marriage is premised in part on individualism and the belief that the other gender is not needed for one's happiness. This is not as God has intended it and same-sex marriage will lead to confused roles for partners in the relationship and the confusion will spread to any children involved. This will eventually have consequences for society at large.[23]

Because same-sex marriage is contrary to creation, there will continue to be resistance to its acceptance. When the judicial system enforces the gay agenda by, for example, compelling a school board to add gay-friendly books to its elementary book list as happened in a ruling by the Supreme Court of Canada in 2002, it ignores the conflict of competing worldviews in the name of toleration. The result of such a ruling is that we can expect gay marriage to be included in the public school curriculum and that those teachers who resist will be punished. "All this amounts to state-sponsored social engineering on the basis of a state-supported ideology—which is tantamount to an official state

---

20. Young and Nathanson, "The Future of an Experiment," 48–49, 59–60 and Rekers, "Psychological Foundations for Rearing Masculine Boys and Feminine Girls," 294–311.

21. A fact also recognized in Article 7 of "Convention on the Rights of the Child."

22. Somerville, "What About the Children?" 78. Also see Marquardt, *The Revolution in Parenthood*.

23. See further Young and Nathanson, "The Future of an Experiment," 50–53.

religion."[24] Same-sex marriage has the potential to deprive a nation of its freedom of religion.[25]

Finally, with the redefinition of marriage, defending traditional marriage in the courts becomes very difficult. The question arises: if we can define marriage as we like, why can other forms of cohabitation not be legal, such as having several lovers with the consent of all involved (polyamory) or having several wives (polygamy)? These are relevant concerns. Researchers studying polyamory estimate that "openly polyamorous families in the United States number more than half a million, with thriving contingents in nearly every major city."[26] Both the United States and Canada have polyamory societies.[27] With respect to polygamy, the Fundamentalist Church of the Latter Day Saints in both the United States and Canada practice it. Furthermore, Islam allows polygamous marriages. The number of those involved in the United States has been estimated to range from fifty to one hundred thousand. With respect to Canada, the Muslim community in Toronto alone has at least one hundred such multiple unions.[28]

The Role of Government

What is the task of government in all of this? As a servant of God (Rom 13:4), government has the obligation to represent God's interests and wishes for society. In a democracy that may not always be easy or even possible. But government has the first responsibility with respect to marriage and not the courts. In redefining marriage, the Canadian federal government has not involved the people in the process but simply followed the courts. Its American counterpart seems to be doing the same. This is not how it should be in a democracy. The legislature is accountable to the people. The appointed courts are not.[29] Every legal possibility should be utilized to overturn the legal-

---

24. Young and Nathanson, "The Future of an Experiment," 55.
25. See Reid and Buckingham, "Whose Rights? Whose Freedoms? 79–93.
26. Jessica Bennett, "Only You. And You. And You. Polyamory."
27. E.g., Loving More based in the United States (http://www.lovemore.com) and the Canadian Polyamory Advocacy Association (http://polyadvocacy.ca/).
28. See Sinclair, "The Polygamists," 34–61; Bradley Hagerty, "Some Muslims in U. S. Quietly Engage in Polygamy," and Dueck, "Polygamous Challenge: A Case of Lost Common Sense."
29. On the trend of judges determining legislation, see, e.g., for America and Canada Bork, *Coercing Virtue*, 21–105 and for Canada Leishman, *Against Judicial Activism*.

ization of same-sex marriage as dictated by the courts. In Canada that can include invoking the notwithstanding clause (Section 33) of the *Charter of Rights and Freedoms*, which allows legislators to opt out of a court decision which is found to be unacceptable. Courts can make mistakes and when that happens they should not have the last say.[30]

Marriage as the lawful union of one man with one woman to the exclusion of all others is a creation ordinance and should be accepted as such by government. No human being or institution has the right to change the conditions God has set for it. Once that has been done and marriage is redefined, we find ourselves in unfamiliar territory and no one really knows how this will impact society in the future. The very least that should be done at this point is that government remove the designation "marriage" to describe the same-sex relationship. If it lacks the political will to do so, the issue should be opened up for full public discussion—something which has not happened up to now in Canada and America seems to be heading in the same direction.[31] A problem such as this with potential consequences that are difficult to oversee should never be left to the judgment of a court. The legislative branch and ideally the input of all the important institutions of society should be involved.

If a democratic society clearly desires to recognize or regulate same-sex unions, then any name for the relationship other than marriage should be used. Christians can acknowledge the fact that legally recognizing a relationship such as same-sex cohabitation, need not imply ethically approving it, just as recognizing a divorce need not mean agreeing with it. Recognition or regulation should go hand in hand with spelling out the legal obligations and responsibilities that the same-sex relationship requires.[32] It should be obvious from the

---

30. See further Morton, "Taking Section 33 Seriously," 135–54.

31. As indicated by President Obama's determination that the Defense of Marriage Act is unconstitutional without a full public discussion preceding this pronouncement. See note 16 above. Canada's federal Bill C-38, passed in 2005, specifically speaks of same-sex marriage. The Bill is available at http://www.parl.gc.ca/.

32. Cf. the proposed solutions in Farrow, "Facing Reality," 159–68. A Reformed Dutch political think tank proposed registering all non-marriage relationships that share a dwelling, including same-sex cohabitation, as the political answer to the problem of how to regulate gay unions. See Haasdijk et al., *Zo Zijn Wij Niet Getrouwd*. A follow-up study emphasized the legal obligations. Bos et al., *Samenwonen Verplicht*. On the distinction of law and morality, see McIlroy, "The Role of Government in Classical Christian Thought," 98–102 and Rivers, "Government," 144.

law of the land that marriage is and remains a unique institution that cannot be redefined by humans.

The need to defend traditional marriage is also obvious from the challenges that polyamory and polygamy present. With respect to polyamory, there are no laws in North America explicitly addressing a situation of more than two people living in an informal sexual relationship with one another. Although polyamorous arrangements would like to have parental and custodial rights,[33] such relationships should receive no legal recognition since they undermine marriage and family bonds. Polygamy is illegal in both the United States and Canada, but so far authorities have not succeeded in stopping the practice. Polygamy is abusive for women.[34] Documented evidence produced before the Supreme Court of British Columbia in 2011 showed that polygamy within the fundamentalist Mormon sect in Bountiful, British Columbia, abuses the young by forcing underage girls into marriages and by shunning or evicting the "surplus" boys from the community, with all the associated problems these practices create.[35] Polygamy is clearly no way for society to go.

What should be done? The law of the land should be enforced. Monogamous marriage is the biblical norm and departing from this norm does much harm.

As just noted, in Canada, the matter was before the British Columbia Supreme Court in 2011. Freedom of religion is often appealed to. However, an historical factor that can be noted is that when the Mormons came to Canada in 1887, they were aware of this country's negative stand on polygamy. After they failed to persuade the Prime Minister, John A. MacDonald, in 1888 to allow plural marriages, the Canadian parliament passed legislation specifically forbidding the practice in 1890. Most Mormons complied with the law, but not all.[36] Those who continued with polygamy were breaking the law. Muslim immigrants coming to Canada know the law. If they do not like it, they are free not to come to this country.[37] A country has the

---

33. Bennett, "Only You. And You. And You. Polyamory."
34. Hassouneh-Phillips, "Polygamy and Wife Abuse," 735–48.
35. *Affidavit #1 of Joseph Henrich*. Also, Kent, "A Matter of Principle: Fundamentalist Mormon Polygamy, Children, and Human Rights Debates," 7–29 and Wall, *Stolen Innocence*.
36. Card, Northcott, and Foster, eds., *The Mormon Presence in Canada*, 143.
37. One could argue that those who came to Canada as refugees with a polyga-

right to preserve its Christian heritage of monogamous marriage and can expect compliance by newcomers. The appeal to freedom of religion should not be done at the expense of the ethical heritage of the host nation. It would be self-destructive. There has to be an absolute norm. For Canada the preamble of *The Charter of Rights and Freedoms* should be decisive. "Canada is founded upon principles that recognize the supremacy of God." A similar argument can be made for America, with its motto: "In [the Christian] God we trust."

It has been said that a state that believes itself competent to redefine marriage is a dangerous state. "It is a state that no longer acknowledges the supremacy of God . . . and is prepared . . . to alter the nature and structure of the family as such. Before that sort of state a precipice yawns. As G. K. Chesteron once said. 'This triangle of truisms, of father, mother and child, cannot be destroyed; it can only destroy those civilizations which disregard it.'"[38] Indeed, God warns us in his Word that to ignore his will for his creation ordinance of marriage will result in his judgment on society. The moral chaos so evident today is part of that judgment (cf. Rom 1:18–32).

Children

When marriage and family are discussed, children must enter the picture. They have already been mentioned as being at risk in alternate forms of cohabitation and the duty of government to consider their plight. Now we need to consider other aspects of the role of the state with regard to children. But first, what does the Bible tell us about the desirability of receiving children?

A Blessing

The Lord God gave history's first couple the mandate to "be fruitful and increase in number" (Gen 1:28). These words form part of a divine blessing and show that procreation is an integral part of God's plan for marriage. Marriage and children normally go together. In our shortsighted, individualistic, and narcissistic culture, children are

---

mous household with nowhere else to go could be tolerated by way of exception. After all, their relationships were solemnized in a country where it was considered legal and presumably solemnized under oath. The toleration of polygamy in the Old Testament (although never presented as normative or ideal) also points in this direction. See De Vries, "Polygamie, de Bijbel en de Praktijk."

38. Farrow, "Facing Reality," 170.

often regarded as a nuisance best done without. But the Bible rejoices in the gift of offspring. Blessing and prosperity mean that "your wife will be like a fruitful vine within your house; your sons will be like olive shoots around your table. Thus is the man blessed who fears the Lord" (Ps 128:3–4). "Sons are a heritage from the Lord, children a reward from him" (Ps 127:3). To be barren was a tragedy of immense proportion (cf. Gen 30:1) and to have that condition removed was an indication of divine favor (Gen 30:23; Ps 113:9). Children are a great blessing which is to be greatly desired.

With the advance of sophisticated conception control and abortion, birth rates in the Western world have plunged. This development has gone hand in hand with a growing trend of individualism. "Sexual intercourse has been transformed from being valued primarily for its role in procreation and in cementing a marriage relationship to being a pleasurable and typically essential component of intimate adult romantic relationships."[39] The birthrate has fallen below replacement values in the United States and Canada. Were it not for the often higher fertility rate of immigrants, the overall birthrate would be even lower. This low birthrate has and will have enormous consequences. For example, current American and Canadian demographics will not be able to continue to support the health care systems. It could eventually collapse as an aging population incurs unsustainable expenses. Fewer workers in the work force means increasingly more immigrants are needed, gradually changing the character and makeup of the host nation and often depriving developing countries of needed talent and wealth. Many other social, economic, and cultural consequences can be mentioned, but the point is that receiving children is a blessing and the state should have a vital interest in the birthrate of the nation.[40]

There are several ways in which the state can encourage a higher birthrate. One is giving a financial bonus for each child received. As an illustration of such a policy, consider the province of Quebec. Its birthrate was one of the lowest in the world and the government was concerned that its distinctive French culture was increasingly at risk. To encourage the birth of children, the government paid non-taxable

---

39. Kuehne, *Sex and the iWorld*, 74.

40. For the statistics, see Statistics Canada, "Declining Birth Rate and the Increasing Impact of Immigration," the DVD "Demographic Winter: The Decline of the Human Family," and Phillip Longman, *The Empty Cradle*, 7–27, 89–112.

$500 for the first child, $1,000 for the second, and $8,000 for the third one. There were no restrictions as to who would get the allowance. The sole condition was being a resident of Quebec. The program, Allowance for Newborn Children, was announced in 1988, upgraded in 1992, and discontinued in 1997, for the officially stated reason that it did not work. However independent study indicated otherwise. The result of the program was a robust 12% average increase in the birthrate. This study also noted successes with incentive programs in other countries. The above is simply an example. The point is that government should encourage the birth of children. Financial incentives, in whatever way is most appropriate, do appear to work, but other policy decisions have an impact as well.[41]

Nurturing and Educating Children

This brings us to a related point. Government should also encourage and enable mothers not only to give birth but also to nurture their offspring. Motherhood should not be restricted to the labor room and maternity leave. In other words tax laws should favor stay-at-home moms. This would be most in keeping with the Lord's design for the family unit. No day care center can match the biological nurturing bond that exists between a mother and her child. Mothers are uniquely qualified to raise and nurture their young. Their task and role is indispensable. The old Jesuit saying is true: "Give me a child until he is seven, and I will give you the man." What we sow in childhood, we reap in adulthood (cf. Prov 22:6). Mothers lay the life-long foundation for their children's values and worldview.[42] One implication of the important place of the mother is that government should stay out of the universal child care business and make it attractive for mothers to stay at home. For example, government can insure that tax laws are equitable and do not tax one-earner families unfairly.[43] The first re-

---

41. Milligan, *Subsidizing the Stork* and Longman, *The Empty Cradle*, 177, 196. A Rand study showed that a combination of policies is usually involved in affecting birth rates. This combination can include a mix of financial incentives. Grant and et al., *Population Implosion*

42. See further Patterson, "The High Calling of Wife and Mother in Biblical Perspective," 369–73.

43. As illustrations for these concerns, see for the United States: Fathers for Life, "Marriage: A Taxing Affair," and for Canada: Mintz, "Taxing Families: Does the System Need an Overhaul?" 15–17. On getting the Canadian government out of the child care business, see Mrozek, "Getting Children Out of the House," 10–14.

sponsibility for a child's nurture and thus education is with the parents rather than the state.

This principle is clearly taught in the Bible. Parents had to educate their children in the great deeds of the Lord (Exod 10:2; 12:26–27; 13:8) and this was to be an ongoing instruction, making use of every opportunity (Deut 6:4–9). The teaching of God's Word which is "useful for teaching, rebuking, correcting and training in righteousness" results in one being "thoroughly equipped for every good work" (2 Tim 3:16–17). When God's salvation and grace are taught, godliness and upright living are passed on (Titus 2:11–12). Both parents have this responsibility (Prov 1:8; 6:20; 23:22) and they should use disciplinary measures fitting for the occasion (Prov 15:10; Heb 12:7–10), including as necessary appropriate corporal punishment (Prov 13:24; 23:13–14).

These basic biblical principles need to be recognized by the state. As noted earlier in chapter 4, the United Nation's Convention on the Rights of the Child states that a child's education is to be directed to the development of respect for the child's parents and values (Article 29). Such a statement rightly underlines the primary place of parents in determining the education of their children. The implication is that the educational tax dollar should follow the child for the parents to use as deemed best. This is generally not the case in either the United States or Canada. In Ontario, for example, Roman Catholic schools do get public funding but no other religiously based schools do. In protest a complaint was lodged with the United Nations Human Rights Committee. In 1991 and again in 2005, this Committee demanded that the government of Canada "eliminate discrimination on the basis of religion in the funding of schools in Ontario."[44] Whatever one may think of this ruling, nothing changed, but it did underline the inequity of current educational policies. Government has an obligation to give parents more control over the education that takes place outside the home.

Related to this issue is having a school curriculum that is sensitive to the morals and responsibilities of the parents. The first responsibility for sex education, including the teaching of biblical morals, rests with the parents and whatever is taught in school should rein-

---

44. See Vanderheyden, "UN Rules Government Funding of Catholic Education in Ontario 'Discriminatory.'"

force what parents teach in the home. A related growing concern is the issue of disciplining children. Government has every obligation to combat child abuse but it should not infringe on the right of parents to discipline their offspring. The rightful authority of the parents to educate and discipline their children according to biblical norms has been and continues to be under the pressure of court challenges with the possibility of further state encroachment of the unique responsibilities of parents.[45] Government should never allow court decisions that undermine the family unit to stand.

In summary, government has the right and duty to protect and uphold God's creational gifts of marriage and family. These are the basic building blocks of society. If they are not healthy and sound, society has a dark future.

SUGGESTED READING

Marriage and Divorce

Burnside, Jonathan. *God, Justice, and Society: Aspects of Law and Legality in the Bible*. Oxford: Oxford University Press, 2011, pages 317–387. A detailed scholarly look at the biblical legislation and noting its relevance for today.

The Centre for Faith and Public Life, *When Two Become One: The Unique Nature and Benefits of Marriage*. 3rd ed. Markham, ON: Faith Today Publications, 2006. An excellent survey touching on all the major issues.

Dere, Daniel and Douglas Farrow, ed. *Divorcing Marriage: Unveiling the Dangers in Canada's New Social Experiment*. Montreal and Kingston: McGill-Queen's University Press, 2004. The essays in this book make a compelling case to retain the biblical understanding of marriage.

Farrow, Douglas. *Nation of Bastards: Essays on the End of Marriage*. Toronto: BPS Books, 2007. A powerful exposé of the implications of same-sex marriage and what it takes for society to undo the damage.

---

45. See for America, Sears and Osten, *The ACLU Vs America*, 34–98 and for Canada, Leishman, *Against Judicial Activism*, 165–88.

Köstenberger, Andreas with David W. Jones. *God, Marriage, and Family: Rebuilding the Biblical Foundation*. 2nd ed. Wheaton, IL: Crossway, 2010. A very readable, comprehensive treatment, including children and parenting.

Same-Sex Marriage

Gagnon, Robert A. J. *The Bible and Homosexual Practice: Texts and Hermeneutics*. Nashville: Abingdon, 2001. A thorough academic study.

Kuehne, Dale S. *Sex and the iWorld: Rethinking Relationship beyond an Age of Individualism*. Grand Rapids, MI: Baker Academic, 2009. A professor of politics considers the aftermath of the sexual revolution and asks and answers the question: where are we heading.

Satinover, Jeffrey. *Homosexuality and the Politics of Truth*. Grand Rapids, MI: Baker, 1996. This solid study shows that homosexuality is neither innate nor unchangeable and offers compassion and hope.

Stanton, Glenn T. and Bill Maier. *Marriage on Trial: The Case Against Same-sex Marriage and Parenting*. Downers Grove, IL: InterVarsity Press, 2004. An incisive treatment, mostly in question and answer form.

Children

Gairdner, William D. *The War Against the Family: A Parent Speaks Out*. Toronto: Stoddart Publishing, 1992. A Canadian bestseller which touches on a wide variety of modern problems threatening the family, not just in Canada, but also the United States.

Grudem, Wayne. *Politics According to the Bible: A Comprehensive Resource for Understanding Modern Political Issues in Light of Scripture*. Grand Rapids, MI: Zondervan, 2010, pages 245–260 dealing with the family.

Longman, Phillip. *The Empty Cradle: how falling birthrates threaten world prosperity and what to do about it*. New York: Basic Books, 2004. A most stimulating secular study of a disastrous trend that the media and political elite do not talk about but should.

7

Work and Rest

A GIFT OF GOD which is easily overlooked is the creation ordinance of labor. It is also a mandate. Although the fall into sin made working much more difficult, work in and of itself was given to man in an unspoiled perfect world. God placed man in the Garden of Eden for the express purpose that he "work it and take care of it" (Gen 2:15). The Lord God however did not want man to labor without interruption. Right from the beginning, he also granted a weekly day of rest. This day of rest is also a creation ordinance and a gift from God's hand.

This chapter considers work and rest and what obligations these ordinances entail for government today—a most relevant topic considering, for example, work related issues such as the need for both work and time off in an increasingly uncertain and hectic world. The topic of work and rest is large and multifaceted. We will necessarily restrict ourselves to briefly defining the important ideas and then considering whether government has a role and if so, what that role should be.

WORK

The Divine Mandate

The creation ordinance of labor was already implied in the blessing God pronounced after he had created man, male and female. God had then said: "'Be fruitful and increase in number; fill the earth and subdue it. Rule over the fish of the sea and the birds of the air and over every living creature that moves on the ground.' Then God said, 'I give you every seed-bearing plant on the face of the whole earth and every tree that has fruit with seed in it. They will be yours for food.'"

(Gen 1:28–30). These blessings were followed with the explicit charge to work the Garden of Eden and to take care of it (Gen 2:15). In effect these blessings and the garden instructions gave humanity the agenda for the work that needs to be done.

The fall into sin has not changed this basic task. It has however made it much more difficult to realize because work is now done in a world which has fallen from its perfect beginnings into a state of sin and grief. As God said to Adam after the fall: "Cursed is the ground because of you; through painful toil you will eat of it all the days of your life. It will produce thorns and thistles for you, and you will eat the plants of the field. By the sweat of your brow you will eat your food until you return to the ground, since from it you were taken; for dust you are and to dust you will return" (Gen 3:17–19). But the original mandate remained, as is also evident from the blessing God pronounced over those who survived the Noachian flood, a blessing very similar to that given in paradise (Gen 9:1–4, 7; cf. 1:28–30). The mandate to work is also part of the fourth commandment as given at Mount Sinai. "Six days you shall labor and do all your work" (Exod 20:9). Idleness is therefore condemned (Prov 18:9; 2 Thess 3:6).

Some Implications of this Mandate

The mandate to work, as given in the description of man's task, needs to be understood in the context of man's being created in God's image. The Bible links the two together. God had said: "Let us make man in our image, in our likeness, and let them rule over the fish of the sea and the birds of the air, over the livestock, over all the earth, and over all the creatures that move along the ground" (Gen 1:26; also cf. vv. 28–30). To put it differently, man's assignment to work came with his being a human made in God's likeness.[1] Not to work would entail missing something of what it means to be human. It is unnatural. God has created and designed men and women to labor. To work is therefore a God-given right. Since God has ultimately given a person his task in life (unless it is a sinful occupation), one's labor is an honorable and noble enterprise. It has dignity, regardless of what one's line of work may be. It should not be avoided or shunned.

Another implication of being made in God's image is that people are to labor as God's representatives acting for God's interests on earth.

---

1. For a discussion on the image of God, see Merrill, "Image of God," 441–45.

His goals need to be kept in mind if their labor is not to be in vain. Whether it be in the home as mother and homemaker or whether it be in any occupation outside the home, all human labor in the end is to contribute to bringing that grand blessing of being fruitful, filling the earth, and subduing creation to fruition. This task is often called the cultural mandate, an expression which underlines that all aspects of human endeavor are included in God's mandate to work. Every task ultimately needs to be done with God's purpose in mind so that it is all to his glory (Rom 11:36; 1 Cor 10:31). Obviously Christians cannot engage in work that is not to his glory. For human labor to be truly successful, God's norms need to be followed.

When that happens, Christians reflect something of God's image in very concrete ways. For example, by his diligence in working the soil, the farmer shows an aspect of God's purpose in giving the good earth to us. By being honest, a bookkeeper displays something of God's integrity and truth. By being a moral example, a teacher exhibits something of God's standard of holiness. By making the most of the time while on the job, the employee displays God's desire for good stewardship and for the effective use of his resources such as time. By doing one's best, God's desire for perfection is reflected. And so one could go on.

God put man in the garden "to work it and take care of it" (Gen 2:15). Working the garden can be understood as tilling the ground and developing the garden. In other words, man's work as God's representative involves getting out of creation something of its potential to the glory of God. This endeavor is also included in the divine command to subdue the earth (Gen 1:28); that is, to control and govern it. Subduing the earth also includes "harnessing and utilizing of the earth's resources and forces."[2] God has endowed man with curiosity and clear thinking to unravel much of the potential that is in God's creation. The inventions enjoyed today are astounding and they have literally come from the possibilities for development that God put into the earth. Man also had to take care of the garden. This task implies being careful to use its resources wisely so that man's needs can be satisfied and the beauty of the garden remain intact. Man is a steward of the gifts God has entrusted to him. There are implications here

---

2. Murray, *Principles of Conduct*, 37.

for taking good care of the environment as we will see in the next chapter.

Work as a Blessing in a Sinful World

Since being able to work is embedded in the very identity of a human being as made in God's image, work can give much satisfaction and joy. God had designed humanity to this end and so one can experience a deep sense of self-fulfillment when working. In doing their daily labor, people can use and develop their gifts and creativity in response to the God-given cultural mandate. Furthermore, God designed work so that through it one can support oneself and one's family (cf. 2 Thess 3:10). But that is not all. God also wants one's labors to help others. One "must work, doing something useful with his own hands, that he may have something to share with those in need" (Eph 4:28). Being unemployed, not being able to enjoy the satisfaction that comes with working, and basically being declared dispensable and unwanted can therefore be devastating to one's self-esteem, lead to depression, and create considerable stress in the family that is impacted.

For work to be truly beneficial it must be done with the right attitude and goals. Work will not be a joy if one has purely materialistic goals and buys into the egoistic consumerism which only wants more and more. "Do not wear yourself out to get rich" (Prov 23:4). Working for purely materialistic goals is in essence rebellion against God and his design for work, and one's efforts become a form of idolatry in the service of money (1 Tim 6:9–10). The greatest joy from working comes to those who seek to do it according to God's norms and to his glory. One's daily work, whether as a home maker or as a retired person doing volunteer work, as a company executive or plumber, can have meaning because it is not just a job. It is a task and calling which God has given in accordance with one's talents and his providential provision. The words the apostle Paul wrote initially to slaves applies to all Christians: "Whatever you do, work at it with all your heart, as working for the Lord, not for men, since you know that you will receive an inheritance from the Lord as a reward. It is the Lord Christ you are serving" (Col 3:23–24).

Besides the obvious blessings just mentioned there are also other less tangible and nonetheless very real benefits from working. Being on the job and interacting socially with others takes a major block of one's time, time which can have enormous positive impact on one's life and the life of others. Working develops one's gifts, makes oneself useful to others, and contributes to the well being or the betterment of society by providing necessary labor and services.

Sometimes, however, one can experience work more like a curse than a blessing. The long hours on boring assembly line shifts, or the constant bickering in the office, or the exhausting routines, to mention some examples, can get people down. What is the sense of it all? Indeed, such thinking has been vocalized by the Teacher of Ecclesiastes when he considered all the results of his toil meaningless, a chasing after the wind (Eccl 2:11) and he began to despair over all his toilsome labor (Eccl 2:20). Today there are not a few who beginning on Monday already look forward to the weekend.

This is a burden which Christians in such a predicament can see as a cross they have to carry, but they can do so in faith and with a positive outlook. "Work can be cross bearing, self-denying, and life-sacrificing; because work is following the Lord in ways of service, be that in ways hidden to all but God alone or at an envied occupation demanding sacrifices only the doer can know." In faith a Christian can go on, knowing that in it all, he is making a contribution to the world in which he lives and helping to build the civilization and society with benefits that are easily taken for granted. "Work is the gift of self to the service of others that becomes the fabric of civilization. Civilization is the gift of others to the service of ourselves." At the end of the day, "work is the form in which we make ourselves useful to man and thus to God!"[3] And therefore, the Teacher of Ecclesiastes could also say: "A man can do nothing better than to . . . find satisfaction in his work. This too, I see, is from the hand of God, for without him, who can eat or find enjoyment? " (Eccl 2:24–25; see also 5:18).

Because work is integral to being human, finding oneself without a job can be a devastating and demoralizing experience. There is however a productive way out of this conundrum. While one is actively looking for work, one can make satisfying and productive use of one's available time and gifts by volunteering. Helping others gives the joy of being useful and a sense of fulfillment. For Christians it can be a powerful witness of consecrated love.

---

3. DeKoster, *Work: The Meaning of Your Life*, 37–54. The quotations are from pp. 37, 54, and 62.

Since working is such an important part of human life, the question arises: does the state have a role to play with respect to work? If so, what is its task?

The Task of Government

Scripture gives very few concrete principles on government involvement in labor and unemployment issues that are readily applicable to today.[4] However, since government is God's servant and God has ordained and mandated man to work, the basic task of the state with respect to work can be seen in especially three areas.

First, the state has the obligation to ensure and maintain righteousness and justice in the work place. This responsibility includes such diverse matters as minimum standards for working conditions with respect to issues such as hygiene, safety, and the length of the workday. Government involvement can also include ensuring freedom of association for workers who, for example, should be at liberty to join or not join a labor union. Furthermore, the state can encourage good relationships between management and workers by organizing forums with the purpose of discouraging the adversarial "them-against-us" attitudes that poison so many management-labor relationships and encouraging cooperation and worker-input into aspects of production that workers are familiar with.[5]

Second, although the creation of work is best left to those economic units and institutions which provide products and services and so create employment, the reality is that government is a major employer. The modern state retains many people in exercising its responsibilities in areas such as tax collection, defense, building infrastructure, welfare, and consular services. Government can also produce new employment by building and maintaining mega-projects, such as power-generating plants which the private sector may not be able to finance. Furthermore, it can enhance employment opportunities for its citizens by using its influence to bring in foreign investment in the form of new factories, especially if the labor resources for the needs of a particular industry are available in the country. Government can be

---

4. See, e.g., Rogerson, "The Use of the Old Testament with Reference to Work and Unemployment," 100–108.

5. See, e.g., Sutherland, ed., *Us and Them*.

involved in using its legitimate authority to stimulate the economy in the hope of creating jobs.[6]

Third, the state can assist those looking for work by setting up employment offices which bring those who seek jobs and who need workers together, by providing opportunities for training such as in apprenticeships, and by providing a good environment for business to create jobs.

Although the topic of helping the unemployed is outside the scope of the subject of work as such, a few comments on government's role in helping the unemployed is appropriate. In general, government should be the last institution of society to which one should need to turn for help. There is first of all one's personal responsibility. All avenues need to be exhausted before declaring oneself unemployed (cf. 2 Thess 3:7–12). Next in line in terms of responsibility is the family of the unemployed. This principle is clearly outlined in the apostle Paul's discussion of needy widows. He urged that the children or grandchildren take care of such needy (1 Tim 5:4) and then enunciated a general principle. "If anyone does not provide for his relatives, and especially for his immediate family, he has denied the faith and is worse than an unbeliever" (1 Tim 5:8). Any government initiatives that would make it financially easier through tax legislation or otherwise for relatives to take care of the needy unemployed in their families would be consistent with this principle. For Christians, the larger family, the church, provides through members helping each other, including through diaconal aid (cf. 1 Tim 3:8–13). A key rule for Christians is: "Carry each other's burdens, and in this way you will fulfill the law of Christ" (Gal 6:2; cf. Matt 7:12). Governments can assist private organizations and churches helping the unemployed by offering tax breaks for charitable contributions to such organizations. Although the unchurched needy often do not realize this, they can seek assistance from the church which has been charged to "do good to all people" (Gal 6:10).

---

6. Government spending in the hope of creating jobs and stimulating the economy out of a recession is controversial, but this strategy has been used. The economists advising the Obama administration and those in Congress supporting the American Recovery and Reinvestment Act of 2009 were convinced it was a good idea. (For the bill, see http://www.recovery.gov/About/Pages/The_Act.aspx). For a negative assessment of this strategy, see, e.g., Riedl, "Why Government Spending does not Stimulate Economic Growth."

Last in line to assist the unemployed should be the state. Because current culture is secular and very individualistic, many people think of government handouts as the first source of help when facing unemployment. Although this is not an ideal priority, government does have an obligation and North American governments have varying degrees of legislated courses of action, such as unemployment benefits, for financially assisting those without work. This also follows biblical principles. Government as a servant of God (Rom 13:4) is expected to fulfill God's expectations for those who rule nations. Those expectations include protecting the legitimate rights of the poor and needy and intervening for their sakes as necessary. This is evident, for example, from King Solomon's prayer for the Davidic king: "May he defend the cause of the poor of the people, give deliverance to the children of the needy" (Ps 72:4 ESV). This king is characterized as one who "delivers the needy when he calls, the poor and him who has no helper. He has pity on the weak and the needy, and saves the lives of the needy" (Ps 72:12–13). Of King Josiah it was said that "he defended the cause of the poor and needy, and so all went well" (Jer 22:16). Indeed, "if a king judges the poor with fairness, his throne will always be secure" (Prov 29:14). This judging refers in particular to protecting the rights of the poor and their well-being as covered by legislation given by God himself.

Welfare in ancient Israel seems to have been decentralized, with the emphasis on the involvement of the local community.[7] But the king in executing justice could be called upon to enforce legislation pertaining to the poor such as ensuring that the triennial tithe be available to the needy (Deut 14:28–29) and that the sabbatical year provisions be maintained. These provisions would include ensuring that what grew of itself during the sabbatical year was available to the poor (Exod 23:10–11) and that debts were suspended during the sabbatical year (Deut 15:1–11).

Today too an emphasis on the involvement of the local community in distributing welfare should be kept in mind and stimulated. However, such decentralization does not absolve the modern state from responsibility in welfare since it, like Israel's kings, are in God's

---

7. On the principles for caring for the poor by family, church, and state see Van Dam, *Perspectives on Worship, Law and Faith*, 67–82 and Schluter, "Welfare," 181–87.

service for the good of its citizens (Rom 13:4). In a secular, individualistic society where the support of family and church has declined, the state's working for good needs to include helping those who cannot provide for themselves and who have no recourse to assistance from family members or a church community.[8]

The Old Testament legislation pertaining to poverty contains many fundamentals that are of great value in coming to a biblical view of economic principles and the care for the poor, principles that can be applied to issues we are facing today. This is a vast and rich topic which cannot be entered into here,[9] but one simple example related to work comes to mind. In helping the needy, ancient Israel's welfare system in many ways maintained the honor and dignity of the poor. So, by way of illustration, rather than simply prescribing handouts, a practice which can be demeaning, the LORD provided help by giving opportunity for employment. In harvest time some of the produce had to be left behind for the poor to gather (Lev 19:9–10; Deut 24:19–22). This was hard work (cf. Ruth 2:7, 17) but it gave a sense of satisfaction and dignity for the poor were providing for themselves. The lesson to be learned is that government assistance tied to some form of employment and so enhancing the feeling of personal worth for the unemployed is better than simply handing out a check.

Indirectly and proactively government can also help mitigate the effects of sudden unemployment by discouraging the accumulation of excessive personal debt and therefore discouraging consumerism and materialism, and encouraging charitable giving. These are all biblical principles.[10] Saving for the rainy day should be encouraged, also by legislation rewarding those who save.[11] Personal debt levels appear to be at an all-time high in North America. This circumstance leaves families very vulnerable to sudden unemployment since they have lit-

---

8. John Boersema, *Political-Economic Activity*, 111–16.

9. Cf. e.g., Burnside, *God, Justice, and Society*, 219–52.

10. Prov 15:16; 30:7; Mark 10:21–25; 1 Tim 6:9–10; Acts 20:35. The Old Testament laws discouraged long-term debt, encouraged self-sufficiency as a family unit, and preventive strategies. See Schluter, "Welfare," 178–81 and how this can be translated into modern action, pp. 187–92; also, Wright, *Old Testament Ethics for the People of God*, 164–69, 171–79.

11. This type of legislation exists in Canada in the form of Tax Free Savings Account which seems to be similar to the American Roth Individual Retirement Account.

tle or nothing to fall back on for financial emergencies. Governments should set a good example and be very cautious with taking on long term debt for the negative consequences are many, including risking higher unemployment.[12]

When God established work as the normal activity of man, he also established a day of rest, a topic to which we now turn.

REST

A Creation Ordinance

A weekly day of rest was established by God after he had finished his work of creation. Genesis 2 tells us that "By the seventh day God had finished the work he had been doing; so on the seventh day he rested from all his work. And God blessed the seventh day and made it holy, because on it he rested from all the work of creating that he had done" (Gen 2:2–3). In this way God set the seventh day apart and separated it as special from the preceding days of work. Herewith God established a rhythm of work and rest with a view to the welfare of the human race. Man as created in God's image and likeness could be expected to reflect this pattern which God had established and enjoy regular periods of rest from his labor. Furthermore, by blessing this day and setting it apart as holy, God made this day of rest available for man to worship and have fellowship with God.[13]

To be sure, no explicit order is given in Genesis 2 that man should adopt a weekly day of rest. "Like the institution of marriage, the day of rest is not commanded for man. A creation ordinance is not an order. Rather it is an institution for the welfare and good of man which God has built into the way things are. It is the way the human mechanism works best."[14] The fall into sin undoubtedly corrupted humanity's understanding and observance of this day. Later when God renewed his covenant with his people, the LORD explicitly incorporated remembering the Sabbath as the fourth commandment in the Decalogue (Exod 20:8–11; Deut 5:12–15). However, there is no reason to deny that the rhythm of a week, along with a day of rest, was known

12. See Boersema, *Political-Economic Activity*, 96–99.
13. Calvin, *Commentaries on the First Book of Moses Called Genesis*, 1:105–7.
14. Townsend and Schluter, *Why Keep Sunday Special*, 11.

from the beginning. The unit of a week is referred to in Jacob's marriage to Leah and Rachel (Gen 29:27–28). Also, Israel had to honor the Sabbath day about a month before receiving the Ten Commandments at Mount Sinai. The context implies that this day was known to them and needed no further elaboration (Exod 16:1, 22–30; cf. 12:6, 17). And so although the fourth commandment was specifically directed to Israel at Mount Sinai in the first instance, a weekly day of rest was known prior to this time and as a creation ordinance it was meant for all mankind. As the Lord Jesus said: "The Sabbath was made for man" (Mark 2:27), that is "humanity."[15]

This creation ordinance took on additional meaning when the LORD commanded his covenant people to remember this day.

A Covenant Sign for the People of God

When the LORD gave his people Israel the fourth commandment at Mount Sinai, he said: "Remember the Sabbath day by keeping it holy. Six days you shall labor and do all your work, but the seventh day is a Sabbath to the LORD your God. On it you shall not do any work, neither you, nor your son or daughter, nor your manservant or maidservant, nor your animals, nor the alien within your gates. For in six days the LORD made the heavens and the earth, the sea, and all that is in them, but he rested on the seventh day. Therefore the LORD blessed the Sabbath day and made it holy" (Exod 20:8–11). As already evident from the Sabbath as a creation ordinance, this day was to be a day of rest, a day of cessation from labor. All were to share in the rest, including the animals. The reason for the rest is God's rest from his work of creation on the seventh day. As God rested and rejoiced, he made it possible for man to partake in this rest and joy. Such a blessed rest could only be had if one remembered this day "by keeping it holy" and keeping in mind that it was to be "a Sabbath to the LORD your God." In other words, it was to be a day of worship and fellowship with God.

A second reason for the day of rest was given when Moses repeated the Ten Commandments prior to Israel's entry into the Promised Land. This reason was: "Remember that you were slaves in Egypt and that the LORD your God brought you out of there with a

---

15. The generic article in the Greek original points to this understanding. Robertson, *Word Pictures in the New Testament* on Mark 2:27. For a fuller treatment, Zorn, "The New Testament and the Sabbath-Sunday Problem," 48–49.

mighty hand and an outstretched arm. Therefore the LORD your God has commanded you to observe the Sabbath day" (Deut 5:15). Thus the Sabbath day was to recall not only God's work of creation, but also his acts of redemption and salvation. In this way the Sabbath was to serve as a covenant sign for God's people and profaning that day would result in death (Exod 31:13–17; Ezek 20:12).

As a sign of the covenant, this day also pointed ahead to the full redemption and renewal of all creation. The Lord Jesus Christ, "our Passover lamb" (1 Cor 5:7), set his people free from all bondage and slavery of the Egypt of sin (Col 2:13–15; Heb 9:26), and opened the way to the eternal rest (Matt 11:28–29; Heb 4). Christ accomplished all this with his death on the cross and his resurrection on the first day of the week (Matt 28:1; Rom 4:25; 1 Cor 15:16–20). In this way he fulfilled the Sabbath as an Old Testament redemptive sign of the covenant (Col 2:16–17). He now works towards the perfect new creation (Rev 5; cf. 2 Cor 5:17).

With the fulfillment of the sign, the actual day of rest changed. It is striking that Christ choose the day of his resurrection, the first day of the week, to appear to his disciples before his ascension (Matt 28:1, 9; Luke 24:1, 13–14; John 20:19, 26). The church, led by the Spirit, adopted this day as the day of worship (Acts 20:7; 1 Cor 16:2; cf. Rev 1:10). In a sense the original paradisiacal order was restored. Adam and Eve's first full day after creation was the Sabbath. Now Christians, as a new creation (2 Cor 5:17), can start each week with the day of the resurrection, the Lord's Day, and look forward to the fulfillment of the new creation that has been promised (Rev 21:5). This day of worship and rest is to be a foretaste of the eternal rest.[16]

While the Sabbath as a special Old Testament covenant sign has been fulfilled, the creation ordinance of a weekly day of rest remained. From the very beginning, God had blessed this day and set it apart as holy with the intent that all humanity should rest on this day and recognize its holiness by using it for worship and fellowship with God. The fall into sin meant that God's intentions were not fully honored. Christians however seek to do justice to God's original design for this day, not only as a creation ordinance of rest, but also as the day of the

---

16. For a fuller treatment of the Sabbath and Sunday, see Murray, *The Claims of Truth*, 205–28; Van Groningen, "The Sabbath in the Old Testament," 9–45; and Zorn, "The New Testament and the Sabbath-Sunday Problem," 46–61.

resurrection to be used for worship and praise to God. The question that arises is this: Does the state have an obligation with respect to a day of rest as a creation ordinance? And what about the Sunday and civil law? What is the duty of the state as God's servant?

In answering these questions, it may be helpful to consider first in summary fashion some relevant historical highlights which illustrate why and how governments have dealt with these issues in the past and then reflect on the current situation.

The State and Sunday: A Brief Historical Overview

THE ROMAN EMPIRE

On March 3, 321, Emperor Constantine decreed complete public rest "on the most honorable day of the sun," with the exception of farmers who were free to work "lest haply the favorable moment sent by divine providence be lost" and agriculture suffer. Constantine used the planetary name "day of the sun" and made no reference to Christianity. It is therefore not clear whether he was referring primarily to the popular pagan day of the sun or to the Christian Lord's Day.[17] In any case this was in effect the first state regulation of the Sunday since Christians were now completely free from working on their day of worship. This day could now be fully utilized as they saw fit in the service of God. It is difficult to overestimate the impact that this decree had on the subsequent history of the Western world.

Constantine's decree was followed by others dealing with the Sunday as a statuary day of rest. But it was not until the year 386 that the term "the Lord's Day" appears in Roman imperial legislation dealing with this day. In 399 a law was passed which decreed that "on the Lord's Day . . . there be no celebration of theatrical sports, nor races of horses, nor any shows in any city, which are found to enervate the mind." In 409 a humanitarian law was put in force which dictated that "prisoners be brought out of prison on all of the Lord's days" so that food and bathing be available to the prisoners.[18] While the church

---

17. For the text of the decree and discussion, see Rordorf, *Sunday*, 162–64 and Lewis, *A Critical History*, 18–35. For a positive evaluation of Constantine's legislation as having primarily the Christian Sunday in view, see De Vries, *Overheid en Zondagsviering*, 134–35.

18. Lewis, *A Critical History*, 36–39, 42–43.

benefited from the state's recognition of Christianity and its protecting the Lord's Day as a special day, the cost of such benefits was very high. With imperial recognition of Christianity and its day of worship, it became beneficial to be a Christian whether one was truly committed or not. Such an expansion of the church did not make a stronger church. Furthermore, the precedent of state involvement did not stop with Sunday legislation but led to government interference and rule in all sorts of church issues as Constantine's involvement in the Council of Nicea in 325 and 327 shows. The church's close relationship with those in high civil office also tempted it to use worldly power for its own ends.[19]

Medieval Europe

During the Middle Ages, the civil authorities continued making laws concerning the Sunday. As communities in the European mainland became more Christianized, the laws became stricter reflecting the tremendous influence of the church on society and its laws. For example, when the Franks were dominant in Western Europe during the time of the Merovingian kingdom (481–751) and the Carolingian empire (751–843), decisions of church councils on the Lord's Day were reflected in civil law. This included forbidding all labor (including agricultural) and to rest on Sundays so that worship and praising God could take place. Interestingly, these laws were based not on the day of rest as a creation ordinance, but on the basis of Sunday as an ecclesiastical feast day which had taken the place of the Jewish Sabbath. Unfortunately this rationale for Sunday observance meant that the fundamental difference between Sunday as a creation ordinance for all humanity (and thus within the jurisdiction of the state) and church festivities (about which the church alone should determine) was erased. The state's penalties for non-compliance varied greatly, ranging from monetary fines to physical punishment and even death.[20] Needless to say, these early laws had an enormous influence on society until the time of the Reformation.

---

19. For as favorable reading as possible of Constantine's involvement in church affairs and the church's relationship to imperial power see Leithart, *Defending Constantine*, 164–89.

20. De Vries, *Overheid en Zondagsviering*, 147–63. Also helpful is the overview by Glazebrook, "Sunday," 105–6.

Meanwhile across the English Channel in Britain, similar developments took place in Anglo-Saxon civil law. This is not surprising since the church was a unifying force that provided leadership for all of Christendom and the political powers issued laws that conformed to the will of the church. It appears however that the Sunday laws in medieval England were stricter than elsewhere. Travel on Sunday was forbidden with only rare exceptions being allowed. Also, the duration of the Sunday was officially from Saturday noon to the dawn of Monday.[21] Through these early laws Christianity exerted a significant influence on the development of English common law and so on the English speaking world.[22]

The Reformation

In jurisdictions affected by the Lutheran Reformation, not much changed. The population was to celebrate the Sunday as determined by the church and articulated in civil law. There was as yet no distinction made between the specific responsibilities of the state and the church. For example, civil law demanded that government officials were obliged to attend church on the Lord's Day and some civil laws even decreed that people should serve God wholeheartedly, attend the worship services, and read the Bible.[23]

As we saw in chapter 3, Calvin recognized that the church and the state had different jurisdictions and he wanted to keep them separate. Calvinist influence in the Republic of the Seven United Netherlands resulted in sixteenth-century civil decrees on the Lord's Day which appealed not to the authority of the church (as had been done previously) but to God's command that this day be hallowed.[24] Keeping the dictates of the church out of civil law was a step in the right direction. However, not surprisingly in this time of transition, the different jurisdictions of state and church were not consistently recognized. This lack was especially evident in England where the monarch became the head of the church, but the Dutch Republic struggled with this issue as well. In England and Scotland, as well as in the United Netherlands,

---

21. De Vries, *Overheid en Zondagsviering*, 186–87 and Lewis, *A Critical History*, 74–77.

22. Perks, *Christianity and Law*, 43–54.

23. De Vries, *Overheid en Zondagsviering*, 216–21.

24. De Vries, *Overheid en Zondagsviering*, 249–50.

the civil authorities made wide-ranging determinations as to precisely what could and could not transpire on the Lord's Day. Civil prohibitions were legislated which went far beyond forbidding work on the Lord's Day. Again, English law tended to be more stringent. The underlying rationale was the spiritual well-being of the people and to encourage them to go to church. The degree to which these goals were pursued depended on the circumstances. The most rigorous legislation was enacted when Puritanism was strong in England. The Lord's Day was basically equated with the Old Testament Sabbath and civil law reflected this view. With civil legal demands such as compulsory church attendance (the laws of 1644 and 1656), the distinctions between the separate jurisdictions and legitimate concerns of state and church were blurred.[25]

Subsequent Developments in the United States and Canada

Those who crossed the Atlantic to America took their Puritan inheritance along with them. This influence was strongest in the colonies of New England. Its seventeenth century colonial Sunday laws decreed, among other things, that church attendance was compulsory and that it was illegal to sleep in church. These laws were enforced. State and church worked in unison without any clear demarcation of their respective responsibilities. This was typical of New England Sunday legislation, but similar legislation was also found in Virginia. On the other hand, the colonies in Rhode Island, New York, and Pennsylvania passed Sunday legislation which consciously did not compel people to go to church but allowed for freedom of religion. The credit for this approach goes in part to the Dutch colony in what is now New York. This legislation shows that Sunday laws can be enacted without the pressures of an official state church and without the goal of getting people to go to church. It was promoted simply as a day of rest. This rationale became more or less universal after the American Revolution. In time practically all the American states had Sunday laws but eventually they were relaxed and subsequently for the most part either repealed or treated as a dead letter. The decline of Christian cultural influence and the rise of secularism undoubtedly contributed to the demise. By

---

25. For detailed accounts, see De Vries, *Overheid en Zondagsviering*, 236–64, 354–71, 381–84, 388–97 and Lewis, *A Critical History*, 92–152; for a brief overview, Glazebrook, "Sunday," 107–8.

the second half of the twentieth century people wanted to go shopping on Sunday.[26]

With respect to the history of Canada, the scattered British colonies in that country were largely under the laws of England until most colonies were federated under the Constitution Act of 1867 which established the Dominion of Canada. Uncertainty and disputes about whether legislating on the Sunday was a federal or provincial jurisdiction led in time to the adoption of the federal Lord's Day Act in 1906. The Lord's Day Alliance had been very influential in drafting this Act. This Alliance was founded under the aegis of the Presbyterian Church but had the support of many Protestant churches, as well as the French Canadian Roman Catholic hierarchy. Its primary purpose was "the prevention of the profanation of the Lord's Day" with the secondary purpose of "protecting the working man." Not surprisingly, the Act had fairly stringent measures to protect the Sunday. It prohibited "sales, business, transportation, employment, games, performances or public meetings where an admission fee is charged on Sunday."[27] However, provinces were able to opt out of the major prohibitions and virtually all provinces took advantage of this provision in one form or another. The Act was further weakened by the fact that most provinces had secular laws with special Sunday prohibitions where necessary. This reality raised the question of the constitutional role of provincial legislation. Additional uncertainly resulted from a lack of clarity about the works of necessity or mercy as allowed on Sundays by the Act. Also there were issues of religious freedom and tolerance that remained unresolved. For all these reasons the Law Reform Commission of Canada recommended in a 1976 report that the 1906 Act be repealed.[28]

That did not happen. Instead, some years later, in 1985, the Supreme Court of Canada struck it down as unconstitutional. The Court considered the Lord's Day Act to be an infringement of the

---

26. De Vries, *Overheid en Zondagsviering*, 413–23; Lewis, *A Critical History*, 160–256; Raucher, "Sunday Business and the Decline of Sunday Closing Laws," 13–33.

27. Law Reform Commission of Canada, *Report on Sunday Observance*, 1, 27; Laverdure, *Sunday in Canada*, 27–44, 197–200; for the Presbyterian influence, see also Laverdure, "Canada's Sunday," 83–99.

28. Law Reform Commission of Canada, *Report on Sunday Observance*, 2–3, 27–59. For a detailed history, Laverdure, *Sunday in Canada*, 45–187.

freedom of conscience and religion as defined in Canada's Charter of Rights and Freedoms. Since the purpose of the Lord's Day Act is

> the compulsion of religious observance, that Act offends freedom of religion. . . . It binds all to a sectarian Christian ideal, works a form of coercion inimical to the spirit of the *Charter*. . . . Non-Christians are prohibited for religious reasons from carrying out otherwise lawful, moral and normal activities. Any law, purely religious in purpose, which denies non-Christians the right to work on Sunday denies them the right to practice their religion and infringes their religious freedom. The protection of one religion and the concomitant non protection of others imports a disparate impact destructive of the religious freedom of society.[29]

The demise of the Lord's Day Act, along with growing public pressure for permissive legislation, eventually led to widespread Sunday shopping across most of Canada. Indeed, most provinces now have no specific legislation restricting work or retail business on Sundays.[30]

Summary

On the basis of this brief historical overview we can note the following.

First, Sunday as a common day of rest commenced with the Christianization of the Roman Empire under Constantine. Prior to that, no one, including Christians, had a public day of rest. In God's providence the church nevertheless managed for centuries to worship and honor God on the Lord's Day before it became a general day of rest.

Second, starting with Constantine, the different responsibilities of the state and church were not always recognized and honored. This led in medieval times to the church using civil authorities to impose on society its ecclesiastical holidays and its prevailing view of how the Sunday should be honored. Even after the Reformation the distinctive tasks of church and state were not always respected so that civil legislation even dictated that citizens attend church and not sleep but listen to the sermon.

---

29. The Supreme Court of Canada, "R. v. Big M. Drug Mart Ltd. [1985];" Laverdure, *Sunday in Canada*, 188.

30. For more detail on the process leading to widespread Sunday shopping, see Human Resources and Skill Development Canada, "Sunday Closing and Weekly Rest Periods;" also Laverdure, *Sunday in Canada*, 191–96.

Third, some pre-revolutionary American colonies did enact Sunday legislation which nevertheless allowed freedom of religion. These laws illustrate that the Sunday can be protected by the civil authorities without imposing Christianity on society.

Fourth, a major current issue is how a Christian conviction of a day of rest can be squared with notions of freedom of religion in a multicultural society. What is the proper role of government with respect to the Christian Sunday in an increasingly secular and postmodern society, a society which nevertheless has a strong Christian heritage? These concerns bring us to our next topic.

The State and Sunday Today

One lesson to be learned from the history of Sunday legislation is that the state should be careful not to go beyond its jurisdiction. Clearly the state cannot, for example, legislate a day of rest with the express purpose of compelling people to go to church. It is the task of the church to exhort the citizens of the nation to believe and worship God on the Lord's Day. The different responsibilities of church and state have been discussed in chapter 3. If civil Sunday legislation cannot be based on the need for people to go to church, should the state get out of Sunday legislation? No, for a weekly day of rest is not only a Christian day of worship, it is also a creation ordinance which God designed for the benefit of all humanity.

A Creation Ordinance with Benefits

God as Creator knows best how his creation works. He ordained a weekly day of rest and it would be impudent for society to deprive itself of this gift of God. Apart from the fact that God ordained a weekly day of rest—and that fact itself should be sufficient to end all dispute—there is significant empirical evidence to suggest that humanity cannot really do without a weekly day of repose. Consider the following failed attempts of those who tried to do away with this creation ordinance. The French Revolution abolished the Christian calendar and decreed that every tenth day should be a day of rest. While this decree was more or less enforced, it was not successful. The 1804 Napoleonic Code restored Sunday as the day of rest. About a century later, Communist Russia tried to break away from the Christian week by experimenting with five and six day weeks. It did not work. World War II restored the Sunday. It is of interest to note that China adhered to the Chinese moon calendar but in 1912 switched to the seven day week beginning with the Sunday. The Communist takeover in 1949 did not change this. A final example, when Britain tried to boost productivity during World War II, it experimented with weeks without days of rest or with extra days. But total output fell and there were more sick employees. God designed humans with the need for a weekly day of rest.[31]

Sunday as a day of rest benefits society in many ways. Since the vast majority of Americans and Canadians still consider themselves Christian, and since Sunday is the day of Christian worship, protecting the Sunday as a day of rest makes it possible for Christian worship to take place with the least amount of hindrance and distraction. Considering the great blessing that Christianity has been, it is wise for government to protect this day and give the church the full freedom it needs to do its work and encourage people to attend worship. The weakening of Christian influence which has been so beneficial to society is detrimental to the nation.

A work-free Sunday also benefits society by providing a regular common day of rest which breaks the routine of work and shopping. It therefore acts as a deterrent for people to be consumed by work and to idolize the materialistic impulse of modern living.

Furthermore, withdrawing from the daily rat race once a week makes it possible for families to have a day of shared time off. Not having such time together and not being able to coordinate periods of rest makes it very difficult for many working families to have down time together. Consequently not having a common day of rest can place great strains on the family unit and be a contributing factor to family breakdown.[32]

In addition, having a common day of rest with no shopping makes good economic sense. Businesses would be spared the expense of being open that extra day.

---

31. Kistemaker, "The History of the Lord's Day," 74; Mills, "A Brief Theology of Time," 3, and *Industry and Sunday* (London: Lord's Day Observance Society, n.d.), 12–15.

32. For more detail on these and related issues, see Townsend and Schluter, *Why Keep Sunday Special*, 40–79.

Objections and Concerns

But what about the duty of the state in a pluralistic society? What about Muslims who honor Friday as their special day of prayer and Jews whose day of rest is the Saturday? These are valid concerns since government serves all its citizens and should respect the minority religious traditions and accommodate where possible. However, this respect should not be an occasion to do away with the Christian values that have shaped the identity and practices of the nation to which those of other faiths have come. But, where possible, laws should take into consideration non-Christian religious needs and promote societal peace.

Another objection is that the state has no business in protecting any day as special. Government should be secular. By treating Sunday differently, is the state not imposing Christianity on the population? No. Such would be the case if the state used its power to coerce people to attend church on the Lord's Day. The church and not the state should determine how the day of rest is to be used in a Christian manner. However, the civil authorities, as God's servant, have the duty to respect and defend God's ordinances such as a weekly day of rest. God's creational designs are good for society. History has shown this and the state has the obligation to seek the best for its nation. It is therefore important that government makes clear the benefits of a weekly day of rest when proposing any such legislation. Obviously, Christians also have a responsibility in promoting its social benefits.[33]

The Task of Government

Due to the nature of the issue at hand, government is the only entity in society that is able to legislate a common day of rest. It therefore has responsibilities in this area. The task of the civil authorities as servant of God with respect to the Sunday can be summarized as follows.

First, the state has the duty to honor God's creation ordinance of a weekly day of rest. This obligation means that as much as possible society as a whole should have a common day of no work. Considering North America's heritage, that should be Sunday. Exceptions should of course be made for works of necessity and mercy. Where possible, al-

---

33. See further Townsend and Schluter, *Why Keep Sunday Special*, 76–79, Stott, *Issues Facing Christians Today*, 50–52 and Woolley, *Family, State, and Church*, 30–32.

lowance should also be made for adherents of religions with a different day of rest.[34] Although legislation for a weekly work-free day would counter current trends in North America and face resistance, it would be good for government to bring the issue into public discussion. Not having a common day of rest is very detrimental to society and families. This truth is causing many on the other side of the Atlantic to agitate and lobby for a work-free Sunday in the European Union.[35]

Second, the state does not have the duty to enforce the Lord's Day as a holy day of worship and compel its citizens to go to church.[36] Since the majority of Americans and Canadians still profess to be Christian, the state should make it possible for the church to function and worship in freedom on the Lord's Day. But the state does not have the authority to impose Christianity on the population even if it were possible to pass such legislation. Furthermore, the church is not dependent on the state and its protection of the Sunday to survive and prosper. The history of the early church illustrates both the church's ability through the enabling Spirit to carry on in times of persecution and without an officially sanctioned day of rest, as well as the dangers of government sponsorship of the church and its day of rest. Also today the growth of the church in jurisdictions hostile to Christianity, such as China, shows that the church does not need government support to flourish.

Third, any Sunday legislation should contain provisions to protect the rights of workers such as being able to refuse to do non-essential

---

34. E.g., observant Jewish shop keepers who close their stores on their Sabbath could be allowed to be open on Sunday. A historical example from Canada illustrates this point. Ontario's Retail Business Hours Act, which had allowed for a business to be open on a Sunday, if it was closed for religious reasons on another day of the week, was found to be constitutional even though the court acknowledged that there was a violation of the right to freedom of religion for those worshipping on Saturday. A key consideration for the Supreme Court's decision was the Act's secular purpose of providing a uniform holiday. Hence the abridgement of the freedom of religion was justifiable as a reasonable limit. The Supreme Court of Canada, "R. v. Edwards Books and Art Ltd. [1986]." Also see Smeenk, *Christelijk-Sociale Beginselen*, 1:286.

35. On June 20, 2011, the European Sunday Alliance, a network of 65 civil society organizations, trade unions, and churches, asked the European Union's Economic and Social Committee to declare Sunday a work-free day in its new working guidelines for member states. "Religious Liberty Wary of Europe's Sunday Law."

36. As noted earlier, Canada's 1906 Lord's Day Act was struck down as unconstitutional because its purpose was the compulsion of religious observance. This object made it offensive to freedom of religion.

work on Sunday and to be given the opportunity to rotate with others when needing to work in essential services on the day of rest.

SUGGESTED READING

Work

Boersema, John. *Political-Economic Activity to the Honour of God.* Winnipeg, MB: Premier Publishing, 1999. A comprehensive look at biblical principles for all economic matters, including work and unemployment by interacting with policies developed by Reformed Christians in the Netherlands.

DeKoster, Lester. *Work: The Meaning of your Life. A Christian Perspective.* 2nd edition. Foreword by Stephen J. Grabill and afterword by The Oikonomia Network. Grand Rapids, MI: Christian's Library Press. A very stimulating look at the meaning of work which integrates Christian understanding of the purpose of life into the workplace.

Ryken, Leland. *Work and Leisure in Christian Perspective.* Portland, OR: Multnomah, 1987. A very informative and useful overview of all the important facets of work and leisure.

Van Dam, Cornelis. *Perspectives on Worship, Law and Faith: The Old Testament Speaks Today.* Kelmscott, Western Australia: Pro Ecclesia Publishers, 2000, pages 59–92. These pages show the relevance and richness of the Bible in informing us today on principles for taking care of the poor.

Wright, Christopher J. H. *Old Testament Ethics for the People of God.* Downers Grove, Ill: InterVarsity Press, 2004, pages 146–181. These pages deal with economics and the poor and give good insight into the principles of work and welfare articulated in the Old Testament and how they can apply to today.

Rest

Beckwith, Roger T. and Wilfrid Stott. *The Christian Sunday. A Biblical and Historical Study.* Grand Rapids, MI: Baker Book House, 1978. A detailed yet accessible treatment of the subject.

Lee, Francis Nigel. *The Covenantal Sabbath. The Weekly Sabbath Scripturally and Historically Considered*. London, UK: The Lord's Day Observance Society, 1966. An exhaustive work.

Lewis, A. H. *A Critical History of Sunday Legislation from 321 to 1888 A.D.* New York: D. Appleton and Company, 1888. Available at Internet Archive (http://www.archive.org/). A very interesting and full treatment.

Townsend, Christopher and Michael Schluter. *Why Keep Sunday Special*. Foreword by Sir Norman Anderson. Cambridge, UK: Jubilee Centre Publications, 1985. This booklet of 87 pages was published as part of a political campaign lobbying for a public weekly day of rest in Britain and giving arguments from both Scripture and the realities of modern living.

Van Groningen, G., ed. *The Sabbath-Sunday Problem*. Geelong, Australia: Hilltop Press, 1968. A stimulating collection of essays that deal with all aspects of the biblical meaning of Sunday and the implications for today.

8

The Environment

THE ENVIRONMENT IS A hot issue. Media attention is constantly focused on it and government agencies have been created to avoid or lessen any negative impact of what is generally seen as an ecological crisis. Pollution and global warming are major North American concerns and on the world stage, many worry that continued population growth in the face of diminishing resources is not sustainable. Indeed, not a few blame environmental problems on there simply being too many people.

Christians should be particularly concerned and interested in the ongoing discussions and debates in this area for at least two basic reasons. First, they confess that "This is my Father's World," to quote a well-known hymn. As steward of planet earth entrusted to its charge by God, humanity has great responsibility to take good care of it and Christians especially should be interested in doing so. Second, Christianity is often blamed for the present crisis. One author has even suggested that the only way out of the ecological conundrum is to "find a new religion, or rethink the old one."[1] Have the Bible and Christianity put the world on the wrong track? Christians need to be informed and to be part of the ongoing discussion in the public square. Understanding some of the basic issues involved will also enable one to ask what the role of government as a servant of God is to be.

In order to get a handle on this whole area, this chapter will first consider what the Bible says and what impact its message has on our understanding of the issues. Next it will introduce radical environ-

---

1. Lynn White, "The Historical Roots of Our Ecological Crisis," 1203–7. This article became famous and started considerable discussion. It has often been reprinted, including in Schaeffer, *Pollution and the Death of Man*, 97–115 (the quote is from p. 112).

mentalism and survey key environmental concerns along with the role of government. Finally, it will offer some reflections on moving forward.

THE BIBLE AND THE ENVIRONMENT

A basic question that needs to be addressed is: to whom does the world belong and what are the consequences of this ownership for environmental issues? Secondly, what do God's charges to humanity at the dawn of creation say to us today? Thirdly, what other biblical principles need to be taken into consideration? These topics will now be dealt with in turn.

Whose World is It?

The answer to this question is in a sense obvious. The earth belongs to the One who created all things. "The earth is the Lord's, and everything in it" (Ps 24:1). Addressing God, the psalmist declares: "The heavens are yours, and yours also the earth" (Ps 89:11; also Ps 50:12). But there is more to it. The planet also belongs to humanity. "The highest heavens belong to the Lord, but the earth he has given to man" (Ps 115:16). In other words, man has been entrusted with the care of the world. It is ultimately not his but it has been given to him in trust. To put it differently, we are but tenants on this world and we are ultimately responsible to God for what we do with it. "God himself remains (in the most literal sense) the 'landlord', the Lord of all the land."[2]

This relationship to God is articulated in the biblical account of creation with man's being created in God's image and likeness (Gen 1:26). As we saw in the previous chapter this identity means that mankind has been charged to be God's representatives in this world and to act for his interests. Human beings can therefore never act as if the earth is solely theirs to do with as they please. The world's environmental concerns are also God's concerns. He has a vital interest in how we treat and manage his creation. It is not just ours to do with as we please.

At creation, God gave man clear instructions which further defined his identity and outlined his duties. It will be helpful to consider these, especially from the perspective of current environmental concerns.

---

2. Stott, *Issues Facing Christians Today*, 111.

Rule Creation

When God decided to make human beings in his image, he determined that they had the duty to "rule over the fish of the sea and the birds of the air, over the livestock, over all the earth, and over all the creatures that move along the ground" (Gen 1:26; similarly Ps 8:6–8). Several consequences of this task description can be noted.

First, by being set over creation, humanity is clearly positioned between God and the world. Mankind's identity is connected to the dust of the earth from which it was made (Gen 2:7). However, its identity is also heavenward for God breathed into the first human nostrils the breath of life and then set male and female over the created world as his representative (Gen 1:26; 2:7). So there is a hierarchy of God, humanity, and the rest of creation. Furthermore, as part of and yet distinct from the rest of creation, mankind is ideally suited for the task of ruling in a way that honors the Creator. As part of creation, humanity can be expected to be empathetic to creation's needs and as made in God's image, it can be sensitive to God's wishes.

Second, since God made everything well (Gen 1:22, 31) and continues to care for his creation (Ps 145:15–16; Matt 6:26), he can expect the human race as his representatives on earth to respect his work as that which he blessed and cares for. Mankind should therefore do likewise and not harm but attempt to protect creation and seek its well being (cf. Rom 8:19–22). This means, for example, no plundering and willful destruction but wise and careful stewardship of the natural resources on which life on earth, including humanity's, depends.[3] Human beings as rulers for God have the duty, as much as possible, to make God's beautiful handiwork of creation continue to be recognizable as such, so that it reflects something of the divine glory (Ps 19:1–6; Rom 1:19–20). In this way, rightful honor and recognition can be given to the Creator.

Third, ruling implies being in charge of the situation and not letting matters get out of hand. When environmental issues are not addressed in a timely manner and spin out of control, God's expectations for humanity are not being met. Thus, for example, when overfishing is pushing a particular species to the point of extinction, remedial action must be taken as soon as possible. Whether it be marine resources or

---

3. See further Burnside, *God, Justice, and Society*, 152–55.

good farmland, conservation and a careful use of finite resources are a high priority for those who rule wisely.[4]

Fill the Earth and Subdue It

After God had made man in his own image, male and female, he "blessed them and said to them, 'Be fruitful and increase in number; fill the earth and subdue it. Rule over the fish of the sea and the birds of the air and over every living creature that moves on the ground.' Then God said, 'I give you every seed-bearing plant on the face of the whole earth and every tree that has fruit with seed in it. They will be yours for food. And to all the beasts of the earth and all the birds of the air and all the creatures that move on the ground—everything that has the breath of life in it—I give every green plant for food.' And it was so" (Gen 1:28–30). These exhortations were essentially repeated after the Noachian flood (Gen 9:1–3).

Passages such as these have been used to show that the Judeo-Christian heritage is insensitive to caring for the environment and protecting it.[5] How can these biblical words be taken seriously when the world is already overpopulated and subdued to the point of endangering entire ecosystems both on land and in the oceans? In the light of such sentiments, we need to look more closely at the divine commands given at the beginning of history and consider their abiding implications for today.

"Be Fruitful and Increase in Number"

God commanded Adam and Eve to have offspring and to multiply. They were to fill the earth. These commands are part of the blessing with which he blessed them. And blessings from God are very good. These blessings and commands were repeated after the devastation of the Noachian flood (Gen 9:1, 7). But, many suggest, surely these commands do not apply to us today? Is the world not overpopulated right

---

4. Environmental issues such as overfishing are very difficult to resolve since international treaties usually need to be signed to make any course of remedial action effective. Furthermore, since livelihoods are at stake, human needs must be balanced with those of the environment. See further on ruling creation, Bullmore, "The Four Most Important Biblical Passages for a Christian Environmentalism," 153–57.

5. For some examples, see Stott, *Issues Facing Christians Today*, 116–17.

now?[6] In reflecting on this contentious issue, there are several things we need to keep in mind.

First, there is no indication in Scripture that these blessings and commands have ever been abrogated. The fact that God repeated them after the Noachian flood indicates that the mandate to be fruitful and multiply still holds true in a world struggling with sin in a groaning creation. The gift of children is always mentioned as a blessing to be welcomed and not avoided (Deut 7:13–14; Ps 127:3–5; 128:3–4). The Creator had designed the world to be filled with people. "He did not create it to be empty, but formed it to be inhabited" (Isa 45:18).

Second, although it may seem counterintuitive, considering the perspective that some scientists and the mainstream media often give to these issues,[7] the world is not suffering from overpopulation. Studies indicate that there is plenty of room for more people and plenty of food as well. The fear of overpopulation and looming shortages of food and other necessities of life is misplaced. The ability of humanity to provide a growing population with the necessities of life has more than sufficiently kept pace with demand. Indeed, a recent article noted that "confidence in our capacity to adapt is growing, easing primordial fears about the consequences of unchecked procreation." The debate about overpopulation "is increasingly framed by thinkers who view population growth as an expansion of human capital, rather than simply a drain on resources." An expert has even stated that "ten billion people is only about one-third more than we already have, and we have plenty of land and activities to occupy them. . . . We're not going to run out of food, and we won't run out of factories to employ them. I'm very optimistic that progress will not only continue, but accelerate."[8] The hunger that some parts of the world experience is not

---

6. For examples see Glover and Economides, *Energy and Climate War*, 156–58; Grudem, *Politics According to the Bible*, 327–28.

7. E.g., McDougall, "Too Many People: Earth's Population Problem" and Duke, "Earth Population 'Exceeds Limits.'"

8. The quotes are from a recent article in a mainstream news magazine, and the expert quoted is Robert Fogel, Nobel laureate in economics and head of the Center for Population Economics at the University of Chicago's Booth School of Business. Gillis and Lunau, "A World of 10 Billion." See further for the facts exposing the myth of overpopulation Beisner, *Prospects for Growth*, 52–81 and Grudem, *Politics According to the Bible*, 332–39. These works are based on data from official government and respected academic sources.

due to the inability of the planet to provide them with food. It is due to a host of other factors both political and economic.[9]

Third, rather than fearing overpopulation, the world (and the Western nations in particular) should fear the looming disastrous "demographic winter" mentioned in chapter six. The only way to solve the horrendous social, political, and economic upheavals that could follow current declining population trends is for the Western nations "to be fruitful and multiply" and see children as a blessing rather than a burden.[10] It is not politically correct to encourage having more children, since it goes against an individualistic materialistic culture that depreciates motherhood and children; but being fruitful and multiplying is the best way forward.[11]

Fill and Subdue the Earth

To the dismay of many environmentalists, the Bible not only mandated the first couple to be fruitful and multiply, but also to "fill the earth and subdue it" (Gen 1:28). Both terms speak of taking control of the earth by occupying and mastering it. The emphasis is on the human race actually filling the earth. The term used for filling (*male'*) is not ambiguous. It refers to an abundance of people occupying the entire world. With respect to subduing creation, the original language uses a fairly strong term (*kavash*). It means to overpower, to conquer, to bring under control. This shows that the task of ruling creation is not that easy. Although creation is good, it nevertheless needs to be subjugated in order to fulfill God's wishes for it, namely that humanity rule, fill, and subdue the earth so that it is a fitting place for mankind. God has set a work agenda for humanity. That becomes even clearer when he sets man in the Garden of Eden as we shall see shortly.

It is important to note that God's commands to rule, fill, and subdue the earth indicate that God had created the world as a place for human beings to make their home. The world was not created for its own sake but to provide a place for the crown of creation, mankind, which is to use it to God's glory. Understanding this in a biblical sense has enormous implications for ecology and environment. On the one

---

9. World Hunger Education Service, "2011 World Hunger and Poverty Facts and Statistics" and Gregg, *Beyond Romanticism*, 39–40.

10. See the well-researched study of Longman, *The Empty Cradle*.

11. Also see Beisner, *Prospects for Growth*, 83–103, 175–77, 189–92.

hand, God's good creation is to be respected and protected. It would be a grave mistake to understand subduing creation as a license to mindlessly loot the earth's natural resources. Humanity was not given unlimited sovereignty over the earth and its riches. As God's representatives on earth, human beings are to act according to the designs of the Creator who takes excellent care of his creation (Ps 65:9–13; 104). On the other hand, God expected them to make their home there. They had to be fruitful, fill the earth, and subdue it. They were therefore free to use the resources as needed. As lord over the animal world, humanity could domesticate creatures that were useful. God had put them at the disposal of human beings. They could make use of plant life for food and cut down trees to build a home. Although a plant and a tree can be things of beauty to be admired and respected for their own sake as part of God's beautiful work of creation, God did give human beings dominion over them to be used responsibly. The same goes for the riches found below the surface of the earth.

God elaborated on humanity's duty to rule and subdue the earth when he put Adam "in the Garden of Eden to work it and take care of it" (Gen 2:15).

Tend the Garden

As noted in the previous chapter, to work and to take care of the garden includes tilling the ground and developing the garden. Taken together with the command to subdue the earth, the divine mandate involves harnessing creation's resources and making the most of its potential while being careful to use the resources wisely. This was humanity's place in the world.

Now it is important to remember that when God placed the first couple in the Garden of Eden, they were also blessed with the commands to be fruitful and multiply and to fill the earth. Obviously then, the Garden was but a starting point and the intention was that the boundaries of the Garden would gradually increase as the population grew. The ultimate goal was to fill the earth according to God's command. As the prophet Isaiah later said of God: "he who fashioned and made the earth, he founded it; he did not create it to be empty, but formed it to be inhabited" (Isa 45:18).

The realization that the Garden was but the beginning point of tending creation, as well as subduing and filling it, gives one a greater appreciation for the instruction to work and take care of the Garden. Working Eden and increasing the productivity of the land was obviously essential for a growing population. Similarly it was necessary to take care of the available resources with a view to an increasing number of people. So taken together the obligation to work the Garden and to take care of it speaks of economic growth and using the available resources wisely. The fall into sin did not fundamentally change these obligations. Adam and Eve were evicted from the Garden of Eden but the obligation to work the soil and take care of creation and its resources remained. It did, however, become more difficult.

As humanity labored to provide for itself and utilized the accessible resources at its disposal, the resulting economic growth eventually meant building cities. This development should not be regarded in a negative way. There is no return to the illusionary so-called noble savage living in pristine romantic primitive innocence. God intended human beings as his representatives to make creative use of the resources with which the Creator had endowed the world and make a cultural contribution. The ongoing development of creation, which can profoundly affect the physical environment, is part of God's plan for this world. It is telling that although the world began with a garden it will end with a great and beautiful city, the new Jerusalem according to God's promise (Rev 21–22).

Several principles can be deduced from the above. First, there should be no hesitation to make use of the resources with which God has endowed the earth. The key condition is that such usage be done carefully and with integrity, with due respect to the Creator, the great Landlord, and his wishes. Second, using earth's resources to develop countless inventions and consumer goods is a good thing. Humanity recovers something of the potential that God placed in his creation and generates wealth. What is not good is the misuse of resources. Third, natural is not always best. Even before the fall into sin, man was instructed to work the garden. To take care of the earth does not mean leaving it untouched. For example, rivers that destroy fields and human habitat can be tamed with prudently placed dams and so provide both a safer environment for human beings and beast as well as valuable recreation areas and water resources. Insecticides can be used to kill disease-carrying pests. The assumption that whatever is natural is best is wrong as the need to fight all sorts of natural calamities both in terms of weather and diseases shows.[12]

Other Biblical Principles

Besides the basic principles derived from God's intentions for his creation as seen in the two opening chapters of the Bible, others need to be noted as well.

First, there is of course the reality of sin. We live in a world that has fallen from its original perfect state because of the sin of Adam and Eve. This truth has several obvious consequences. A fallen creation experiences God's curse because of sin and its harmony with mankind has been broken. It is full of strife, imperfection, competition, and sorrow. The ecology is no longer at peace with itself or humanity (Gen 3:18–19; cf. Rom 8:18–25). The fear and dread of all creatures for human beings is now the order of the day (Gen 9:2).

Because of sin, there is an ongoing temptation to base environmental decisions not on what God would like to see but on wrong motives such as profit, the way of least resistance, and whatever seems to work best for humanity in the short term—all to the detriment of the environment (cf. Hos 4:1–3). It is obvious that with the reality of sin, human beings, even with all their knowledge and technology, cannot bring paradise to this earth.[13]

Second, in spite of sin, God has nevertheless endowed humanity as crown of creation with the insight necessary to rule creation as his representative (cf. Ps 8:5–8). He who gave Adam the ability to name the animals and so discern their place in creation (Gen 2:19–20) continues to make it possible for human beings to make wise decisions respecting the environment. But they can make the most of this capability only by listening to the wisdom of God's Word (Ps 111:10; Prov 9:10; Eccl 2:26).

Third, God revealed in Mosaic law environmental fundamentals that are still applicable today. God values his creation and does not want to see it abused or needlessly harmed. This fact is evident from Mosaic legislation. Animals had to be given rest on the Sabbath, just

---

12. For examples, see Beisner, *Prospects for Growth*, 152, Grudem, *Politics According to the Bible*, 322–23.

13. For a detailed look at biblical data on sin and the environment, see Burnside, *God, Justice, and Society*, 162–171.

like human beings, even at harvest time (Exod 20:10; 34:21) and treated well (Deut 25:4; cf. Prov 12:10). Fruit trees were to be spared when a city was besieged. Their food value made them a valuable part of the ecosystem and not even military conflict could justify their destruction (Deut 20:19–20). Israelites were allowed to eat wild young birds, but not the mother, no doubt to protect the future sustainability of the species. This in turn would ensure Israel's well-being (Deut 22:6–7).[14]

Fourth, when God's designs for his creation are honored, his blessing follows and the environment flourishes. If the contrary is the case, then his curse ensues in the form of environmental degradation and destruction with negative consequences for humans. These truths are obvious from the blessings and curses pronounced over Israel at Mount Gerizim and Mount Ebal (Deut 11:29; 28).

Fifth, although humanity has been set over creation to rule it as God's representative, human capacities are limited. The knowledge of the world entrusted to humanity remains limited. Human beings must stand in awe of what God has made (Ps 8:1, 9; 104). Their control over the created world and the environment also has its limits as God made clear when he addressed Job from the storm (Job 38–39). These limitations do not negate the tremendous damage that human activity can do to creation, but they do underline humanity's powerlessness in the face of forces far greater than itself. Think only of such natural phenomena as tornados, earthquakes, and tsunamis. These should keep man humble and ever more diligent to be good stewards of that which has been entrusted to him.

Having seen some key biblical principles on the environment, we need to consider our current situation and apply these fundamentals. But first, in order to understand our present context, we need to take a brief look at radical environmentalism.

RADICAL ENVIRONMENTALISM

Environmental issues often cause heated discussion. Feelings run high and passionately held beliefs are vocalized. Why is that? Surely a major part of the reason is that environmental concerns touch the very core of what it means to be an occupant of planet earth; that is, underlying religious beliefs often fuel much of the fervor in current debates.

---

14. For a detailed look at these and other laws and their relevance for environmental issues, see Richter, "Environmental Law in Deuteronomy," 355–76.

Christian environmentalists have their starting point in what the Bible teaches, but others also hold core values whether they are consciously articulated as such or not. It is therefore important first to take a look at radical environmentalism and then move on to some actual issues of the day and how society and the state interact with them.

Radical environmentalism is a diverse movement with many components. These include activist organizations such as Greenpeace and Earth First! which use creative confrontation to expose environmental problems and so try to force solutions. Politically, green parties are most favorably inclined to the tenets of radical environmentalism. On the religious and philosophic fronts green spirituality and philosophies such as deep ecology share the basic outlook of radical environmentalism. A movement as diverse as this has no officially agreed-upon set of beliefs. However, there are foundational principles and convictions that are representative of most, if not all, of its different adherents.

Although Christians share many of their concerns, such as the need to take good care of the environment and use our resources wisely, some of the core beliefs of radical environmentalists run counter to biblical teaching. Perhaps the foundational belief of radical environmentalism is its essential deification of the earth and its resources. This faith can show itself in the idea of Gaia which regards the earth and all that is in it as a single living superorganism. This notion has led some wishing to revive Earth worship.[15] For our purposes, such pagan convictions show themselves in at least three ways.

First, the deification of the earth means that the natural world is good and sacred. Because it is holy, it is not to be desecrated by humanity tampering with it in any way for it is best preserved in its untouched natural condition. Of course to leave the earth in its supposedly pristine state denies the reality of a fallen world and makes any intervention in creation suspect. On the basis of this type of thinking, environmentalists have protested against any interference with nature on a wide range of issues from the culling of deer to prevent them from overwhelming a national park to the use of pesticides to kill malaria-carrying mosquitoes. Furthermore this mind-set makes any development of the earth's "sacred" resources a fearful enterprise, leading people to oppose necessary developments such as hydroelectric

---

15. Whelan, "Greens and God," 47 and Gregg, *Beyond Romanticism*, 7.

dams because they may harm fish and nuclear plants because there may be an accident.[16]

Second, according to radical environmentalism man has not been set above creation. Humanity is simply part of the natural world. One adherent of this movement therefore spoke of all creation as people: "The tree people, the rock people, deer people, grass-hopper people and beyond."[17] There is no qualitative difference between humans and the rest of the world. This notion further justifies the opposition to any development of civilization and technological progress. Man should step back from his exalted position.[18] As a matter of fact, since the human race is the main cause of the environmental problems, the world population needs to be drastically reduced. The best decision couples can make for the environment is to have fewer children.[19] Another consequence of making people simply part of creation and nothing special is that human rights need to be balanced off with animal rights. Now it is imperative that animals be treated humanely, as God desires (Exod 20:10; Deut 22:12); but, to place animals and humans on the same level is unbiblical (cf. Ps 8:4–8; Luke 12:7). Followed through consistently this notion of equating the position of humans with animal life would mean not intruding into the habitat of any creature and making humanity go "back to nature." Indeed, some radical environmentalists want to return to the hunter-gatherer lifestyle of pre-urban civilization.[20] But, as we have seen earlier in this chapter, this is not what God had in mind when he created humanity. He wanted mankind to subdue the world and have dominion over it. He did not want the crown of his creation to live a subsistence existence.[21]

Being aware of how radical some sectors of environmentalism have become equips one to ask questions and be discerning when it comes to the major environmental concerns and claims of the day. Not all in the environmental movement are led by the facts. There

---

16. For details see Grudem, *Politics According to the Bible*, 322–23, 326–27; Repanshek, "Judge Clears Way for Deer Culling."

17. Mike Roselle of Earth First! as quoted by Whelan, "Greens and God," 27.

18. Whelan, "Greens and God," 27–28.

19. Grudem, *Politics According to the Bible*, 327–28 and Gregg, *Beyond Romanticism*, 35–37.

20. See Whelan, "Greens and God," 27 and Gregg, *Beyond Romanticism*, 37. For more on animal rights see, e.g., Kirwan, "Greens and Animals," 102–23.

21. See also Grudem, *Politics According to the Bible*, 328–29.

are also quasi-religious passions at work. Indeed, it has been said that "one of the most powerful religions of the Western world is environmentalism."[22] The intent of what follows is to highlight briefly two of the most important topics that are being discussed today and to ask what the role of the state should be.

THE STATE AND THE ENVIRONMENT

The environmental issues of the day are many and complex. Earlier in this chapter the matter of overpopulation and limited resources has already been briefly addressed. We will now turn to issues related to climate change and energy resources and subsequently consider the obligations of the state.

Climate Change

The atmosphere encircling the earth enables heat from the sun to be trapped so that life on earth is possible—somewhat similar to what happens in a greenhouse where the heat from the sun is trapped by the glass. Since the industrial revolution that began in the eighteenth century greenhouse gases have become more concentrated in the earth's atmosphere. The net result, according to the vast majority of scientists, is an increasing greenhouse effect whereby less of the sun's radiant heat striking the earth can escape back into space. Instead it is reflected back to earth causing an increase in the average temperature of the earth. According to a report of the United Nations' Intergovernmental Panel of Climate Change (IPCC), the average global surface temperature (over land and sea) has risen about .76 degrees centigrade from 1850 to 2005. The most important greenhouse gas is carbon dioxide (CO_2) which is essential for life on earth. Burning fossil fuels—coal, oil, and natural gas—releases this gas. International efforts are underway to reduce the amount of greenhouse gases released into the atmosphere. An important milestone was the Kyoto Protocol (1997) by which industrialized countries committed themselves to reduce the six more important greenhouse gases by at least 5.2% from 2008 to 2012.[23] Although Canada has signed and ratified the Protocol (1992,

---

22. Michael Crichton as quoted in Glover and Economides, *Energy and Climate Wars*, 11, 113–14.

23. "IPCC, 2007: Summary for Policymakers," 5–6; Bayer, "Climate Change," 248–49.

2002), it has taken little action towards meeting its emission targets. The United States signed (1998) but never ratified the treaty.

The Kyoto Protocol and the ongoing climate change negotiations are complex and there are different reasons for the reluctance of countries like Canada and the United States to pursue international control measures. But two underlying reasons are important to note.

First, although the official position of the IPCC on the reality and causes of global warming is widely embraced as scientific truth, not all experts agree on how to interpret the evidence. There is not even agreement whether carbon dioxide emissions are indeed causing global warming. A 2009 U.S. Senate Environment and Public Works Committee report lists over 700 international scientists who dissent over man-made global warming claims. Although they do not all think the same, they generally agree on several key points. 1. The earth's temperature fluctuations is currently well within natural climate variability; 2. almost all climate fear is generated by unproven computer model predictions; 3. an abundance of peer-reviewed studies continue to debunk rising CO2 fears; and 4. "consensus" has been manufactured for political, not scientific purposes.[24] The uncertainty of what is going on is also underlined by the fact that there was first talk about global warming and then it became climate change in order to bring any and all observations under the same umbrella of concern since the term global warming might be too narrow a focus.[25]

Second, at least two high profile events have eroded public confidence in the science of climate change, confirmed that experts are far from unified on the issue, and raised questions about the motives of some climate change activists. Al Gore's 2006 documentary film, *An Inconvenient Truth: a Global Warning*, pushed an alarmist scenario on global warming. However, a British court judged in 2007 that it was unsuitable for viewing in schools as it was because of the untruths and exaggerations it contained as well as the propagandistic and politically charged nature of the film. If the film was to be shown in schools it had to be accompanied by guidance notes giving the other side of the argument. Two of the errors identified were the claims that sea-levels

---

24. *U.S. Senate Environment and Public Works Committee Minority Staff Report (Inhofe)* (2009).

25. As a matter of fact, in 1970's there was fear of earth's cooling too much. See "Another Ice Age?" For a current cooling trend, Glover and Economides, *Energy and Climate Wars*, 98 and Mooney, "Scientific Evidence Now Points to Global Cooling."

would rise twenty feet by melting ice and that snow was melting on Mount Kilimanjaro due to global warming.[26]

Far more dramatic was "Climategate" which undermined the credibility of the IPCC which had been established to provide authoritative scientific climate information to decision makers. The IPCC and national governments relied on data from the Climatic Research Unit at the University of East Anglia in Britain, NASA's Goddard Institute for Space Studies, the National Oceanic and Atmospheric Administration, the National Center for Atmospheric Research, the National Climatic Data Center, the UK Meteorological Office, and others. The accuracy and reliability of all this information was called into question when leaked e-mails and documents from the Climatic Research Unit in Britain, one of the world's premier repositories of climate information, showed that for the last decade scientific evidence had been manipulated and doubts concealed about the validity of the claims of global warming. There was even a long series of communications discussing how best to marginalize and professionally hurt scientists who did not agree with the so-called consensus on global warming or climate change. These revelations were obviously a serious blow to climate change advocates for it called into question their scientific objectivity. What is truly remarkable is that the fallout was not more negative. The IPCC stayed the course and climate change is still the politically correct orthodoxy. One wonders whether this does not betray the power of vested interests and the fervent ideology driving some of the climate debate.[27]

Government would do well to know all the facts before binding the country to abide by international climate control measures. Sober science often neither supports the scary scenarios portrayed nor justifies the drastic actions demanded. Also, the high financial costs could jeopardize the economic well-being of the nation and lead to "economic suicide."[28]

---

26. "Gore Climate Film's Nine 'Errors.'" Also see Monckton, "35 Inconvenient Truths."

27. For more detail on the scandal and fallout, see Glover and Economides, *Energy and Climate Wars*, 108–14 and Grudem, *Politics According to the Bible*, 374–76.

28. Glover and Economides, *Energy and Climate Wars*, 12, 104–105.

Energy Resources

Concerns about global warming and climate change motivate environmental lobbies to pressure government to end our dependence on fossil fuels—coal, oil, and natural gas—as a source of energy. Other considerations factor in as well for moving away from these fuels. Retrieving the coal or oil comes at a cost. Mining can leave waste materials, scar the landscape, and generate waste water that pollutes streams. Drilling for oil brings with it the potential for accidents that can contaminate the landscape or offshore waters with severe consequences for plant and wildlife. Furthermore, using these fuels generates pollution which can cause respiratory diseases in humans and acid rain in the environment.

Western governments are responding by attempting to reduce dependency on fossil fuels, seeking more green and renewable sources of energy, and bringing down the total amount of energy used. Enormous amounts of money have been and continue to be invested in searching for alternative green renewable sources of energy.[29] The most promising for many seems to be wind power, the flagship of the green energy industry. However, there are significant challenges. Without hefty government subsidies, that is, tax payers' money, no one would be interested in investing in wind power. Judging from the experiences of Britain, reportedly the windiest country in Europe, there is no viable future for wind power without sustained and massive injection of public funds which need to be recovered through high domestic energy costs to consumers. Moreover, according to one expert, the science of wind power is flawed. A renewable energy source like wind and water "are *mathematically* unable to produce the industrial scale energy *essential* to keeping the lights on in an industrialized society. . . . industrial scale renewable energy is, realistically and mathematically, an economic, geographical and social non-starter."[30] Environmentalists do not accept these politically incorrect conclusions, but economic and physical realities can cause a rethinking of positions. In February, 2011, the Ontario government called for a moratorium on offshore wind farms, citing

---

29. "By the end of 2009, the US taxpayer had subsidized the American climate industry to the tune of $79 billion—with trillions more to come." Glover and Economides, *Energy and Climate Wars*, 124.

30. Glover and Economides, *Energy and Climate Wars*, 56–64, the quotations can be found on pp. 62–63 and are from William Tucker, "Understanding E=mc2*", adapted from his book *Terrestrial Energy* (2008). The emphases are in the original.

the need for further scientific study and implicitly admitting they had not thought the issues through carefully enough. The hard reality is that renewable energy plants need a much larger environmental footprint, "anywhere from 100 to 10,000 times the land area compared to conventional resources."[31] Much needs to happen before renewable energy sources such as wind and, for that matter also the sun, become viable.

Currently about 84% of world energy production comes from fossil fuels, and, given the state of science, technology, and political realities, that is not likely to change in the foreseeable future.[32] Government should not be embarking on large scale so-called green energy programs without being sure that it is a viable and secure alternative to fossil fuels. Indeed, in the words of two experts: "governments *must* restore the use of coal and oil, and particularly cleaner-burning natural gas, to the heart of rational energy strategies and policies. And that will mean understanding that the on-going primacy of hydrocarbons in the energy mix, and for future national stability, is a far higher priority than the alleged nebulous threat from continued hydrocarbon use."[33] Additionally, nuclear power should not be overlooked when alternatives are studied. It has proven itself to give clean power; the technology and safety have greatly improved; and it continues to show much promise.[34]

---

31. Nathwani, "Red Flags on Green Energy." Nathwani is a professor and Ontario Research Chair in Public Policy for Sustainable Energy Management at the University of Waterloo. Also see Glover and Economides, *Energy and Climate Wars*, 63.

32. Grudem, *Politics According to the Bible*, 355; Glover and Economides, *Energy and Climate Wars*, 195.

33. Glover and Economides, *Energy and Climate Wars*, 231. Emphasis in the original. See also Linowes, "Wind Energy's 'Trail of Broken Promises' (USA)." Evangelical scholars opposed forced reduction in fossil fuel use because among other things it would hurt the world's poor the most. See *A Renewed Call to Truth, Prudence, and Protection of the Poor*."

34. This valuation is true even after Japan's nuclear disaster caused by a tsunami. See, e.g., Spencer, "U.S. Nuclear Policy after Fukushima: Trust but Modify." On nuclear energy see Tucker, *Terrestrial Energy*. On the safety of nuclear reactors also see Beisner, *Prospects for Growth*, 122–24. "Both the US administration and the EU have set themselves on course to develop a new generation of domestic nuclear power plants." Glover and Economides, *Energy and Climate Wars*, 234, also see 235–40. Ontario is planning to depend on nuclear power for 50% of its future energy needs. The Independent Electricity System Operator (IESO), *Ontario's Long Term Energy Plan*.

Of course larger questions and issues remain about government's role in the areas of climate change and energy. We turn to these now.

The Obligations of the State

There is little agreement among Christians as to what the role and direction of government should be when it comes to environmental concerns. Some of the dissension stems from evaluating climate scare scenarios differently and being more optimistic about a growing reliance on secure renewable green energy.[35] However, in spite of these differences, there are underlying biblical principles that should find agreement with Christians from all quarters.

First, since the earth is the Lord's (Ps 24:1), government as God's servant (Rom 13:4) and as the highest authority in the land should do everything possible to protect the riches of God's creation entrusted to its care. With respect to the environment, this means protecting air quality by enforcing economically achievable standards for clean air. Fighting pollution has many angles and can include such diverse tactics as encouraging the use of public transit for commuting to work and enforcing the use of scrubbers on industrial chimneys. Safeguarding the environment also includes a responsible program for protecting endangered species, setting high standards for land restoration after quarrying or mining operations are completed, and urban planning with the wise use of green space.

Second, government is expected to show good stewardship of natural resources and seek to encourage a wise use of resources among its citizens. Waste should not be tolerated. For that reason recycling programs, for example, are excellent. Landfill sites last much longer and waste is drastically reduced. Good stewardship also includes the careful management of tax dollars. Government should not embark on so-called green programs that have not been thoroughly thought through and tested as to their feasibility. Green ideology should not override the common sense use of available resources. It remains a fact that God has put an incredible amount of fossil fuel energy in the earth at our disposal and more is being discovered all the time.[36] Not

---

35. E.g., the approach taken by Grudem, *Politics According to the Bible* is generally quite different from that taken in the essays found in White, *Creation in Crisis*. The latter usually follows the lead of the United Nations and the mainstream media.

36. Glover and Economides, *Energy and Climate Wars*, 69–89.

to make use of such resources because of ideology is irresponsible and wastes billions of dollars.³⁷

Third, government should stimulate research and innovation, also in the energy sector. A respect for the environment and the created world does not mean leaving untapped resources untouched. Man has been set over creation and government can use its considerable authority to encourage the wise use of earth's bounty for the benefit of society.

Fourth, prior to any new legislation government should take the time to properly inform the public of its intentions and invite feedback. If necessary, formal consultations can be organized. For environmental law to work, the public needs to be on side, understand the rationale for the law, and support it fully.

Sometimes government in an attempt to show goodwill to the environmental lobbies quickly passes legislation that seems innocent and beneficial. However, due to a lack of adequate study it may simply solve one problem only to create another. A simple case in point is the somewhat hasty banning of incandescent light bulbs in the United States and Canada in 2007 for environmental reasons. However, compact florescent lights, their replacement, contain mercury, a significant environmental hazard. So are we really making progress here?³⁸ A larger problem is the massive public investment in harvesting energy from wind farms. Apart from the concerns mentioned above, from an environmental perspective they are not only an eyesore, but more importantly can decimate bird populations especially if they are on migration routes. For this reason, even the environmental group Greenpeace has opposed a huge wind farm development in the Western Isles of Scotland. Furthermore, human health in the vicinity of wind farms is becoming an issue as research has confirmed that

---

37. There is truth in the following question raised by energy experts. "Why are we wasting billions of dollars fighting pointless battles against an enemy that is really no enemy at all ($CO2$) to win a fight (to change global climate) that's entirely beyond us? And where is all this finite resource—money—all going?" Glover and Economides, *Energy and Climate Wars*, 122.

38. See, e.g., The editors, "Light-Bulb Ban Has Voters Incandescent with Rage," 4–5. A similar problem may be legislating ethanol content in gasoline. This makes little environmental sense since if it takes more fossil fuel energy to get a unit of ethanol than it can yield. Scientific opinion is divided on the topic. Fischer, "Is Ethanol from Corn bad for the Climate?"

people living within two kilometers of wind farms can get sick from Wind Turbine Syndrome.[39]

Fifth, government should safeguard the freedom of its citizens as much as possible. When government makes laws with respect to the environment, the state can become very intrusive and regulate the lives of its people in many ways. The political left's leaning for a strong centralized government could be one reason why so many environmentalists do not mind the state controlling more and more of the lives of its citizens. The thinking is that enlightened government officials can run people's lives better than the citizens themselves can. "Regulating people's use of energy is an incredibly effective way of increasing the control of central governments over our entire lives. If the government can dictate how far you drive your car, how much you heat or cool your home, how much you will use electric lights or computers or a TV, how much energy your factory can use, and how much jet fuel you can have to fly an airplane, then it can control most of the society."[40] But government should never use energy as a tool for social engineering.

Also in the international forum, democratic freedoms should never be sacrificed on the altar of climate control. "The necessary corollary of a trans-national, legally-binding, accord . . . for the lofty purpose of 'saving the planet,' of necessity, would require a new world order, a one world governance." This would create "a ruthless power elite."[41]

And last but not least, in the sixth place, Western governments should be sensitive to the needs of the developing world and be mindful of how the Western world has benefited from industrialization. In light of the inconclusive evidence of the role of carbon dioxide in global warming, the West should not make the developing world feel guilty about using cheap and efficient fossil fuels for their economic development. Rather, the West should encourage them to do so and

---

39. "Greenpeace Opposes Wind Farm Plan;" Nina Pierpont, *Wind Turbine Syndrome*. For other studies see Industrial Wind Action Group's website, http://www.windaction.org/?tab=topdocs.

40. Grudem, *Politics According to the Bible*, 380. Also see Glover and Economides, *Energy and Climate Wars*, 9.

41. Former British Prime Minister Margaret Thatcher put it this way: "Since clearly no plan to alter climate could be considered on anything but a global scale, it provides a marvellous excuse for worldwide, supra-national socialism." All quotes are from Glover and Economides, *Energy and Climate Wars*, 149, also see 150–67.

be prepared to assist them with anti-pollution technology as much as possible. In the global village, loving the neighbor includes doing everything possible for weaker nations to benefit from relatively cheap energy. Energy is a key ingredient for economic growth and prosperity.[42]

THE WAY FORWARD

Limitations

When we reflect on environmental issues and the role of government, it becomes quite obvious that there are some severe limitations. Due to the nature of environmental problems, the state has a large role to play by way of legislation and passing laws that seek to protect the environment from harm. However, creation is bigger than any human government. And while citizens and legislators may be very busy with environmental concerns, natural calamities happen regardless of what is on the law books. Forest fires, earthquakes, tornadoes, hurricanes, and volcanic eruptions can all have an enormous impact on the environment. Furthermore, man is unable to control the daily weather. What comes, comes. No human activity can determine the next day's temperatures or wind direction. Man is also unable to make climates suit his preferences. Quite simply, on several environmental fronts man is not in control. Humanity has great responsibilities which he must carry out regarding the environment. But at the end of the day the ability of human beings to actually bring overall lasting change, for example, to the climate is either minuscule or non-existent. The earth will continue to go through inexplicable periods of warming and cooling as it has for millennia.[43] Humanity's influence on the physical geography is much more impressive. Cities rise out of the landscape and super highways curve elegantly through the wilderness. But here too there are forces greater than mankind. One only needs to think of recent events such as what happened to New Orleans with hurricane Katrina (2005) or to northern Japan during the 2011 tsunami or Christchurch, New Zealand during the 2011 earthquake.

---

42. Grudem, *Politics According to the Bible*, 360–61, 381. Also see Glover and Economides, *Energy and Climate Wars*, 5–7, 150.

43. NASA Science, "Earth's Fidgeting Climate" and Whelan, Kirwan, and Haffner, "Science Facts," 134–38.

There is another considerable limitation for dealing with environmental issues which is much closer to home. It is human nature which tends to be self-centered, materialistic, and pragmatic. Government can and should pass good environmental laws but, the state can only do so much. Legislation is only the beginning. The citizens of the land must fully support government's efforts to be good stewards of the natural resources entrusted to them. This can include simple things like recycling and car pooling to fight waste, traffic congestion, and pollution, as well as more complex initiatives such as providing input into government sponsored planning forums for city or highway developments. However, there is a larger issue. For citizens to truly make a difference, the outward actions must be motivated by a change of mind-set which becomes genuinely altruistic, caring less about material things and convenience and being more concerned about protecting the environment. After all one's mind-set governs all the day-to-day decisions and it is these daily mundane choices by millions of citizens that have enormous repercussions for the environment.

Clearly we need to approach environmental concerns holistically. Government, citizen participation, and the mind-set of a nation are all important. However, if we are truly to achieve a holistic approach, we must also include the One who made all things, namely God. As Creator, he also left us instructions on how to use his handiwork. His wisdom as given in Scripture will give direction on how to deal with current environmental issues. Christians have the first responsibility to make God's wisdom known, but as we shall see there is also a task for government here, be it mostly indirectly. In briefly mapping out a holistic Christian approach, we will draw on the earlier sections of this chapter.

A Holistic Christian Approach

Christians have the duty to share their biblically informed vision on environmental matters with the population at large. When this vision is accompanied with solid facts they will make an important contribution to the ongoing debate in the public square. They will also bring hope and realism to the discussion. Key components of a biblical grasp of environmental issues include the following.

Environmental concerns must be taken very seriously because this world is God's world. This topic is not one to dismiss lightly as sometimes happens in Christian circles. It is God's world and all people should be in awe of its splendor and magnificence and in the spirit of Psalm 8 exclaim: "O Lord, our Lord, how majestic is your name in all the earth!" (Ps 8:1). One should also marvel at the high position in which God has placed humanity over the earth and address him in amazement: "You made him ruler over the works of your hands; you put everything under his feet" (Ps 8:6). In spite of the fall into sin and the accompanying grief for creation, God still gives man the responsibility and therefore the ability to take care of planet earth and to develop its resources. Surely, the fact that God is the one who has put us in charge should give hope and confidence that solutions can be found to today's challenges. One must never underestimate the wisdom with which God has made all things. Creation's robustness and resilience have often surprised scientists. For example, predictions of doom and gloom with respect to food supply and the ability of the earth to support its growing numbers have continually been put to shame.[44] The same is happening with the energy supply. There is a Creator who has put much more into this planet than seems obvious at first. Indeed, new secrets of the world are constantly being discovered.

All of this does not take away from the need for careful stewardship and responsible development of the resources available. It does however mean that one should not be too easily frightened by the scary scenarios of radical environmentalists but carefully dissect fact from fiction. This exercise is not done enough. Fooled by one-sided and often sensational mass media coverage of the issues, people can too easily jump on the radical environmentalist bandwagon and unwittingly adopt its unproven assumptions. Too many people seem simply to repeat the current unproven environmentalist slogans without checking the facts and probing deeper. Citizens also have the responsibility to do their homework and attempt to get beyond environmentalist scare tactics to the actual facts. They can then interact meaningfully with their elected representatives on the issues of the day.[45] One must also

---

44. Perhaps the most famous of such predictions are those contained in the 1972 Club of Rome report: Meadows et al., *The Limits to Growth*. It predicted, e.g., that almost all earth's resources would be exhausted by 2010. See further Glover and Economides, *Energy and Climate Wars*, 69–70.

45. Very helpful guides in this respect are Grudem, *Politics According to the Bible*, 329–86 and the book he draws much of his information from: Lomborg, *The Skeptical Environmentalist*.

remember that God created a resilient earth and he promised that "as long as the earth endures, seedtime and harvest, cold and heat, summer and winter, day and night will never cease" (Gen 8:22). In other words, the seasonal cycles sustaining life would continue.[46]

A wise biblical use of resources also includes helping the less fortunate inhabitants of this world and sharing the wealth and the resources that Canada and the United States have. That includes encouraging the type of development and industrialization which has made the West prosperous while minimizing the impact on the environment.

Another component of a holistic Christian approach to environmental issues is to remember that God made no mistake when he told man to subdue the earth and fill it. The command to subdue implies that government must not hesitate to promote the development and use of a country's resources. God endowed the nation with them to benefit the country. That includes both the resources that are technically finite, such as fossil fuels, and renewable, like the trees of the forest. It has been well documented that a nation's prosperity is in proportion to its energy usage. In other words, taxing energy to make it less affordable can negatively impact a country's prosperity.[47]

The state should also promote the development of its human resources. The point here is not such matters as education, but the natural increase of population. Fostering population growth is implied with the command to fill the earth. Raising families, even large families, is politically incorrect from the point of view of radical environmentalists, since they consider too many humans as the biggest danger to the earth. But God knew what he was doing when he blessed man with the command to procreate and fill the earth. The state should be proud of the large families in the nation and assist them in every way, not least with favorable tax laws. After all, large families help fuel the future economic well-being of the nation.

People need a place to live and so another aspect of nurturing a country's human resources is developing cities and towns. A huge

---

46. See also Grudem, *Politics According to the Bible*, 367–70.

47. The term "finite" is used of fossil fuels because that is technically the reality. However, in terms of ongoing discoveries from a human perspective and considering long range future, the fossil fuel resources seem infinite. See Grudem, *Politics According to the Bible*, 356–57 and Glover and Economides, *Energy and Climate Wars*, 69–91.

environmental issue is the redevelopment of decaying inner cities. As suburbs grow, downtown areas can get neglected and need to be revitalized and repopulated. An example is Hamilton, Ontario. As is probably typical, the city's long term development plan for a vibrant, healthy, and sustainable downtown regrettably made virtually no mention of the role of churches. A Christian think tank submitted a white paper to city hall and community leaders pointing out that churches can play a vital role in urban renewal.[48] Government should take heed and invite submissions from churches for urban renewal. After all, not only would such participation affect the urban environment in terms of social and economic benefits from having a church building with the human traffic that comes from that, but a living faith community would above all positively influence the spiritual climate.

The Bible teaches that there is a connection between environmental crises and the spiritual health of a nation. When morals go down and all people are out for themselves, then God's judgment comes also in the form of environmental disasters. After listing the sins of a decadent society, the prophet Hosea noted: "Because of this the land mourns, and all who live in it waste away; the beasts of the field and the birds of the air and the fish of the sea are dying" (Hos 4:4). When the spiritual health of a nation is very good, environmental issues can be dealt with in the best possible manner. Special interests will yield for the common good and facts rather than faulty ideological dreams will shape policy. Government must therefore give the church all the room and opportunity it needs to fulfill its mandate so that the church can seek to raise the moral environment of a city and so the nation. Such a positive change will impact positively on addressing the physical environmental issues. After all, everything is interconnected and a holistic approach which recognizes the importance of the moral ecology is necessary.[49]

The United States and Canada have been richly blessed with abundant natural resources and opportunities. Also with a view to the environment that has been entrusted to us we need to remember Christ's words. "From everyone who has been given much, much will be demanded; and from the one who has been entrusted with much, much more will be asked" (Luke 12:48).

---

48. Van Pelt and Greydanus, *Living on the Streets*.
49. See further on this point Gregg, *Beyond Romanticism*, 40–45.

SUGGESTED READING

A Renewed Call to Truth, Prudence, and Protection of the Poor: An Evangelical Examination of the Theology, Science, and Economics of Global Warming. This 76 page document is available at http://www.cornwallalliance.org/. It calls for stopping policies requiring drastic reductions in carbon dioxide emissions as unrealistic, threatening prosperity, and hurting earth's vulnerable poor the most. It has been endorsed by scientists, economists, and theologians.

Beisner, E. Calvin. *Prospects for Growth: A Biblical View of Population, Resources, and the Future.* Westchester, ILL: Crossway, 1990. The topics are covered from a biblical perspective, backed by solid scientific evidence, and is a refreshing and encouraging read.

Glover, Peter C. and Michael J. Economides. *Energy and Climate Wars: How Naive Politicians, Green Ideologues, and the Media Elites are Undermining the Truth About Energy and Climate.* New York: Continuum, 2010. A hard-hitting survey based on solid data which exposes many fallacies and myths behind the drive for alternate renewable energy.

Grudem, Wayne. *Politics According to the Bible: A Comprehensive Resource for Understanding Modern Political Issues in the Light of Scripture.* Grand Rapids, MI: Zondervan, 2010, pages 320–386. An excellent chapter on the environment, including biblical teaching and a detailed look at all the hot topics.

Whelan, Robert, Joseph Kirwan, and Paul Haffner. *The Cross and the Rain Forest. A Critique of Radical Green Spirituality.* Grand Rapids, MI: Acton Institute for the Study of Religion and Liberty / Eerdmans, 1996. A thoroughgoing critique of the origins and implications of radical environmentalism.

9

Multiculturalism

MUCH OF THE WESTERN world has been expounding the virtues of multiculturalism. The colorful mosaic of many nationalities and cultures now characterizes major cities in Europe and North America. The old melting pot norm by which immigrant cultures assimilated into the host culture has, for the most part, been replaced by the new ideal of foreign cultures, many non-Western, retaining their identity in the new homeland and coexisting peacefully alongside others.

What are we to make of this state of affairs? How should we evaluate it? Is it something that Scripture encourages or discourages? To get a handle on the issues that multiculturalism raises and the role that government should play, we will consider what the Bible tells us about being a nation. There is, after all, a close relationship between culture and nationhood.[1] We will also examine what Scripture says about the place of immigrants and their reception into the host nation. After that we will consider our current multicultural challenges and how best to meet them.

WHAT IS A NATION?

God ordained the existence of nations. This truth is evident both in the nations spread over the world and also in the existence of that special nation of Israel. Being a nation is therefore a positive entity and Scripture gives us principles about nationhood that we can use today.[2]

---

1. A culture can be defined as "the customary beliefs, social forms, and material traits of a racial, religious, or social group." *Merriam-Webster's Collegiate Dictionary*, 282. A culture binds a group together and characterizes people who live together and form a cohesive group. Such a group when politically organized can be called a nation.

2. Helpful resources on being a nation include: Block, "Nations/Nationality;"

Nationhood is a Divine Ordinance

The Beginning of Nations

It was God's idea to cover the face of the earth with nations. We read in Acts 17:26-27 "From one man he made every nation of men, that they should inhabit the whole earth; and he determined the times set for them and the exact places where they should live. God did this so that men would seek him and perhaps reach out for him and find him, though he is not far from each one of us." From this passage, several things can be noted. First, as Creator of humanity, God is sovereign over all nations. As sovereign God he wants people to seek him. The nations have this obligation (Acts 17:27; cf. Ps 96:6; 67:3-5; Rom 1:20-21). Indeed, there are many examples of God holding nations accountable for what they do and judging them for violating his will (e.g., Gen 15:16; Deut 20:17-18). Second, God wanted the nations to be dispersed over the whole earth (cf. Gen 1:28). For each he set the place where they should live. Third, God "determined the times set" for the nations (Acts 17:26); that is, as Job put it: "He makes nations great, and destroys them; he enlarges nations, and disperses them" (Job 12:23; also Dan 2:21). Nations have their times of greatness and demise as God determines.

The beginning of the nations is recounted in Genesis 11. The people that lived on earth originally spoke one language. Because they wanted to remain together to provide mutual security and to make themselves a name and a reputation, they decided to build a city and a tower that reached to the heavens. By doing so they arrogantly disobeyed God's creation ordinance that they fill the earth (Gen 1:28). God therefore came down to their city and scattered them by confusing their language so that they could no longer understand each other (Gen 11:1-9). As a result people who were once united, dispersed and nations with different languages were formed. The preceding chapter, Genesis 10, details how the descendants of Noah's three sons developed into nations. Noteworthy is the mention of territories, clans, and languages as a refrain after the descendants of each son have been listed (Gen 10:5, 20, 31). This refrain indicates that nations are defined by geography, ethnicity, and language.

A consideration of Israel as a political entity will yield further understanding in what it means to be a nation.

Köstenberger, "Nations," 676-78; Hays, *From Every People and Nation*.

The Nation of Israel

As God's chosen nation (Exod 19:6), Israel provides a paradigm at least in part of what the Lord conceives a nation to be—in part, because no modern nation can identify itself as God's elect people.[3] God's chosen nation today is the church (1 Pet 2:9). However, ancient Israel as a nation, that is, as a civil society and people, not only gives additional depth of field to some of the features of nationhood mentioned in Genesis 10, but also provides important additional characteristics of a nation that are instructive for us today.

Like the nations mentioned in Genesis 10, Israel as a nation also had a specific territory allotted to it, namely the land of Canaan (Gen 12:1–7). Ethnically, Israel was descended from Abraham, Isaac, and Jacob (or Israel) and therefore known as "the children of Israel" (Gen 32:28, 32; Exod 1:7). This name underlined Israel's ethnic unity in spite of the existence of twelve tribes. Although there were regional disparities (cf. Judges 12:6), they all shared the same basic language. In addition, what is noteworthy about God's chosen nation is that it had a shared past, a history that gave the people an identity throughout their nationhood. They were in covenant with God who had delivered them from Egyptian bondage, an event they were never to forget (Exod 19–20; Deut 26:1–10; Ps 105; Hos 2:14–20). This common past gave them a united identity as a nation. Coupled with this was the demand from God that his covenant nation truly serve him. As his chosen people that was the overriding obligation. The people were to reject the gods of the other nations and be true only to the Lord God who had delivered them (Deut 6). In this way they would be the holy nation, set apart from all others, and be an example to them (Deut 4:1–10). Israel's unfaithfulness eventually led to its downfall as a nation, first the northern kingdom and then Judah (2 Kings 17, 24–25).

The Principles Involved

There is no nation today that can be reckoned as God's special people. That is now, as just mentioned, the church (1 Pet 2:9). However, the Bible gives political truths and principles in general about the origin of nations and specifically about Israel that are abiding. Although Israel

---

3. In the past England and the United States have been identified in greater and lesser extent with Israel, as God's chosen nation. See, e.g., Grosby, *Biblical Ideas of Nationality*, 217–31.

did not live up to all these principles and neither do modern nations today, it is good to remember these fundamentals. They are the ideal to keep in mind as the opportunity or need for change arises. These principles, in no particular order, are as follows.

First, nationhood is a biblical idea and being a nation and having a culture are identity markers that one can be proud of and defend. The current pressures for more and more world government through entities like the United Nations, or the perceived need for more regional government such as through the European Union, should not go at the expense of one's identity as a nation. Being a nation is a gift of God.

Second, a nation has a territory assigned to it by God's providence. There is a geographical dimension to nationhood.

Third, the Lord has used language and common ancestry to create nations. The cohesion given by common ethnicity and language cannot be overlooked.

Fourth, the identity of a nation is shaped in great part by a common past, a story, a meta-narrative, that all can identify with. Collective memory of the past functions as a cohesive in the present and gives shared values for the future.

Fifth, God ordained nations "so that men would seek him and perhaps reach out for him and find him" (Acts 17:27). A nation can only experience lasting blessing if it heeds the will of the God who created all things and who also providentially provided for its existence as a nation. For this reason it is important that a nation with a Christian past not neglect what has been entrusted to it but makes full use of its Christian heritage. A nation ignores this to its hurt for God is sovereign and his blessing will only be lasting where his will for his creation is honored. Otherwise, his judgment eventually follows.

If a nation is ideally to have a homogeneous population, for that is what some of these principles seem to suggest, must doors to immigrants and refugees from other cultures then be closed? No, for multiculturalism is not a new phenomenon and there is more in God's Word about what being a nation entails.

MULTICULTURAL ISRAEL

In some ways, ancient Israel was also a multi-cultural society and it is helpful to reflect on this phenomenon. We will consider the situation in ancient Israel and how this translates into principles for us today.

The Situation in Ancient Israel

A Multi-ethnic Society

When Israel was delivered from Egypt, "many other people went up with them" (Exod 12:38). The Hebrew term for "other people" (*'ereb*) indicates they did not share a common racial origin with Israel. It is a word used elsewhere to describe foreigners (Jer 25:20; Neh 13:3). Given the historical circumstances at the time of the Exodus, it is likely that Egypt had thousands of slaves and laborers from other nations, both Semitic and non-Semitic. Probably black Africans from Cush were among them (cf. Num 12:1).[4] Many of these people joined Israel on their exodus from Egypt. Thus, at the defining moment of Israel's being set free from oppression to be a free nation under God, Israel as a political entity was not ethnically homogeneous but had multi-cultural aspects to it.

This plurality of backgrounds continued through Israel's long history. Doeg the Edomite served as Saul's head shepherd (1 Sam 21:7). David's army included people like Uriah, the Hittite (2 Sam 11), Zelek, the Ammonite (2 Sam 23:37), and Ittai, the Gittite. Ittai was a Philistine from Gath who had six hundred Philistines under his command. During Absalom's rebellion he was in charge of a third of David's forces (2 Sam 15:18–22; 18:2). David's army also included a Cushite (2 Sam 18:21). Kerethites, who were probably from Crete, and Pelethites, whose origin is uncertain, served in David's and Solomon's body guard (2 Sam 8:18;1 Kings 1:38). Resident aliens (*gerim*), including Hittites, Amorites, Perizzites, Hivites, and Jebusites, numbered 153,600 during the time of Solomon. He made use of their labor in building the temple (1 Chron 22:2; 2 Chron 2:16–17; 8:7–8). Such a large number of resident aliens would have been a significant part of Israel's population (cf. 2 Sam 24:9, 15).

Israel's strategic geographical position was a factor in maintaining a diverse mosaic of racial backgrounds in society. Canaan was at the center of the crossroads of commerce and travel between Egypt to the south and the nations to the north. The porous nature of ancient national boundaries ensured that a variety of peoples would remain a part of the Israelite population.

---

4. For an overview of the evidence see Hays, *From Every People and Nation*, 67–68.

Resident Aliens

Not surprisingly, the Lord gave extensive direction in his law for dealing with resident aliens. Underlying all the laws and regulations was the command of love. "The alien [*ger*] living with you must be treated as one of your native-born. Love him as yourself, for you were aliens [*gerim*] in Egypt. I am the LORD your God" (Lev 19:34; similarly Deut 10:19). This generosity of love, treating the alien as native-born, needs to be appreciated within the overall context of Israelite society. It not only had resident aliens, but also true foreigners [*nokrim*]. These happened to be in Israel but had no real attachment to that nation. God's law treated the resident aliens [*gerim*] differently from these foreigners.

In order to comprehend what was all involved it is first necessary to have a clear understanding of who constituted the resident aliens [*gerim*] and what their place in society entailed.[5] These were people who had left their homeland because of political, economic, or other reasons and settled in another country, seeking its protection and being given a special status there. In this sense Abraham was a resident alien in Hebron (Gen 23:4), the entire people of Israel were so in Egypt (Exod 23:9), and Elimelech with his family had that position in Moab (Ruth 1:1). The status of such resident aliens would be roughly comparable to that of our immigrants today. When such people left their homeland and joined Israelite society, they intended to establish themselves there. As circumstances would have it, they usually placed themselves in a relationship of dependency to their Israelite hosts. As such they were vulnerable and associated with the poor, the widows and orphans, and the hired man. God however gave these people a legal status by giving them rights, as well as obligations.

No one was to take advantage of these resident aliens. They were to be helped (Exod 23:9). Although they were not allowed to own land because Canaan was Israel's inheritance (Gen 12:7; Deut 31:7; cf. Ezek 47:22), they nevertheless were to enjoy the benefits of the land. They had the right to glean, that is to gather grain, grapes, or olives left by the harvesters (Lev 19:10; 23:22; Deut 24:19–21), to partake of the festivities of the offering of the first fruits (Deut 26:11) and every three years they could participate in enjoying the tithe of the produce of the land (Deut 14:29; 26:12–13). Furthermore, they could share in the fes-

---

5. For what follows, see H. H. Schmid, "*gûr* to sojourn," 308–9. Another term, *toshav*, is sometimes used as a synonym (Gen 23:4; Ps 39:12).

tivities (and food) during the annual Feasts of Weeks and Tabernacles (Deut 16:11, 14; cf. 12:7) and every Sabbath year they could freely eat what the land produced (Lev 25:6). God "loves the alien, giving him food and clothing" (Deut 10:18). The Babylonian exile was in part divine punishment for not protecting and treating the aliens fairly (Jer 7:6–7; Ezek 22:29–31; Zec 7:10–14).

The resident aliens were not slaves but were free. They could even become wealthy (Lev 25:47). Israelites were not to oppress them, for example, by withholding wages (Deut 24:14–15) or denying justice (Exod 23:6–9). They had the same judicial protection of the law as a native-born Israelite and were to be given a fair hearing (Deut 1:16; 24:17). An alien who accidentally killed someone could, like a native-born Israelite, flee to a city of refuge (Num 35:15). Both native-born Israelites and resident aliens were also subject to the same penalties of the law (Exod 12:19; Lev 20:2; 24:16, 22; Num 15:29–30; Josh 8:35).

It is telling that the resident aliens, simply by being part of Israelite society, were also subject to the prohibitive religious laws that the covenant nation had to submit to and in this way had to acknowledge the God of Israel. It was therefore not unexpected that they were included in the covenant renewal ceremony in Moab prior to entering the promised land (Deut 29:10–11) and were in the audience to hear the reading of the law (Deut 31:11–13).[6] Like the Israelites, resident aliens were not to blaspheme the Name of the Lord (Lev 24:16) nor to sacrifice a child to Molech (Lev 20:2). They were not to eat blood (Lev 17:10), to engage in illicit sexual relations (Lev 18:6–30), to have leaven in their homes during the Feast of Unleavened Bread (Exod 12:19), and to work on the Sabbath day (Exod 20:10) or on the Day of Atonement (Lev 16:29). The resident alien was bound by all these prohibitive commands. Violations of these and, for example, the command against murder, constituted sins of commission and they polluted the land (Lev 18:27–28; 20:3; Num 35:33–34).

The resident alien was, however, not bound by the performative commandments, that is, those positive commandments that enjoined Israel in the true worship of God. For example, he was allowed to offer sacrifices to God as long as this was done in the prescribed manner (Lev 17:8–9; 22:17–25; Num 15:14–16), but he was not under compul-

---

6. Tigay, *Deuteronomy*, 278. For a discussion of the prohibitive and performative commands and the resident alien, see Milgrom, *Numbers*, 399–401.

sion to do so. If a resident alien did not bring these sacrifices, he did not pollute the land.

One implication of the laws governing the resident alien is that they encouraged the assimilation of the aliens into Israel. This encouragement is also obvious from the Passover legislation. Although this was the defining meal of Israel and was central to their identity as a nation, yet the resident aliens were welcome to join as full participants, if they committed themselves to the Lord and the males underwent circumcision (Exod 12:48–49; Num 9:14). In this way they would be integrated into Israel (cf. Gen 17:10–14). The rules for participating in the Passover that applied to the native-born Israelite applied to the resident aliens as well (Num 9:14). It is significant that this possibility of being part of the people of the covenant was given right at the beginning of Israel's existence as an independent nation in their exodus from Egypt. There was openness to outsiders right from the outset.

There is some evidence to suggest that resident aliens who loved the Lord and so in all likelihood had become full members of the covenant community of Israel, nevertheless retained their ethnic identity. For example, Uriah is still identified as the Hittite even though he clearly honored God. He refused to sleep with his wife while the ark and Israel were in tents on the battlefield (2 Sam 11:11; cf. 1 Sam 21:5).

Foreigners

A true foreigner [*nokrim, ben-neker*] had no real vested interest in the land or people of Israel but was there on a temporary basis, for example, as a mercenary (2 Sam 15:19). Since foreigners were truly outsiders and worshipped other gods and had different customs, they were generally regarded somewhat more negatively in Scripture. Whereas one had to "love those who are aliens, for you yourselves were aliens in Egypt" (Deut 10:19), the attitude to foreigners was more restrained. "Do not abhor an Edomite, for he is your brother. Do not abhor an Egyptian, because you lived as an alien in his country" (Deut 23:7–8).

The law also dealt differently and less generously with the foreigners. This was especially noticeable in economic matters. If an animal has died of its own, the native Israelite was not to eat it. He could give it to a resident alien, but was allowed to sell it to a foreigner (Deut 14:21). When it came to loaning money, every seven years outstanding debts owed by a native Israelite had to be released or deferred. The reason for what was probably a deferral, rather than a complete cancellation of the debt, is that every seventh year was a sabbath year with the fields laying fallow. Income would have been low in such a year making repayment of a debt much more difficult and taking away from the celebrated rest that was to characterize such a year. This law of deferral probably applied to the resident alien as well (cf. Lev 25:1–7). However, this privilege did not apply to a foreigner (Deut 15:2–3) whose occupation as a merchant or something else would not have been directly dependent on the land. Also, a native-born Israelite could borrow money without interest, but that was not the case with a foreigner. He could be charged interest on loans (Deut 23:30).

Whereas a resident alien could partake of the Passover on meeting certain conditions, this was not possible for a foreigner. He was forbidden to partake and no allowance was made for his participation (Exod 12:43). Sometimes specific nations were singled out. Moabites or Edomites were not allowed to enter the assembly of the Lord, that is, the covenant people of God gathered in worship, because of their past hostility to Israel. However, third generation children from Egyptian and Edomite parents could enter this assembly (Deut 23:3–8).

The Principles Involved

In light of the legislation just considered, the following principles can be articulated.

First, although God ordained the existence of nations, multi-ethnic societies are a reality in this world. We must learn to deal biblically with varying degrees of the occurrence of different races and cultures co-existing in one nation.

Second, host nations should show love and concern for immigrants. God demanded that Israel love the resident aliens or immigrants in its midst. The patriarchs, Israel's ancestors, had been resident aliens in Canaan (Gen 23:4) and God's command to love the alien was often accompanied with the reminder that Israel herself had had that status in Egypt (Exod 22:21; 23:9; Lev 19:34; Deut 10:19). These reminders "stood in the way of an all-too self-glorifying separation from other strangers."[7] Today many share with Israel the legacy of having been a stranger. The immigrant origins of the vast majority of those living in the United States and Canada should, therefore, caution citizens of these and similar countries not to look down on the new immigrants in their midst. Furthermore, the seriousness of

---

7. Burnside, *The Status and Welfare of Immigrants*, 8.

the command to love the stranger was underlined in two ways. The implications were spelled out very concretely in terms of equal justice, sharing in the resources of the land, and having fair wages. Also, if the admonition to love the stranger was not heeded, there was the threat of divine judgment (Jer 7:6; Zec 7:10; Mal 3:10).

Third, resident aliens had to acknowledge the God of Israel by submitting to his prohibitions. There was no compulsion to worship God alone, to be circumcised, and be bound to the performative commandments; but, the resident aliens were to honor the prohibitive religious laws lest the land become unclean and face God's anger (Lev 18:27–28). Religious identity was more important than ethnic identity. Foreign religious influences were to be feared, rather than foreigners as such. Faith and religion were critical in shaping Israel's distinctiveness as a nation. Ethnic origins were less important.[8]

Fourth, the resident aliens were encouraged to assimilate into Israelite society. The most complete integration involved accepting Israel's God as their own and submitting to circumcision and the other demands of the covenant. Even then, there are hints and suggestions in Scripture that a resident alien never lost his ethnic label.

Fifth, since Israel's laws encouraged integration, it is not surprising that not all outsiders were treated alike. Important distinctions were made. The resident alien was treated more favorably than the foreigner, and the resident alien who wished to integrate had more advantages than those that did not want to do so. Commitment to the host nation of Israel and identification with its values were rewarded. In this way the biblical approach to race relations and immigration has a double-edge. "It is positive in its attitude towards immigrants who are willing to assimilate and it is tolerant of non-hostile foreigners who are not willing to assimilate. But this open and welcoming approach is not achieved at the expense of national or religious identity."[9]

Sixth, there were limits to the integration of the resident alien. For example, if they became rich (cf. Lev 25:47) and purchased property, they could not own the land permanently but had to give up whatever land they may have purchased in the year of Jubilee (Lev 25:28). The one exception was city property (Lev 25:29–30). Full and complete integration could only come with subsequent generations of those

---

8. Burnside, *The Status and Welfare of Immigrants*, 80.
9. Burnside, *The Status and Welfare of Immigrants*, 81.

who were willing to assimilate and who intermarried with the native Israelites. The example of Ruth comes to mind. Her permanent integration into Israel by marriage resulted in sharing in the inheritance of the land and eventually, in a subsequent generation, even having a descendant, David, become king of God's people (Ruth 2:10; 4:13–22; cf. Deut 17:15).

THE CURRENT MULTICULTURAL CHALLENGE

Our Western world and culture is light years away from ancient Near Eastern society and from ancient Israel in particular, but we can and need to learn from the principles articulated in Scripture. In the biblical principles we have divine guidance for the challenges facing our society today. We will first consider the broad underlying issue of nationhood and then continue with more specific questions about immigration and multiculturalism.

Who are We? The Importance of a National Identity

The influx of large numbers of immigrants into Western countries and the emphasis on multiculturalism has resulted in an eroding or downplaying of a country's national identity. Samuel P. Huntington has documented much of this for the American scene while the issue for Canada sometimes seems to be whether that country has ever had a national identity! Such hyperbole when voiced is mainly due to the fact that Canada's culture is so similar to the American that it is sometimes difficult to differentiate between the two.[10] Canada clearly has a dominant Western culture that is heavily influenced by its European origins.

Over the past decades there has been a clear shift away from the melting-pot ideal according to which immigrants blend into the language and culture of their new home, to the multicultural vision of different languages and cultures co-existing in the host nation. Multiculturalism fits the post-modern mind-set of our times—a mind-set that espouses that everything is relative and that there is no

---

10. For America, see Huntington, *Who Are We?*. The situation in Canada has been summed up by the late Canadian icon, Pierre Berton. According to him, "One of the unifying forces of Canada is the long debate about who we are. No other country debates the way we do, and that is because of the presence of the [United] States" as quoted by Stanbury, "Canadian Content Regulations," 31.

standard of truth by which we can judge a culture, religion, or life style. All are equally valid; all should be promoted. There is no absolute right or wrong.

To be sure, multiculturalism has its attractions in displaying a stimulating diversity of ethnic specialties and traditions across the fabric of society. The downside is that some cultures make no attempt at assimilation and multiculturalism encourages the formation of cultural ghettos. These enclaves begin by living on the margins of the dominant society but end up creating their own isolated world that becomes virtually autonomous and self-sufficient. Such developments are not good for the unity of a country.

One needs to remember that nationhood is a divine ordinance (Acts 17:26). Being a nation is God's idea and having a distinctive culture are identity markers that one can be proud of and defend. For a people to be a nation, therefore, there needs to be cohesion and a meaningful national unity among its citizens. Since nationhood is a biblical principle, government has the obligation to protect the distinctiveness of their nation and not let it be fragmented into many diverse groups, each with its own culture, identity, language, and aspirations. There has to be something for people coming to their new country to be part of. Having a national identity as a nation that a country is prepared to defend is honorable. One way to achieve this is to teach each generation the story and aspirations of the nation's past and to inculcate love of and gratitude for the country without idolizing it.

Such an educational goal would follow an important biblical principle. Israel as a nation had to remember their communal past and pass it on to the next generation. In this way they would safeguard their identity, in their case, their identity as a nation in covenant with God (e.g., Ps 78, 105). The need to remember one's history and heritage, one's story as a nation, is vital for retaining one's national identity. Government must see to it that the national history is taught in the schools. The American and Canadian heritages are rooted in Western Christian civilization and that background needs to be taught in a constructive way, remembered, and safeguarded. A nation needs to entrust this legacy to the next generation so that each generation understands and appreciates the institutions and values of their nation. Then they will be prepared to defend them. One example to illustrate the importance of this should suffice. America and Canada fought in two World Wars to preserve Western democracy and freedoms. Other more localized wars with the same basic rationale have followed. We cannot take these liberties for granted. This treasured heritage needs to be passed on and taught to the next generation, including the immigrants entering the land. This is particularly important with immigrants coming from non-Western countries with non-democratic traditions. Unless such traditions and values like democracy and liberty are cherished by the entire population, the unity of a nation is at risk. Only citizens who understand the price paid in the past will realize the importance of retaining the liberties and rights which are so easily taken for granted and, if necessary, will fight for them.

A question arises. Does the need to retain one's national identity then preclude immigration? Should a nation bar all foreigners from entering? Such a suggestion is of course unreal and probably impossible to carry out given the falling birthrates in the West. But even if it were possible, such a suggestion need not be entertained. Scripture does not forbid the receiving of foreigners. To the contrary, it tells us to love those who are disadvantaged and seek refuge, help, and a better life in another country. As Israel had to love the resident aliens in their midst, so should Western nations today.

Today many have misgivings about the numerous foreigners coming into the West. But North Americans must remember that they too were probably once immigrants, either in the current or in a previous generation, and the command to love the neighbor whom God puts on their path, is applicable also for them. In this one needs to follow the example of the Lord Jesus who showed compassion, also to that despised part of Israel's population, the Samaritans (John 4:1–26; cf. Matt 22:37–40; Luke 10:29–37). Furthermore, there is one humanity with a divinely ordained diversity of races and languages. We share the same human nature with those who come to us from distant shores. We are to welcome them as fellow humans and show them love.

At the same time, we need to protect and safeguard our national heritage and culture. This necessitates considering some of the positives and pitfalls of multiculturalism as it is promoted today. We will subsequently move on to how we should welcome the immigrant into our midst.

Pitfalls of Multiculturalism

A great benefit of the current multicultural reality is that it promotes an appreciation for the strengths of other cultures and in this way combats racial prejudices. Furthermore, the reality of people of different racial origins living on the same street underlines our common humanity and thus promotes tolerance and respect for each other. Having diverse cultures living side by side also emphasizes that all should be treated alike which is a solid biblical principle. These are all very positive consequences of a multicultural society. Few would dispute them. There are however pitfalls and dangers to the dogma of multiculturalism that need to be noted.

To understand the main dangers of multiculturalism as a normative philosophy, one needs first of all to remember that nations were formed and scattered by God's judging the earth's population for their pride and arrogance in wanting to stay together and build a tower to heaven (Gen 11:1–9). Since God's judgment is involved, it is not surprising that the history of the world is a history of conflict and conquest as each nation tries to get the better of the other. The humanistic dream of uniting all peoples in a single multicultural society is therefore doomed to fail. This dream goes against God's expressly stated purpose of scattering by creating different languages, races, countries, and cultures. The only bond that will truly transcend different cultures and unite peoples of different backgrounds is the Holy Spirit who brought together different tongues and nationalities on the Day of Pentecost (Acts 2). God still brings Christians from different cultures together. But, even on the Day of Pentecost the different languages and cultures were not eliminated, but miraculously overcome. Perfect harmony will only be achieved when the "great multitude that no one could count, from every nation, tribe, people and language, [is] standing before the throne and in front of the Lamb" (Rev 7:9; cf. 5:9; 15:4; Gen 10:5, 20, 31).[11]

For Christians this grand picture injects a biblical realism into what is often an overly optimistic and somewhat naive push for a peaceful, multi-racial, and multicultural society in which all will get along. This dream is not doable for some of the presuppositions shaping government decisions on multicultural policies are not sound. Let us consider three such presuppositions.

---

11. See the discussion in Hays, *From Every People and Nation*, 193–99.

Are Cultures Morally Equivalent?

First, multiculturalism assumes that all cultures are somehow morally equivalent and agreeable and that the mixing of completely different cultures presents no threat to national unity. But such an assumption denies the reality of competing cultures and religions and is premised on the view that there is no absolute truth and that everything is relative. If all cultures are equal, then we should be prepared to welcome cultural norms in our society as diverse as the Hindu caste system, Sharia or Islamic Qur'an-based law, and the all-covering Muslim burqa as the normal expected dress for women outside their home. Only those who have absolutely no commitment to any culture or religion could even begin to entertain consenting to this. For cultures are not only different, but their values and beliefs are often not compatible. Since there is much immigration to North America from Islamic countries, we can use the Muslim faith and culture as an example.

Although there are areas of commonality between Western and Islamic cultural heritages, it is important to be aware of the vast differences that separate them. What follows are some important areas where they do not agree.

Christianity supports freedom of religion (cf. Matt 13:24–30, 36–42). Indeed, this is one of the reasons why multiculturalism comes up in Western societies influenced by Christianity and the Enlightenment and not in countries like Japan or China. They have absolutely no interest in it and oppose it. Of course Christianity, while endorsing freedom of religion, does have the mission to bring the gospel to the ends of the earth and to convince people of salvation in Christ alone (Matt 28:19–20). But missionaries are not to use force to do so. The sword of the Spirit is the Word of God (Eph 6:17). Whenever Christians have sought to subjugate others by force to the Christian faith, they have not acted in accord with Christ's teachings (cf. John 18:36). Freedom of religion means, for example, that Muslims are free to build mosques and practice their faith in Western nations.

Islam however has no interest in such freedom except when they are a minority and utilize Western freedoms to their advantage. Wherever Muslims are the majority of the population the trend is to lay obstacles to the spread of Christianity and to impose Islam wherever possible. Islam is a religio-political system. "Church and state" are so to speak one.¹² Christians are persecuted in many Muslim countries. Indeed, there are very few Islamic countries where religious oppression does not take place. Such persecution is apparently in accordance with the Qur'an.¹³

Another major difference is that cultures influenced by Christianity generally have a free press. The Muslim world despises freedom of the press. The press must serve the political and religious agenda of those in power.¹⁴ To be sure there is agitation in some Muslim countries for more freedom, but traditional Islam is opposed to it. Indeed, Muslims are even trying to curb the freedom of publishing in the West by launching libel suits against Western companies for what they consider to be publications hostile to Islam. Publishers and courts have caved in to the pressure. An example is Sheikh Khalid Bin Mahfouz who has brought lawsuits against Western publishers. In one case he successfully sued Cambridge University Press in a British court for publishing *Funding Evil. How Terrorism is Financed and how to Stop it* by Rachel Ehrenfeld. This court action has had a chilling effect, also in America, and other publishers have stopped publication of material critical of Islam.¹⁵

Democracy does not function naturally in Islamic societies as the political map of the world indicates. Many Muslims are working to change this but there is an inner resistance to democracy by fundamentalist Muslims who argue that only the laws of Allah are legitimate.

---

12. Miller, *A Christian's Response to Islam*, 94.

13. See, e.g., Jamie Glazov, "Symposium: The Muslim Persecution of Christians." For a Qur'anic justification to persecute Christians, see Surah 9:29, 73. "Fight those who believe not in Allah nor the Last Day nor hold that forbidden which hath been forbidden by Allah and His Messenger, nor acknowledge the Religion of Truth, from among the People of the Book, until they give the *Jizyah* [poll tax] with willing submission, and feel themselves subdued. . . . O Prophet! strive hard against the Unbelievers and the Hypocrites, and be firm against them. Their above is Hell—an evil refuge indeed." Quotations from the Qur'an are taken from 'Ali, *The Meaning of the Holy Qur'ān*.

14. See, e.g., Turki, "Muslim World Despises Freedom of Press."

15. See, e.g., Huston, "Islamists Rule American Publishing Industry." Other examples include: Lopez, "Is the Encyclopedia of Christian Civilization 'Too Christian'?" and Cohen, "Yale Press Bans Images of Muhammad in New Book."

Can Diverse Cultures Always Co-exist Peacefully?

A second and related presupposition is that multiculturalism assumes that diverse cultures can always coexist peacefully. Coexistence is possible in some cases. The Chinese communities in major American and Canadian cities attest to that. But such harmony is not always the case. This is particularly obvious where Islamic and Western cultures meet.[16]

Today massive Muslim immigration into Western nations is a fact of life and with it we are witnessing a clash of civilizations. Islamic and Western cultures are clearly not compatible on a whole range of issues: human rights, the place of women, Sharia law, democracy and others. Consistent Muslims who hold that truth is only found in the Qur'an are hostile to the Western culture of their new homeland. Indeed, classic Islamic teaching according to the Qur'an calls for the conquest of all things not Islamic because the whole world must be in favor of Islam.[17] The Egyptian born, British historian, Bat Ye'or, has shown that a coordinated Islamic jihad is being waged against the West. She has documented that Europe is already subject politically to Islam as witnessed by fervent anti-Americanism, the unconditional support given to Islamic efforts to repudiate Israel's legitimacy as a nation, and the de facto acceptance of a jihadist world order. This makes Europe, Eurabia, a land of dhimmitude, that is, a land subordinate to Islam. This status was evident when a Danish newspaper published cartoons of Mohammed. A firestorm of Islamic protest was ignited for, according to Islamic law, those in subjection to Islam are not allowed to criticize the Prophet Mohammed or any Islamic law without risking death.[18] As Europe has found out, the message, verbalized or not, is often, if you don't satisfy our Islamic demands, there will be social unrest, riots, and possibly even terrorist attacks. A consistent Muslim cannot and will not integrate into their host nation. The American and Canadian nations need to recognize Europe's gradually being sub-

---

16. This is true both politically and culturally, both in the past but also in the present. See, e.g., Huntington, *The Clash of Civilizations*, 198–204, 209–18.

17. The Qur'an states: "fight those who believe not in Allah . . . until they pay the *Jizyah* [poll tax] with willing submission, and feel themselves subdued" (Surah 9:29).

18. See Bat Ye'or, *Eurabia* and more briefly Bat Ye'or, "Europe and the Ambiguities of Multiculturalism."

jected to Islamic ways and losing its cultural sovereignty. The process of catering to Islam has also started in North America.[19]

Must One Respect the Culture to Respect the Individual?

A third important presupposition is that multiculturalism sometimes assumes that to respect an individual we must respect his or her native culture.[20] But this is not logical. Persons of a different culture whom we respect may reject their native culture because it has wronged or abused them. Respect for other cultures does not imply approval of everything which that culture practices. One can think of the Hindu religious practice of *suttee* according to which a widow is to be cremated on her husband's funeral pyre as an indication of her devotion to him; or, the Muslim practice of killing a woman for bringing "dishonor" to the family, even if such dishonor consisted of no more than refusing to wear the hijab, the traditional Islamic head scarf for women.[21] With respect to this last example, it is remarkable how most of the mainline media went to great lengths to deny that this was actually an honor killing, but simply an instance of domestic violence gone too far. Such obvious media bias in favor of presenting a positive image of Islam makes one wonder whether the politically correct multiculturalism does not harbor hostility to white culture and Christianity. Indeed, this opposition to white culture has been called the "ugly secret of multiculturalism."[22]

There are two other aspects to the assumption that one needs to respect the culture in order to respect the individual. This way of

---

19. See, e.g., in the area of education, Bat Ye'or, *Eurabia*, 253–57; for the world of finance, e.g., Zaidi, "U.S. Government Embraces Islamic Banking;" for the mainline media tiptoeing around Islam but not respecting Christianity in the same way, see Steel, "Drawing the Line."

20. This point and what follows is dependent on Burnside, *The Status and Welfare of Immigrants*, 61–62.

21. For the custom of *suttee* see Doniger, "Suttee." With respect to honor killing, a Toronto area Muslim father was charged with the murder of his daughter who had refused to continue to wear the hijab. Wattie, "Dad Charged After Daughter Killed in Clash Over Hijab." The practice of honor killing has followed Muslim immigrants into many western nations. See Chesler, "Are Honor Killings Simply Domestic Violence?"

22. Arthur M. Melzer, in *Multiculturalism and American Democracy*, as quoted by Burnside, *The Status and Welfare of Immigrants*, 63. For media bias against Christianity, see, e.g., Limbaugh, *Persecution*, 265–85.

thinking can easily encourage people of a foreign culture to claim that they have been victimized or oppressed because of their culture. Such claims are often based on flimsy evidence, but it seems to be politically correct to side with the supposed victim.[23] Furthermore, by catering to the perceived needs to protect and honor every culture in the country, a divided society results. The danger is that each cultural group lives in isolation from the other and that a nation becomes fragmented.

Anyone familiar with urban life in a multi-ethnic city and in tune with the media can see a confirmation of the pitfalls and the dubious presuppositions of the dogma of multiculturalism. The dream of a peaceful society where a consistent multiculturalism is promoted by the state is just that—a dream which is premised on the humanistic assumption of the basic goodness of man and his ability to bring all cultures together in harmony.

If some of the pitfalls of multiculturalism are to be avoided, then assimilation needs to be encouraged. Such assimilation need not go at the expense of the culture of the immigrant but the immigrant should reckon with the norms of his new homeland.

Welcoming Immigrants: The Need to Assimilate

Earlier in this chapter we saw that immigrants were welcomed into ancient Israel and had to be shown love. But, God's law also encouraged non-Israelites to assimilate into the population and culture of Israel by being more favorable to immigrants willing to assimilate than to foreigners not willing to become part of the nation. It is important to note that this open and welcoming policy is not enacted at the cost of national or religious identity. This approach "undercuts both traditional political perspectives. It undercuts traditional right-wing xenophobia and mean mindedness. It also undermines left-wing slowness to unashamedly protect the interests and values of the host culture."[24] The two biblical impulses of hospitality and nationalism come together in the worship of the Lord.

---

23. See Burnside, *The Status and Welfare of Immigrants*, 64. Citizens of a minority race can easily invoke victimization on the basis of racial profiling. A high profile case of alleged racial profiling involved the arrest of a black Harvard professor by a white police officer. President Obama even got involved by siding with the professor and it all led to a reconciliation summit around a drink of beer. Cooper and Goodnough, "Over Beers, No Apologies, but Plans to Have Lunch."

24. Burnside, *The Status and Welfare of Immigrants*, 81.

In today's context of non-theocratic nations, one might say that the idea of allegiance to the adopted country should be the basis for an ethical race relations and immigration policy. A nation can maintain both a welcoming stance towards newcomers as well as a strong sense of its national identity, provided that immigrants realize that they are expected to show loyalty to their new homeland and are willing to assimilate in the host culture. In line with the biblical principles, such immigrants should be treated as much as possible as the native-born. But those foreigners who are not inclined to show allegiance or who do not intend to settle and make the host nation their own, can be treated less generously than those who wish to assimilate.[25]

These principles show that Western governments today should give a high priority to encouraging assimilation rather than promoting multiculturalism. Multiculturalism has the tendency to treat all cultures and traditions as equal. This trend endangers the unity, identity, and the very economic and political structures and freedoms that have made the Western world such an attractive destination for countless immigrants from other backgrounds.[26] Government should therefore stress integration and assimilation and promote a national identity that builds on a nation's past. But how should governments go about doing this?

Admitting Immigrants

Ideally, governments should only allow into the country those who wish to assimilate. However, we do not live in an ideal world and rich nations have a responsibility to help those who come knocking on their doors as religious or economic refugees. In any case, governments should let non-Western immigrants know that they are expected to assimilate. This expectation means that immigrants adopt the country's language as their own so that they can interact meaningfully with the culture of their new home and work towards making their first loyalty to the nation that welcomed them and whose beneficiaries they are. Since many immigrants come from countries where freedom of religion and the rule of law are either non-existent or leave much to be desired, their assimilation must include adopting as their basic values the rule of law, democratic institutions, and freedom of religion

---

25. Burnside, *The Status and Welfare of Immigrants*, 81.
26. For more on this, see Burnside, *The Status and Welfare of Immigrants*, 63.

that form the Western heritage. For example, Muslim immigrants should acknowledge the justice system of our land, rather than the supremacy of Sharia law, and disown and reject Muslim institutions that are at odds with Western norms and culture, such as, polygamy, honor killings of daughters or daughters-in-law, female circumcision, and other practices that demean the position of women.

Unfortunately many of these practices still continue in North America. The demands of political correctness often cover up or tolerate these traditions. However, by so doing government and the media do a gross disservice to both the immigrants and the nation. Government has the duty to safeguard the Western heritage and should therefore take strong action against practices that are contrary to the country's laws and traditions. For example, polygamous marriages are illegal in Canada. Yet, they are de facto being recognized. Muslim men in the Greater Toronto Area who are in polygamous marriages are receiving provincial and city welfare and social benefits for each of their wives.[27] The government refuses to face the problem and even denies polygamy exists. The situation in the United States does not appear to be much different.[28]

North Americans, informed by politically correct media, can be quite naive about Islamic culture. But one must realize that, according to Islam, every Muslim has the duty to propagate Islam wherever he or she may be. Militant Muslims exploit Western freedoms for their own end and use the multicultural programs, political correctness, legal institutions, and the political institutions through lobbying for their purposes. By all accounts the Islamic cause is making progress.[29]

The point is that government needs to take consistent and firm action that will protect the national heritage and historical legacy that is America's and Canada's. The first order of the day is to ensure that immigrants are prepared to assimilate. Government should set immigration policy so that when the country allows genuine refugees and others from non-Western backgrounds on compassionate grounds, such immigrants should be given a choice, at the point of entering the

27. Godfrey, "Harems Pay Off for Muslims."

28. Turley-Ewart, "Sharia by Stealth — Ontario Turns a Blind Eye to Polygamy." For the situation in America, see, e.g., Bradley Hagerty, "Some Muslims in U.S. Quietly Engage in Polygamy."

29. Solomon and Maqdisi, *Modern Day Trojan Horse*, Pipes, *Militant Islam Reaches America*, and Spencer, *Stealth Jihad*. Also see, above notes 17, 19, and 22.

country, whether they wish to assimilate (and therefore, in the case of Muslims, disown Muslim cultural practices that are repugnant to traditional Western culture) or whether they wish to remain in the host country as foreigners who do not wish to assimilate. Their choice would affect their status as residents and have practical implications, with economic and social incentives being given for those wishing to assimilate. Those not open to assimilation, but only wanting to benefit from being in the host country, should not be given the right to become citizens and have a say in the land.[30] Indeed, they really do not belong and should feel free to leave if they do not like its institutions. Such policy would be in accord with the biblical principles considered earlier in this chapter. When immigrants are admitted on other than compassionate grounds, the interests of the country should come first and it may be necessary to refuse entry to those not wishing to integrate into the host society.[31] Multiculturalism should not be allowed to become a Trojan horse which will eventually destroy the historic fabric and heritage of the nation.

Helping Immigrants

Once immigrants have been admitted, government has the responsibility to show love to the newcomers and to protect the interests of the nation. These goals could be achieved by following through on the following duties.[32]

The government, at whatever level would be most effective, should inform those who wish to integrate what their responsibilities are and give them a suggested timetable for learning the language and becoming familiar with the country's institutions and values. Follow up should be organized within the relevant cultural community with those best able to help the process along.[33]

Government can provide assistance to those looking for work. Indeed, it would be in accord with biblical principles, to encourage

---

30. See also Burnside, *The Status and Welfare of Immigrants*, 84, 86.

31. For suggestions to this effect for the United States, see, e.g., Spencer, *Stealth Jihad*, 278–79, and for Canada, Bissett, *Demography is Destiny*, 16.

32. European nations have been struggling for some time how to deal most effectively with the many immigrants who are not assimilating. What follows is in part dependent on solutions being sought in the Netherlands. Voogel, "Integratie in de Gemeente."

33. Cf. Fennema, Van Middelkoop, et al., *Integratie en Verzuiling*, 26.

new and needy immigrants to work for their needs rather than to rely on free handouts. As noted earlier, the resident alien in ancient Israel had access to charity in the form of working for his own harvest by gleaning leftover grain, olives, and grapes (Lev 19:9–10; 23:22; Deut 24:19–22). The dignity of labor, rather than free handouts, gives an enhanced sense of worth to the immigrants. This is love for the neighbor in action. There is something drastically wrong when, for example, in Denmark, the Muslim immigrant population (which is 5% of the total) is allowed to consume up to 40% of the welfare budget.[34] Love for the neighbor would ensure that needy immigrants are put to work. Finding work would also reinforce the need to learn the language of their new homeland. Government should also assist those with professional training to find work in their field. This could involve making sure their credentials match those in North America or assisting them in upgrading their qualifications if necessary.

In order to encourage assimilation and to protect its heritage, government also needs to act positively to preserve the collective memory of the nation, especially through education and so cultivate and encourage the allegiance of the newcomers. As we saw earlier, this is a particularly important area since elementary and secondary schools teach less and less history and even current citizens in North America are not as familiar with the history of their nation as the previous generation was.[35] Governments therefore need to insist on the teaching of compulsory core history courses. When a nation forgets its history, it loses its sense of identity and is in danger of taking its freedoms and institutions for granted. If a country forgets its past, how can it expect newcomers to become familiar with it? Both citizens and newcomers need education in the history of the nation. Otherwise, America and Canada could eventually lose their distinctive identities as Western countries with a Christian heritage and all the benefits that have come from that.

Developments in Europe are a warning to North America. There the process of fragmentation of society with the accompanying diminishing influence of freedom of expression in the face of Islam is well underway and a lack of education in the host country's values is a big

---

34. See MacAllen, "Salute the Danish Flag!"

35. For the United States, see, e.g., Streich, "American Students and the Decline in History;" for Canada, see, e.g., Chalifoux and Stewart, "Canada is Failing History."

part of the problem.[36] Indeed, the need to encourage assimilation has become urgent. Recently the heads of state in Germany, the United Kingdom, and France have declared that multiculturalism has been a failure in their countries. As a result, national unity and Western political values are endangered.[37]

While government has the duty to safeguard the heritage and identity of the nation, it also has the obligation to protect the individual rights of immigrants coming from different cultural and religious backgrounds. While assimilation and cultural integration should be promoted wherever possible, the state is obliged to combat discrimination against immigrants and to protect the individual liberties of those whom it has admitted into the country. This includes freedom of religion. However, where the demands of a foreign religion transgress the norms of a Western society, which has been influenced by Christianity, limits need to be set.

There are therefore tensions. On the one hand immigrants need to assimilate but as much as possible they should be allowed to express their cultures freely. On the other hand, the host country needs to protect and retain its historic identity as a nation.

A basic rule is that government show love to immigrants and make it possible for love to be shown to them. The fullest expression of love for the neighbor includes the desire to share the gospel and show all immigrants the love of God in Jesus Christ. The state has no mandate here. The institution in society whose responsibility it is to show this love is the Christian church. A government that seeks the unity of a nation on the basis of its heritage will therefore give the church the necessary freedom to pursue its mission. Giving the church free rein to pursue its calling is in the best interests of America and Canada.

---

36. See, e.g., Bat Ye'or, *Eurabia*, 10–11. The teaching of Islam in public schools contributes to fragmentation and loss of Western identity. It promotes the division of society into Muslim and other sectors. Bawer, *While Europe*, 208–10.

37. See, e.g., Connolly, "Angela Merkel Declares Death of German Multiculturalism," BBC, "State Multiculturalism Has Failed, Says David Cameron," and Agence France-Presse, "Multiculturalism 'clearly' a Failure: Sarkozy."

SUGGESTED READING

Bat Ye'or. *Islam and Dhimmitude: Where Civilizations Collide.* Madison, NJ: Fairleigh Dickinson University Press, 2002. A scholarly history, with many lessons for today, of Islamic expansion using dhimmitude, a process of concession, surrender, and appeasement to Islamic demands.

Burnside, J. P. *The Status and Welfare of Immigrants: The Place of the Foreigner in Biblical Law and its Relevance to Contemporary Society.* Cambridge, UK: The Jubilee Centre, 2001. A study of the biblical material with practical applications for today.

Huntington, Samuel P. *Who are We? The Challenges to America's National Identity.* New York: Simon & Schuster, 2004. A clarion call for reflecting on the impact foreign cultures are having on America. A call Canadians also need to heed.

Rivers, Julian. "Multiculturalism," *Cambridge Papers* 10:4 (2001). Available online at http://www.jubilee-centre.org. This paper takes a critical, biblical look at multiculturalism in Britain and the lessons to be learned.

Spencer, Nick. *Asylum and Immigration: A Christian Perspective on a Polarized Debate.* Milton Keynes, UK: Paternoster, 2004. A very helpful look at important immigration issues.

Part D

Working for Change

10

Getting Involved

WHEN CONSIDERING THE CONTENTIOUS but ethically important issues government faces and the apparent slide in Western morals along with the decreasing influence of Christianity, the question arises: what can be done? Should the church "do something?" Chapter 3 explained that the task of the church as an institution is very limited in terms of interacting with government. The church has neither the charge nor the expertise to do so. However, what about church members? Do Christians have a distinctive task in a postmodern democracy? If so, why? And what is the duty of Christians in today's context? How can Christians be most effective? This chapter addresses these issues.

THE BIBLICAL DEMAND

The Bible makes clear that Christians should get involved politically; that is, they should seek to influence the current political scene and the direction and life of their city or town, state or province, and nation. Two biblical passages can serve to make this point clear. They also give us principles for today.

Jeremiah's Letter to the Exiles

Jeremiah was a prophet who ministered to God's people before and during the first part of the Babylonian exile in the sixth century B.C. The people who had been exiled for their sins did receive the promise that they or their descendants would eventually return to the promised land (Jer 32). But in the meantime, what were they to do in a strange country with a culture foreign to them? They were in a land whose armies had destroyed their country. These exiles must have felt out of place as they settled in Babylon.

Now what was their attitude to their new surroundings to be like? Jeremiah sent them a letter with very specific instructions. We read in that letter, as recorded in Jeremiah 29:5-7

> This is what the LORD Almighty, the God of Israel, says to all those I carried into exile from Jerusalem to Babylon: "Build houses and settle down; plant gardens and eat what they produce. Marry and have sons and daughters; find wives for your sons and give your daughters in marriage, so that they too may have sons and daughters. Increase in number there; do not decrease. Also, seek the peace and prosperity of the city to which I have carried you into exile. Pray to the LORD for it, because if it prospers, you too will prosper."

In other words, they were told to participate in the culture and business of their new dwelling place. That included seeking the peace and prosperity of the city in which they lived. The term used for peace is *shalom*, a very comprehensive term, covering all of life. It can also be translated by "welfare" — "seek the welfare of the city" (NASB).

This advice to exiles is without parallel in the Old Testament and in the literature of antiquity. They were to seek the welfare of their captors and pray for them. They were to work for the good of the country and society of those who would one day destroy their holy city of Jerusalem. To seek their welfare would have meant getting involved culturally and also politically to the extent that this was possible. They were to give their best efforts for that. And they had something to give. The heritage of godly wisdom in the Scriptures they had received was something to be shared. Indeed, had God not said to Abraham already that his descendants were to be a blessing to the nations (Gen 12:2-3)? Was Israel not to be a light to all peoples on earth? (cf. e.g., Isa 42:6; Deut 4:6; Ps 67). The example of Daniel, serving in the royal palace, must have been an inspiration for the Jewish people.

At the same time, the exiles had to realize that they would eventually return. For Jeremiah also said: "This is what the Lord says: 'When seventy years are completed for Babylon, I will come to you and fulfill my gracious promise to bring you back to this place'" i.e. Jerusalem (Jer 29:10). In other words, their staying in Babylon was ultimately to be temporary. They had to keep that in mind.

There are some relevant principles to note. Christians today are in some ways like the Judean exiles living in Babylon. They also are not of this world, though living in it (John 17:16, 18). Their sojourn here is ultimately temporary and they look forward to the promised land of the new world that is coming. And so on one level, this world is a hostile place for Christians, a temporary place. The temptation can arise to say: "Forget about the godless society around us." That is a response that could have been expected from the Babylonian exiles. However, God said otherwise. His children have an obligation towards the society in which they live, even if that society is hostile to their faith and values. That obligation toward society also involves the political sphere. After all, like the Judean exiles, Christians too have explicit instructions to pray for those in authority over them. "I urge, then, first of all, that requests, prayers, intercession and thanksgiving be made for everyone—for kings and all those in authority, that we may live peaceful and quiet lives in all godliness and holiness" (1 Tim 2:1–2). But how can Christians pray for those in authority if they do not do what they can to witness to God's norms for our society and nation? Those in authority should not be regarded as adversaries but as those to whom Christians owe respect and obedience. They have been placed there by God himself (Rom 13:1–5). Christians today should get involved in one way or another and again the example of Daniel can be an inspiration.

Salt and Light

Another biblical warrant for Christians to get involved is found in the Sermon on the Mount. The Lord Jesus said to his followers:

> You are the salt of the earth. But if the salt loses its saltiness, how can it be made salty again? It is no longer good for anything, except to be thrown out and trampled by men. You are the light of the world. A city on a hill cannot be hidden. Neither do people light a lamp and put it under a bowl. Instead they put it on its stand, and it gives light to everyone in the house. In the same way, let your light shine before men, that they may see your good deeds and praise your Father in heaven (Matt 5:13–16).

The Lord Jesus used two images. The first is salt. Salt prevents or slows down decay by being rubbed into meat. Christians by living out their faith unashamedly combat the moral and spiritual decay of the society of which they are part. The imagery is grand. "Salt of the earth!" Not salt of our home or church, but of the earth! In other words, nothing is to be left outside the influence of Christians. Also society, culture, and politics need to feel the effect of the Christian testimony. Wherever this testimony is experienced, there is resistance against the moral decay of this age and it can ultimately have political consequences. If Christians don't live out their faith in the fullness of life, their words will mean little and their testimony will be compromised.

The other image Christ used is light. Light is used in Scripture for many positive things such as righteousness and truth which Christians are to embody (Eph 5:8–9). Again the image is grand and comprehensive. "You are the light of the world!" Everything needs to be illumined by the gospel and Christian principles, including the often sordid world of politics. It is unthinkable to let the light be hidden under a bushel. Light is meant to shine! The positive impact must be such that "men may see your good deeds and praise your Father in heaven." Indeed, everything Christians do must be to the glory of God. "Whether you eat or drink or whatever you do, do it all for the glory of God" (1 Cor 10:31).

God enables Christians to shine their light by equipping them with his Word. The Bible is relevant for today. It shows the way for all of life. Christians who get involved in the political process in a responsible way can "take captive every thought to make it obedient to Christ" (2 Cor 10:15) and so shed the light of the gospel on the issues of the day and that's good for the nation. After all, biblical principles and solutions work! And as the Psalmist put it: "Your word is a lamp to my feet and a light for my path" (Ps 119:105). That truth is also relevant for the nation. The more a nation is in tune with God's wishes, the more blessed it is as a people. "Righteousness exalts a nation, but sin is a disgrace to any people" (Prov 14:34).

Jesus is Lord

But what if it looks hopeless? To use the words of psalmist: "When the foundations are being destroyed, what can the righteous do?" (Ps 11:3). The implication is: nothing! If a building is on shaky ground, as our society seems to be at the moment, what can be done about it?

Nothing, many say. However, David in this particular psalm refuses to flee from the problem and avoid the hard reality. In a simple child-like faith he goes on to remind us that "the LORD is in his holy temple; the LORD is on his heavenly throne. He observes the sons of men; his eyes examine them" (Ps 11:4). God's throne may be highly exalted, but he knows what's going on in this world. He sees what people are doing!

Now David is realistic, as Christians today also have to be. David knows that you can not always change a bad situation. But he comforts himself with the thought that God is on his throne and therefore sovereign and in control. Furthermore, he is just. There is a day of judgment coming "for the Lord is righteous, he loves justice; upright men will see his face" (Ps 11:7). Meanwhile, David will do what he can and not flee from the problems of the moment.

This is the attitude believers today can also take. It is possible because "Jesus is Lord!" (1 Cor 12:3). Well, if he is Lord of heaven and earth, and he is; and if all power and authority has been given to him, and it has (Matt 28:18), then such a confession like "Jesus is Lord" encourages Christians to do whatever is possible to influence the political direction of those set above them in government. As Abraham Kuyper once put it: "There is not a square inch in the whole domain of our human existence over which Christ, who is Sovereign over *all*, does not cry: 'Mine!'"[1] The confession "Jesus is Lord" cannot, by its very nature, be confined to the privacy of a Christian's personal life. It is a confession that clamors to be heralded in the life of a nation for all governments will eventually have to answer to the king of kings and Lord of Lords what they have done with the authority God has given to them. The children of God owe it to those in authority to pass on what they know with respect to God's demands for our society today. After all, applying biblical principles to the issues of the day is good for society. Christians may labor in the joyful realization of the triumphant Christ, but they must do so soberly, realizing that cherished goals will not necessarily be met and that ultimately believers are strangers and pilgrims in this world.[2] But no matter how gloomy the current circumstances may be, Christians need never give up but

---

1. Kuyper, "Sphere Sovereignty," 488, the emphasis is Kuyper's.

2. For a necessary cautionary note against easy triumphalism in the line of Kuyper, see Mouw, *Uncommon Decency*, 159–69.

continue to be involved in faith in the political arena knowing that in the Lord their work is never in vain (1 Cor 15:58).

Since government as God's servant is accountable to God (Rom 13:4), there can be the time and occasion for Christians to remind the state or its officials that Jesus is Lord. Consistent with Western Christian tradition, British Prime Minister Tony Blair rightly acknowledged that he was accountable to God for his political decisions.[3] As Lord and King over all governing authorities, Christ comes to judge. "God's people have the vital calling to speak the truth to them and call them to account in anticipation of that . . . final day."[4]

In summary, Scripture gives believers a clear mandate to be involved in the affairs of their country and this includes the political issues of the day. The Lord also uses the reality of the moment to encourage Christians to be involved and his Word gives the necessary guidance.

THE PRACTICAL NECESSITY

Most people resist or are reluctant to get entangled in affairs of state and government. However, one has no choice for everyone in the country is already involved whether they realize it or not. Christians also pay their taxes, and are daily affected by the legislation and agenda of the state for which they have contributed. For that reason committed Christians cannot but feel the pressure to let their voice be heard in the cacophony of current political discourse, especially when they see their tax money go to causes inconsistent with God's will. So there is a real practical necessity to become engaged. It is unavoidable for those living in a democracy founded on a Christian heritage.

The Democratic Reality

Christians living in a democracy have an obligation to participate in it. Apathy about government affairs is a temptation for all citizens but Christians should have no excuse. Will they not want the wishes of their King, Jesus Christ, to be made known to the relevant authorities? After all, his will is wise and merciful. In a democratic society there are

---

3. McIlroy, "The Role of Government in Classical Christian Thought," 82.
4. Wright, "Neither Anarchy Nor Tyranny," 75; also see 75–79.

many ways in which to connect with one's elected representative and Christians should seize the opportunities that this system offers.

As noted in chapter 1, God gave ancient Israel a political system that had significant democratic features. However, as a result there were implications and consequences. God held the people accountable for the moral direction of the nation and admonished the nation as a whole to maintain justice in the land (Exod 23:6–8; Deut 16:19–20). God expected his people to use the democratic elements for the well-being of the country. The same principles apply today. In a democracy people share in the responsibilities of state decisions and actions. Christians today are therefore to be no less vigilant than the Israelites of old that God's norms for justice be upheld. As citizens of a democratic society, Christians have their share of the responsibility for the way society goes.

Furthermore, if Christians who accept the Word of God as an infallible rule for life do not stand up to promote Christian values, who will? Liberal mainline churches support policies that contradict clear biblical teaching, such as abortion and same-sex marriage.[5] Government can hide behind the ecclesiastical endorsement that these bodies give to unbiblical legislation. It is therefore imperative that Christians committed to biblical ethics stand up and demand a hearing. The Christian heritage of the United States and Canada gives added justification to speak up.

The Christian Heritage

God is mentioned in the American motto: "in God we trust." He also appears in the preamble to the Canadian Charter of Rights and Freedoms: "Canada is founded upon principles that recognize the supremacy of God and the rule of law." Detractors may scoff at these references but the reality is that whether one is a believer or not there is

---

5. On abortion, the American organization Religious Coalition for Reproductive Choice lobbies for abortion and includes mainline churches (http://www.rcrc.org/about/members.cfm). The issue of same-sex marriage is more contentious but important ecclesiastical bodies such as the United Church of Christ (http://www.ucc.org/) has embraced it and the Episcopal Church allows its clergy to bless it (http://www.integrityusa.org/samesexblessings/index.htm). In Canada, the influential United Church, the largest Protestant body, supports abortion and same-sex marriage (http://www.united-church.ca/). Also see on the American religious left Kupelian, *The Marketing of Evil*, 219–21.

and there always has been a transcendent point of reference in the life of the nation, namely the God of Scripture, and this needs to be taken seriously and retained.[6] If God is removed from public discussion, we are left with what has been called a naked public square. It misses a recognized outside authority that is higher than the community itself with the result that there is no absolute norm by which to debate or criticize. Democracy is however premised on the recognition of transcendent truth to which government is to be held accountable. This is historically the case and continues to be necessary in order for meaningful interaction among citizens on policy issues and good government to be possible.[7]

Without God in the picture, decisions are made on the basis of autonomous human preferences. But in such a normative vacuum what gives one moral opinion legitimacy over another? When the ethical principles of the law of God are outlawed, humans, that is the courts and the state, become the source of law rather than being servants of God and his law (cf. Rom 13:4). Legal and government institutions become as a god, decreeing what should be without any moral accountability to a higher authority. Indeed, a higher authority is ruled out of order, as is traditional morality. In such a case, even the most solemn questions are decided on the basis of the lowest possible factor. When the American Supreme Court legalized abortion (*Roe v. Wade*, 1973) "the questions of the meaning of human life and who belongs to the human community for which we accept common responsibility" were "reduced to the question of 'privacy' . . . It is an instance of law against life, of individualism's assault upon the individual, of the eradication of the personal and communal bonds without which it is not possible to be an individual."[8] No wonder that years after the court's ruling, its decision remains controversial. It has no moral legitimacy in the face of biblical principles and has led to the destruction of millions of human lives.

So what do Christians see as their goal as they work to prevent immoral decisions that have disastrous consequences? Is it the estab-

---

6. Instructive in this regard is Farrow, "Of Secularity and Civil Religion," 140–82.

7. See Neuhaus, *The Naked Public Square*, 76, 120. Neuhaus' book popularized the phrase "naked public square."

8. Neuhaus, *The Naked Public Square*, 259.

lishment of a Christian state? The Lord Jesus has not given us any reason to think that this is the duty of Christians. He himself made no attempt to establish his kingdom in political terms while he was on earth. To the contrary, he emphasized that his kingdom was not of this world (John 18:36) and the parable of the wheat and the weeds teaches that the good and evil be tolerated as much as possible until the great separation takes place on judgment day (Matt 13:24–30, 36–43).[9]

So, if Christians are to participate in the political process, what general principles should govern the goals they set? In a general sort of way what should Christians seek from the state? What should Christians be after? A famous interchange that the Lord Jesus had with the Pharisees helps to put this issue into focus.

GIVE TO CAESAR WHAT IS CAESAR'S . . .

The Savior gave as guideline: "Give to Caesar what is Caesar's and to God what is God's" (Matt 22:21; Mark 12:17; Luke 20:25). How should we interpret this? Does it mean that life is divided into two parts: one part for Caesar, and one part for Christ? That is what is often concluded—in public honor the government and do what it says, and in the privacy of your home or church exercise your religious activities. This is your freedom of religion! Is that what the Lord envisaged and meant? His words deserve a closer look.

The Pharisees wanted to trap Jesus and so discredit him before the people. So they asked: "Teacher, . . . we know you are a man of integrity and that you teach the way of God in accordance with the truth. You aren't swayed by men, because you pay no attention to who they are. Tell us then, what is your opinion? Is it right to pay taxes to Caesar or not?" (Matt 22:16–17). Now if Christ had answered "yes" he would have alienated the Pharisees, the zealots, and every devout freedom-loving Jew. They all hated paying the poll (head) tax to the Romans. But if Christ had said "no", that would have made him liable to being charged with treason. Christ gave neither answer. Instead he said: "'Show me the coin used for paying the tax.' They brought him a denarius, and he asked them, 'Whose portrait is this? And whose inscription?'" Now when Christ asked: "Whose portrait is this?" he literally said: "whose image is this." "Caesar's" they replied (Matt 22:21).

---

9. See further, e.g., Skillen, "The Principled Pluralist," 158–64.

After all, his image is on the coin. The coin therefore belongs to him and so to him it should go. "Give to Caesar what is Caesar's!"

Well, if the coin is Caesar's because his image is on it, what belongs to God? Or, in this particular context: what bears God's image and so belongs to him? Well, people bear God's image. After all, as the Jews fully realized, humans were created after the image of God and they bear the likeness of the Most High (Gen 1:26–27). Well then, if humans bear the image of God, then they ultimately belong to God and should therefore render to God what he has coming. And God who created humans after his image and likeness does demand everything! He is not satisfied with a denarius or a dollar bill, but he wants one's heart, mind, and soul, a total love commitment (Matt 22:38). He must always come first. No government can ever supplant this right of the Creator.[10]

Give to Caesar

We need to take a closer look at these two alternatives—give to Caesar, give to God. First, "give to Caesar what is Caesar's." Give to the Roman government, what is its due. As an authority established by God it has the right to demand taxes so it can do its task such as keeping the peace, providing roads, and enforcing justice. However, by implication, Christ said more, namely, one is only to give to Caesar what belongs to him and what is legitimately his. That means that one must not honor any pretensions to divinity that a Roman emperor may have or worship him. Only God is to be worshipped. This observation raises another point. The tribute coin, the silver denarius, would have had a picture of Tiberius, the reigning emperor at the time, on the front, along with the words: "Tiberius Caesar, son of the Divine Augustus." On the back would have been a female figure designated as "Highest Priest." Such a coin was blasphemous and conscientious Jews considered the minting of such currency a transgression against the first two commandments. Yet Christ had no difficulty using that coin to honor the government. He did not consider such payment to the civil authorities to be compromising his commitment to serve God above all else. Why was that? Palestine was under a pagan government and Christ did not expect it to honor or support the true religion. It was beyond their jurisdiction. The theocratic rule of Old Testament

---

10. Owen-Ball, "Rabbinic Rhetoric," 8–14.

times was over. In that sense, the things of God were not the responsibility of the emperor.[11]

This has implications for what Christians can and should demand from their government today. Now the United States and Canada are not pagan states. However as we have seen in chapter 3, the Bible gives government today no jurisdiction to dictate on religious matters. Christ's teaching with respect to the tribute money reinforces this. A major implication is that Christians should be very careful what they ask the governing authorities to get involved in. For example, Christians should not lobby government to include prayer in public schools. This would require a civil authority to enforce a religious practice. On the other hand, Christians can protest if a government should forbid the teaching of origins from a biblical perspective in public or private schools or force evolutionism as a religious and philosophical system on students. Should Christians in Canada ask the state to support Christian education as a matter of fairness since Roman Catholic schools are already funded? There is some legitimacy in that argument but becoming dependent on the state can be dangerous for the integrity of Christian education. More to the point is that government really has no task to support any religious education although it is fully understandable how the practice developed given Canada's Christian heritage. A related question for both Americans and Canadians is whether the educational tax dollar should not simply follow the child. If this rule were to be adopted and applied to all citizens for all elementary and secondary education, it would be within the jurisdiction of the state since all would be treated alike and it arguably would promote justice and peace in society.[12]

In a general sort of way, one could say that government should stay out of legislating the first four commandments which deal with one's relationship to God and concentrate on the last six dealing with one's relationship to one's neighbor.[13] The two great commandments are to love God and our neighbor (Matt 22:36–40). Government should normally not legislate on the former but the state does have

11. See, also for what follows, Barker, "Theonomy, Pluralism, and the Bible," 233–41.

12. See on a school voucher system Wayne Grudem, *Politics According to the Bible*, 250–56.

13. Barker, "Theonomy, Pluralism, and the Bible," 237–39. Woolley, *Family, State, and Church*, 30–46. For the fourth commandment, see chapter 7.

the duty to regulate the relationship citizens have with their compatriots so that justice, peace, freedom, and the well-being of society are maintained. For this reason, laws against abortion and pornography, for example, are fully justified.[14]

Give to God

Now we need to consider briefly further implications of the second half of Christ's words. After telling his audience to give to Caesar what was Caesar's the Lord Jesus had added: "[give] to God what is God's." We have noted that one's entire life as made in God's image belongs to God. No government can ever legitimately make a total claim on any human made in God's image. The point of the Lord Jesus is that if everything belongs to God, the demands of the state must always be very limited for the state does not own its citizens. God does. For that reason obedience to God must always takes priority over obedience to men (Acts 5:29).

How do Christians give to God what belongs to him? One thing that God demands from all his creation is recognition and worship. After all, he has written enough evidence of himself and his greatness in the created world and in the very lives of mankind that he be acknowledged and adored (Rom 1:19–21; 2:14–15). In the context of the present discussion, Christians must therefore always have the freedom to be able to worship God in a manner pleasing to him. The state therefore has the obligation to make that possible.

Furthermore, in giving to God what is his due, Christians have the sacred obligation to defend the good name of God in the public square (cf. Rom 2:24). This can include mentioning God in public debate. The state must provide the necessary freedom for so speaking. Christian legislators need not always specifically mention God to fulfill their duty to honor him. After all, they speak from the basic assumption that Jesus is Lord and therefore point out to their fellow citizens the necessity and blessing of acknowledging the wisdom God gives in his Word for the life of the nation. They do this by articulating and defending biblical principles for social, economic, and political life.[15]

Without taking anything away from the need to honor God in public life, there are limitations to what a Christian is able to do. It

---

14. See for more examples Woolley, *Family, State, and Church*, 30–46.
15. On these issues see Chaplin, *Talking God*, 38–46.

can be argued that in a multi-cultural democracy, religious reasons for supporting a certain policy should be permitted maximum expression during the debate leading up to a decision. But the official government justification for a new law or policy which has been passed should show religious restraint since the law or policy decided on needs to appeal and be acceptable to as many as possible within the wide spectrum of beliefs found in current society in order to keep the civil peace. The office of government has constraints in a secular democracy and a Christian legislator can live with that.[16]

North American society, however, very much resists introducing any reference to God and biblical principles during any interaction in the public square. People say: we are a free and democratic society which can set its own rules. The public square should be neutral and introducing God in a public debate takes away from objectively looking at the issues at hand. In response it should be noted that there is no such thing as a perfectly neutral person or ethic. All values and preferences are informed by underlying presuppositions which are religious, that is, ultimately accepting either the God of Scripture or autonomous man as authoritative. Those who reject the biblical ethic and wish more freedom for themselves are just as biased and prejudiced as those who hold to biblical norms. Secularism is in itself a religion based on certain beliefs such as the ability of man to determine what is best and what is right for him without any reference to God's will. These beliefs are evident, for example, when a policy is pursued in the name of some imagined right, although such a course of action is clearly detrimental to society. Faith in the correctness of a particular human right at stake trumps other considerations.[17] Indeed, secularism as a religion "claims sovereignty in the public sphere to the exclusion of other religions." In spite of protestations to the contrary, secularism is actually intolerant.[18]

---

16. See on this Chaplin, *Talking God*, 18, 58–72.

17. E.g., George Smitherman, Ontario's gay Minister of Health and Long Term Care (2003–2008), vigorously opposed a Health Canada guideline that classifies active homosexual men as a "high risk" for disease for purposes of organ donation. White, "Ontario's Gay Health Minister Blasted."

18. Sampson, *Sustaining Democracy*, 7. Also see pp. 10–12. For the position that faith is a precondition to any reasoning, religious or secular, see Chaplin, *Talking God*, 18.

If a secular government is not to become oppressive, it is especially Christians who must be vigilant to safeguard liberty as much as possible. After all, it is the Christian heritage that is responsible for the many benefits North American democracies enjoy today. Also, Christians are aware that they can only serve the state and be obedient to it in a manner pleasing to God. This realization limits what the state can request from them. As the apostles put it: "We must obey God rather than men" (Acts 5:29). Christians therefore need to be involved in public political dialogue to work for the necessary freedoms so that all segments of society are at liberty to fulfill their respective God-given responsibilities.

SECURING AND PRESERVING FREEDOM

Recognizing the importance of freedom is fundamental. The true freedom is the freedom to observe the will of God and to live according to his Word (Ps 119:44–45). This is historically the freedom that many died for in the religious persecutions in Europe or came to North America for. This is the freedom that Christians have an obligation to continue to defend and if necessary do everything legally possible to maintain. It can only be done by acknowledging God's sovereignty.

God alone is sovereign over everything. No human government is nor should be. However, human nature being what it is, there is always a tendency or temptation for government to keep adding power to its already vast portfolio of authority and control. Since secularism has banished God from the public square, a spiritual vacuum exists and the way is open for government to virtually take the place of God. Through the courts and the legislature, the state is now in the business of establishing a new moral code that is sometimes diametrically opposed to God's own directives in his Word. Since Christians understandably resist whatever is contrary to God's will, the new morality needs to be imposed from above through the sheer force and power of legal declarations from the courts and legislation from the government. Since the latter should have the final say over judicial pronouncements, the net effect will ultimately be that the state gives itself the place once reserved for God. It will pass into law and enforce whatever morality it wishes or society demands from it.

But the voice of the people is not the voice of God. As laws contrary to God's will are passed, freedom becomes more and more limited. This is inevitable since only God knows perfectly how his creation works best and can fulfill its potential. God designed the role of government to be limited so that other sectors of society such as the family unit, the church, and educational and economic institutions can fulfill their God-given responsibilities without government interference.[19] These institutions when functioning properly make it more difficult for government to infringe on their jurisdictions. The secular denial of the divine design can, however, lead to state encroachment on their spheres of authority and consequently result in a loss of freedom. This loss includes the inevitable tyranny of a political majority over the rest of the population since secularism confers sovereignty on such a majority.[20]

What can or should be done about this? There is of course a need to be frank about this situation and have an open public discussion about it. Chapter 4 dealt with this area by addressing the issue of public debate and finding a justifiable civic consensus, along with the pitfalls involved. In addition and critical for a good response to the challenges of diminishing freedoms is that Christians live their faith in a robust and unapologetic manner and seek in whatever way is feasible to work to protect the freedoms enjoyed today.

Living the Faith

Because North American culture generally considers religion to be a matter of the privacy of one's home, it is of great consequence that Christians live their faith to the full publicly and not be shy about it. Living the faith does however start in the home.

It is difficult to overestimate the significance of the home because what Christian parents do there affects an entire future generation. This impact begins with raising a family. Children are welcomed into the home and not considered an inconvenient burden. A new generation of citizens is born which will contribute to the well-being of the nation. In a Christian home abortion is never an option and even handicapped infants are received with love. Children learn Christian

---

19. See further, e.g., Woolley, *Family, State, and Church*.

20. See on these themes, e.g., Groen van Prinsterer, *Unbelief and Revolution*, 207–12; Ovey, "Beyond Scrutiny?" 1–4; Groen van Prinsterer, *Unbelief and Revolution*, 207–12; as translated and found in the second half of Van Dyke, *Groen Van Prinsterer's Lectures on Unbelief and Revolution*, and Koyzis, *Political Visions and Illusions*, 136–38.

values from the example set by their parents. In an age when there is much disrespect and disdain for authority, Christians should be at the forefront to honor the civil authorities as set over them by God (John 19:11; Rom 13:1–2). Showing this respect includes obeying the authorities (1 Pet 2:12–17), and praying for the government in good and bad times, when policies are favorable to Christians and when they are not (1 Tim 2:1–2). Even in times of persecution, Christians are to pray for those set above them (Matt 5:44). Christians are to honestly pay taxes and set an example as law-abiding citizens (Rom 13:6–7).

Society must see that Christians are not weird extremists as they are often portrayed by liberal media, but conscientious citizens who seek the best for their country. Their Christian life style should therefore include getting involved outside their immediate circles, bonding with the neighborhood, striking friendships, and demonstrating Christian love and concern to those in need. This is all about trying to shift the civic culture into a more biblical direction so that politics can change for the better. Unless the mind-set and moral outlook of the voting population changes, there is little hope of changing the views of those who determine the direction of government.

In several ways the situation of North American Christians today is somewhat similar to that experienced by the early Christian church. Western society is showing more and more pagan characteristics as its culture continues to drift from its Christian moorings. This development is obviously disheartening given the rich history of Western Christianity. However, Christians can also take much encouragement from the example of the early Christian church which found itself in a pagan culture under much more trying circumstances. They did not count in the Roman Empire. They were despised and persecuted because they confessed that Jesus is Lord over all worldly authorities and powers (1 Cor 12:3). Because of this core confession they refused the Roman duty of burning incense to the gods and of worshipping the emperor as a god. As a consequence they were feared and charged with atheism and treason. Christians did not participate in the immoral culture of the public games with its cruel entertainment of watching people being killed and many refused public office. Consequently they were regarded with suspicion, considered intolerable, and were oppressed.

These early Christians however steadfastly maintained their faith and showed it, not just in what they did not do, but also and perhaps especially in their positive counter-cultural activities. Unlike the surrounding pagan culture they maintained the sanctity of matrimony and honored the important place of the woman in marriage. They showed Christian love to each other and to those in the community outside, including their enemies. They cared for the poor and sick, condemned abortion, rescued exposed infants from death and placed slaves and masters on the same level before God. All this was in sharp contrast to the pagan culture and non-Christians noticed and were favorably impressed.[21]

The end result was that after centuries of hardship that involved much persecution the empire was Christianized. Although from a human perspective many factors were involved in the Spirit's work of spreading the gospel, there is no doubt that the clear and consistent Christian witness in their life style and morals was a major contributing factor for a changing cultural environment in which the gospel was accepted and the empire was eventually Christianized.[22] This is a truth that can inspire Christians today to lead robust Christian lives and assert biblical values. It is also a truth that keeps one sober and realistic. It took many years and enormous hardship to turn the empire from paganism to Christianity. The Christian life is part of being "the salt of the earth" (Matt 5:13) and salt works slowly. It has taken many years for North America to deny its Christian roots. And, should it happen, it will take a long time to turn things around. All the important media and political, legal, educational, and cultural institutions in the land are by and large firmly in the grip of the prevailing secular spirit. A national culture has to change. Ultimately the real power that will bring truly positive change is the power of the gospel (cf. Rom 1:16; 2 Cor 10:4). The freedom for preachers to continue to proclaim it in fullness is critically important for sustaining Christians to live their faith and for arming them to be a salt and light seeking cultural

---

21. See Cadoux, *The Early Church and the World, passim*; on public office, pp. 393–395; 558–561; on the place of the woman in marriage, pp. 281, 443, 597; and Schaff, *Ante-Nicene Christianity A.D. 100–325*, 338–77, 385–86.

22. See Cadoux, *The Early Church*, 302–2, 470–73 and Adamopoulo, "The Triumph of the Gospel of Love."

change. The gospel is the sword of the Spirit who alone can renew the hearts of men (1 John 5:4; cf. Zec 4:6).[23]

Christians today are in many respects in a much more favorable situation than those in the early Christian church. Unlike the dictatorship of the Roman Empire, a democracy offers many possibilities which were then non-existent. Democracy welcomes the input of all its citizens. Christians need to make full use of the opportunities, let their light shine, defend the right to express their faith publicly, and work to have society benefit from it.

Defending Freedom

Since political leaders follow the culture, changing the culture should be a top priority also when it comes to defending our freedoms. Living one's faith to the full and publicly should include coming out of the comfort zone of the church and church related activities and seizing every opportunity to become involved in community affairs and networking and interacting with those involved in institutions that affect the direction of our culture. Christians in education will do so with those in their field and similarly those in the arts, in the business world, in the legal profession, in agriculture, in the media, or whatever field. By acting on their faith presuppositions robustly, wisely, and confidently, Christians can have significant impact in whatever place in society the Lord has put them. Consistent Christians have much to contribute. Since this is a cultural conflict, change will come very slowly, but every person who witnesses a Christian approach to the issues of the day and sees the positive benefits will reflect and not too quickly dismiss the input of Christians in the issues of the day. Furthermore, by building relationships with colleagues and friends, it becomes possible to develop coordinated strategies to address specific issues within one's area of expertise and so move forward on an agenda of gradual cultural change.[24]

---

23. On the task of preaching and the political process see the helpful study of Trumper, *Preaching and Politics*.

24. Helpful on this general topic is Ray Pennings, "Influencing for Good," 13–21. There is ongoing discussion on how best to influence culture from individual Christians living the faith, as emphasized, e.g., by Colson and Pearcey, *How Now Shall We Live?*, to underlining the importance of the faithful presence of believers in the institutions and structures of power that form the infrastructure of culture, as in Hunter, *To Change the World*. See Pennings, "Embracing the Paradox."

In order to be well-informed and effective, Christians should make use of the work of policy institutes, think tanks, and activist groups that they can identify with, and support them. (Chapter 11 lists some of the more prominent.) The internet has become a very effective tool for gaining up-to-date information from such organizations and disseminating it. Alternate news media can have a considerable beneficial effect in giving opposing or different views on current hot button issues.[25]

An important area for defending freedom is the courts. The gay movement has reshaped how current culture thinks of gay rights and same-sex marriage by using the courts to further their cause. Christians can and should make use of the judiciary as well and use it for positive change. As detailed in the next chapter, organizations to defend these freedoms exist in both the United States and Canada. The freedoms of religion and speech are especially important since they are at the very basis of being able to function as a Christian in today's society. They allow for peaceful assembly in worship, the full proclamation of the Word, the establishing of Christian schools, and free expression in the media, be it printed or electronic. All these activities are essential if Christians are to be a salt and light in today's world. Yet these freedoms are severely under threat since secular humanism in spite of the rhetoric is very intolerant.

It is instructive to consider briefly the situation in Canada where cherished freedoms are in jeopardy due to intrusive officially appointed human rights commissions on both the federal and provincial level. These commissions "have quasi-legal powers that should be offensive to the citizens of any free country. They are kangaroo courts, in which the defendant's right to due process is withdrawn. They reach judgments on the basis of no fixed law. Moreover, 'the process is the punishment' in these star chambers—for simply by agreeing to hear a case, they tie up the defendant in bureaucracy and paperwork, and bleed him for the cost of lawyers, while the person who brings the complaint, however frivolous, stands to lose nothing."[26] Indeed, the Commission pays the legal costs of the complainant and often reimburses other expenses as well. On what basis can a complaint be brought? According

---

25. See, e.g., Farah, *Stop the Presses!* Farah founded WorldNetDaily, an independent news website which attracts over eight million unique visitors a month.

26. Warren, "Suing for Silence."

to Section 13 of the Canadian Human Rights Act any matter which is "likely to expose a person or persons to hatred or contempt" can be the basis of a complaint. Crucially, as the record shows, truth is not considered a defense for the accused—with negative implications for, among others, preachers of the gospel.[27] Not surprisingly, for thirty years (up to about 2007) not a single defendant charged with "hate speech" had ever been acquitted. There have been calls for the repeal of Section 13 but that has not happened.[28] The United States also has a growing number of human rights commissions. It is to be hoped that the lessons learned in Canada will not be lost on Americans.[29]

In defending freedom, more Christians should also become directly involved in politics. Since the reach of government is intruding in ever increasing ways into daily life, it is becoming increasingly necessary for the Christian voice to be heard in the political forum. In its simplest form political involvement means being informed and voting on election day. But also between elections, Christians should be involved to defend the freedoms that are so easily taken for granted. A fundamental prerequisite is of course that Christians keep up to date on what is going on in the corridors of power. Then they are able to engage their elected representatives on the issues of the day. But this should not be done lightly. In the first place, a good contact with those in government means having a positive relationship with them and not just writing when something is wrong, but also thanking them for the work they do well. Second, when writing about an issue, one should make sure that one's facts are accurate and that the argumentation brought to bear is clear and convincing for someone who disagrees with the position taken. Third, in obvious issues such as abortion and marriage the biblical message is very clear. However one should bear in mind that in some issues Christians may differ in how to apply biblical principles to contemporary issues and may come up

27. The ordeal of Pastor Stephen Boissoin is a case in point. Shaidle and Vere, *The Tyranny of Nice*, 52–55.

28. One example of such a call for repeal was made by *MacLeans* magazine which had itself been hauled before human rights commissions. The editors, "Harper Must Act Now to Protect Free Speech." The literature on the subject is vast. A good entry is Levant, *Shakedown* and the website of Stand up for Freedom Canada: http://humanrightscommissions.ca.

29. Levant, "Human Rights Commissions in the United States." Levant was an expert witness to the U.S. Congress' bi-partisan human rights caucus on July 11, 2008. His prepared comments are found in Levant, "Levant to Congress."

with different solutions or approaches. It is therefore important when writing not to say too quickly "thus says the Lord." Also it is essential to show how one's solution or view helps society and is workable. Fourth, use the local and electronic media to broadcast your views with letters to the editor or otherwise. For example, if the issue is important enough, make your letter to your elected representative an open letter which also gets printed in your local newspaper. Fifth, work together with others wherever possible to make a political point. This applies to getting good information and making use of a lobby group or think tank that specializes in the area of concern. Cooperation can also involve supporting organizations which promote ideas consistent with biblical teaching.

Christians can also become involved by joining a traditional or mainstream political party, provided it does not involve endorsing immoral or unbiblical principles. Their influence can then be exerted to try to bring official party policy closer to the biblical ideal. As members of such a party, they can also seek to run for public office. Not all Christians agree that it is possible to work through mainline parties because of strictures such as party discipline. In Canada, Christians formed an officially recognized federal political party in 1987. The Christian Heritage Party develops policy, participates in policy forums, and runs candidates in national elections. The first-past-the-post method of electing members to the legislature, whereby the candidate in a constituency with the most votes wins, does not favor small political parties. All votes cast for other parties, even if over 50% of the total votes cast, are essentially wasted. A small party can however present a distinctive testimony and witness in the debate in the public square and hold high the banner of biblical truth and principles.[30] Deciding how to be involved in the strict political sense of the term will depend on how one can be most effective in fulfilling Christ's demand to be a salt and light in society and so making a difference.

There are many ways for Christians to become involved and not everyone will agree on what is the best strategy. That also depends

---

30. The official website of the Christian Heritage Party is http://www.chp.ca/. See further, Vanwoudenberg, *A Matter of Choice*. It is interesting to note that in the 1970's H. Evan Runner and Bob Goudzwaard advocated the forming of a Christian political party with some caveats. Runner, *Scriptural Religion and Political Task*, 99–102 and Goudzwaard, *A Christian Political Option*, 63–66. Also cf. Redekop, *Politics Under God*, 155–69.

on the circumstances. But the main thing is that Christians should get involved. Christians have much to contribute and historically have been a major source of the betterment of society. The danger of apathy is real especially when the cultural war seems hopelessly tilted against Christian values and the hostility against Christian principles is openly articulated in the media. As the saying goes: "All that is necessary for evil to triumph is for good men to do nothing."[31]

Christians need to be mentally prepared for strident opposition to biblical views that go against current cultural norms. The conflict is after all ultimately spiritual. But how Christians respond to the challenge of opposition is extremely important. Christians should remain calm and graceful when interacting with opponents and so show love and consideration even to their enemies.[32] "Do to others as you would have them do to you" (Luke 6:31). Christians must simply carry on in spite of resistance. The Lord never promised a bed of roses in testifying to his will, even if done as carefully as possible and with a view to the good of society. "No servant is greater than his master. If they persecuted me, they will persecute you also" (John 15:20). As a matter of fact, in Revelation 11, the two witnesses representing the faithful testimony of God's people, are eventually killed as martyrs on the streets of the great city, figuratively called Sodom and Egypt (Rev 11:1–8). The people of God will seem to go down in defeat in an ungodly world but in the end of time they will triumph (Rev 11:1–11).[33] These biblical passages inject a sober realism into what Christians are up against but they also encourage for ultimately Jesus is Lord and he simply demands obedience.

SPECIAL ISSUES

But what does that obedience entail? The current state of affairs raises questions such as: is compromise possible for Christians seeking to be active in the political affairs of the nation? At what point should Christians refuse to obey the government? When is civil disobedience in accord with God's will? We will consider each issue in turn.

---

31. On being involved also see Redekop, *Politics Under God*, 109–25.

32. Helpful reading include: Chamberlain, *Talking About Good and Bad* and Mouw, *Uncommon Decency*.

33. Beale, *The Book of Revelation*, 572–76, 590–93, 596–97.

Compromise

The topic of compromise often divides committed Christians when considering strategy in trying to be a light and salt in society. To make the issue concrete, we will use the problem of abortion as an example. In the fight against abortion, a question often raised is whether a Christian can support a law that offers less than one would wish to see. Some maintain that no law can be supported unless it outlaws abortion outright, except by way of rare exception to save the physical life of the mother. Would supporting a less than ideal abortion law not mean that you give your approval to the killing that is still being done under that law? It comes down to whether Christians should take an all-or-nothing approach, or work incrementally, one small step at a time for change. Those who go for all or nothing often consider it a matter of conscience, a position which is difficult to argue against. However, to get a handle on this issue we need to consider the different factors.

First of all, what exactly is compromise? In a most basic sense it means coming to an agreement with each party making concessions. Given the nature of a democratic pluralistic society, it could not function without compromise. There are strongly held beliefs that divide segments of society and without mutual concessions society would fracture. But some would protest and say that Christians can never compromise. Is Christ not king of all creation and must the moral direction of his Word not be heeded? Yes, and if there is a way to make that happen, that route should surely be pursued. But it is not always possible. Society's morals and attitudes can be so entrenched that proposed legislation that decrees otherwise is simply not doable. So there is a need to compromise, that is, to settle for less than one would prefer. However, such compromise does not mean that this is the end of the road. Rather, Christians will continue to work for a better solution with a view to honoring God and his Word. Is this approach warranted?

Is Compromise Biblical?

It is remarkable that the Lord God often showed much patience and understanding for our fallen nature in situations where we might be less tolerant. Here are some examples. In Exodus 12 God had set the date for the Passover, but a mere two years later, God accommodated his people by setting a second date for this feast so that those ceremonially unclean on the first date could still celebrate the feast (Num 9). God did not strictly insist that the original date be maintained at all costs, although this was his clearly expressed divine will. Another example: God forbade the eating of an animal that was found dead (Lev 7:24; Deut 14:21). Yet, he reckoned with the weakness of his people and made provision for disobedience to this ordinance (Lev 11:40). A final example: God hates divorce (Mal 2:16), but knowing the hardness of men's hearts, he showed considerable tolerance (Deut 24:1–4; Matt 19:8). In all these examples, God was willing to settle for a situation that was less than he would have liked for he reckoned with the reality of the power of sin. But, God was working towards the long term goal of the redemption and holiness of his people.

There is however more to God's accommodation. God certainly did not condone sin or minimize the seriousness of disobedience. But by accommodating to the hardness of men's hearts, God moderated the effects of sin. For example: by allowing for divorce, he provided a legal framework to part ways and prevent worse things happening. By giving a second date for the Passover, he still enabled his people to benefit from this feast. By working this way, God showed his patience and love to his people. He knew that they could not be a new creation overnight and that life is a long pilgrimage in which the progress in holiness and commitment is not without struggle and falling. That reality is still very much with us today as we seek sanctification in all our life.

Now if God was and is willing to factor in the reality of the sin-ridden world in which we live, should Christians then not also be willing to settle for less than the ideal and likewise reckon with the hard reality of a fallen creation, which we share with our fellow citizens? Is it not sometimes necessary to compromise to prevent worse things from happening? Take the example of abortion. Canada has the dubious distinction of being the only country among developed nations that has absolutely no limitation on abortion and no unborn human being within the womb has legal protection. This is in reality "the law" of the land.[34] Now if a country has always had full protection for the life of the unborn children, one could convincingly argue

---

34. For an overview of abortion in Canada, see Dunsmuir, "Abortion: Constitutional and Legal Developments."

that it is unjustifiable, should legislation for abortion on demand be proposed, to begin with seeking a compromise solution. Then one is legislating the killing of unborn children, even if one seeks to limit the damage. However both Canada and the United States are far beyond such a situation. Very liberal abortion policies are in place. In such a situation, "we should seize every improvement that can lead to fewer victims, even though we will be unable to totally reverse pro-abortion legislation."[35] If we strive for the very best, we may end up losing even second best. It is therefore better to settle for the second best, not with joy, but with sincere regret and with the realization that the ideal is not yet attainable. This is also a guideline for elected representatives to follow.

In this connection, it is good to remember the sober word of Ecclesiastes. "Do not be overrighteous" (7:16a). The context of these words is the helplessness that the Preacher experiences in watching evil apparently triumph over good. The righteous one dies in spite of his doing good, but the wicked man seems to live forever in his evil doing (Eccl 7:16). The Teacher then counsels that the righteous should not think that they can rectify all evil and wrongs. It is beyond their power to do so and trying to achieve this end will destroy them. And therefore, "Be not overrighteous." There is also a great danger in such an attitude. One could not only end up overestimating one's own abilities, but also be critical of God for not doing more to curb evil. One should rather comprehend the power of sin and fear God (cf. Eccl 7:18).[36]

Scripture does not forbid compromise in the political arena. The indications are that it can be pursued as part of a Christian acknowledgement of the limitations of a world and society fallen in sin. There are also the hard political realities. Should there be any movement towards a greater protection and sustaining of society's foundational values and institutions, compromise is a necessary part of the process. Indeed, it has been well said that "the exercise of political authority is the search for a compromise which, while bearing the fullest witness to the truth that can in the circumstances be borne, will, nevertheless lie within the scope of possible public action in the particular community of fallen men which it has to serve."[37]

---

35. Douma, *Responsible Conduct*, 193.
36. Kelley, *The Burden of God*, 116–17; also Douma, *Responsible Conduct*, 191.
37. O'Donovan, *Resurrection and the Moral Order*, 130. Also see Neuhaus, *The*

Incrementalism

With issues like abortion, the approach to take may be one small step at a time and to support legislation which although far from ideal nevertheless gives some limitation or additional curbs to abortion.[38] History teaches that a dedicated Christian approach to eradicating evil structures and practices from society by small incremental steps, which involve compromise, can be blessed and has been blessed by the Lord. A famous case is that of William Wilberforce (1759–1833). He was instrumental in outlawing slavery and banishing this evil from the British empire. But it did not come overnight. It took much perseverance and much compromise to reach his goal. Unable to abolish slavery outright, he first worked for the regulation of the slave trade which succeeded in 1788, then worked on the abolition of the slave trade and not slavery itself. Such a bill eventually passed in 1807. The actual abolition of slavery itself took another 26 years. However, in the meantime, he supported legislation that seemed to go against his cause. For example, he backed a bill that would regulate the number of slaves allowed on a single ship, as well as supporting measures that ameliorated the condition of the slaves. Both actions implicitly continued to legalize slavery, but Wilberforce saw, correctly, that these incremental changes were good for the slaves and so he supported them while continuing his struggle to outlaw slavery altogether.[39]

A recent Canadian example is the struggle to raise the age of consent for sexual activity. In 2008, the national Parliament raised the age of consent from 14 to 16.[40] This was a positive development. But one should realize that the United Nations Conventions on the Rights of the Child (Part I, Article 1), to which Canada is signatory, defines a child as being under age 18. It would, therefore, have been better to raise the age of consent to 18. However, under the circumstances that would not have happened. Less is better than nothing.

Naked Public Square, 124.

38. So, e.g., Frame, *The Doctrine of the Christian Life*, 732.

39. See Belmonte, *William Wilberforce*, 102–7, 150–51, 332 and Wolffe, *The Expansion of Evangelicalism*, 193–208.

40. The law was passed on February 28, 2008. See "Bill C-2: An Act to Amend the Criminal Code."

IN CONCLUSION

Christians need to exercise patience with a society that is increasingly secular and neo-pagan. Change will not come overnight. As the Lord has exercised great patience and love with a rebellious Israel and often lapsing church, Christians today must show love and endurance in seeking to influence the culture and the political process in a Christian manner. This has nothing to do with giving up the truth and compromising in the sense of denying the Lord and his place in life. It means that Christians should not be overrighteous and think that they can eradicate all evil quickly and on their terms. Rather one should try to move ahead as the Lord gives opportunity, if necessary, one baby step at a time. Slow incremental change will act like a leaven in our society and under God's blessing lead to bigger and better things.[41]

However, there can be situations where compromise is not possible and when Christians have to say no. That can even lead to civil disobedience.

Civil Disobedience

The Bible is clear about the Christian's duty to obey the governing authorities (e.g. Rom 13:1–7; 1 Pet 2:13–17), but it is also obvious that one's preeminent duty is to obey God above all else. When faced with the demands of the Jewish Sanhedrin not to teach in Christ's name, "Peter and the other apostles replied: 'We must obey God rather than men!'" (Acts 5:29; cf. 4:19). This truth is evident throughout the biblical account of God's people. Think of the following examples. The believing Hebrew mid-wives did not listen to Pharaoh's decree that they kill the baby boys when they were born. They let them live and gave the excuse that the boys were born before they arrived (Exod 1:15–20). They refused to murder the male offspring of God's people. Another example: the high government official, Obadiah, did not cooperate with the royal house of King Ahab. When Queen Jezebeel was persecuting the prophets of the Lord, he hid one hundred of them (1 Kgs 18:3–16). He knew that these servants of the LORD needed to be protected. A final example: when everyone in Babylon had been commanded to worship no one but King Darius, Daniel still kept on praying three times a day to the true God and he did not attempt to hide

---

41. See also Mouw, *Uncommon Decency*, 36–38.

that action from those who hated him (Dan 6:7–11). Like his fellow countrymen, Shadrach, Meshach and Abednego (Dan 3), Daniel was prepared to pay the ultimate price for his obedience. He was thrown to the lions, but the Lord shut their mouths and so rescued Daniel (Dan 6:22).

Now all these examples are taken from situations which are far removed from our present democratic context. Pharaoh and Darius were absolute monarchs and King Ahab and Queen Jezebeel also clearly acted like that. What they wanted happened even if it meant corrupting justice and disregarding the rights of the people (cf. 1 Kgs 21). But notice, in all these examples, the believers simply did what they could. When it came to clear and obvious demands from God, they disobeyed man in order to honor God and left the consequences to God.

If necessary, Christians today must be prepared to do the same. But, one may ask, what constitutes the right conditions for civil disobedience? It is indeed not something to be taken lightly. Believers are not interested in being revolutionaries who destabilize the legitimate authorities. Furthermore, engaging in civil disobedience can make the reputation of Christians odious among their fellow citizens. Clearly explaining what is at stake should there be civil disobedience is therefore an absolute must. However, living in freedom in a democracy should mean that needing to resort to civil disobedience is relatively rare. All legal avenues to effectuate change need to be exploited first before any sort of disobedience is contemplated.

The topic of civil disobedience is a broad one and can involve issues such as conscientious objection and the right of rebellion or resistance to the authorities. It is far beyond the limitations of this book to go into all these aspects. To keep this discussion focused we define civil disobedience as a refusal by citizens to obey a law or command from a higher authority when obedience to such a demand would constitute disobeying God's law. Those refusing have exhausted legal or other avenues for change, do not use violence, are motivated by a love for the neighbor, are prepared to pay the price for their disobedience, and hope to force change with respect to the demands made to them.

To illustrate we go back to the example of abortion. On an individual level, if a nurse is asked to assist in an abortion and she has exhausted all avenues to be released from this demand, she can refuse such an order since God's law against murder overrides the civil law allowing abortion. What about picketing outside abortion clinics and thereby violating local ordinances or court orders? Some would argue that this type of civil disobedience is never permitted for it undermines the rule of law and democratic institutions.[42] Others would say that the government does not compel you to have an abortion and do evil, and so the law does not affect you directly. It only permits someone else to sin. You therefore have no business getting involved.[43] A third option is to agree with such a course of action because the object is to save the human lives of those who are completely unable to defend themselves. "Rescue those who are being led away to death" (Prov 24:11). The entire matter of civil disobedience is very contentious but it would seem that the third option is a position that is very difficult to condemn with biblical arguments. We are, after all, to be our brothers' keepers. At the same time, one cannot be everywhere at once and to demand that one join others in such activity is a step too far. In deciding on civil disobedience, each should be free to make one's own decision before God.[44]

THE RETURN OF THE KING

Both government and its citizens are ultimately responsible to the living God of heaven and earth. He gave each their task and he will one day call all to account (Ps 2; Rom 13:1–7; 2 Cor 5:10). In the meantime, Christians live in the tension of the return of the Lord Jesus Christ.

On the one hand, this reality calls for much patience and hard work. The date of his return is unknown and the state gives virtually no recognition to the reality of the kingship of Jesus Christ. Vigilance to protect God-given freedoms and rights are the order of the day. Christians need to be vigorously watchful for the freedom of reli-

---

42. Douma, *Politieke Verantwoordelijkheid*, 189–93. A brief English summary can be found in Douma, *The Ten Commandments*, 204–5.

43. J. S. Feinberg, P. D. Feinberg, and Huxley, *Ethics for a Brave New World*, 93–96.

44. Frame, *The Doctrine of the Christian Life*, 619–21. Frame does emphasize using educational, political, and religious approaches consistent with the law of the land to fight abortion but also affirms that using civil disobedience, as once practiced by Operation Rescue, was not sinful. For an overall and balanced treatment of this topic, see Redekop, *Politics Under God*, 171–82.

gion and expression of their views in the public square. They should jealously guard the uniqueness of marriage and the privileges and prerogatives of the family over against any encroachment by the increasingly long arms of the state. Indeed, Christians need to continue to confront the authorities with the clear demands of God's law over the entire spectrum of societal concerns, especially in such obvious areas as abortion and euthanasia. Christians can expect heated opposition from those adhering to secular humanism. Christ warned that those who believe in him will suffer as he did (John 15:20). They will need to persevere.

On the other hand, Christians can be confident and live in joyful expectation even as they struggle for the realization of God's claims on the life of their nation. After all, the Savior has not only died but he rose again in real time on this earth (Matt 28:1–10; 1 Cor 15:20). In his resurrection body he then ascended triumphantly into heaven. He did so assuring those who believe in him that all authority in heaven and on earth had been given to him and he promised that he will be with his people until the end of the age (Matt 28:17–20). At that time he will return to judge the living and the dead (2 Thess 1:6–10). Right now he rules at the right hand of his heavenly Father (Col 3:1). Christians can therefore work with the confidence that if a nation adheres to God's norms, that nation will experience the blessings that come with obeying God's ordinances and honoring his creation gifts. "Righteousness exalts a nation" (Prov 14:34), that is practicing justice and uprightness raises the power, prosperity, and prestige of the nation. This blessing comes from Christ who is in control. He sovereignly rules over this world (Eph 1:19–23). Christians can therefore engage the current culture and interact with their politicians knowing that their labors are not in vain (1 Cor 15:58). They can rejoice, without triumphalism, but in the sure conviction that one day Christ will establish his kingdom in perfection and usher in the new world where righteousness and peace dwell. Christians are ultimately on the winning side! Their Lord and King has the last word.

SUGGESTED READING

Douma, J. *Responsible Conduct: Principles of Christian Ethics.* Translated by Nelson D. Kloosterman. Phillipsburg, NJ: P&R, 2003. This Reformed study of ethics deals with many of the issues Christians face in living their faith.

For the Health of the Nation: An Evangelical Call to Civic Responsibility (2004), Online at http://www.nae.net/images/content/For_The_Health_Of_The_Nation.pdf. The political action of the National Association of Evangelicals is based on this document. It justifies Christian civic engagement and highlights seven important issues.

Marshall, Paul. *God and the Constitution.* Lanham, MD: Rowman & Littlefield, 2002. A scholarly call for Christian involvement in politics as a God-given duty.

Redekop, John H. *Politics Under God.* Foreword by John A. Lapp. Waterloo, ON / Scottdale, PA: Herald Press, 2007. Written by a political scientist of Anabaptist persuasion, this popularly written book shows how Christians should be involved in the political process and what the limitations of government are.

Wagner, Michael. *Christian Citizenship Guide: Christianity and Canadian Political Life.* Lethbridge, AB: ARPA Canada, 2010. A very helpful and practical guide for Canadians which highlights Canada's Christian heritage, human rights issues, and how to get involved.

11

Resources: A Selection of Helpful Organizations

A NUMBER OF ORGANIZATIONS stand out in terms of giving up-to-date and relevant resources to equip those who wish to get involved in the issues of the day in a meaningful manner. This chapter gives a brief introduction to twelve such organizations from both the United States and Canada, and, by way of exception one from Britain as well. A wealth of information is available simply by going to their websites.

The selection is no doubt subjective, but turning to these organizations for facts and assistance will lead you to others. Furthermore, just because an organization is outside one's country does not diminish its usefulness since the issues of the day are very similar in the global village of Western democracies. It is of course always advisable to be discerning and understand the source of the data being presented. However, these and similar organizations make an incredible amount of good data available that can be used profitably to inform oneself and to influence legislators and policy makers.

All direct quotations, as well as virtually all information, are taken directly from the website of the organization being discussed.

AMERICA

Acton Institute

The Acton Institute for the Study of Religion and Liberty (http://www.acton.org) was founded in 1990 and seeks to integrate Judeo-Christian truths with free market principles. Its staff of more than forty has as its mission "to promote a free and virtuous society characterized by individual liberty and sustained by religious principles." To that end it "organizes seminars aimed at educating religious leaders of all denominations, business executives, entrepreneurs, university professors, and academic researchers in economic principles, and in the connection that can exist between virtue and economic thinking." The Institute also has a wide-ranging publishing program from the popular to the rigorously academic. It produces a weekly, *Acton Commentary*, a bi-monthly newsletter, *Acton Notes*, a quarterly journal called *Religion & Liberty* that engages the intellectual reader on issues in religion, politics, economics, literature, and culture, and the biannual *Journal of Markets & Morality*, a refereed academic and inter-disciplinary journal that brings together economics, theology, and philosophy. In addition, the Institute publishes monographs on economic issues that have direct impact on Christian theology as part of a collection called the *Christian Social Thought Series*. It also disseminates its views through special lecture series, Acton University which is an annual four day event, the podcast *Radio Free Action*, and its Impact Campaigns which uses print advertisements to focus attention on important faith and policy issues.

It is of interest to note that Acton Institute and Kuyper College, which are both in Grand Rapids, Michigan, are partnering together to translate Abraham Kuyper's three-volume work on common grace. Kuyper basically argued that God is not absent from the non-church areas of our common life but bestows his gifts and favor indiscriminately to all people.

Alliance Defense Fund (ADF)

The ADF (http://www.alliancedefensefund.org) defines itself as "a servant organization that provides the resources that will keep the door open for the spread of the Gospel through the legal defense of religious freedom, the sanctity of life, marriage, and the family." Because of the urgent need for a strong, coordinated legal defense of religious freedom, the leaders of more than 35 ministries—including the late Dr. Bill Bright, the late Larry Burkett, Dr. James Dobson, the late Dr. D. James Kennedy, and the late Marlin Maddoux—came together and launched ADF in 1994 to aggressively defend religious liberty.

The ADF is unique in that it accomplishes its work through strategic coordination with like-minded organizations, training Christian attorneys and future leaders, funding key, precedent-setting cases, and when necessary, direct litigation through their in-house team of Christ-centered attorneys. The ADF has taken part in defending some of the most significant, precedent-setting cases threatening religious freedom. It has been successful in more than three out of every four of these cases litigated to conclusion.

Those who have their constitutionally protected rights violated are encouraged to contact the ADF Legal Intake Team. The ADF alliance includes more than 2,000 attorneys that are located in virtually every community across the United States. Extensive print, online and video resources are available through their website.

American Family Association (AFA)

The AFA (http://www.afa.net) is "one of the largest and most effective pro-family organizations in the country with over two million online supporters and approximately 180,000 paid subscribers to the *AFA Journal*, the ministry's monthly magazine. In addition, AFA owns and operates nearly 200 radio stations across the country under the American Family Radio (AFR) banner." The AFA's mission is "to inform, equip, and activate individuals to strengthen the moral foundations of American culture, and give aid to the church here and abroad in its task of fulfilling the Great Commission." To that end AFA has an online news provider which is syndicated around the world (through http://www.onenewsnow.com) and maintains activist websites such as OneMillionMoms.com and OneMillionDads.com. Part of their strategy is to hold accountable companies that sponsor programs attacking traditional family values and to commend those companies that act responsibly regarding programs they support. The overall aim of AFA is "to communicate an outspoken, resolute, Christian voice throughout America."

Americans United For Life (AUL)

Founded in 1971, AUL (http://www.aul.org) is the first national pro-life organization in the United States. Its mission is "to defend human life through vigorous legislative, judicial, and educational efforts, on both the state and national level." An important part of this organization's strategy is the production of an annual resource manual, *Defending Life: A State-by-State Legal Guide to Abortion, Bioethics, and the End of Life*. This manual combines AUL's "model legislation, expert analysis, and 50 state report cards into a single nonpartisan guide for legislators, policy makers, the media, and interested Americans. It comprehensively addresses abortion, protection of the unborn (in contexts outside of abortion), bioethics, the end-of-life, and health care freedom of conscience." It also tackles legal and policy challenges for the pro-life movement, reports on recent legislative and courtroom victories and emerging issues and trends. AUL also produces groundbreaking legal research and writing, hosts Legislator Educational Conferences, and develops educational resources and programs. It has founded Advocates for Life, a national, nonpartisan association of pro-life law students and supports pregnancy centers. AUC has also created Lawyers for Life, an intellectual network that seeks to educate lawyers about life-issues and the law and to provide encouragement for pro-life advocacy. On the international front, AUL is establishing a strategic network with pro-life leaders outside America and contributing to pro-life legal developments abroad through consulting, filing briefs, and speaking engagements.

Brookings Institution

The Brookings Institution (http://www.brookings.edu) was founded in 1916 by Robert S. Brookings. It is a nonprofit public policy organization based in Washington, DC. Its mission is to conduct high-quality, independent research and, based on that research, to provide innovative, practical recommendations that advance three broad goals: first, to strengthen American democracy, second, to foster the economic and social welfare, security and opportunity of all Americans, and third, to secure a more open, safe, prosperous, and cooperative international system. It is consistently ranked as the most influential, most quoted, and most trusted think tank.

This reputation of quality, independence, and impact is based on research done by over 200 resident and nonresident fellows who write books, papers, articles, and opinion pieces. They also testify before congressional committees and participate in dozens of public events each year.

The research is spread over many specialized and diverse Brooking's policy centers such as Brown Center on Education Policy, Center on Children and Families, Saban Center for Middle East Policy, and Urban-Brookings Tax Policy Center. Brookings Institution Press publishes many books that result from this research. Research papers are also available online. One can subscribe to a wide variety of more than two dozen newsletters that keeps the reader up to date on the latest research and commentary.

Cato Institute

The Cato Institute (http://www.cato.org) founded in 1977 and located in Washington, D.C., is "a public policy research organization—a think tank—dedicated to the principles of individual liberty, limited government, free markets and peace. Its scholars and analysts conduct independent, nonpartisan research on a wide range of policy issues."

Cato is "dedicated to providing clear, thoughtful, and independent analysis on vital public policy issues. Using all means possible—from blogs, Web features, op-eds and TV appearances, to conferences, research reports, speaking engagements, and books—Cato works vigorously to present citizens with incisive and understandable analysis."

The breadth of Cato's work is considerable. Because the principles of liberty and limited government impact nearly every dimension of public policy, Cato scholars focus on a wide range of issues. Included are policies about education, energy, finance, health, taxes, trade, and immigration. The Cato Institute commissions and publishes more than a dozen books a year and produces *The Cato Journal* three times a year, a quarterly magazine, *Regulation*, a bi-monthly Policy Report, an annual *Cato Supreme Court Review*, and many other publications. Cato's website provides continually updated resources on all sorts of issues.

Center for Bioethical Reform (CBR)

Both CBR (http://www.cbrinfo.org) and their Canadian sibling CCBR (see below) have the goal of making abortion unthinkable in the United States and Canada by using words and pictures to show the reality of what abortion does. They organize the Genocide Awareness Project displays on university campuses, drive massive billboards of aborted babies through cities, and train people to defend the humanity and worth of the unborn.

Although their graphic, in-your-face approach is controversial, the organization has played a big role in sparking societal discussion about abortion in ways that political organizations never could.

The Center for Public Justice (CPJ)

The Center for Public Justice (http://www.cpjustice.org) was established in 1977 in Washington, D.C. as the Association for Public Justice. The following year James Skillen was named executive director and he has headed the organization until 2009. The CPJ defines itself as "an independent, non-partisan organization dedicated to public policy research, leadership development, and civic education." With its distinctive Christian-democratic perspective, it helps "citizens, policy makers, and government respond to the call to pursue justice for all."

The CPJ believes that Christians should contribute to the renewal of public life. It approaches government and citizenship from a wide-ranging, comprehensive perspective. It recognizes different religions and points of view and wants to keep the public square open to people of all or no faiths. The Center believes government's authority is not limitless and that it should respect the responsibilities and rights of individuals and organizations. It seeks to act with a comprehensive, constitutional concern for political life in all of its dimensions—domestic as well as international.

The Center's philosophy of principled pluralism flows directly from its conviction that governments have not been ordained by God for the purpose of separating believers from unbelievers, giving privilege to Christians and the church, or serving the interests of one nation over others. This is a religious conviction that mandates publicly established religious freedom for all.

The Center has published a large number of books which are available through their website. The CPJ also produces a quarterly *Public Justice Report*, a biweekly *Capital Commentary*, periodic commentaries called *Root & Branch*, and *Citizen e-Link*, the Center's free, periodic electronic news bulletin. It also sponsors an annual Kuyper Lecture and runs two one-week inter-disciplinary summer programs about the Christian faith and politics called Civitas and The Civitas School.

CitizenLink

This organization (http://www.citizenlink.com) is an affiliate of Focus on the Family (http://www.focusonthefamily.com) which is a global Christian ministry dedicated to helping families thrive. CitizenLink is "a family advocacy organization that inspires men and women to live out biblical citizenship that transforms culture." It therefore provides "resources that equip citizens to make their voices heard on critical social policy issues involving the sanctity of human life, the preservation of religious liberties, and the well-being of the family as the building block of society." CitizenLink also helps "citizens understand and passionately engage in policy issues relevant to families from a foundation firmly established in a biblical worldview" and encourages them to participate in the democratic process in order to forge a better future for their children and their culture. After all, "Christians have a responsibility to promote truth and social policy that improves the strength and health of the family, and to preserve the proper roles for government, church and family, as God designed them."

To equip men and women for their task, CitizenLink provides resources that seek to educate, activate, and motivate or inspire. The following means are used to educate: daily emails, video features, *Rising Voice*, a policy outreach to the millennial generation, white papers with in-depth background information on current issues, *DriveThru Blog* which provides expert commentary, and *True Tolerance*, which helps parents create a safe school environment for children and their faith. The Action Center helps activate citizens by assisting them in getting access to legislators so that their voice can be heard. To inspire and motivate, CitizenLink reports on successes, both the high-profile ones and the involvement of ordinary citizens producing extraordinary results.

Heritage Foundation

Founded in 1973, The Heritage Foundation (http://www.heritage.org) is "a research and educational institution—a think tank—whose mission is to formulate and promote conservative public policies based on the principles of free enterprise, limited government, individual freedom, traditional American values, and a strong national defense." Heritage is one of the largest public policy research organizations in the United States. More than 710,000 individual members make it the most broadly supported think tank in America.

To accomplish its aims, Heritage has over a dozen policy centers which cover a wide diversity of issues such as foreign policy, judicial studies, health, religion and civil society, data analysis, and economic studies. These centers publish their research which is packaged in different formats to reach the target audience. Heritage's primary audiences are members of Congress, key congressional staff members, policy makers in the executive branch, the news media, and the academic and public policy communities.

In 2007, Heritage undertook a 10-year campaign for freedom, the Leadership for America campaign. It is a new effort to conserve liberty, and a sustained program to rebuild the foundations for the future.

National Association of Evangelicals (NAE)

The National Association of Evangelicals (http://www.nae.net) was founded in 1942, "represents more than 45,000 local churches from over 40 different denominations, and serves a constituency of millions." This diverse body seeks to stand publicly for biblical truth. Among its different interests, such as helping churches and giving humanitarian assistance to those suffering, it has the desire to bring biblical values to the political sphere. The NAE's political action is based on the document *For the Health of the Nation: An Evangelical Call to Civic Responsibility* which is available on their website. It outlines seven different issues important to evangelicals: religious freedom, children and family, the sanctity of life, the poor and vulnerable, human rights, peace, and creation care. In all these areas the NAE seeks to involve and mobilize its membership in the public sphere, drafts policy resolutions on a wide variety of issues, and takes legal action in select court cases. It also publishes a quarterly newsletter, *Insight*.

Witherspoon Institute

The Witherspoon Institute (http://www.winst.org) is "an independent research center that works to enhance public understanding of the moral foundations of free and democratic societies. Located in

Princeton, New Jersey, the Institute promotes the application of fundamental principles of republican government and ordered liberty to contemporary problems through a variety of research and educational ventures." This conservative think tank does its ambitious research agenda through six Research Programs: Science and Ethics; Business and Ethics; Ethics, Culture, and Economic Development; Family, Marriage, and Democracy; Political Thought and Constitutional Government; and Religion and Civil Society. Its extensive educational mission is realized through the scholarly work of the Simon Center and the Center on Ethics and the University.

It publishes a quarterly newsletter, *Public Discourse: Ethics, Law, and the Common Good*, an online journal, and books. The most recent publications include studies on diverse topics such as the cost of pornography, a defense of marriage, and the human embryo as a human person worthy of full moral respect. The website also has helpful links to recent relevant articles published by others.

CANADA

The Canadian organizations are generally much smaller and fewer in number than their American counterparts, even on a per capita basis. The level of political engagement among evangelicals in Canada has declined noticeably in the last decade. Roman Catholics and Reformed Christians make up a large percentage of the active groups. Of the groups below, most have only a handful of employees.

Association for Reformed Political Action (ARPA) Canada

Its website (http://www.arpacanada.ca) states that "the mission of ARPA Canada is to educate, equip, and encourage Reformed Christians to political action and to shine the light of God's Word to Canada's municipal, provincial, and federal governments."

ARPA Canada has seen huge growth and interest since it started in 2007. The organization is devoted to political advocacy by equipping grassroots Christians with the tools they need to be a salt and light in secular Canada. It is also increasingly bringing a Christian perspective to Canada's national Parliament, provincial legislatures, and the courts. Furthermore, ARPA Canada established the *Stand Up for Freedom Canada!* campaign, to protect fundamental freedoms from Canada's human rights commissions (http://www.humanrightscommissions.ca).

Visitors to ARPA's website can make use of their Easy Mail technology, subscribe to their newsletter, and explore their extensive resources: everything from government submissions to audio clips of talks ARPA hosted.

There are numerous local ARPA chapters that exist across Canada, each of which is operated independently of ARPA Canada. This allows the local groups to pursue the issues they want in a way that works for the people involved. Their locations are available at ARPA's website.

Campaign Life Coalition (CLC)

CLC (http://campaignlifecoalition.com) calls itself "the premiere advocate for legal and cultural change in Canada with respect to protecting human life and the family" and organizes the annual March for Life in Ottawa. This national organization makes many resources available through its extensive website and its online store. It also publishes a monthly *Newsletter* and a monthly newspaper called, *The Interim* (http://www.theinterim.com). Furthermore, CLC is the founder of LifeSite News website (http://www.lifesitenews.com) which features Canadian, American, and international news, as well as news in Spanish.

Canadian Centre for Bioethical Reform (CCBR)

The CCBR (http://www.unmaskingchoice.ca) is the Canadian sibling of its American counterpart, the CBR, mentioned above. Their goals and methods are similar.

Canadian Centre for Policy Studies (CCPS)

The CCPS (http://www.policystudies.ca) is "an independent, not-for-profit institution dedicated to the advancement of freedom and prosperity through the development and promotion of good public policy." Its guiding principles include limited, constitutional government; free markets; a justice system that holds everyone equally accountable, punishing criminal offenders and protecting the law-abiding; responsible, fact-based stewardship of the environment; respect for the natural family as the essential building blocks of a free, prosperous and democratic society; and respect for the intrinsic value of all human life, from conception to natural death.

The Centre pursues its agenda by promoting its principles, by encouraging sensible public laws, policies and practices in Canada that reflect and respect those principles, and by providing Canadians with the knowledge, skills, and support necessary to effectively promote these goals. The Centre conducts independent analysis of existing policy and legislation, develops and promotes policy alternatives, and educates policy-makers and the general public through publications, conferences, seminars and public lectures. The Centre's online public library is a rich resource on a wide range of issues.

Cardus

Cardus (http://www.cardus.ca) describes itself as "a think tank dedicated to the renewal of North American social architecture." Drawing on more than 2000 years of Christian social thought, it works "to enrich and challenge public debate through research, events and publications, for the common good." Their research focuses on four key areas of North American public life: cities, civic core, education and culture, and work and economics. Cardus publishes three journals: *Comment* which especially targets young intellectuals, *Policy in Public*, an occasional journal of political and policy analysis, and *LexView* which deals with court decisions. Its purpose is "to review cases that have important social, cultural, public policy, human rights and moral implications."

Centre for Faith and Public Life (CFPL)
of the Evangelical Fellowship of Canada (EFC)

The EFC (http://www.evangelicalfellowship.ca) "promotes an evangelical Christian understanding on matters of law and public policy. Through its Centre for Faith and Public Life in Ottawa, it intervenes before government and the courts on issues of concern to Evangelicals, seeking to uphold care for the vulnerable, religious freedom, sanctity of human life, marriage and family, and freedom of conscience. The EFC develops guiding principles for response to these issues in a manner that reflects our Christian citizenship."

The Centre for Faith and Public Life has a team of experienced employees including two lawyers. The Centre has intervened in numerous court cases, up to the Supreme Court of Canada, on a wide variety of issues such as reproductive technologies, same-sex marriage, and religious freedom. The Centre has earned a reputation as a solid, trustworthy source for research and analysis of political and legal issues. They are well-grounded in biblical truth and do their best to avoid sensationalism.

Christian Heritage Party of Canada (CHP)

The CHP (http://www.chp.ca) was registered as an official federal political party in 1986. "The CHP is Canada's only pro-Life federal political party, and the only federal party that endorses the Judeo-Christian principles enshrined in the Canadian Constitution: 'Canada was founded upon principles that recognize the supremacy of God and the rule of law.'"

The CHP was not set up because there were no Christians in the other federal parties. However, party discipline was considered too restrictive so that "Christian members of Parliament in the major parties are not permitted to bring their deepest convictions into parliamentary debates: they are told by their caucuses what to say, and when."

While it desires to honor Canada's Christian heritage, the CHP has no intention to force all Canadians to become Christian. Freedom of religion is one of the things the Party is fighting for. The CHP does however derive its "policies and platform from the ultimate authority, the Word of the Living God." The party website details their platform on a variety of political issues including immigration, economy, family, health care, justice, and the environment.

Christian Legal Fellowship of Canada (CLF)

The CLF (http://www.christianlegalfellowship.org) is "is a national not-for-profit, charitable organization founded in 1978 out of the conviction that the vocation of law is a calling from God." It is "dedicated to uniting Christians involved in the administration, practice, teaching and study of law by supporting their efforts to love and serve Jesus Christ and by equipping and motivating them to advocate for justice and religious freedom. The CLF is dedicated to serving the body of Christ by informing the Christian community about legal issues affecting them and by advocating a biblical Christian worldview of law and justice in the public sphere."

This association of lawyers, law students, and others participates in legal interventions on constitutional cases impacting the unborn, the family, and religious freedom. It hosts numerous conferences, seminars, and institutes devoted to challenging Christian lawyers and law students to boldly apply their skills to God's glory. It also makes submissions to government and provides legal support on public issues to other Christian organizations. Furthermore, the CLF has a lawyer referral service that is available through their website.

It publishes a *Newsletter*, including *Law Watch* which reports on current legal issues, and the *Christian Legal Journal*, a scholarly quarterly which addresses relevant legal issues from a Christian perspective.

Fraser Institute

The Fraser Institute (http://www.fraserinstitute.org) is a conservative economic think tank whose vision "is a free and prosperous world where individuals benefit from great choice, competitive markets, and personal responsibility." Their mission "is to measure, study, and communicate the impact of competitive markets and government interventions on the welfare of individuals." Its success has been heralded by leaders from across the political spectrum. It develops research that is meant to be easily understood and accessible. The Institute is Canada's leading public policy think tank. It is credited with shaping Canadian economic policy, both provincially (especially British Columbia, Alberta, and Ontario) and federally (beginning with the Paul Martin Liberal government, 2003–2006) and giving Canada a fiscally conservative reputation.

The Institute publishes a detailed annual report which covers a wide array of policy issues including such diverse topics as health care, energy, and education. It also produces a monthly magazine, *Fraser Forum* which offers analysis and perspectives on a wide range of issues, a quarterly, *Canadian Student Review*, with articles on public policy and current affairs, and a French-language public policy magazine, *Perspectives*. The Institute also runs various educational programs geared to students, teachers, parents, and journalists.

Institute of Marriage and Family Canada (IMFC)

After years of trying to react to the many political and legal challenges against marriage and the family (divorce, same-sex marriage, three-parent families) Focus on the Family Canada took a different approach. In 2006 it started the IMFC (http://www.imfcanada.org) in Ottawa with the aim of bringing good research into the hands of the decision-makers.

Since the family is the foundation of society, the IMFC "conducts, compiles, and presents the latest and most accurate research to ensure that marriage and family-friendly policy are foremost in the minds of Canada's decision makers."

The IMFC has already seen great success in its short existence. It regularly publishes studies, hosts conferences, and makes numerous appearances in the mainstream media. If the federal government is considering a new policy related to the family, it is likely that the IMFC will be called upon for its perspective.

The IMFC website makes much research available, both for ordinary Canadians and those seeking more specialized studies. The Institute also publishes a bi-weekly email, *eReview*, written by IMFC researchers.

Justice Centre for Constitutional Freedoms (JCCF)

The JCCF (http://www.jccf.ca) was founded in 2010 by constitutional lawyer John Carpay. It is a non-religious charity with the mission to advance "the human rights and constitutional freedoms of each and every Canadian through research, education and litigation to safeguard individual freedom and equality before the law." The organization has taken on two key areas of focus: defending student pro-life groups that have been the subject of censorship across Canada and defending those who are subject to the country's infamous human rights commissions.

Manning Centre

The Manning Centre (http://www.manningcentre.ca) has the mission "to identify, develop, and support political entrepreneurs who can advance our common vision of a free and democratic Canada guided by conservative principles." Its vision is for "a free and democratic Canada where conservative principles are well articulated, understood, and implemented." This vision is fuelled by values that include: individual freedom, worth, and responsibility; free markets, freedom of choice, and limited government; Canada's cultural, religious, and democratic traditions; strong families and communities; and grassroots, democratic participation and decision-making.

The Centre seeks to implement their vision by offering courses for people wanting to get involved in politics through their School of Practical Politics; organizing an annual Manning Networking Conference; encouraging and equipping people of faith through its Faith-political Interface Program; encouraging and supporting research and policy innovation; and training and encouraging the next generation of conservative leaders, activists, and policy innovators through their intern and mentorship programs.

BRITAIN

Jubilee Centre

The Jubilee Centre (http://www.jubilee-centre.org) was founded in 1983 in Cambridge. It "is a Christian social reform organisation that offers a biblical perspective on issues and trends of relevance to the general public." It holds that "the Bible describes a coherent vision for society that has enduring relevance for Britain and the world in the twenty-first century. At the heart of this social vision is a concern for right relationships." It seeks "to study, disseminate and apply this vision in order to provide a positive response to the challenges faced by individuals, communities and policy makers." The Jubilee Centre maintains that "there is and ought to be a constructive relationship between social reform and the advance of the gospel. The fruitfulness of this relationship was understood by nineteenth-century reformers like Wilberforce, but too often neglected by the church in the twenty-first century. 'Love of neighbour' requires us to take an interest in reforming the structures of society, not just in alleviating symptoms."

The Centre sponsors or is involved in much published research on how the Bible gives direction to current challenges and difficulties. This can take the form of books, such as the important *Jubilee Manifesto: A Framework, Agenda, and Strategy for Christian Social Reform* (2005). The Centre also produces reports presenting interim or final conclusions on their research of issues facing Britain such as co-habitation, marriage, homosexuality, education, health, the West's Christian heritage, justice, the environment, and many other topics. Other resources coming from the Jubilee Centre include the *Cambridge Papers*, a quarterly peer-reviewed publication which helps Christians respond to the ideas shaping society, *Bible Studies* that apply biblical teaching to a wide array of contemporary issues, and multimedia resources. The determination of the Centre to be relevant is also evident from its Fair Sex Movement, "an informal movement that seeks to promote a greater awareness of the personal, social, and economic consequences of sexual relationships."

Questions for Further Discussion

THE QUESTIONS LISTED ARE meant to encourage further discussion and ideally should only mark a beginning point. Additional resources are listed at the end of each chapter.

CHAPTER 1: THE HERITAGE OF THE WESTERN WORLD

1. What evidence of Christian heritage can you see in your country's politics?
2. What evidence of humanism can you see in the current political scene?
3. The majority can be wrong. So, what is good about democracy?
4. If true freedom is freedom from the dominion of sin, what implications does this truth have for the type of legislation that should be passed? What are the challenges in this regard?
5. Are the foundational natural rights of humanism (life, liberty, and property) incompatible with scripture? Or is it only the foundation that departs from God?

CHAPTER 2: THE ORIGIN AND TASK OF GOVERNMENT

1. What are the practical implications of government being God's servant for good with respect to your relationship to the governing authorities? Discuss in relation to your expectations and responsibilities.
2. Do you think your local, regional, or national government is being unnecessarily intrusive or not? Discuss.
3. Why do the labels of liberal or conservative not really cover the options that a Christian faces in evaluating the role of government?

4. Should government have any role in funding or regulating early childhood education? Primary school? Secondary school? Post-secondary education? Why?

5. How would you prioritize the tasks of government and why?

CHAPTER 3: CHURCH AND STATE

1. Discuss a historical example of the state having too much say over the church and an example of a church meddling in political affairs. What lessons do these situations teach us?

2. What is the relationship between church and state in voluntaryism, in theonomy, in principled pluralism?

3. What is the difference between the church and God's kingdom? What practical impact does this difference have for a political agenda?

4. Does the church have to be silent about the affairs of the state? How is the church's role different than the role of the members of the church?

5. Should government require prayer in public schools?

CHAPTER 4: HUMAN RIGHTS, MORAL NORMS, AND TOLERATION

1. What is a biblical understanding of human rights and how does it help to address current human right issues? How does the understanding of human rights in the American Bill of Rights and the Canadian Charter of Rights and Freedoms affect current discussion?

2. What did Thomas Jefferson have to say about liberty? Who is giving this message in Western society today?

3. What are some biblical examples of tolerating sin in a fallen world? What prompted this toleration and does it give a general license to tolerate evil?

4. What are some prerequisites for ensuring a fair and open debate in public life?

5. In what ways can government show moral leadership and guide the nation in a manner that is in harmony with its Christian heritage?

CHAPTER 5: LIFE AND DEATH

1. How is Exodus 21:22–25 read to condone abortion? How is this a misunderstanding of the text? What other passages affirm this misunderstanding?
2. Why is it so difficult to talk about abortion in our society?
3. What is Scripture's response to the argument that disabled people should be able to end their lives because they no longer enjoy sufficient quality of life?
4. How can Christians best meet the challenge offered by those lobbying for legalizing euthanasia?
5. How would following biblical principles dramatically reduce the likelihood of an unjust conviction in a murder trial?

CHAPTER 6: MARRIAGE AND FAMILY

1. How does marriage speak to humanity's uniqueness in creation?
2. How can Christians strengthen their marriages and show the beauty of this institution to a culture and society where this institution is weakening and underappreciated?
3. What are some consequences of legislation creating the new category of same-sex marriage?
4. What is the role of government in upholding marriage as God defined it?
5. What are some consequences of a falling birth rate? What, if anything, should government do about it?

CHAPTER 7: WORK AND REST

1. How is work a blessing from God given at creation?
2. How should Christians decide on a career?
3. What are the tasks of government with respect to work? How do they impact on your occupation?
4. How have the duties of church and state with respect to the Lord's Day been confused in Western history? What lessons can we draw from that today?

5. How important is a weekly day of rest? Should the state enforce such a day? What day should that be and why? What are the implications for a multi-cultural society?

CHAPTER 8: THE ENVIRONMENT

1. Does the divine mandate to "fill the earth" still apply today? If it does, will the time come when that mandate has been fulfilled?
2. What do the commands to subdue the earth and take care of the garden (Gen 1:28; 2:15) mean and not mean?
3. Give some recent examples of radical environmentalism that you have noticed in the media recently. How would you respond?
4. Is sharing a holistic Christian approach to the environment part of our mission task? Is it a good way to evangelize? Why or why not?
5. How can Christians help revitalize urban downtown areas? Why is this important from an environmental perspective? Should more consideration be given to locating new churches downtown rather than in the suburbs?

CHAPTER 9: MULTICULTURALISM

1. How is nationhood a divine ordinance? What are the implications?
2. How were resident aliens and foreigners treated in Israel? What does that teach us today? How can biblical guidelines realistically be incorporated into current law?
3. What presuppositions of multiculturalism are flawed and why?
4. How can immigrants be encouraged to assimilate?
5. How can you as a Christian help your immigrant neighbor?

CHAPTER 10: GETTING INVOLVED

1. What are some parallels between the recipients of Jeremiah's letter to the exiles and us today?
2. What is the meaning and message of Christ's words: "Give to Caesar what is Caesar's, and to God what is God's"?

3. Should Christians ask for public funding of Christian schools?
4. How should you interact with your elected representatives? Give some guidelines.
5. What is compromise and how can it be biblically justified? What are the limits of compromise?

Bibliography

Aalders, G. Ch. *Genesis*. 2 vols. Translated by William Heynen. Bible Student's Commentary. Grand Rapids, MI: Zondervan, 1981.
Adamopoulo, Themistocles. "The Triumph of the Gospel of Love." In *Orthodox Research Institute* (October-November 1988). No Pages. Online: http://www.orthodoxresearchinstitute.org/articles/church_history/themistocles_triumph_love.htm.
Adams, James Luther. *On Being Human Religiously: Selected Essays in Religion and Society*. 2nd ed. Edited by Max L. Stackhouse. Boston: Beacon Press, 1986.
Affidavit #1 of Joseph Henrich Sworn July 15th, 2010 in the Supreme Court of British Columbia. Online: http://www.vancouversun.com/pdf/affidavit.pdf.
Agence France-Presse. "Multiculturalism 'clearly' a Failure: Sarkozy," *National Post* (February 10, 2011). No Pages. Online: http://www.nationalpost.com/news/Multiculturalism+clearly+failure+Sarkozy/4261825/story.html.
Aguirre, M. Sophia, and et al. *Marriage and the Public Good: Ten Principles*. Princeton, NJ: The Witherspoon Institute, 2008.
'Ali, 'Abdullah Yūsuf. *The Meaning of the Holy Qur'ān*. Rev. translation, commentary, and newly compiled comprehensive index, 11th ed. Beltsville, MD: Amana, 2006.
American Medical Association. "Opinion 2.21 - Euthanasia." *AMA Code of Medical Ethics*. No Pages. Online: http://www.ama-assn.org/ama/pub/physician-resources/medical-ethics/code-medical-ethics/opinion221.page.
American Medical Association. "Opinion 2.211 - Physician-Assisted Suicide." In *AMA Code of Medical Ethics*. No Pages. Online: http://www.ama-assn.org/ama/pub/physician-resources/medical-ethics/code-medical-ethics/opinion2211.page.
"American Revisions to the Westminster Confession of Faith." No pages. Online: http://www.opc.org/documents/WCF_orig.html.
"Another Ice Age?" *Time Magazine* (June 24, 1974). No Pages. Online: http://www.time.com/time/magazine/article/0,9171,944914,00.html.
Arkes, Hadley. "Always to Care, Never to Kill : A Declaration on Euthanasia." *First Things* 20 (February 1992) 45–47.
Audi, Robert and Nicholas Wolterstorff. *Religion in the Public Square: The Place of Religious Convictions in Political Debate*. Lanham, MD: Rowman & Littlefield, 1997.
Baklinski, Thaddeus. "California Passes Bill Mandating Pro-gay Teaching in Schools, No Parent Opt-out." (July 6, 2011). No Pages. Online: http://www.lifesitenews.com/news/california-passes-bill-mandating-pro-gay-teaching-in-schools-no-parent-opt.

Bahnsen, Greg L. "The Theonomic Position." In *God and Politics: Four Views on the Reformation of Civil Government*, edited by Gary Scott Smith, 21–53. Phillipsburg NJ: Presbyterian and Reformed, 1989.

———. "The Theonomic Reformed Approach to Law and Gospel." In *The Law, the Gospel, and the Modern Christian: Five Views*, edited by Wayne G. Strickland, 93–143. Grand Rapids, MI: Zondervan, 1993.

———. *Theonomy in Christian Ethics*. Nutley NJ: Craig, 1977.

Bakhuizen van den Brink, J. N. *De Nederlandse Belijdensgeschriften*. 2d ed. 1940. Amsterdam: Ton Bolland, 1976.

Barker, William S. "Theonomy, Pluralism, and the Bible." In *Theonomy: A Reformed Critique*, eds William S. Barker and W. Robert Godfrey, 226–42. Grand Rapids, MI: Zondervan, 1990.

Bat Ye'or. "Europe and the Ambiguities of Multiculturalism." (November 2006). No Pages. Online: http://jihadwatch.org/dhimmiwatch/archives/013959.php.

———. *Eurabia: The Euro-Arab Axis*. Madison, NJ: Fairleigh Dickinson University Press, 2005.

———. *Islam and Dhimmitude: Where Civilizations Collide*. Madison, NJ: Fairleigh Dickinson University Press, 2002.

Bavinck, Herman. *Reformed Dogmatics*. 4 vols. Edited by John Bolt. Translated by John Vriend. Grand Rapids, MI: Baker Academic, 2003–08.

Bawer, Bruce. *While Europe Slept: How Radical Islam is Destroying the West from Within*. New York: Doubleday, 2006.

Bayer, Stefan. "Climate Change." In *RPP* 3: 248–49.

BBC. "State Multiculturalism Has Failed, Says David Cameron." In *News UK Politics* (February 5, 2011). No Pages. Online: http://www.bbc.co.uk/news/uk-politics-12371994.

Beale, G. K. *The Book of Revelation: A Commentary on the Greek Text*. NIGTC. Grand Rapids, MI: Eerdmans, 1999.

Beckwith, Roger T. and Wilfrid Stott. *The Christian Sunday. A Biblical and Historical Study*. Grand Rapids, MI: Baker Book House, 1978.

Bedau, Hugo Adam. *The Death Penalty in America: Current Controversies*. New York: Oxford University Press, 1997.

Beisner, E. Calvin. *Prospects for Growth: A Biblical View of Population, Resources, and the Future*. Westchester, IL: Crossway, 1990.

———. *Prosperity and Poverty: The Compassionate Use of Resources in a World of Scarcity*. Westchester IL: Crossway, 1988.

Belmonte, Kevin. *William Wilberforce: A Hero for Humanity*. Foreword by Charles Colson. Grand Rapids, MI: Zondervan, 2007.

Bennett, Jessica. "Only You. And You. And You. Polyamory—Relationships with Multiple, Mutually Consenting Partners—Has a Coming-Out Party." In *Newsweek* (July 29, 2009). No Pages. Online: http://www.thedailybeast.com/newsweek/2009/07/28/only-you-and-you-and-you.html.

Berman, Harold. "Religious Foundations of Law in the West: An Historical Perspective." *Journal of Law and Religion* 1 (1983) 3–43.

"Bill C-2: An Act to Amend the Criminal Code." In *Parliament of Canada* (September 7, 2008). No Pages. Online: http://www.parl.gc.ca/legisinfo/billdetails.aspx?Bill=C2&language=e&mode=1&Parl=39&ses=2&view=1.

Birch, Bruce C. *Let Justice Roll Down: The Old Testament, Ethics, and Christian Life*. Louisville: Westminster/John Knox, 1991.

Bissett, James. *Demography is Destiny: Toward a Canada-First Immigration Policy*. Ottawa: Canadian Centre for Policy Studies, 2008.
Blizzard, Rick. "Canadians and the Ethics of Euthanasia." In *Gallup* (July 23, 2002). No Pages. Online: http://www.gallup.com/poll/6442/canadians-ethics-euthanasia.aspx.
Block, Daniel I. "Nations/Nationality." In *NIDOTTE*, 4.966–72.
Boersema, John. *Political-Economic Activity to the Honour of God*. Winnipeg: Premier, 1999.
Bolt, John. "Abraham Kuyper and the Search for an Evangelical Public Theology." In *Evangelicals in the Public Square: Four Formative Voices on Political Thought and Action*, ed. J. Budziszewski, 141–61. Grand Rapids, MI: Baker Academic, 2006.
———. "The Background and Context of Van Ruler's Theocentric (Theocratic Vision)." In *Calvinist Trinitarianism and Theocentric Politics: Essays Toward a Public Theology*, by Arnold A. Van Ruler, translated by John Bolt. Lewiston: Edwin Mellen, 1989.
Book of Praise: Anglo-Genevan Psalter. Authorized provisional version. Winnipeg: Premier, 2010.
Bork, Robert H. *Coercing Virtue: The Worldwide Rule of Judges*. The Barbara Frum Lectureship. Toronto: Vintage Canada, 2002.
Bos, E., et al. *Samenwonen Verplicht: Aanzet Voor Een Regeling Van Niet-Huwelijkse Samenlevingsvormen*. Groen Van Prinsterer-Reeks. Groningen: De Vuurbaak, 1995.
Bradley Hagerty, Barbara. "Some Muslims in U. S. Quietly Engage in Polygamy." In *NPR* (May 27, 2008). No Pages. Online: http://www.npr.org/templates/story/story.php?storyId=90857818.
Brandon, Guy. *Just Sex: Is It Ever Just Sex?* Nottingham, UK: Inter-Varsity Press, 2009.
Bremmer, R.H. *Reformatie en Rebellie: Willem Van Oranje, de Calvinisten en Het Recht Van Opstand. Tien Onstuimige Jaren 1572–1581*. Franeker: Wever, 1984.
Broeckaert, Bert, and Rien Janssens. "Palliative Care and Euthanasia: Belgian and Dutch Perspectives." In *Euthanasia and Palliative Care in the Low Countries*, edited by Paul Schotsmans and Tom Meulenbergs, 35–69. Leuven: Peeters, 2005.
Brutus, Junius. *A Defence of Liberty Against Tyrants or, of the Lawful Power of the Prince Over the People and of the People Over the Prince*. With an introduction by David E. Goodrum. Edmonton: Still Waters Revival Books, 1989 (reprinted from the 1689 translation).
Bullmore, Michael A. "The Four Most Important Biblical Passages for a Christian Environmentalism." *Trinity Journal* NS 19 (1998) 139–62.
Burnside, Jonathan, and Nicola Baker, eds. *Relational Justice: Repairing the Breach*. Winchester: Waterside Press, 1994.
Burnside, Jonathan, P. *God, Justice, and Society*. Oxford: Oxford University Press, 2011.
———. *The Status and Welfare of Immigrants: The Place of the Foreigner in Biblical Law and Its Relevance to Contemporary Society*. Cambridge: The Jubilee Centre, 2001.
Cadoux, Cecil John. *The Early Church and the World: A History of the Christian Attitude to Pagan Society and the State Down to the Time of Constantinus*. Edinburgh: T. & T. Clark, 1925.

Calvin, John. *Commentaries on the First Book of Moses Called Genesis*. Translated from the original Latin and compared with the French edition by John King. 1847. Grand Rapids, MI: Eerdmans, 1948.

———. *Letters of John Calvin. Compiled from the Original Manuscripts and Edited with Historical Notes by Jules Bonnet*. 4 vols. Philadelphia, PA: Presbyterian Board of Publication, 1858.

———. *On God and Political Duty*. 2nd ed. Ed. with an introd. by John T. McNeill. Indianapolis: Bobbs-Merrill, 1956.

"Canada's Christian Heritage Web Site." No pages. Online: http://www.ccheritage.ca.

"The Canadian Charter of Rights and Freedoms." In *Part I of the Constitution Act, 1982*. No Pages. Online: http://lois.justice.gc.ca/eng/charter/page-1.html.

Canadian Medical Association. "Euthanasia and Assisted Suicide (Update 1998)." In *CMA*. No Pages. Online: http://www.cma.ca/index.php/ci_id/3214/la_id/1.htm.

Card, Brigham Young, Herbert C. Northcott, and John Foster, eds. *The Mormon Presence in Canada*. Edmonton, AB: The University of Alberta Press, 1990.

The Centre for Faith and Public Life, *When Two Become One: The Unique Nature and Benefits of Marriage*. 3rd ed. Markham, ON: Faith Today Publications, 2006.

Cere, Daniel. "War of the Ring." In *Divorcing Marriage: Unveiling the Dangers in Canada's New Social Experiment*, edited by Daniel Cere and Douglas Farrow, 9–28. Montreal and Kingston: Mc-Gill Queen's University Press, 2004.

Chalifoux, Marc, and J. D. M. Stewart. "Canada is Failing History." In *The Globe and Mail* (June 18, 2009). No Pages. Online: http://www.theglobeandmail.com/news/opinions/canada-is-failing-history/article1184615.

Chamberlain, Paul. *Talking About Good and Bad Without Getting Ugly: A Guide to Moral Persuasion*. Downers Grove, IL: InterVarsity Press, 2005.

Chaplin, Jonathan. "Political Eschatology and Responsible Government: Oliver O'Donovan's 'Christian Liberalism'." In *A Royal Priesthood? The Use of the Bible Ethically and Politically. A Dialogue with Oliver O'Donovan*, eds. Craig Bartholomew, Jonathan Chaplin, Robert Song, and Al Wolters. Scripture and Hermeneutics Series, vol. 3. Carlisle, U.K. / Grand Rapids, MI: Paternoster. Zondervan, 2002.

———. *Talking God: The Legitimacy of Religious Public Reasoning*. London: Theos, 2008.

Chesler, Phyllis. "Are Honor Killings Simply Domestic Violence?" *Middle East Quarterly* 16:2 (Spring 2009) 61–69. Online: http://www.meforum.org/2067/are-honor-killings-simply-domestic-violence.

Chewning, Richard C., ed. *Biblical Principles and Economics: The Foundations*. Colorado Springs CO: NavPress, 1989.

Cochrane, Arthur C., ed. *Reformed Confessions of the 16th Century*. Philadelphia: Westminster, 1966.

Cohen, Patricia. "Yale Press Bans Images of Muhammad in New Book." In *The New York Times* (August 12, 2009). No Pages. Online: http://www.nytimes.com/2009/08/13/books/13book.html.

Colijn, H. *Van de Overheid en 's Heeren Wet:Overdruk Van Artikelen Uit De Standaard*. 'S-Gravenhage: Dr. A. Kuyperstichting, [1925].

Colson, Charles W. and Nancy Pearcey. *How Now Shall We Live?* Wheaton, IL: Tyndale, 2000.

Colson, Chuck. "Illegal Immigration: The Real Root of the Problem." In *BreakPoint* (April 11, 2006). No Pages. Online: *http://thepoint.breakpoint.org /bpcommentaries/entry/13/13595*.

Connolly, Kate. "Angela Merkel Declares Death of German Multiculturalism." In *Guardian, UK,* (October 17, 2010). No Pages. Online: http://www.guardian.co.uk/world/2010/oct/17/angela-merkel-germany-multiculturalism-failures.

"The Constitution of the Reformed Presbyterian Church." No Pages. Online: http://reformedpresbyterian.org/download/constitution.pdf

"Convention on the Rights of the Child." In *Office of the United Nations High Commissioner for Human Rights*. No Pages. Online: http://www2.ohchr.org/english/law/crc.htm.

Cooper, Barry. *Sins of Omission: Shaping the News at CBC TV*. Toronto; Buffalo: University of Toronto Press, 1994.

Cooper, Helen, and Abby Goodnough. "Over Beers, No Apologies, but Plans to Have Lunch." In *New York Times* (July 30, 2009). No Pages. http://www.nytimes.com/2009/07/31/us/politics/31obama.html.

Corbella, Licia. "Christ's Name Banned from Memorial." *The Calgary Sun* (13 December 1998). No pages. Online: http://fathersforlife.org/rights/swiss_air_111_crash.htm.

Craine, Patrick B. "Toronto School Board: Parents Can't Opt Kids Out of Pro-homosexual Curriculum" (June 8, 2011). No Pages. Online: http://www.bcptl.org/gay.htm.

D'Souza, Dinesh. *What's So Great About Christianity*. Washington: Regnery, 2007.

de Greef, Wulfert. *The Writings of John Calvin: An Introductory Guide*. Translated by Lyle D. Bierma. Louisville: Westminster John Knox Press, 2008.

de Gruchy, John W. *Christianity and Democracy*. Cambridge: Cambridge University Press, 1995.

de Vries, J. P. "Polygamie, de Bijbel en de Praktijk." *Nederlands Dagblad*, 30 March 1992.

de Vries, Tiemen. *Overheid en Zondagsviering*. Leiden: A. W. Sijthoff, 1899.

De Young, James B. *Homosexuality: Contemporary Claims Examined in the Light of the Bible and Other Ancient Literature and Law*. Grand Rapids, MI: Kregel, 2000.

DeKoster, Lester. *Work: The Meaning of Your Life. A Christian Perspective*. 2nd ed. With a foreword by Stephen J. Grabill, with an afterword by The Oikonomia Network. Grand Rapids, MI: Christian's Library Press, 2010.

DeMar, Gary. *America's Christian History: The Untold Story*. 1995. Powder Springs, GA: American Vision, 2008.

"Demographic Winter: The Decline of the Human Family." No pages. Online: http://www.demographicwinter.com/index.html.

Department of Justice. "Capital Punishment in Canada." In *Department of Justice Canada*. No Pages. Online: http://www.justice.gc.ca/eng/news-nouv/fs-fi/2003/doc_30896.html.

Dobbin, Jim, and et al. "Memorandum by the All-Party Parliamentary Pro-Life Group" (August 2004). In *Parliament UK Publications and Records*. No Pages. Online: http://www.publications.parliament.uk/pa/ld200405/ldselect/ldsdy/86/86we26.htm.

Doniger, Wendy. "Suttee," in *Encyclopaedia Brittanica*. No Pages. Online: http://www.britannica.com/EBchecked/topic/575795/suttee.

Douma, J. *Another Look at Dooyeweerd*. Trans. from the Dutch. Winnipeg: Premier, n.d.
———. *Politieke Verantwoordelijkheid*. Ethische Bezinning. Kampen: Van den Berg, 1984.
———. *The Ten Commandments: Manual for the Christian Life*. Translated by Nelson D. Kloosterman. Phillipsburg NJ: P & R, 1996.
———. *Responsible Conduct: Principles of Christian Ethics*. Translated by Nelson D. Kloosterman. Phillipsburg, NJ: P&R, 2003.
Dueck, Lorna. "Polygamous Challenge: A Case of Lost Common Sense." In *The Globe and Mail* (September 28, 2009). No Pages. Online: http://www.theglobeandmail.com/news/opinions/polygamous-challenge-a-case-of-lost-common-sense/article1302275/.
Duke, Steven. "Earth Population 'Exceeds Limits.'" In *BBC News* (March 31, 2009). No Pages. Online: http://news.bbc.co.uk/2/hi/7974995.stm.
Dunsmuir, Mollie. "Abortion: Constitutional and Legal Developments." In *Government of Canada Depository Services Program* (August 18, 1998). No Pages. Online: http://dsp-psd.pwgsc.gc.ca/Collection-R/LoPBdP/CIR/8910-e.htm.
Eberstadt, Mary, and Mary Anne Layden. *The Social Costs of Pornography: A Statement of Findings and Recommendations*. Princeton, NJ: The Witherspoon Institute, 2010.
The editors. "Harper Must Act Now to Protect Free Speech." In *Macleans* (September 20, 2009). No Pages. Online: http://www2.macleans.ca/2009/09/20/harper-must-act-now-to-protect-free-speech.
———. "Light-Bulb Ban Has Voters Incandescent with Rage." *Maclean's Magazine* 124:28 (2011) 4–5.
"Effects of Abortion." No Pages. Online: http://www.abortionfacts.com/effects/effects.asp.
Farah, Joseph. *Stop the Presses! The Inside Story of the New Media Revolution*. Los Angeles, CA: WND Books, 2007.
Farrow, Douglas. "Facing Reality." In *Divorcing Marriage: Unveiling the Dangers in Canada's New Social Experiment*, edited by Daniel Cere and Douglas Farrow, 155–73. Montreal and Kingston: Mc-Gill Queen's University Press, 2004.
———. "Of Secularity and Civil Religion." In *Recognizing Religion in a Secular Society: Essays in Pluralism, Religion, and Public Policy*, edited by Douglas Farrow, 140–82. Montreal and Kingston: McGill-Queen's University Press, 2005.
———. *Nation of Bastards*. Foreword by William D. Gairdner. Toronto: BPS Books, 2007.
Fathers for Life. "Marriage: A Taxing Affair." In *Fathers for Life* (March 14, 2001). No Pages. Online: http://fathersforlife.org/feminism/us_family_tax_plan.htm.
Feinberg, J. S., P. D. Feinberg, and A. Huxley. *Ethics for a Brave New World*. Wheaton, IL: Crossway, 1996.
Fennema, Meindert, Eimert Van Middelkoop, et al. *Integratie en Verzuiling: Bezinning Op de Multiculturele Samenleving*. Kort Commentaar. Amersfoort: Mr. G. Groen van Prinsterer Stichting / Wetenschappelijk Instituut ChristenUnie, 2003.
Fergusson, Sinclair B. "An Assembly of Theonomists? The Teaching of the Westminster Divines on the Law of God." In *Theonomy: A Reformed Critique*, eds William S. Barker and Godfrey W. Robert, 315–49. Grand Rapids, MI: Zondervan, 1990.

Fischer, Douglas. "Is Ethanol from Corn Bad for the Climate?" *Scientific American* (February 12, 2010). No Pages: Online: http://www.scientificamerican.com/article.cfm?id=ethanol-corn-climate&page=2.
For the Health of the Nation: An Evangelical Call to Civic Responsibility (2004). Online: http://www.nae.net/images/content/For_The_Health_Of_The_Nation.pdf.
Frame, John M. "Abortion from a Biblical Perspective." In *Thou Shalt not Kill*, edited by Richard L. Ganz, 43–75. New Rochelle, NY: Arlington House, 1978.
———. *Medical Ethics: Principles, Persons, and Problems*. Phillipsburg, NJ: Presbyterian and Reformed Publishing Company, 1988.
———. "Toward a Theology of the State." *Westminster Theological Journal* 51 (1989) 199–226.
———. *The Doctrine of the Christian Life*. A Theology of Lordship. Phillipsburg, NJ: P&R, 2008.
Fries, Paul Roy. "Religion and the Hope for a Truly Human Existence: An Inquiry Into the Theology of F. D. E. Schleiermacher and A. A. Van Ruler with Questions for America." Ph.D. diss. Utrecht: Rijksuniversiteit in Utrecht, 1979.
Frijhoff, Willem. "Religious Toleration in the United Provinces: From 'Case' to 'Model.'" In *Calvinism and Religious Toleration in the Dutch Golden Age*, eds R. Po-Chia Hsia and Henk van Nierop, 27–52. Cambridge: Cambridge University Press, 2002.
Gaer, Joseph, and Ben Siegel. *The Puritan Heritage: America's Roots in the Bible*. Toronto: Mentor Books, 1964.
Gagnon, Robert A. J. *The Bible and Homosexual Practice: Texts and Hermeneutics*. Nashville: Abingdon, 2001.
Gairdner, William D. *The War Against the Family: A Parent Speaks Out*. Toronto: Stoddart Publishing, 1992.
Gamble, Richard C. "Presbyterianism, Politics, and Westminster Theology." In *Unity in Diversity: Studies Presented to Prof. Dr. Jelle Faber on the Occasion of His Retirement*, edited by Riemer Faber. Hamilton: Senate of the Theological College of the Canadian Reformed Churches, 1989.
Gardoski, Kenneth M. "The Implications of Living Together Before Marriage." *Journal of Ministry and Theology* 7:1 (2003) 91–113.
George, Robert P. and Christopher Tollefsen. *Embryo: A Defense of Human Life*. New York: Doubleday, 2008.
Gilbert, Kathleen. "Americans Favor Laws Reducing Abortion, Shy Away from Outlawing Procedure: Polls." (March 14, 2011). No Pages. Online: http://www.lifesitenews.com/news/americans-favor-laws-reducing-abortion-shy-away-from-outlawing-procedure-po/.
———. "Roundup: Sudden Surge of Pro-Life Legislation in Numerous States." (March 4, 2011). No Pages. Online: http://www.lifesitenews.com/news/roundup-sudden-surge-of-pro-life-legislation-in-numerous-states/.
Gillis, Charlie, and Kate Lunau. "A World of 10 Billion." In *Macleans* (June 15, 2011). No Pages. Online: http://www2.macleans.ca/2011/06/15/a-world-of-10-billion/.
Glazebrook, M. G. "Sunday." *ERE* 12: 103–11.
Glazov, Jamie. "Symposium: The Muslim Persecution of Christians." In *Front Page Magazine* (October 10, 2003). No Pages. Online: http://archive.frontpagemag.com/readArticle.aspx?ARTID=15988.
Gleason, Ron. *The Death Penalty on Trial*. Ventura, CA: Nordskog Publishing, 2008.

Glover, Peter C., and Michael J. Economides. *Energy and Climate Wars: How Naive Politicians, Green Ideologues, and Media Elites Are Undermining the Truth About Energy and Climate.* New York: Continuum, 2010.

Godfrey, Tom. "Harems Pay Off for Muslims." In *Toronto Sun* (December 31, 2008). No Pages. Online: http://www.torontosun.com/news/torontoandgta/2008/12/31/7891231.html.

Godfrey, W. Robert. "Church and State in Dutch Calvinism." In *Through Christ's Word: A Festschrift for Dr. Philip E. Hughes,* eds W. Robert Godfrey and Jesse L. Boyd III, 223–43. Phillipsburg, NJ: Presbyterian and Reformed, 1985.

Gootjes, N. H. *Both in Life and Death: Biblical Notions in Connection with Today's Tendency Towards Euthanasia.* London ON: Inter-League Publication Board, 1994.

Gordis, Robert. "Democratic Origins in Ancient Israel - the Biblical 'ĒDĀH.'" In *Alexander Marx Jubilee Volume on the Occasion of His Seventieth Birthday, English Section,* 369–88. New York: The Jewish Theological Seminary of America, 1950.

"Gore Climate Film's Nine 'Errors.'" In *BBC News* (October 11, 2007). No Pages. Online: http://news.bbc.co.uk/2/hi/7037671.stm.

Gorman, Michael J. *Abortion and the Early Church.* Downers Grove, IL: InterVarsity Press, 1982.

Goudzwaard, Bob. *A Christian Political Option.* Trans. from the Dutch. Toronto: Wedge, 1972.

Grant, Jonathan, et al., *Population Implosion? Low Fertility and Policy Responses in the European Union.* Cambridge, UK: Rand Europe, 2005. Online: http://www.rand.org/content/dam/rand/pubs/research_briefs/2005/RAND_RB9126.pdf.

Green, Jennifer. "Christians Livid as CRTC Denies Religious Radio, but OKs Porn TV." *Ottawa Citizen,* April 7, 2009. No Pages. Online: http://www.ottawacitizen.com.

"Greenpeace Opposes Wind Farm Plan." In *BBC News* (April 6, 2005). No Pages. Online: http://news.bbc.co.uk/2/hi/uk_news/scotland/4415787.stm.

Gregg, Samuel. *Beyond Romanticism: Questioning the Green Gospel.* CIS Occasional Papers. St. Leonards, Australia: The Centre for Independent Studies, 2000.

Groen van Prinsterer, G. *Unbelief and Revolution: A Series of Historical Lectures,* 1847.

Grosby, Steven. *Biblical Ideas of Nationality: Ancient and Modern.* Winona Lake, IN: Eisenbrauns, 2002.

Groseclose, Tim, and Jeffrey Milyo. "A Measure of Media Bias." *The Quarterly Journal of Economics* 120 (2005) 1191–1237.

Grudem, Wayne. *Politics According to the Bible.* Grand Rapids, MI: Zondervan, 2010.

Haasdijk, Th., et al. *Zo Zijn Wij Niet Getrouwd: Over de Registratie Van Niet-Huwelijkse Samenlevingsvormed.* Groen Van Prinsterer-Reeks. Groningen: De Vuurbaak, 1992.

Hall, David W. *Calvin in the Public Square: Liberal Democracies, Rights, and Civil Liberties.* Phillipsburg, NJ: P&R, 2009.

Hart, D. G. *Defending the Faith: J. Gresham Machen and the Crisis of Conservative Protestantism in Modern America.* Baltimore: John Hopkins University Press, 1994.

———. *A Secular Faith: Why Christianity Favors the Separation of Church and State.* Chicago: Ivan R. Dee, 2006.

Hartwig, Mark. "Spread by the Sword?" In *Answering Islam*. No Pages. Online: http://answering-islam.org/Terrorism/by_the_sword.html.

Haskell, David M. *Through a Lens Darkly: How the News Media Perceive and Portray Evangelicals*. Toronto: Clements Academic, 2009.

Hassouneh-Phillips, Dena. "Polygamy and Wife Abuse: A Qualitative Study of Muslim Women in America." *Health Care for Women International* 22 (2001) 735–48.

Hays, J. Daniel. *From Every People and Nation: A Biblical Theology of Race*. New Studies in Biblical Theology. Leicester, UK / Downers Grove, IL: Apollos / Inter Varsity Press, 2003.

Hayward, John, and Guy Brandon. *Cohabitation in the 21st Century*. Cambridge, UK: Jubilee Centre, 2010.

———. "Our Forgotten Christian Heritage." No Pages. Online: http://www.jubilee-centre.org/blog/136/our_forgotten_christian_heritage.

Helmholz, R. H. "Western Canon Law." In *Christianity and Law: An Introduction*, eds John Witte Jr. and Frank S. Alexander, 71–87. Cambridge / New York: Cambridge University Press, 2008.

Henrich, Joseph. *Affidavit #1 of Joseph Henrich Sworn July 15th, 2010 in the Supreme Court of British Columbia*.

Hesselink, I. John. *Calvin's Concept of the Law*. Allision Park, PA: Pickwick, 1992.

Hobbes, Thomas. *Leviathan*. Edited with an introduction and notes by J.C.A. Gaskin. Oxford World's Classics. Oxford ; New York: Oxford University Press, 1998.

Hoffner, Harry. "Hittite Laws." In *COS*, 2:106–19, 2000.

Hudson, Winthrop S. "Democratic Freedom and Religious Faith in the Reformed Tradition." *Church History* 15 (1946) 177–94.

Human and Constitutional Rights Documents. No Pages. Online: http://www.hrcr.org/docs/frenchdec.html.

Human Resources and Skill Development Canada. "Sunday Closing and Weekly Rest Periods: Historical Evolution and Current Situation." No Pages. Online: http://www.hrsdc.gc.ca/eng/labour/labour_law/esl/weekly_rest.shtml.

Hunter, Ian. "If Life is Cheap, Death is Cheaper." *The Globe and Mail*, Friday, December 1 2000, A15.

Hunter, James Davison. *To Change the World: The Irony, Tragedy, and Possibility of Christianity in the Late Modern World*. New York: Oxford University Press, 2010.

Huntington, Samuel P. *The Clash of Civilizations and the Remaking of the World Order*. New York: Simon & Schuster, 2003.

———. *Who Are We? The Challenges to America's National Identity*. New York: Simon & Schuster, 2005.

Hurley, Dan. "Divorce Rate: It's not as High as You Think." In *New York Times* (April 19, 2005). No Pages. Online: http://www.nytimes.com/2005/04/19/health/19divo.html.

Huston, Warner Todd. "Islamists Rule American Publishing Industry." No Pages. Online: http://www.familysecuritymatters.org/publications/id.830/pub_detail.asp.

The Independent Electricity System Operator (IESO). *Ontario's Long Term Energy Plan: Building Our Clean Energy Future*. In *Ontario Ministry of Energy* (2 March 2011). Online: http://www.ieso.ca/imoweb/pubs/consult/sac/sac-20110302-Item5_LTEP.pdf.

The Islamisation of Britain: And What Must Be Done to Prevent It. A Pilcrow Press Report. N.p.: Pilcrow Press, 2007.

Industry and Sunday. London: Lord's Day Observance Society, n.d.

Institute of Marriage and Family Canada. "Cohabitation Statistics." In *Quick Stats*. No Pages. Online: http://www.imfcanada.org/article_files/Cohabitation%20Statistics.pdf.

"IPCC, 2007: Summary for Policymakers." In *Climate Change 2007: The Physical Science Basis. Contribution of Working Group I to the Fourth Assessment Report of the Intergovernmental Panel on Climate Change*, edited by Susan et al. Solomon, 1–18. Cambridge, UK: Cambridge University Press.

Isaacs, Nathan. "The Influence of Judaism on Western Law." In *The Legacy of Israel*, eds Edwyn R. Bevan and Charles Singer, planned by I. Abrahams, 377–406. Oxford: Clarendon Press, 1927.

James, Stephen A. "Divine Justice and the Retributive Duty of Civil Government." *Trinity Journal* NS 6 (1985) 199–210.

Janse, A. *Burgerlijke of Kerkelijke Politiek*. Aalten: De Graafschap, 1932.

Jansen, Joh. *Korte Verklaring Van de Kerkenordening*. 2nd ed. Kampen: Kok, 1937.

Jefferson, Thomas. "Quotations on the Jefferson Memorial." No Pages. Online: http://www.monticello.org/site/jefferson/quotations-jefferson-memorial.

Johnson, Dennis E. "The Epistle to the Hebrews and the Mosaic Penal Sanctions." In *Theonomy: A Reformed Critique*, eds William S. Barker and Godfrey W. Robert, 171–92. Grand Rapids, MI: Zondervan, 1990.

Joüon, Paul. *A Grammar of Biblical Hebrew*. Reprint of first edition, with corrections. Trans. and rev. T. Muraoka. Subsidia Biblica. Rome: Pontifical Biblical Institute, 1993.

Keil, C. F., and F. Delitzsch. *Commentary on the Old Testament*. Peabody, MA: Hendrickson, 2002.

Keller, Timothy J. "Theonomy and the Poor: Some Reflections." In *Theonomy: A Reformed Critique*, eds William S. Barker and Godfrey W. Robert, 263–94. Grand Rapids, MI: Zondervan, 1990.

Kelley, Michael W. *The Burden of God: Studies in Wisdom and Civilization from the Book of Ecclesiastes*. Minneapolis: Contra Mundum Books, 1993.

Kelly, Douglas F. *The Emergence of Liberty in the Modern World: The Influence of Calvin on Five Governments from the 16th Through 18th Centuries*. Phillipsburg NJ: P & R, 1992.

Kent, Stephen A. "A Matter of Principle: Fundamentalist Mormon Polygamy, Children, and Human Rights Debates." *Nova Religio* 10:1 (August 2006) 7–29.

Kirwan, Joseph. "Greens and Animals." In *The Cross and the Rain Forest: A Critique of Radical Green Spirituality*, Robert Whelan, Joseph Kirwan, and Paul Haffner, 102–23. Grand Rapids, MI: Acton Institute / Eerdmans, 1996.

Kistemaker, Simon. "The History of the Lord's Day." In *The Sabbath-Sunday Problem*, edited by G. Van Groningen, 62–76. Geelong, Australia: Hilltop Press, 1968.

Knight III, George W. *The Pastoral Epistles*. NIGTC. Grand Rapids, MI / Carlisle, UK and: Eerdmans / Paternoster, 1992.

Knudsen, Robert D. "May We Use the Term 'Theonomy' for our Application of Biblical Law?" In *Theonomy: A Reformed Critique*, eds William S. Barker and Godfrey W. Robert, 17–37. Grand Rapids, MI: Zondervan, 1990.

Köstenberger, A. J. "Nations." In *New Dictionary of Biblical Theology*, edited by T. Desmond Alexander and Brian S. Rosner, 676–78. Downers Grove, IL: InterVarsity, 2000.

———. "Marriage and Family in the New Testament." In *Marriage and Family in the Biblical World*, edited by Ken M. Campbell, 240–84. Downers Grove, IL: InterVarsity, 2003.

Koyzis, David T. *Political Visions and Illusions: A Survey and Christian Critique of Contemporary Ideologies*. Downers Grove, IL: InterVarsity, 2003.

Kuehne, Dale S. *Sex and the iWorld: Rethinking Relationship Beyond an Age of Individualism*. With a foreword by Jean Bethke Elshtain. Grand Rapids, MI: Baker Academic, 2009.

Kuiper, R. *Dienstbare Overheid: Christelijke-Staatkundige Visie Op Politiek en Overheid*. Mr. G. Groen van Prinsterer stichting - wetenschappelijk instituut ChristenUnie, 2003.

Kupelian, David. *The Marketing of Evil: How Radicals, Elitists, and Pseudo-Experts Sell Us Corruption Disguised as Freedom*. Nashville, TN: WND Books, 2005.

———. *The Marketing of Evil: How Radicals, Elitists, and Pseudo-Experts Sell Us Corruption Disguised as Freedom*. Nashville, TN: WND Books, 2005.

Kuyper, A. *The Problem of Poverty*. Edited by James W. Skillen. 1891. Grand Rapids, MI: Baker, 1991.

———. "Maranatha." In *Abraham Kuyper: A Centennial Reader*, edited by James D. Bratt, 205–29. Grand Rapids, MI: Eerdmans, 1997.

———. "Sphere Sovereignty." In *Abraham Kuyper: A Centennial Reader*, edited by James D. Bratt, 461–90. Grand Rapids, MI; Carlisle, UK / Eerdmans; Paternoster, 1998.

Laverdure, Paul. "Canada's Sunday: The Presbyterian Contribution, 1875–1950." In *The Burning Bush and a Few Acres of Snow: The Presbyterian Contribution to Canadian Life and Culture*, edited by William Klempa, 83–99. Ottawa: Carleton University Press, 1994.

———. *Sunday in Canada: The Rise and Fall of the Lord's Day*. Yorkton, SK: Gravelbooks, 2004.

Law Reform Commission of Canada. *Report on Sunday Observance*. Ottawa: The Commission, 1976.

Lee, Francis Nigel. *The Covenantal Sabbath. The Weekly Sabbath Scripturally and Historically Considered*. London, UK: The Lord's Day Observance Society, 1966.

Leishman, Rory. *Against Judicial Activism: The Decline of Freedom and Democracy in Canada*. Montreal; Kingston: McGill-Queen's University Press, 2006.

Leithart, Peter J. *Defending Constantine: The Twilight of an Empire and the Dawn of Christendom*. Downers Grove, IL: IVP Academic, 2010.

Levant, Ezra. "Human Rights Commissions in the United States." In *Ezra Levant* (July 10, 2008). No Pages. Online: http://ezralevant.com/2008/07/human-rights-commissions-in-th-1.html.

———. "Levant to Congress." In *Ezra Levant* (July 11, 2008). No Pages. Online: http://ezralevant.com/2008/07/levant-to-congress-put-canada.html.

———. *Shakedown: How Our Government is Undermining Democracy in the Name of Human Rights*. With a foreword by Mark Steyn. Toronto: McClelland & Stewart, 2009.

Lewis, A. H. *A Critical History of Sunday Legislation from 321 to 1888 A.D.* New York: D. Appleton and Company, 1888.

Liddell, Henry George, Robert Scott, and Henry Stuart Jones. *A Greek-English Lexicon*. 9th ed. Oxford: Oxford University Press, 1968.

Limbaugh, David. *Persecution: How Liberals Are Waging War Against Christianity*. Washington, D.C.: Regnery Publishing, 2003.

Linowes, Lisa. "Wind Energy's 'Trail of Broken Promises' (USA)." In *Wind Turbine Syndrome* (July 16, 2011). No Pages. Online: http://www.windturbinesyndrome.com/news/2011/wind-energys-trail-of-broken-promises-usa/.

Lomborg, Bjorn. *The Skeptical Environmentalist: Measuring the Real State of the World*. Cambridge / New York: Cambridge University Press, 2001.

Longman III, Tremper. "God's Law and Mosaic Punishments Today." In *Theonomy: A Reformed Critique*, eds William S. Barker and Godfrey W. Robert, 41–54. Grand Rapids, MI: Zondervan, 1990.

Longman, Phillip. *The Empty Cradle: How Falling Birthrates Threaten World Prosperity and What to Do About It*. New York: Basic Books, 2004.

Lopez, C. L. "Is the Encyclopedia of Christian Civilization 'Too Christian'?" In *Christianity Today* (February 2009). No Pages. Online: http://www.christianitytoday.com/ct/2009/februaryweb-only/108-43.0.html.

MacAllen, Susan. "Salute the Danish Flag! - It's a Symbol of Western Freedom." In *Family Security Matters* (July 23, 2007). No Pages. Online: http://www.fsmarchives.org/article.php?id=1172085.

Mansbridge, Peter, and Stephen Harper. "Interview with Stephen Harper." In *The National*. No Pages. Online: http://www.cbc.ca/thenational/indepthanalysis/story/2011/01/17/national-stephenharperinterview.html.

Marquardt, Elizabeth. *The Revolution in Parenthood: The Emerging Global Clash Between Adult Rights and Children's Needs*. New York: Institute for American Values, 2006.

Marshall, I. Howard. *A Critical and Exegetical Commentary on the Pastoral Epistles*. ICC. Edinburgh: T&T Clark, 1999.

Marshall, Paul. *God and the Constitution. Christianity and American Politics*. Lanham, MD: Rowman & Littlefield, 2002.

Martinuk, Susan. "Women Who Have Abortions Face Numerous Health Issues." *Christian Legal Journal* (Summer 2008) 6.

McConville, J. G. *Deuteronomy*. Apollos Old Testament Commentary. Leicester, England / Downers Grove, Ilinois: Apollos / InterVarsity, 2002.

———. *God and Earthly Power: An Old Testament Political Theology, Genesis-Kings*. Library of Hebrew Bible/Old Testament Studies. London: T & T Clark, 2008.

McDougall, Rosamund. "Too Many People: Earth's Population Problem." Online: http://www.optimumpopulation.org/opt.more.earth.pdf.

McGrath, Alister E. *A Life of John Calvin: A Study in the Shaping of Western Culture*. Oxford: Blackwell, 1990.

McIlroy, David. "The Role of Government in Classical Christian Thought." In *God and Government*, edited by Nick Spencer and Jonathan Chaplin, 81–107. London: Society for Promoting Christian Knowledge, 2009.

———. *A Biblical View of Law and Justice*. Milton Keynes: Paternoster, 2004.

McKeating, Henry. "Sanctions Against Adultery in Ancient Israelite Society, with Some Reflections on Methodology in the Study of Old Testament Ethics." *JSOT* 11 (1979) 57–72.

McNeill, John T. "Calvin and Civil Government." In *Readings in Calvin's Theology*, edited by Donald K. McKim, 260–74. Grand Rapids, MI: Baker, 1984.

McNeill, John T., ed., Ford Lewis Battles, trans. *Calvin: Institutes of the Christian Religion.* LCC. Philadelphia: Westminster, 1960.
Meadows, Donella, and et al. *The Limits to Growth: A Report for the Club of Rome's Project on the Predicament of Mankind.* New York: Universe Books, 1972.
Megivern, James J. *The Death Penalty: An Historical and Theological Survey.* New York: Paulist Press, 1997.
Melzer, Arthur M. "Introduction." In *Multiculturalism and American Democracy*, edited by Arthur M. Melzer, Jerry Weinberger, and M. Richard Zinman. Lawrence, Kan.: University Press of Kansas, 1998.
Merkle, Benjamin L. *The Elder and Overseer. One Office in the Early Church.* Studies in Biblical Literature. New York: Peter Lang, 2003.
Merriam-Webster's Collegiate Dictionary. 10th ed. Edited by Frederick C. Mish. Springfield, MA: Merriam-Wesbster, 1996.
Merrill, E. H. "Image of God." In *Dictionary of the Old Testament: Pentateuch*, edited by T. Desmond Alexander and David W. Baker, 441–45. Downers Grove, IL: InterVarsity, 2003.
Melzer, Arthur M., Jerry Weinberger, and M. Richard Zinman, ed. *Multiculturalism and American Democracy.* Lawrence, KS.: University Press of Kansas, 1998.
Milgrom, Jacob. *Leviticus 1–16.* AB, vol. 3. New York: Doubleday, 1991.
———. *Numbers: The Traditional Hebrew Text with the New JPS Translation.* The JPS Torah Commentary. Philadelphia: Jewish Publication Society, 1989.
Miller, William M. *A Christian's Response to Islam.* Nutley, NJ: Presbyterian and Reformed, 1977.
Milligan, Kevin. *Subsidizing the Stork: New Evidence on Tax Incentives and Fertility.* Research rept. Vancouver, BC: Department of Economics, University of British Columbia, 2004. Online: http://faculty.arts.ubc.ca/kmilligan/research/babies2004.pdf.
Mills, Paul. "A Brief Theology of Time: Part 2: Resisting the Tyranny of Time." *Cambridge Papers* 11:4 (December 2002) 1–4.
Mintz, Jack. "Taxing Families: Does the System Need an Overhaul?" *IMFC Review*, Spring/Summer 2008, 15–17.
Monckton, Christopher. "35 Inconvenient Truths: The Errors in Al Gore's Movie." In *Science and Public Policy Institute.* No Pages. Online: http://Scienceandpublicpolicy.Org/Monckton/Goreerrors.Html.
Monsma, Stephen V. and J. Christopher Soper. *The Challenge of Pluralism. Church and State in Five Democracies.* 2nd ed. Lanham, MD: Rowman & Littlefield, 2009.
Montgomery, John Warwick. "Demos and Christos." In *Christians in the Public Square: Law, Gospel and Public Policy*, C. E. B. Cranfield, David Kilgour, and John Warwick Montgomery, 23–26. Edmonton: Canadian Institute for Law, Theology, and Public Policy, 1996.
———. "Should We Legislate Morality?" In *Christians in the Public Square: Law, Gospel, and Public Policy*, C. E. B. Cranfield, David Kilgour, and John Warwick Mojntgomery, 69–79. Edmonton: Canadian Institute for Law, Theology, and Public Policy, 1996.
———. *The Law Above the Law.* Minneapolis MN: Bethany House, 1975.
Mooney, Kevin. "Scientific Evidence Now Points to Global Cooling, Contrary to U.N. Alarmism." In *The Washington Examiner* (April 8, 2009). No Pages. Online: http://washingtonexaminer.com/blogs/beltway-confidential/2009/08/scientific-evidence-now-points-global-cooling-contrary-un-alarmism.

Moore, David W. "Three in Four Americans Support Euthanasia." In *Gallup* (May 17, 2005). No Pages. Online: http://www.gallup.com/poll/16333/three-infour-americans-support-euthanasia.aspx.

Morris, Edward D. *Theology of the Westminster Symbols. A Commentary Historical, Doctrinal, Practical, on the Confession of Faith and Catechisms and the Related Formularies of the Presbyterian Churches.* Columbus, OH: Champlin Press, 1900.

Morton, F. L. "Taking Section 33 Seriously." In *Divorcing Marriage: Unveiling the Dangers in Canada's New Social Experiment*, edited by Daniel Cere and Douglas Farrow, 135–54. Montreal and Kingston: Mc-Gill Queen's University Press, 2004.

Mouw, Richard J. *Uncommon Decency: Christian Civility in an Uncivil World*. Revised and Expanded ed. Downers Grove, IL: IVP Books, 2010.

———, and Sander Griffioen. *Pluralisms and Horizons: An Essay in Christian Public Philosophy*. Grand Rapids, MI: Eerdmans, 1993.

Mrozek, Andrea. "Getting Children Out of the House." *IMFC Review*, Spring/Summer 2008, 10–14.

Murray, John. *Principles of Conduct: Aspects of Biblical Ethics*. Grand Rapids, MI: Eerdmans, 1957.

———. *The Claims of Truth*. Vol. I of *Collected Writings of John Murray*. Edinburgh: Banner of Truth, 1976.

———. *The Epistle to the Romans*. 2 Volumes in 1. 1965. NICOT. Grand Rapids, MI: Eerdmans, 1968.

Nabuco, J. "Papal Ceremony and Vesture." *NCE* 10: 972–73.

NASA Science. "Earth's Fidgeting Climate." In *NASA Science News* (October 20, 2000). No Pages. Online: http://science.nasa.gov/science-news/science-at-nasa/2000/ast20oct_1/.

Nathwani, Jatin. "Red Flags on Green Energy." In *The Globe and Mail* (February 16, 2011). No Pages. Online: http://www.theglobeandmail.com/news/opinions/opinion/red-flags-on-green-energy/article1908668.

National Desk. "Gov. Lamm Asserts Elderly, If Very Ill, Have 'duty to Die.'" In *The New York Times* (March 29, 1984). No Pages. Online: http://www.nytimes.com/1984/03/29/us/gov-lamm-asserts-elderly-if-very-ill-have-duty-to-die.html.

National Right to Life. "Abortion Statistics: United States Data and Trends." Online: http://www.nrlc.org/factsheets/fs03_abortionintheus.pdf.

Nazir-Ali, Michael. "Breaking Faith with Britain." In *Standpoint Magazine* (June 2008). No Pages. Online: http://www.standpointmag.co.uk/node/85.

Neuhaus, Richard John. *The Naked Public Square: Religion and Democracy in America*. 2nd ed. Grand Rapids, MI: Eerdmans, 1986.

Niederwimmer, K., and H. W. Attridge. *The Didache: A Commentary*. Hermeneia. Minneapolis: Fortress Press, 1998.

Noll, Mark A. *What Happened to Christian Canada?* Vancouver, B.C.: Regent College Publishing, 2007.

———, Nathan O. Hatch, and George M. Marsden. *The Search for Christian America*. Westchester, IL: Crossway, 1983.

O'Donovan, Oliver, and Joan Lockwood O'Donovan, eds. *From Irenaeus to Grotius: A Sourcebook in Christian Political Thought, 100–1625*. Grand Rapids, MI/Cambridge, UK: Eerdmans, 1999.

O'Donovan, Oliver. *Resurrection and the Moral Order: An Outline for Evangelical Ethics*. Leicester, UK / Grand Rapids, MI: Inter-Varsity / Eerdmans, 1986.
———. *The Christian and the Unborn Child*. Bramcote, UK: Grove Books, 1975.
———. *The Desire of the Nations: Rediscovering the Roots of Political Theology*. Cambridge: Cambridge University Press, 1999.
Ovey, Michael. "Beyond Scrutiny? Minorities, Majorities and Post-Modern Tyranny." *Cambridge Papers* 13:2 (June 2004) 1-4.
Owen-Ball, David T. "Rabbinic Rhetoric and the Tribute Passage (Mt. 22:15-22; Mk. 12:13-17; Lk. 20:20-26)." *Novum Testamentum* 35 (1993) 1-14.
Owens, Erik C. "Death Penalty: Law." In *RPP* 3: 704-6.
Paas, Stefan. *Vrede Stichten: Politieke Meditaties*. Zoetermeer: Boekencentrum, 2007.
Parker, Geoffrey. *The Dutch Revolt*. 2nd ed. Harmondsworth, UK: Penguin, 1985.
Patterson, Dorothy. "The High Calling of Wife and Mother in Biblical Perspective." In *Recovering Biblical Manhood and Womanhood: A Response to Evangelical Feminism*, edited by John Piper and Wayne Grudem, 364-77. Wheaton, IL: Crossway, 1991.
Peet, Garnet. "The Protestant Churches in Nazi Germany." *Clarion* 37 (1988) 440-41, 463-65, 487-89, 526-27; also available online: http://www.spindleworks.com/library/peet/german.htm.
Penninga, Mark. *Building on Sand: Human Dignity in Canadian Law and Society*. Winnipeg: Premier / ARPA, 2009.
Pennings, Ray. *Church and Ceasar. A Legal Primer for Church Office-bearers*. Grand Rapids, MI / Mitchell, ON: Reformation Heritage Books / Free Reformed Publications, 2008.
———. "Embracing the Paradox." In *Cardus* (June 25, 2010). No Pages. Online: http://www.cardus.ca/comment/article/2049.
———. "Influencing for Good." *Clarion* 55 (2006) 13-21.
Perks, Stephen C. *A Defence of the Christian State: The Case Against Principled Pluralism and the Christian Alternative*. Taunton, England: The Kuyper Foundation, 1998.
———. *Christianity and Law: An Enquiry Into the Influence of Christianity on the Development of English Common Law*. With an appendix containing a translation of *The Laws of King Alfred the Great*. Whitby, England: Avant, 1993.
Pierpont, Nina. *Wind Turbine Syndrome*. Santa Fe, NM: K-Selected Books, 2009.
Pipes, Daniel. *Militant Islam Reaches America*. New York: W.W. Norton, 2003.
Popenoe, David. "Cohabitation, Marriage, and Child Wellbeing: A Cross-National Perspective." *Society* 46:5 (September 2009) 429-36.
Poythress, Vern Sheridan. *The Shadow of Christ in the Law of Moses*. Brentwood, Tennessee: Wolgemuth & Hyatt, 1991.
Rankin, James. *The Church of Scotland. Books II.-III*. Vol. 2 of *The Church of Scotland, Past and Present: Its History, Its Relation to the Law and the State, Its Doctrine, Ritual, Discipline, and Patrimony*. Edited by Robert Herbert Story. London: William Macknezie, 1890.
Raucher, Alan. "Sunday Business and the Decline of Sunday Closing Laws: A Historical Overview." *Journal of Church and State* 36 (1994) 13-33.
Redekop, John H. *Politics Under God*. With a foreword by John A. Lapp. Waterloo, ON/Scottdale, PA: Herald Press, 2007.
Reid, Darrel, and Janet Buckingham. "Whose Rights? Whose Freedoms?" In *Divorcing Marriage: Unveiling the Dangers in Canada's New Social Experiment*, edited

by Daniel Cere and Douglas Farrow, 79–93. Montreal and Kingston: McGill-Queen's University Press, 2004.

Reid, W. Stanford. *Trumpeter of God: A Biography of John Knox.* Grand Rapids, MI: Baker, 1974.

Rekers, George Alan. "Psychological Foundations for Rearing Masculine Boys and Feminine Girls." In *Recovering Biblical Manhood and Womanhood: A Response to Evangelical Feminism*, edited by John Piper and Wayne Grudem, 294–311. Wheaton, IL: Crossway, 1991.

"Religious Liberty Wary of Europe's Sunday Law." In *Record: The Official News Magazine of the Seventh Day Adventist Church.* No Pages. Online: http://record.net.au/items/religious-liberty-wary-of-europe-s-sunday-law.

"A Renewed Call to Truth, Prudence, and Protection of the Poor: An Evangelical Examination of the Theology, Science, and Economics of Global Warming." No Pages. Online: http://www.cornwallalliance.org/articles/read/an-evangelical-declaration-on-global-warming.

Repanshek, Kurt. "Judge Clears Way for Deer Culling." In *National Parks Traveller* (November 1, 2010). No Pages. Online: http://www.nationalparkstraveler.com/2010/11/judge-clears-way-deer-culling-valley-forge-national-historical-park-friends-animals-plans-protest7145.

Richter, Sandra. "Environmental Law in Deuteronomy: One Lens on a Biblical Theology of Creation Care." *Bulletin for Biblical Research* 20 (2010) 355–76.

Riddell, Peter G., and Peter Cotterell. *Islam in Context: Past, Present, and Future.* Grand Rapids, MI: Baker Academic, 2003.

Ridderbos, H. N. *Matthew.* Translated by Ray Togtman. 1950–51. BSC. Grand Rapids, MI: Zondervan, 1987.

———. *The Coming of the Kingdom.* Edited by Raymond O. Zorn. Translated by H. de Jongste. Philadelphia: Presbyterian and Reformed, 1962.

Riedl, Brian M. "Why Government Spending Does not Stimulate Economic Growth: Answering the Critics." *Backgrounder*, 2354 (January 5, 2010). No Pages. Online: www.heritage.org/Research/Economy/bg2354.cfm.

Rivers, Julian. "Disestablishment and the Church of England." In *Christianity in a Changing World: Biblical Insight on Contemporary Issues*, Michael Schluter and the Cambridge Papers Group, 63–80. London: Marshall Pickering, 2000.

———. "Government." In *Jubilee Manifesto*, edited by Michael Schluter and John Ashcroft, 138–53. Leicester: InterVarsity, 2005.

———. "Multiculturalism," *Cambridge Papers* 10:4 (2001).

Robertson, A. *Word Pictures in the New Testament.* Oak Harbor, WA: Logos Research Systems, 1997.

Rogerson, John William. "The Use of the Old Testament with Reference to Work and Unemployment." In *Theory and Practice in Old Testament Ethics*, ed & introd by M. Daniel Carroll R. JSOTSup 405, 100–108. New York: T&T Clark, 2004.

Rordorf, Willy. *Sunday: The History of the Day of Rest and Worship in the Earliest Centuries of the Christian Church.* London: SCM, 1968.

Rose, H. J. "Euthanasia." In *ERE* 5:598–601.

Roth, Martha. "The Laws of Hammurabi." In *COS* 2:335–53, 2000.

———. "The Laws of Lipit-Isthar." In *COS* 2:410–14, 2000.

———. "The Middle Assyrian Laws." In *COS* 2:353–60, 2000.

Rouvoet, A. *Reformatorische Staatsvisie: De RPF en Het Ambt Van de Overheid*. Marnix Van St. Aldegonde Stichting. Nunspeet: Marnix van St. Aldegonde Stichting, Wetenschappelijk Studiecentrum van de RPF, 1992.
Runner, H. Evan. *Scriptural Religion and Political Task*. Toronto: Wedge, 1974.
Rusch, William G. "Innocent III." In *EC* 2: 710–11.
Rushdoony, Rousas John. *The Institutes of Biblical Law*. 3 Vols. Nutley, NJ/Vallecito, CA: Craig Press / Ross House Books, 1973–99.
Rutherford, Samuel. *Lex Rex*. Harrisonburg, Virginia: Sprinkle, 1982.
Ruys Jr., Th. *Petrus Dathenus*. Utrecht: G. J. A. Ruys, 1919.
Ryken, Leland. *Work and Leisure in Christian Perspective*. Portland, OR: Multnomah, 1987.
Sampson, Philip J. *Sustaining Democracy*. Cambridge: Jubilee Centre, 2009.
Satinover, Jeffrey. *Homosexuality and the Politics of Truth*. Grand Rapids, MI: Baker, 1996.
Savage, Charlie, and Sheryl Gay Stolberg. "In Shift, U.S. Says Marriage Act Blocks Gay Rights." In *New York Times* (February 23, 2011). No Pages. Online: http://www.nytimes.com/2011/02/24/us/24marriage.html?_r=1.
Schaeffer, Francis A. *Pollution and the Death of Man: The Christian View of Ecology*. Wheaton IL: Tyndale, 1970.
Schaff, P., and D. S. Schaff. "Westminster Standards." In *The New Schaff-Herzog Encyclopedia of Religious Knowledge*. 13 vols, edited by S. M. Jackson, 12:324–28. Grand Rapids, MI: Baker, 1949.
Schaff, Philip. *Ante-Nicene Christianity A.D. 100–325*. Vol. II of *History of the Christian Church*. 3rd ed. Grand Rapids, MI: Eerdmans, 1910.
———. *Modern Christianity. The Swiss Reformation*. Vol. VIII of *History of the Christian Church*. 3rd ed. rev. Grand Rapids, MI: Eerdmans, 1910.
———. *The Creeds of Christendom*. 1877. Grand Rapids, MI: Baker, 1966.
Schlossberg, Terry and Elizabeth Rice Achtemeier. *Not My Own: Abortion and the Marks of the Church*. Grand Rapids, MI: Eerdmans, 1995.
Schluter, Michael, and the Cambridge Papers Group. *Christianity in a Changing World: Biblical Insight on Contemporary Issues*. London: Marshall Pickering, 2000.
Schluter, Michael. "Welfare." In *Jubilee Manifesto: A Framework, Agenda, and Strategy for Christian Social Reform*, edited by Michael Schluter and John Ashcroft, 175–92. Leicester, UK: Inter-Varsity Press, 2005.
Schmid, H. H. "*gûr* to sojourn." In *TLOT*, 1.307–10.
Schreiner, Thomas R. *Romans*. ECNT. Grand Rapids, MI: Baker, 1998.
Schrotenboer, Paul G. "The Principled Pluralist Response to Theonomy." In *God and Politics: Four Views on the Reformation of Civil Government*, edited by Gary Scott Smith, 54–60. Phillipsburg NJ: Presbyterian and Reformed, 1989.
Sears, Alan, and Craig Osten. *The ACLU Vs America: Exposing the Agenda to Redefine Moral Values*. Nashville, TN: Broadman & Holman, 2005.
Shaidle, Kathy, and Peter Vere. *The Tyranny of Nice: How Canada Crushes Freedom in the Name of Human Rights (and Why It Matters to Americans)*. With an introduction by Mark Steyn. Toronto: Interim Publishing, 2008.
Sinclair, Stephanie. "The Polygamists." *National Geographic* 217:2 (February 2010) 34–61.
Ska, Jean Louis. "Biblical Law and the Origins of Democracy." In *The Ten Commandments: The Reciprocity of Faithfulness*, edited by William P. Brown.

Library of Theological Ethics, 146–58. Louisville: Westminster John Knox Press, 2004.
Skillen, James W. "The Principled Pluralist Response to Christian America." In *God and Politics: Four Views on the Reformation of Civil Government*, edited by Gary Scott Smith, 158-64. Phillipsburg, NJ: Presbyterian and Reformed, 1989.
Smeenk, C. *Christelijk-Sociale Beginselen*. Kampen: Kok, 1934–36.
Social Contract: Essays by Locke, Hume, and Rousseau. With an introduction by Sir Ernest Barker. New York: Oxford University Press, 1962.
Solomon, Sam and E. Al Maqdisi. *Modern Day Trojan Horse: Al-Hijra, the Islamic Doctrine of Immigration, Accepting Freedom or Imposing Isla?* Charlottesville, VA: ANM Publishers, 2009.
Somerville, Margaret. "Birth, Death, and Technoscience: Searching for Values at the Margins of Life." In *Recognizing Religion in a Secular Society*, edited by Douglas Farrow, 99–115. Montreal & Kingston / London: McGill-Queen's University Press, 2004.
———. "Euthanasia Would Hurt Doctors." In *Ottawa Citizen* (November 6, 2009). No Pages. Online: http://www.christianity.ca/netcommunity/page.aspx?pid=7016.
———. "The Secular Case Against Legalizing Euthanasia." *Christian Legal Journal* (Winter 2008) 18–23.
———. "What about the Children?" In *Divorcing Marriage: Unveiling the Dangers in Canada's New Social Experiment*, edited by Daniel Cere and Douglas Farrow, 63–78. Montreal and Kingston: McGill-Queen's University Press, 2004.
Sossin, Lorne. "The 'supremacy of God,' Human Dignity and the Charter of Rights and Freedoms." *University of New Brunswick Law Journal* 52 (2003) 227–41.
Spencer, Jack. "U.S. Nuclear Policy After Fukushima: Trust but Modify." *Backgrounder* 2557 (18 May 2011) 1–5. Online: http://thf_media.s3.amazonaws.com/2011/pdf/bg2557.pdf.
Spencer, Nick. *Asylum and Immigration: A Christian Perspective on a Polarized Debate*. Milton Keynes, UK: Paternoster, 2004.
Spencer, Robert. *Stealth Jihad: How Radical Islam is Subverting America Without Guns or Bombs*. Washington, D.C.: Regnery Publishing, 2008.
Spykman, Gordon J. "Sphere-Sovereignty in Calvin and the Calvinist Tradition." In *Exploring the Heritage of John Calvin: Essays in Honor of John Bratt*, edited by David E. Holwerda, 163–208. Grand Rapids, MI: Baker, 1976.
———. "The Principled Pluralist Position." In *God and Politics: Four Views on the Reformation of Civil Government*, edited by Gary Scott Smith, with a foreword by John H. White, 78–99. Phillipsburg, NJ: P&R, 1989.
Stanbury, W. T. "Canadian Content Regulations: The Intrusive State At Work." *Fraser Forum*, August 1998, 4–90.
Stanton, Glenn T. and Bill Maier. *Marriage on Trial: The Case Against Same-sex Marriage and Parenting*. Downers Grove, IL: InterVarsity Press, 2004.
Statistics Canada. "Canada Abortion Rates 1974 to 2005." Online: http://www.abortionincanada.ca/stats/.
———. "Declining Birth Rate and the Increasing Impact of Immigration." No Pages. Online: http://www.statcan.gc.ca/kits-trousses/issues-enjeux/edu01c_0002-eng.htm.
———. "Divorces (March 9, 2005)." No Pages. Online: http://www.statcan.gc.ca/daily-quotidien/050309/dq050309b-eng.htm.

Stavleu, Cees. "De Bijbel as Inspiratiebron Voor Politiek." *DenkWijzer* 6:2 (April 2006) 9–10.
Steel, Kevin. "Drawing the Line." In *Western Standard* (February 27, 2008). No Pages. Online: http://www.westernstandard.ca/website/article.php?id=1473.
Stewart, Gary P. et al. *Basic Questions on Suicide and Euthanasia. Are They ever Right?* Bio Basics Series. Grand Rapids, MI: Kregel, 1998.
Stott, John. *Issues Facing Christians Today*. Basingstoke, Hants UK: Marshalls, 1984.
Streich, Michael. "American Students and the Decline in History: Generations of Citizens Are Ignorant of Basic Civics and US History." In *Educational Issues @Suite 101* (February 27, 2009). No Pages. Online: http://www.suite101.com/content/american-students-and-the-decline-in-history-a99242.
Strohm, Theodor. "Democracy and Christianity." In *EC* 1: 792–94.
Supreme Court of Canada. "R. v. Big M Drug Mart Ltd., [1985] 1 S.C.R. 295." In *Judgments of the Supreme Court of Canada*. No Pages. Online: http://scc.lexum.org/en/1985/1985scr1-295/1985scr1-295.html.
———. "R. v. Edwards Books and Art Ltd. [1986] 2 S.C.R. 713." In *Judgments of the Supreme Court of Canada*. No Pages. Online: http://scc.lexum.org/en/1986/1986scr2-713/1986scr2-713.html.
Sutherland, John R., ed. *Us and Them: Building a Just Workplace Community*. Mississauga ON: Work Research Foundation, 1999.
Taylor, E. L. H. "The Death Penalty." In *Essays on the Death Penalty*, edited by T. Robert Ingram, 13–44. Houston, TX: St. Thomas Press, 1971.
"Thirty Years of Surveys Show Canadians Oppose Unrestricted Abortion." No Pages. Online: http://www.abortionincanada.ca/history/Polls_Say_Canadians_Favor_Laws_Governing_Abortion.html.
Tigay, Jeffrey H. *Deuteronomy: The Traditional Hebrew Text with the New JPS Translation*. The JPS Torah Commentary. Philadelphia: Jewish Publication Society, 1996.
Tödt, Heinz Eduard. "Freedom: Theological." In *EC* 2: 350–54.
Townsend, Christopher, and Michael Schluter. *Why Keep Sunday Special*. Cambridge: Jubilee Centre Publications, 1985.
Trumper, Tim J. R. *Preaching and Politics: Engagement Without Compromise*. Eugene, OR: Wipf & Stock, 2009.
Tucker, William. *Terrestrial Energy: How Nuclear Energy Will Lead the Green Revolution and End America's Energy Odyssey*. Savage, MD: Bartleby Press, 2008.
Turki, Fawaz. "Muslim World Despises Freedom of Press." In *Deseret News* (April 23, 2006). No Pages. Online: http://www.deseretnews.com/article/635201511/Muslim-world-despises-freedom-of-press.html?pg=2.
Turley-Ewart, John. "Sharia by Stealth — Ontario Turns a Blind Eye to Polygamy." In *National Post* (May 29, 2008). No Pages. Online: http://network.nationalpost.com/np/blogs/fullcomment/archive/2008/05/29/john-turley-ewart-sharia-by-stealth-ontario-turns-a-blind-eye-to-polygamy.aspx.
Turnau III, Theodore A. "Speaking in a Broken Tongue: Postmodernism, Principled Pluralism, and the Rehabilitation of Public Moral Discourse." *Westminster Theological Journal* 56 (1994) 345–77.
U. S. Senate Environment and Public Works Committee Minority Staff Report (Inhofe), 2009. Online:http://hatch.senate.gov/public/_files/USSenateEPWMinorityReport.pdf.

van Asbeck, F. M. *The Universal Declaration of Human Rights and Its Predecessors (1679–1948)*. Textus Minores. Leiden, 1949.

Van Dam, Cornelis. *Divorce and Remarriage: In the Light of Old Testament Principles and Their Application in the New Testament*. Winnipeg: Premier, 1996.

———. *Perspectives on Worship, Law and Faith: The Old Testament Speaks Today*. Kelmscott, Western Australia: Pro Ecclesia, 2000.

———. *The Elder: Today's Ministry Rooted in All of Scripture*. Phillipsburg, NJ: P&R, 2009.

van der Zwaag, K. *Onverkort of gekortwiekt? Artikel 36 van de Nederlandse Geloofsbelijdenis en de spanning tussen overheid en religie: een systematisch-historische interpretatie van een 'omstreden' geloofsartikel*. Diss. Heerenveen: Groen, 1999.

Van Dyke, Harry. *Groen Van Prinsterer's Lectures on Unbelief and Revolution*. Jordan Station ON: Wedge, 1989.

Van Groningen, G. "The Sabbath in the Old Testament." In *The Sabbath-Sunday Problem*, edited by G. Van Groningen, 9–45. Geelong, Australia: Hilltop Press, 1968.

van Middelkoop, E. *Reformatie en Tolerantie*. Apeldoorn: Willem de Zwijgerstichting, 1985.

Van Pelt, Michael, and Richard Greydanus. *Living on the Streets: The Role of the Church in Urban Renewal*. Hamilton, ON: Work Research Foundation, 2005.

van Riessen, H. *The Society of the Future*. Translated and edited by David Hugh Freeman. Philadelphia: Presbyterian and Reformed, 1952.

van Ruler, Arnold A. *Calvinist Trinitarianism and Theocentric Politics: Essays Toward a Public Theology*. Trans. from the Dutch by John Bolt. Lewiston: Edwin Mellen, 1989.

Vanwoudenberg, Ed. *A Matter of Choice*. Winnipeg: Premier, 1989.

Vanderheyden, Terry. "UN Rules Government Funding of Catholic Education in Ontario 'Discriminatory.'" (November 18, 2005). No Pages. Online: http://www.lifesitenews.com/news/archive/ldn/2005/nov/05111803.

VanDrunen, David. "The Two Kingdoms and the *Ordo Salutis*: Life Beyond Judgment and the Question of a Dual Ethic." *Westminster Theological Journal* 70 (2008) 207–24.

Veling, K. *De Dienst Van de Overheid: Aard en Grenzen Van de Overheidstaak*. Groen Van Prinsterer Stichting. Barneveld: De Vuurbaak, 1987.

Verbrugh, A.J. *Universeel en Antirevolutionair: Toelichting Bij de Richtlijnen Voor de Nationaal-Gereformeerde, Dat is Universeel-Christelijke en Antirevolutionaire Politiek*. Groen Van Prinsterer Stichting 41,44, 49. Groningen: Vuurbaak, 1980–85.

Voogel, Hetty. "Integratie in de Gemeente." *Denkwijzer* 4:3 (Juni 2004) 22–25.

Walker, Williston, Richard A. Norris, David W. Lotz, and Robert T. Handy. *A History of the Christian Church*. New York: Scribner, 1985.

Wall, Elissa, with Lisa Pulitzer. *Stolen Innocence: My Story of Growing up in a Polygamous Sect, Becoming a Teenage Bride, and Breaking Free of Warren Jeffs*. New York: William Morrow, 2008.

Warren, David. "Suing for Silence." In *Ottawa Citizen* (December 2, 2007). No Pages. Online: http://www.davidwarrenonline.com/index.php?id=819.

Watkins, Frederick M. *The Age of Ideology - Political Thought, 1750 to the Present*. Foundations of Modern Political Science Series. Englewood Cliffs, N.J.: Prentice-Hall, 1964.

Wattie, Chris. "Dad Charged After Daughter Killed in Clash Over Hijab." In *National Post* (December 11, 2007). No Pages. Online: http://www.nationalpost.com/story.html?id=159480.

Wells, Paul. "Reformational Thought and the Social Covenant." *Themelios* 3:3 (2006) 32–47.

Wendel, Francois. *Calvin: The Origins and Development of His Religious Thought*. Trans. from the French. London: Collins, 1963.

"The Westminster Confession of Faith." In *Free Church of* Scotland. No Pages. Online: http://www.freechurch.org/index.php/scotland/resources-article/the_westminster_confession_of_faith/.

"The Westminster Confession of Faith." In *Presbyterian Church in* America. No Pages. Online: http://www.pcanet.org/general/cof_chapxxi-Xxv.Htm#chapxxiii.

Whelan, Robert, Joseph Kirwan, and Paul Haffner. "Science Facts." In *The Cross and the Rain Forest: A Critique of Radical Green Spirituality*, Robert Whelan, Joseph Kirwan, and Paul Haffner, 134–38. Grand Rapids, MI: Acton Institute / Eerdmans, 1996.

———. "Greens and God." In *The Cross and the Rain Forest: A Critique of Radical Green Spirituality*, Robert Whelan, Joseph Kirwan, and Paul Haffner, 7–56. Grand Rapids, MI: Acton Institute / Eerdmans, 1996.

White, Hilary. "Ontario's Gay Health Minister Blasted for Opposing Health Canada Safety Guidelines on Organ Donation." (January 25, 2008). No Pages. Online: http://www.lifesitenews.com/news/archive/ldn/2008/jan/08012511.

———. "Over 30% of Euthanasia Cases in Belgian Region Did not Give Consent: Study." (May 19, 2010). No Pages. Online: http://www.lifesitenews.com/news/archive/ldn/2010/may/10051903.

———. "The Historical Roots of Our Ecological Crisis." *Science* 155 (1967) 1203–7.

White, Robert S. *Creation in Crisis: Christian Perspectives on Sustainability*. London: SPCK, 2009.

Wiesing, Urban. "Hippocratic Oath." In *RPP* 6: 154–55.

Williamson, G.I. *The Westminster Confession of Faith: For Study Classes*. 2nd ed. Phillipsburg, NJ: P&R, 2004.

Witte Jr., John. "Introduction." In *Christianity and Law: An Introduction*, eds John Witte Jr. and Frank S. Alexander, 1–33. Cambridge / New York: Cambridge University Press, 2008.

———. "Law and Legal Theory." In *EC* 3: 218–26.

———. "Rights." In *EC* 4:701–9.

———. *The Reformation of Rights: Law, Religion, and Human Rights in Early Modern Calvinism*. Cambridge / New York: Cambridge University Press, 2007.

Wolf, C. Umhau. "Traces of Primitive Democracy in Ancient Israel." *Journal of Near Eastern Studies* 6 (1947) 98–108.

Wolffe, John. *The Expansion of Evangelicalism: The Age of Wilberforce, More, Chalmers and Finney*. History of Evangelicalism 2. Downers Grove, IL: InterVarsity, 2007.

Woolley, Paul. *Family, State, and Church - God's Institutions*. Grand Rapids, MI: Baker, 1965.

World Hunger Education Service. "2011 World Hunger and Poverty Facts and Statistics." In *Hunger Notes*. No Pages. Online: http://www.worldhunger.org/articles/Learn/world%20hunger%20facts%202002.htm.

Wright, Christopher J. H. *Old Testament Ethics for the People of God*. Downers Grove, IL.: InterVarsity, 2004.

Wright, Tom. "Neither Anarchy Nor Tyranny: Government and the New Testament." In *God and Government*, edited by Nick Spencer and Jonathan Chaplin, 61–80. London: Society for Promoting Christian Knowledge, 2009.

Wyatt, John. "Euthanasia and Assisted Suicide." *Cambridge Papers* 19:2 (June 2010).

Young, Katherine K., and Paul Nathanson. "The Future of an Experiment." In *Divorcing Marriage: Unveiling the Dangers in Canada's New Social Experiment*, edited by Daniel Cere and Douglas Farrow, 41–62. Montreal and Kingston: McGill-Queen's University Press, 2004.

Zaidi, Supna. "U.S. Government Embraces Islamic Banking." In *Middle East Forum* (November 24, 2008). No Pages. Online: http://www.meforum.org/2014/us-government-embraces-islamic-banking.

Zorn, R. O. "The New Testament and the Sabbath-Sunday Problem." In *The Sabbath-Sunday Problem*, edited by G. Van Groningen, 46–61. Geelong, Australia: Hilltop Press, 1968.

———. *Christ Triumphant: Biblical Perspectives on His Church and Kingdom*. Edinburgh: Banner of Truth, 1997.

Scripture Index

OLD TESTAMENT

Genesis

1:22	129, 173
1:26	148, 172, 173
1:26–30	40
1:26–27	113, 120, 234
1:27	79
1:27–28	128
1:28	40, 119, 141, 149, 176, 198, 276
1:28–30	148, 174
1:31	173
2	156
2:2–3	156
2:7	113, 173
2:15	147, 148, 149, 177, 276
2:18	130
2:19–20	179
2:23	130
2:24	130, 131
3:15	40
3:17–19	148
3:18–19	179
4:14	121
4:15	28
6:5–8	71
6:7	119
8:21	71
8:22	194
9:1	174
9:1–2	119
9:1–3	174
9:1–4	148
9:1–7	40
9:2	179
9:5	120
9:6	28, 28n1, 31, 62n31, 79, 113, 114, 119, 120, 122, 123
9:7	148, 174
10	198, 199
10:5	198, 210
10:20	198, 210
10:31	198, 210
11	198
11:1–9	198, 210
12:1–7	199
12:2–3	226
12:3	67
12:7	202
15:16	198
17:1	61
17:10–14	204
18:25	7
19	135
23:4	202, 202n5, 205
25:22	108
25:25–26	107
29:27–28	157
30:1	142
30:23	142
32:28	199
32:32	199
37:22	120
38:28–30	107

Exodus

1:7	199
1:15–20	251
4:22–23	68
10:2	144
12:6	157
12:17	157
12:19	203
12:26–27	144
12:38	201
12:43	205
12:48–49	68, 204
16:1	157
16:22–30	157
18:4	130
18:24–30	71
19:4–6	12
19:6	6, 67, 69, 199
19–20	199
20:1	13
20:3	86
20:8–11	156, 157
20:9	148
20:10	180, 182, 203
20:13	113
20:14	132
20:17	86
21	107
21:12	120
21:12–14	120
21:14	120
21:22–25	106, 275
21:23	107, 120
21:23–24	120, 124
21:28–30	123
21:28–32	122
22:1	43
22:4	43
22:8–9	8
22:19	132
22:21	205
22:25	60
23:1–3	8
23:6–8	8, 231
23:6–9	43, 203
23:9	202
23:9	205
23:10–11	45, 154
23:26	107
24:12	7
31:13–17	158
31:14	60
31:18	7
34:21	180

Leviticus

1:2	6
4:2	6
7:24	248
11:40	248
16:29	203
17:8–9	203
17:10	121, 203
17–25	203
18:6–29	132
18:6–30	203
18:8	62
18:22	82, 135
18:24–30	71
18:26–28	8
18:27–28	203, 206
18:29	62
19:2	61
19:9–10	60, 155, 219
19:10	202
19:33	68
19:34	202, 205
20:2	71, 203
20:3	203
20:7	61
20:10	60, 61n31
20:12–17	132
20:24	61
22	203
22:17–25	203
23:22	202, 219
24:10–16	60

24:15	71	6	199
24:16	55, 203	6:4–9	8, 144
24:17	120	6:5	68
24:21–22	120	6:6–9	5
25	13, 36	7	71
25:1–7	205	7:13–14	175
25:6	203	10:18	44, 203
25:28	206	10:19	202, 204, 205
25:29–30	206	11:29	180
25:47	203, 206	12:7	203
26:3–45	8	13:5	5
		13:5–6	55
		14:21	204, 248
Numbers		14:28–29	154
9	248	14:29	202
9:14	204	15:1–11	154
12:1	201	15:1–18	13
12:12	107	15:2–3	205
15:14–16	203	16:11	203
15:27–31	62n31	16:14	203
15:29–30	203	16:18	4, 5, 8
35:6–34	121	16:19–20	5, 8, 231
35:9–28	121	17:5–7	121
35:12	28n1	17:6	121
35:15	203	17:6–7	123
35:24–25	28n1	17:7	5
35:26–27	123	17:15	207
35:30	121	17:18–20	43, 73
35:31–34	62n31	18:13	61
35:33–34	203	19:6	67, 121
		19:11–13	121
		19:15	31, 121, 123
Deuteronomy		20:17–18	198
1:1	5, 8	20:19–20	45, 180
1:13	4, 5	22:6–7	180
1:13–16	8	22:12	182
1:16	203	22:22	61n31
1:17	8	22:22–24	132
4:1–10	199	23:3–8	205
4:5–8	67	23:7–8	204
4:6	87, 96, 226	23:30	205
4:8	87	24:1	133
5:12–15	156	24:1–4	89, 248
5:15	158	24:4	61

Scripture Index 303

Deuteronomy - continued

24:10–11	33
24:14–15	203
24:17	203
24:19–21	202
24:19–22	155, 219
25:4	180
26:1–10	199
26:11	202
26:12–13	202
28	8, 180
29:10–11	203
31:7	202
31:11–13	203
33:7	130
33:26	130
33:29	130

Joshua

8:35	203
24:14–15	12

Judges

2:16–22	28
12:6	199
16:28–30	113

Ruth

1:1	202
2:7	155
2:10	207
2:17	155
4:13–22	207

1 Samuel

7	67
8:4–5	4
21:5	204
21:7	201

2 Samuel

5:3	4
6–7	67
7:12–16	68
8:2–14	72n47
8:18	201
10:6–19	72n47
11	201
11:11	204
12:13	62n31
12:26–31	72n47
15:18–22	201
15:19	204
18:2	201
18:18	201
18:21	201
23:3–4	43
23:37	201
24:9	201
24:15	201

1 Kings

1:38	201
8:31–32	121
12:20	5
15:11	67
15:12	55
18:3–16	251
20:7–8	5
21	252
21:9–13	8

2 Kings

16:2–4	67
17	199
23	55
24–25	199

1 Chronicles

22:2	201
23–25	55

26:30	73	8:6	193
26:32	73	8:6–8	173
28:5	67	8:9	180
29	55	11:3	228
29:23	56, 67, 73	11:4	229
		11:7	229
		19:1–6	173
2 Chronicles		23:4	115
2:16–17	201	24:1	172, 188
3–6	55	31:15	114
8:7–8	201	33:5	35
9:8	56	33:12	38
17:7–9	9	39:12	202n5
19:6	8	47:2	66
19:11	73	47:6–7	66
23:3	5	50:12	172
26:16–21	33	51:5	108
		58	30
		65:9–13	177
Ezra		67	226
1	97	67:3–5	198
		72	44, 45, 63
		72:4	154
Nehemiah		72:12–13	154
13:3	201	72:12–14	63
		78	208
		78:54	71
Job		82	30
1:21	107	82:3	45
2:10	114	82:3–4	44
10:8–11	108	86:9	79
12:10	114	86:10	79
12:23	198	89:11	172
38–39	180	96:6	198
		96:13	122
		99:1	67
Psalms		99:4	44
2	55, 253	104	177, 180
2:1	67	105	199, 208
2:10–12	43	111:10	179
8	45, 193	113:9	142
8:1	180, 193	115:16	172
8:4–8	182	119:14	13
8:5–8	179	119:44–45	238

Psalms - continued

119:45	13
119:105	4, 85, 228
127:3	142
127:3–5	175
128:3–4	142, 175
139:13–15	107
139:13–16	82
145:15–16	173
146:7–9	37

Proverbs

1:8	144
6:20	144
6:32–35	61n31
9:10	179
12:10	180
13:24	144
14:31	44
14:33	74
14:34	38, 85, 100, 228, 254
15:3	121
15:10	144
15:16	155n10
18:9	148
22:6	143
23:4	150
23:13–14	144
23:22	144
23:26	68
24:11	253
24:21	28
24:23–25	43, 45
29:4	43
29:14	154
30:7	155n10

Ecclesiastes

1:9	36
2:11	151
2:20	151
2:24–25	151
2:26	179
5:18	151
7:16	249
7:18	249
12:13	100

Isaiah

1:16–17	35
1:23	43
3:14–15	36
5:7–8	36
5:23	36
9:6–7	68
10:1–2	43
10:20–22	68
32:17	39
42:3	114
42:6	226
42:6–7	96
44:28	97
45:1	97
45:18	175, 177
45:23	67, 69
51:4	67, 87
53	68
61:8	35

Jeremiah

1:4–5	108
1:5	107
7:6	206
7:6–7	203
7:9–10	37
7:14	37
9:24	35
17:9	4
22:16	154
25:20	201
27:5–6	27
29:5–7	226
29:7	28
29:10	226

31:33	63	**Jonah**	
32	225	3	68n42
33:15	68		
33:20–22	68	**Micah**	
Ezekiel		3:1–2	36
20:7	12	3:9–11	36
20:12	158	5:2	97
22:29–31	203	5:5	14n22
34:22–24	68	**Zechariah**	
39:17–19	61	2:12	61, 71
47:22	202	4:6	57, 242
		7:10	206
Daniel		7:10–14	203
2:21	27, 198		
2:37	27	**Malachi**	
2:37–38	74	2:14	131
3	252	2:16	89, 248
4:24–27	74	3:10	206
4:25	28		
4:32	28	# NEW TESTAMENT	
5:21	28	**Matthew**	
6:7–11	252	2:4–5	68
6:22	252	3:2	68
Hosea		4:17	68
2:14–20	199	5	62
4:1–3	179	5:13	241
4:4	195	5:13–16	227
9:14	107	5:13–20	69
12:6	35	5:17–18	59, 62
		5:19–48	63
Amos		5:31–32	89
5:7	36	5:32	133
5:10–11	36	5:39	31
5:12	36	5:44	240
5:21	37	5:45	72
5:23–24	37	5:47–48	62
5:24	35	6:26	173

Scripture Index

Matthew - continued

7:12	72, 99, 153
11:1–6	68
11:28–29	158
12:20	114
12:22–28	68
13:24–30	70, 211, 233
13:30	43
13:36–42	211
13:36–43	70, 72, 233
18:15–18	5, 62
18:17	5
18:17–18	56
19:8	133, 248
22:16–17	233
22:16–22	28
22:21	9, 233
22:36–40	99, 235
22:37–40	209
22:38	234
24–25	70
25:41–46	115
26:52	31
28:1	158
28:1–10	254
28:9	158
28:17–20	254
28:18	32, 69, 229
28:18–20	60, 69, 74
28:19	86
28:19–20	57, 85, 211

Mark

2:27	157, 157n15
10:21–25	155n10
10:45	69
12:17	233

Luke

1:35	108
1:41	108
2:1–5	97
6:31	246
10:29–37	209
12:7	182
12:48	195
14:23	56
18:1–8	70
20:25	233
24:1	158
24:13–14	158
24:44–48	69

John

4:1–26	209
14:15	69
15:13	113
15:20	246, 254
17:16	227
17:18	227
18:10	31
18:36	56, 73, 211, 233
19:11	28, 240
20:19	158
20:26	158

Acts

2	210
4:19	9, 251
5:29	9, 29, 236, 238, 251
10:42	7
14:23	5
15	5
17:26	198, 208
17:26–27	198
17:27	198, 200
20:7	158
20:28	5
20:35	155n10
25:11	122

Romans

1:16	57, 241
1:18	91
1:18–19	65
1:18–20	88
1:18–21	64
1:18–32	141
1:19–20	173
1:19–21	236
1:20	88
1:20–21	198
1:21–27	82
1:21–32	7, 11
1:26–27	132, 135
2:14	110, 236
2:14–15	11, 64, 87, 236
2:15	7
2:24	236
3:10–12	80, 124
3:23	4
5:12	115
8:7	99
8:18–22	114
8:18–25	179
8:19–22	173
11:36	149
12:19–21	31
13	30, 32, 63, 122
13:1	9, 27
13:1–2	29, 240
13:1–4	43
13:1–5	65, 227
13:1–7	30, 251, 253
13:3–4	97
13:4	930, 31, 33, 34, 39, 41, 56, 63, 70, 74, 118, 122, 138, 154, 155, 188, 230, 232
13:6–7	43, 240
14:10	7
15:25–27	60
16:3–4	113

1 Corinthians

5	62
5:5	56
5:7	158
6:13–20	132
7:13–15	133
10:31	79, 149, 228
12:3	69, 229, 240
13:3	60
15:20	254
15:24	32, 69
15:26	115
15:54–57	115
15:58	230, 254
16:1–2	60
16:2	158

2 Corinthians

5:9	7
5:10	253
5:17	158
6:16–18	62
8:19	5n3
10:4	56, 241
10:15	228

Galatians

5:19	132
6:2	153
6:7	124
6:10	153
6:16	62

Ephesians

1:19–23	254
1:20–21	32
1:22	32, 69
2:21	62
4:28	150
5:8–9	228

Ephesians - continued

5:17	70
6:1–9	33n7
6:17	56, 211

Philippians

1:22–26	114
1:23	115
2:6–7	108
2:9–10	69
4:8	44

Colossians

1:13–20	76
1:17	32
2:10	69
2:13–15	158
2:15	76
2:16–17	158
3:1	254
3:18–4:1	33n7
3:23–24	150

2 Thessalonians

1:6–10	254
3:6	148
3:7–12	153
3:10	150

1 Timothy

2:1–2	45, 90, 227, 240
2:1–3	29
2:1–4	76
2:2	9, 43, 44, 134
3:8–13	153
5:4	153
5:8	45, 153
6:9–10	150, 155n10

2 Timothy

3:16–17	144

Titus

1:5	5n3
2:1–3:2	33n7
2:11–12	144
3:1	29
3:3	99

Hebrews

4	158
4:12–13	56
9:26	158
11:32	113
12:7–10	144

1 Peter

2:5	6
2:9	69, 199
2:9–10	62
2:12–17	240
2:13–14	29, 122
2:13–17	9, 251
2:14	31
2:17	29

2 Peter

3:9	70
3:13	70

1 John

2:1	69
5:4	57, 242

Revelation

1:5	32, 60
1:7	69
1:10	158
5	158
5:9	210
7:9	210
11:1–8	246
11:1–11	246
12:11	113
15:4	210
20:11–15	115
21:5	158
21–22	178

QUR'AN

Surah 2

216	70n45

Surah 9

5	70n45
29	70n45, 212n13, 213n17
73	212n13